Houghton Mifflin English

Grammar and Composition

Third Course

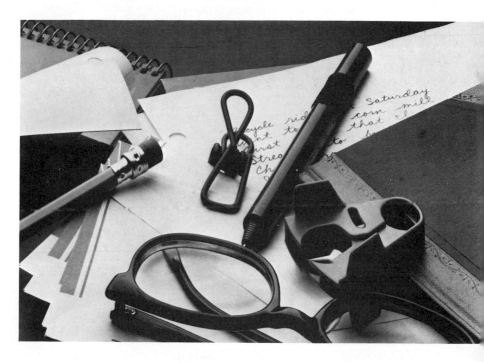

Houghton Mifflin Company • **Boston**

Atlanta   Dallas   Geneva, Illinois
Lawrenceville, New Jersey   Palo Alto   Toronto

Authors

Ann Cole Brown Former Lecturer in English composition and literature at Northern Virginia Community College in Alexandria, Virginia

Jeffrey Nilson Former teacher of English at the Wixon Middle School, South Dennis, Massachusetts, and independent computer software designer

Fran Weber Shaw Assistant Professor of English and Coordinator of the Writing Center at the University of Connecticut, Stamford

Richard A. Weldon Vice Principal, Associate Dean of Studies, and teacher of English at the Christian Brothers High School in Sacramento, California

Editorial Advisers

Edwin Newman Veteran broadcast journalist, author, and chairman of the Usage Panel of the *American Heritage Dictionary of the English Language*

Robert Cotton Vice Principal, Curriculum Director, and former chairman of the English Department at Servite High School in Anaheim, California

Consultant

Nancy C. Millett Professor of Language Arts Education at Wichita State University, Kansas, and co-author of *Houghton Mifflin English, K-8*

Special Contributors

Ernestine Sewell, University of Texas at Arlington

Luella M. Wolff, Washburn University, Topeka, Kansas

Acknowledgments

The Publisher gratefully acknowledges the cooperation of the National Council of Teachers of English for making available student writing from the Council's Achievement Awards in Writing Program.

(Acknowledgments continue on page 694.)

ISBN: 0-395-38549-0

ABCDEFGHIJ-RM-943210/898765

Contents

Part One

Grammar, Usage, and Mechanics

Why do we study the rules of English grammar, usage, and mechanics? Why do we need to know what a direct object is, or whether to use *who* or *whom,* or how to punctuate a sentence? Actually, these rules are simply descriptions of our language today. They form a system that organizes and regulates how we use words whenever we speak and write.

As you study the units in Part One, you will become more familiar with how this system of language works, and you will practice using it to communicate effectively. You will then have at your command a useful, adaptable, and highly powerful tool—the English language.

Unit 1

Parts
of Speech

Unit Preview

Words can be classified into parts of speech, all of which play an important role in helping people to communicate. To see just how important a particular part of speech is in helping you to express yourself, read the following paragraph. What do you think the paragraph is about? What makes it difficult to understand?

Few realize that there are more than one million. Most occur far beneath and do not threaten any. Unfortunately, some occur where there are many, and that which they cause can be enormous. For several after the serious ones there, it was still digging. They are working on them. Let's hope that they find one soon.

The problem in the paragraph is that it does not contain nouns, which name people, places, things, and ideas. The first sentence says that there are over one million, but it does not identify *what* is being discussed. The second sentence says that most occur, but you are not told what occurs.

For Analysis Read the paragraph that follows, and answer the questions.

Few people realize that there are over one million earthquakes a year. Most quakes occur far beneath the surface of the ocean and do not pose a danger to people. Unfortunately, some occur where there are many people, and the damage that they cause can be enormous. For several months after the serious earthquakes in Italy in 1980, the entire region of that country was still digging through the rubble. Scientists are working on ways of predicting earthquakes. Let's hope that they find a way soon.

1. What is the topic of the second paragraph?
2. Which words in the second paragraph helped you figure out the topic?
3. List three important details in the paragraph.
4. Which new words in the rewritten version of the paragraph helped you identify the three details that you listed?
5. Explain how the second paragraph is different from the first.

The second paragraph gives much more complete information because it contains nouns, such as *people, earthquakes, surface, ocean,* and *Italy.* Nouns give vital information. But equally vital are the other parts of speech: verbs, adjectives, adverbs, pronouns, prepositions, conjunctions, and interjections. To communicate clearly, you must understand what the eight parts of speech are and how they fit together to make effective sentences.

1.1   Nouns

A **noun** is a word that names a person, a place, a thing, or an idea.

PERSONS	PLACES	THINGS	IDEAS
teacher	cities	baseball	leadership
Mrs. Chan	Ontario	pole	cowardice
family	Ivory Coast	*Ivanhoe*	liberty

There are several kinds of nouns: proper and common, compound, and collective.

Proper and Common Nouns

A **proper noun** is the name or title of a particular person, place, thing, or idea; it always begins with a capital letter. A **common noun** refers to a category or a class of people, places, things, or ideas. You do not capitalize a common noun unless it begins a sentence.

COMMON NOUN   She is going to **school**.

PROPER NOUN   She is going to **Broadmoor School**.

Exercise 1   Proper and Common Nouns   On your paper, label the following nouns *Proper* or *Common*. For each common noun, write a related proper noun. For each proper noun, write a related common noun.

SAMPLE   city

ANSWER   Common—Phoenix

1. river
2. Nebraska
3. newspaper
4. town
5. automobile

6. October
7. Lassie
8. film
9. orchestra
10. Franklin D. Roosevelt

Compound Nouns

A **compound noun** consists of two or more words used together to form a single noun. One kind of compound noun consists of two or more words joined together.

blue + print   blueprint
base + ball   baseball

Another kind of compound noun consists of words joined by one or more hyphens.

son-in-law   passer-by

A third kind of compound noun consists of two words often used together even though they are not joined.

mountain lion   ice cream

A fourth kind of compound noun is a proper name that consists of more than one word.

Mrs. Hasley   Gulf Stream

Collective Nouns

A **collective noun** refers to a *group* of people, places, things, or ideas.

The **herd** moved slowly across the prairie.
Our **family** discussed vacation plans.
[*Herd* and *family* are collective nouns.]

Exercise 2   Nouns   On your paper, write the nouns in the following sentences. There are thirty nouns in all.

> SAMPLE   The airliner descended through the clouds.
>
> ANSWER   airliner, clouds

1. The wheels of the jet touched the runway at the airport.
2. Soon the first passenger walked down the steps.
3. He was a fellow named Bill.
4. The young man had just completed his tour of duty in the army.
5. Inside his pocket was his discharge from the army.
6. For a moment he paused to enjoy the salty air blowing in from the nearby ocean.
7. However, Bill had little patience on this day, for he was in a hurry to get away from the airport.
8. He headed for the line of taxis outside the terminal.
9. Inside a cab, the former soldier grinned.
10. "The ballpark, please," he said to the driver.

Exercise 3   Kinds of Nouns   Rewrite each of the following sentences by replacing the blank with a noun. Use the kind of noun indicated in parentheses. Underline the noun that you use.

> SAMPLE   The two __?__ were loyal to each other. (common)
>
> ANSWER   The two <u>sisters</u> were loyal to each other.

1. Jean was surrounded by a __?__ of strangers. (collective)
2. __?__ reminded the citizens to vote on election day. (proper)
3. Glen overcame his fear of playing __?__. (compound)
4. Wendy looked with pride at her new __?__. (common)
5. Winters in __?__ were harsh during the 1970s. (proper)
6. Bess works with a great __?__ of doctors. (collective)
7. Mr. Benson makes his living as a __?__. (compound)
8. The __?__ put all of her creativity into the project. (common)

1.2   Pronouns

A **pronoun** is a word that replaces a noun. Pronouns identify persons, places, things, and ideas without renaming them.

> *Joanne* is an athlete. **She** trains every day.
>
> Many *people* attended the *concert*. **They** enjoyed **it**.

The noun that a pronoun replaces is the **antecedent** of the pronoun.

> *Carmen* and *Joan* walked into the *theater*. **It** was so dark that **they** could barely see the floor. [*Theater* is the antecedent of *it. Carmen* and *Joan* are the antecedents of *they*.]

There are seven kinds of pronouns: personal, demonstrative, reflexive, intensive, interrogative, relative, and indefinite.

1.2a   Personal Pronouns

Personal pronouns require different forms to express person, number, and gender. When you write or speak about yourself, you use first-person pronouns: *I, me, we, us.* When you refer to your audience, you use the second-person pronoun, *you.* When you refer to other people or things, you use third-person pronouns, such as *he, she, they, it,* and *them.*

Personal pronouns also indicate whether the antecedent is singular or plural in number. *I, she, he,* and *it* are singular pronouns. *We, they,* and *us* are plural pronouns. *You* can be either singular or plural.

Personal pronouns express gender. *He* and *his* indicate the masculine gender. *She* and *her* indicate the feminine gender. *It* indicates the neuter gender, which you use to refer to things and ideas.

Possessive Pronouns.   Personal pronouns have possessive forms to show ownership or belonging. Such pronouns are possessive pronouns.

The *house* is **ours.**

Is that *pen* **mine**?

The following chart contains the personal pronouns. The possessive forms are in parentheses.

	SINGULAR	PLURAL
FIRST PERSON	I, me (my, mine)	we, us (our, ours)
SECOND PERSON	you (your, yours)	you (your, yours)
THIRD PERSON	he, him (his)	them, they
	she, her (her, hers)	(their, theirs)
	it (its)	

Exercise 1   Personal Pronouns   On your paper, write the two personal pronouns in each of the following sentences. Tell whether each pronoun is in the first person, the second person, or the third person.

SAMPLE   Where are you going with them?

ANSWER   you—second person; them—third person

1. I picked up Sam's paycheck and sent it through the mail.
2. I would like to tell you about last summer.
3. It was a long winter, and to make the time pass more quickly, I took up painting.
4. He couldn't quite hear what you said.
5. We thought that the team was out of the running, but it came back to win the pennant.
6. Is the book Sandy's, and does she want it?
7. Will you please try to write us more often?
8. We should not criticize other people too harshly, for those people may turn around and criticize us.
9. They saw the exhibit when it was at the art museum last year.
10. Brad looked at the painting and knew it was his.

Exercise 2   Personal Pronouns   On your paper, list the pronouns in italic type and their antecedents.

SAMPLE   Lloyd didn't know the name of his neighbor. For some reason *it* escaped *him*.

ANSWER   it—name; him—Lloyd

1. Shelly, will *you* please answer the phone? *It* has been ringing for five minutes.
2. Grandmother said that *she* would love to come for dinner today.
3. Larry will give you the information when you need *it*.
4. Amy said, "*I* can do the repairs on the car. *I* did *them* the last time."
5. Juan should go to the fair before *it* closes on Friday.

6. The owl and the cat were beak-to-nose in the hayloft, and *they* stayed that way for three long minutes.
7. As Laura opened the door, *it* squeaked.
8. Peter and I will practice our duet before *we* come to band practice on Saturday morning.

1.2b   Other Kinds of Pronouns

Demonstrative Pronouns

Demonstrative pronouns tell which one or which group is referred to. A list of demonstrative pronouns follows.

> that   this   these   those

> **This** is a new *book,* and **that** is an old one. [The antecedent of *this* and *that* is *book.*]
> Of the two *pairs* of shoes, **these** are more comfortable than **those.** [The antecedent of *these* and *those* is *pairs.*]

Reflexive Pronouns

Reflexive pronouns are used to indicate that people perform actions *to, for,* or *upon* themselves. You form reflexive pronouns with the suffixes *-self* and *-selves.*

FIRST PERSON	myself, ourselves
SECOND PERSON	yourself, yourselves
THIRD PERSON	himself, herself, itself, oneself, themselves

> *Brad* bumped **himself** in the knee. [Brad performed the action of bumping upon himself.]
> The Hanson *children* built **themselves** a treehouse. [The Hanson children built a treehouse for themselves.]

Intensive Pronouns

Intensive pronouns are the same words as the reflexive pronouns but are used for a different purpose: to draw special attention to the performer of an action.

The *principal* **herself** made the announcement. [The principal, not someone else, made the announcement.]

I didn't like its location, but the *house* **itself** was charming. [The house, but not the location, was charming.]

Interrogative Pronouns

Interrogative pronouns introduce questions. A list of interrogative pronouns follows.

who	which	whose
whom	what	

Who lives here?

What will the future bring?

Whose are these galoshes?

Relative Pronouns

Relative pronouns introduce **adjective clauses** (*Unit 3*), which are word groups that modify a word or a phrase. A list of relative pronouns follows.

who	whose	that
whom	which	

I know the *person* **who** lives here. [*Person* is the antecedent of *who*.]

He planted *flowers* **that** bloom every year. [*Flowers* is the antecedent of *that*.]

Indefinite Pronouns

Indefinite pronouns refer to people, places, and things in general. You can use these pronouns without antecedents.

10

The following list contains some commonly used indefinite pronouns.

all	either	most	other
another	enough	much	plenty
any	everybody	neither	several
anybody	everyone	nobody	some
anyone	everything	none	somebody
anything	few	nothing	someone
both	many	no one	something
each	more	one	

Each helps the **other**.

Some is better than **none**.

Exercise 3 Pronouns Number your paper from 1 to 8. Beside each number write every pronoun in the corresponding line of the following poem. If there are no pronouns in a line, write *None*. Do not let capital letters mislead you. Emily Dickinson often capitalized words that are not ordinarily capitalized.

SAMPLE   Although Emily Dickinson wrote over 1700 poems, only seven of them were published while she was alive.

ANSWER   them, she

1 I'm Nobody! Who are You?
2 Are you—Nobody—too?
3 Then there's a pair of us!
4 Don't tell! They'd banish us—you know!
5 How dreary—to be—Somebody!
6 How public—like a Frog—
7 To tell your name—the livelong June—
8 To an admiring Bog!

Emily Dickinson

Exercise 4 Pronouns On your paper, write the pronouns in the following sentences. If there are no pronouns in a sentence, write *None*. There are fifteen pronouns.

SAMPLE We still have much to learn about the solar system.
ANSWER We, much

1. Of all the planets, Venus is the brightest in the sky.
2. The planet is also a puzzle to us in certain ways, even though it is a close neighbor of ours.
3. For instance, Venus has a very long day compared with ours on Earth.
4. This is true because Venus rotates only once for every 243 of Earth's rotations.
5. What accounts for this?
6. No one is completely sure.
7. Venus has a thick layer of clouds that prevents us from observing the planet directly.
8. However, recent studies conducted with space probes have shown the surface temperature of the planet itself to be high.
9. In fact, it has the highest temperature of all the planets in the solar system.
10. The temperature is over 800°F, which makes the planet uninhabitable.

Exercise 5 Nouns and Pronouns On your paper, rewrite the following sentences by changing the nouns in italic type to pronouns. Underline the pronouns in your sentences.

SAMPLE Edward sang "Melancholy Baby." *"Melancholy Baby"* was a favorite song of *Edward's*.
ANSWER Edward sang "Melancholy Baby." It was a favorite song of his.

1. Linda dreamed of visiting relatives in Alaska, but *Linda* had to earn the money first.
2. Lavonne, do these running shoes belong to *Lavonne*?

3. I helped Beth by packing the suitcase for *Beth*.
4. The workers sprinted for shelter before the storm soaked *the workers*.
5. John, will *John* take this book back to the library?
6. The captain docked the ship perfectly and congratulated *the captain* for a job well done.
7. Looking at *the tennis player* in the mirror, the tennis player said, "*The tennis player* must win today."
8. "Terry," Father called, "when will *Terry* have to leave for the game tonight?"

Exercise 6   Kinds of Pronouns   On your paper, rewrite the following sentences. Replace each blank with a pronoun that fits the meaning of the sentence, and underline the pronoun. Use the kind of pronoun indicated in parentheses.

> **SAMPLE**   Is this shirt the best __?__ is on sale? (relative)
>
> **ANSWER**   Is this shirt the best <u>that</u> is on sale?

1. My brother's name is Jim. __?__ is visiting me for a week. (personal)
2. __?__ of the children is in the kitchen? (interrogative)
3. I don't like the frame, but the painting __?__ is beautiful. (intensive)
4. Sharon is going to win __?__ a trophy if she keeps running like that. (reflexive)
5. Professional athletes __?__ take the time to sign autographs deserve respect. (relative)
6. You did a good job sanding that bookshelf over there, but __?__ is still rough. (demonstrative)
7. Someone could have telephoned while __?__ were gone. (personal)
8. __?__ of the peaks in the Rocky Mountains are over 11,000 feet high. (indefinite)
9. Of the flowers, he likes both __?__ by the doorway and __?__ by the fence. (demonstrative)
10. The president __?__ is expected to attend the dinner. (intensive)

Assignment   Nouns and Pronouns   Read the first five paragraphs of a newspaper or magazine article written about a person. On your paper, list every noun and pronoun that refers to that person.

1.3   Verbs

A **verb** is a word that expresses an action or a state of being. There are three kinds of verbs: action verbs, linking verbs, and auxiliary verbs.

1.3a   Action Verbs

An **action verb** describes the behavior or action of someone or something. Action verbs may describe *physical* actions or *mental* activities.

PHYSICAL   The airplane **landed** on the ground.
              The bell **rang** for supper.

MENTAL   We **hoped** for the best.
              Sammy **wants** a new jacket.

Exercise 1   Action Verbs   Number your paper from 1 to 10, and list the action verbs in each sentence by the sentence number. Some sentences have more than one verb.

SAMPLE   She thought quite a bit about the future.

ANSWER   thought

1. Jill pounded the nail into the wall.
2. The children laughed as they spun on the merry-go-round.
3. Pedro wished for the holidays.

4. She considered the offer of an athletic scholarship.
5. We finally arrived in San Antonio.
6. Sally marched quickly out the door.
7. The couple attended opening night of the opera.
8. Find the telephone number right away!
9. I understand algebra better than geometry.
10. Julie concentrated on the textbook in front of her.

1.3b   Linking Verbs

A **linking verb** connects a noun or a pronoun with words that identify or describe the noun or pronoun. Many linking verbs are forms of the verb *be*. The following chart shows all of the forms of the linking verb *be*.

am	can be	shall have been
are	could be	will have been
be	has been	could have been
being	have been	should have been
is	shall be	would have been
was	should be	
were	will be	
	would be	

We **were** optimistic. [The verb, *were,* links the modifier, *optimistic,* to the pronoun, *we.*]

Cynthia **is** my cousin. [The verb, *is,* links the identifying phrase, *my cousin,* to the noun, *Cynthia.*]

Besides *be,* there are other linking verbs. Some appear in the following list.

appear	feel	seem	sound
become	look	smell	taste

The stew **smelled** delicious. [*Smelled* links the descriptive word, *delicious,* to the noun, *stew.*]

15

Some verbs can be either action verbs or linking verbs.

ACTION   I **tasted** the milk. [*Tasted* describes an action.]

LINKING   The milk **tasted** good. [*Tasted* functions like
              was. It links *good* to *milk*.]

Exercise 2   Linking Verbs   On your paper, write the
linking verbs in the following sentences.

SAMPLE   Your idea seems original.

ANSWER   seems

1. When Mark got up, he felt energetic.
2. Sandra Jenkins is the executor of the estate.
3. The piano sounds out of tune.
4. The paperback book with the torn cover looked well read.
5. The vegetable soup tasted a bit bland.
6. The record sounded scratchy.
7. The sky became cloudy very quickly.
8. Anne was the president of the chamber of commerce last year.
9. If I were there, I would help you dig out of the snow.
10. Just before the curtain went up, Jack appeared nervous.

1.3c   Auxiliary Verbs

Sometimes an action verb or a linking verb needs the help
of one or more other verbs. This other verb is called an
auxiliary verb or **helping verb.** The verb that it helps is called
the **main verb.** Together, a main verb and an auxiliary verb
make up a **verb phrase.** In the following sentences, the
auxiliary verbs are in italic type, and the main verbs are in
boldface type.

I *will* **go** tomorrow.   We *are* **leaving** now.
They *had* **tried.**   Wanda *has been* **studying.**

The most common auxiliary verbs are forms of *be, have,* and *do.* Common auxiliary verbs are in the following list.

am, are, be, been, is, was, were   may, might

have, has, had   can, could

do, does, did   will, would

shall, should   must

A verb phrase may contain two or even three auxiliary verbs as well as the main verb.

She *should have been* **elected** by the class.

When you write, you may have to place other words between the auxiliary and main verbs. Be careful not to place the auxiliary verbs too far away from the main verb.

AWKWARD   The dog *has* for the last nine nights **barked.**

IMPROVED   The dog *has* **barked** for the last nine nights.

In questions the verb phrase is usually interrupted by other words.

Has my little sister **returned** yet?

Do you **want** milk or water?

The words *not* and *never* are not considered part of the verb phrase.

The children *should* not **play** too late.

Some verbs can act as either auxiliary verbs or main verbs.

MAIN VERB   I **have** a trumpet.

AUXILIARY VERB   I *have* **lost** my trumpet.

Exercise 3   Verb Phrases   On your paper, write the verb phrases in the following sentences. Underline the auxiliary verbs once and the main verbs twice.

SAMPLE   Jack Frost is nipping at my nose.

ANSWER   is nipping

1. Margaret is mowing the lawn.
2. Sea gulls were perched on the car.
3. Are all of the parents donating their time?
4. Since last week we have been looking for new jobs.
5. Neither candidate would listen to the reporter's questions.
6. Do not take *no* for an answer.
7. The Simpsons will be leaving for Spain tomorrow.
8. Am I disturbing you?
9. Mary Stewart, a British author, has written three novels about Merlin the Magician.
10. May I see your ID card, please?

Exercise 4   Verbs and Verb Phrases   On your paper, write the following sentences. In place of each blank, write an action verb, a linking verb, or a verb phrase that fits the meaning of the sentence. The kind of verb required is in parentheses. Underline the verbs that you write.

SAMPLE   We _?_ _?_ to the circus today. (verb phrase)

ANSWER   We are going to the circus today.

1. Curt's idea _?_ truly brilliant. (linking)
2. We _?_ not _?_ our kites today. (verb phrase)
3. Because Thomas _?_ more exercise, he _?_ all the way home. (action; action)
4. _?_ you _?_ my message to her? (verb phrase)
5. Lee _?_ _?_ my message to her. (verb phrase)
6. Joan _?_ _?_ happy about her victory in the spelling bee. (verb phrase)

7. The students __?__ quietly in their seats. (action)
8. A cure for the common cold __?__ __?__ __?__ at last. (verb phrase)

1.3d Characteristics of Verbs

A verb has several characteristics that you need to understand in order to use it correctly.

Transitive and Intransitive Verbs

All action verbs are either transitive or intransitive. A verb is **transitive** when a person or a thing directs the action toward someone or something.

> He **slammed** the *door*. [*He* directed the action of slamming toward the door. *Slammed* is transitive.]

The person or thing receiving the action is the **object of the verb.** Usually the object is someone or something different from the performer of the action.

> verb obj.
> Craig **saw** Jack running along the road. [*Jack* is the object of the verb *saw*. *Saw* is transitive.]

Sometimes, however, the object is identical to the performer of the action.

> verb   obj.
> The dog **noticed** itself in the mirror. [*Itself* is the object of the verb, *noticed*. *Noticed* is transitive.]

A verb is **intransitive** when the performer of the action does not direct the action toward someone or something. In other words, intransitive verbs do not have objects. The verbs in the following sentences are intransitive.

Pam **was running.**

The door **slammed** shut. [*Shut* is not an object. It is a descriptive word modifying *slammed*.]

Linking verbs like *be, seem, become, look,* and *appear* are intransitive.

Brenda **was** the captain of the team. [*Was,* a linking verb, is intransitive.]

Exercise 5   Transitive and Intransitive Verbs   Copy each verb or verb phrase on your paper, and label it *Transitive* or *Intransitive*.

> **SAMPLE**   Mona adjusted her eyeglasses. They had slipped.
>
> **ANSWER**   adjusted—Transitive; had slipped—Intransitive

1. I appreciate Dan's patience. He rarely complains.
2. Save your breath, Amy. The others are not listening.
3. Our great-grandparents own a ranch. They raise sheep.
4. Stop that woman! She left her purse on the counter.
5. The boys are shopping now. They should return soon.
6. Do you know the definition? Use a dictionary!
7. The clouds gathered above us. We pedaled our bikes faster toward home.
8. I will not come tonight. The mechanics are fixing my car.

Changes in Verb Form

An important characteristic of the verb is that it changes form according to how it is used. A verb changes form in order to agree in person and number with a noun or a pronoun. A verb also changes form to express tense. The basic forms of a verb are its principal parts. (See Unit 4 for more information on verb forms.)

Using Verbs Effectively

When you write, you should try to use action verbs rather than linking verbs because action verbs are more vivid. Write a paragraph describing one of the scenes suggested below. In writing your paragraph, use action verbs rather than linking verbs to create a scene that your reader can easily visualize.

1. a person catching a fish
2. a mountain climber struggling up the side of a mountain
3. a child opening presents at a birthday party
4. a runner coming around the last turn and heading for the finish line
5. a deer running through a forest

1.4 Adjectives

An **adjective** is a word that modifies a noun or a pronoun. The word *modify* means "to change." An adjective modifies a noun or a pronoun by describing it or making it more specific. Sometimes nouns and certain pronouns can be used as adjectives in sentences. In such cases, consider them adjectives, not nouns or pronouns. An adjective answers one of these questions: *Which? What kind?* or *How many?*

Look at **those** flowers. [*Which* flowers? Those flowers.]

I like **yellow** flowers. [*What kind* of flowers? Yellow flowers.]

There are **twelve** flowers. [*How many* flowers? Twelve.]

More than one adjective may modify the same noun or pronoun.

Do you see **the two green** trucks? [*Which* trucks? The trucks. *How many* trucks? Two trucks. *What kind* of trucks? Green trucks.]

Articles.   The most common adjectives are the **articles,** *a, an,* and *the.* *A* and *an* are **indefinite articles** because they do not specify a particular person or thing. *The* is a **definite article** because it always points out a particular item.

INDEFINITE   **A** minute is long enough.

DEFINITE   **The** minute seemed like two hours.

Placement of Adjectives

Many adjectives appear directly before the nouns or pronouns that they modify.

The farmer looked up at **the cloudy** sky.

However, adjectives do not always appear in that location. An adjective may come after a linking verb and modify the noun or pronoun preceding the verb.

The *dog* was **old,** but *it* seemed **young** at heart.

Sometimes an adjective comes immediately after the noun or pronoun that it modifies. Adjectives in this location are set off with commas.

A *bear,* **large** and **fierce,** stood before us.

An adjective may precede the noun or pronoun that it modifies and be set off with a comma.

Large and **fierce,** the *bear* stood before us.

Exercise 1 Adjectives On your paper, write the adjectives in the following sentences and underline them. Write the noun or pronoun that each adjective modifies. Do not include articles.

SAMPLE   The brave girl stepped slowly into the dark cave.

ANSWER   <u>brave</u>—girl; <u>dark</u>—cave

1. After the sudden shower, the forest smelled clean and fresh.
2. In the last game, we held the best center in the league to five points.
3. She was not afraid because she was not alone.
4. The old waiter, tired and footsore, carried the heavy tray expertly.
5. Jessie was very proud of the new motorized wheelchair.
6. Sunlight came through a narrow hole in the high ceiling.
7. The loud thunder and bright lightning awakened the baby.
8. The trunk was too heavy for Ned to carry.
9. The large metallic meteors burned up in the atmosphere of the earth.
10. The train, large and powerful, steamed toward the station.

Exercise 2 Adjectives in a Paragraph *Step 1:* Number your paper from 1 to 9. *Step 2:* Beside each number write every adjective that appears in the corresponding line of the following paragraph. Do not include articles. If there are no adjectives in a line, write *None. Step 3:* Underline each adjective. *Step 4:* Beside each adjective write the noun or pronoun that it modifies. There are ten adjectives.

SAMPLE   Volcanic eruptions are spectacular but frightening.

ANSWER   <u>Volcanic</u>—eruptions; <u>spectacular</u>—eruptions; <u>frightening</u>—eruptions

1   Violent storms often occur in the hot months of the
2 summer when large amounts of radiant energy from the sun
3 reach the surface of the earth. The energy is then
4 released into the atmosphere and produces spectacular
5 clouds. The clouds, which are huge masses of droplets
6 and crystals, may reach an altitude of ten miles. The
7 storms that result contain tremendous energy and can
8 dump a thousand tons of water on the earth in a short
9 time.

Proper Adjectives

A **proper adjective** is an adjective formed from a proper
noun. Proper adjectives are usually capitalized.

April showers bring out the flowers. [*Which* showers? April
showers. *April* is a proper adjective.]

To create many proper adjectives, you add the suffixes *-n,*
-an, or *-ian* to the proper noun.

PROPER NOUNS	PROPER ADJECTIVES
Europe	European
Puerto Rico	Puerto Rican
Asia	Asian
Florida	Floridian

Nouns Used as Adjectives

Some nouns may function as adjectives without changing
form.

We went to the **automobile** race. [*What kind* of race? An
automobile race.]

Where did you put the **soccer** ball? [*Which* ball? The soccer
ball.]

24

Possessive Nouns

Nouns that show possession function as adjectives in sentences. **Possessive nouns** answer the question *Whose?* or *Which?* You form the **singular possessive** of most nouns by adding *-'s.*

Frank's boat almost tipped over. [*Whose* boat? The boat owned by Frank.]

You form the **plural possessive** of most nouns by adding *-s'* or *-es'* to the singular form of the noun.

The **coaches'** *trophies* were in the case outside the gym. [*Whose* trophies? Those belonging to the coaches.]

Exercise 3   Nouns Used as Adjectives   On your paper, write two sentences for each word listed below. In the first sentence, use the word as a noun. In the second, use the word as an adjective. Identify and underline the word in each sentence.

SAMPLE   head

ANSWER   Noun: I bumped my <u>head</u> against the car door.
Adjective: Many sports require some kind of <u>head</u> protection.

1. silver   3. railroad   5. spring
2. blank   4. model   6. kitchen

Possessive Pronouns Used as Adjectives

Possessive pronouns show ownership or belonging. Some of the possessive pronouns modify nouns and pronouns and, therefore, function as adjectives. The possessive pronouns that function as adjectives are in the following list.

	SINGULAR	PLURAL
FIRST PERSON	my	our
SECOND PERSON	your	your
THIRD PERSON	his, her, its	their

Jerry would like a slice of **your** cantaloupe. [*Whose* cantaloupe? The cantaloupe that you have.]

Did you see **my** portrait? [*Whose* portrait? The portrait of me.]

The words in the preceding list are called *possessive pronouns* throughout this textbook. However, some people use the term *pronominal adjectives* when referring to possessive pronouns that modify nouns or pronouns. You should use the term that your teacher prefers.

Other Pronouns Used as Adjectives

Indefinite pronouns, demonstrative pronouns, and interrogative pronouns may also function as adjectives. Here is a list of pronouns that often function as adjectives.

INDEFINITE	some, many, several, few
DEMONSTRATIVE	this, that
INTERROGATIVE	which, what, whose

Some students are visiting colleges. [*How many* students? Some students.]

Do you want **this** cereal or **that** one? [*Which* cereal? This cereal. *Which* one? That one.]

Which cereal would you like? [*Which* modifies *cereal*.]

Exercise 4   Adjectives On your paper, write the adjectives in the following sentences and underline them. Write the word that each adjective modifies. Do not include articles.

SAMPLE   My cousin Jo would like to be an automobile mechanic.

ANSWER   <u>My</u>—cousin; <u>automobile</u>—mechanic

1. These cards belong to your board game.
2. Stan's leather shoes are behind those canvas shoes.
3. Elizabeth has visited many African countries.
4. Both boys took turns carrying the equipment from the locker room.
5. Daniel's canary has lost its voice.
6. Few soldiers agreed with our attack plan.
7. Several construction workers ordered dinners from the Lebanese restaurant.
8. What method of ground transportation will take us quickly to St. Louis, Missouri?
9. Of these refrigerators, do you prefer this one or that one?
10. Jerry wanted a wood bookcase for his den.

Exercise 5   Adjectives   On your paper, list the adjectives in the following sentences and underline them. Write the word that each adjective modifies. Do not include articles.

SAMPLE   Peter plays the Spanish guitar well.

ANSWER   <u>Spanish</u>—guitar

1. My voice sounds hoarse because I was cheering our team.
2. The arctic wind hurt my tender skin.
3. What difference does that new ingredient make?
4. The little boys came running when their mother called.
5. She wanted her nephew to have the blue cup.
6. The mysterious package contained three ornate earrings.
7. Mrs. Schultz bought fresh bread at Sampson's Bakery.
8. The judge ordered both defendants to pay large fines.
9. The plant seemed healthy.
10. It is my turn to pay for this one.

1.5   Adverbs

An **adverb** is a word that modifies a verb, an adjective, or another adverb.

MODIFIES A VERB   The waves *pounded* **ferociously.**

MODIFIES AN ADJECTIVE   Those were **very** *ferocious* waves.

MODIFIES AN ADVERB   They pounded **quite** *ferociously.*

An adverb answers one of five questions about the word or phrase that it modifies.

1. How or in what manner?
2. When?
3. Where?
4. How often?
5. To what extent or degree?

The band *played* **well.** [*In what manner* did the band play? It played well.]

We *arrived* **early** for the play. [*When* did we arrive? We arrived early.]

Does your uncle *live* **here?** [*Where* does your uncle live? He lives here.]

The owl **rarely** *appears* in the daytime. [*How often* does the owl appear? It appears rarely.]

The party *surprised* him **completely.** [*To what extent* did the party surprise him? It surprised him completely.]

The words *not* and *never* are adverbs. They tell to what extent (not at all) and when (never).

The last goal *did* **not** *count.* [*Not* modifies *did count.*]

Lance *will* **never** *go* to camp. [*Never* modifies *will go.*]

Unless the directions state otherwise, do not include *not* and *never* among the adverbs that you must identify in the following exercises.

Exercise 1   Adverbs   On your paper, write the adverbs in the following sentences. Then state whether each adverb tells how, when, where, how often, or to what extent.

> **SAMPLE**   The farmer walked calmly to the barn.
>
> **ANSWER**   calmly—how

1. The children rose early and dressed for school.
2. Roger danced energetically onto the stage.
3. She closed the front door tightly.
4. Kevin and Doreen ran ahead to meet their Uncle Roy.
5. Ruth will leave tonight.
6. The space shuttle rose slowly into the clear sky.
7. You can always trust Janet to do a good job on her homework.
8. That player scored frequently last season.
9. The engineers worked hard to finish the project on schedule.
10. The huge black stallion sometimes came into the meadow.

1.5a   Adverbs Modifying Verbs

When adverbs modify the verbs in a sentence, they modify the entire verb phrase, which includes the main verb and auxiliary verbs.

> Work *has been going* well. [*Well* modifies the auxiliary verb, *has been,* and the main verb, *going.*]

An adverb that modifies a verb does not have to appear next to that verb. Look at the different positions that the adverb *lately* has in the following sentences.

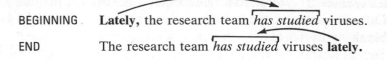

BEGINNING   Lately, the research team *has studied* viruses.

END   The research team *has studied* viruses **lately.**

Exercise 2 Adverbs Modifying Verbs *Step 1:* On your paper, write the adverbs in the following sentences. *Step 2:* Write the verb or verb phrase that each adverb modifies. *Step 3:* State whether the adverb tells how, when, where, how often, or to what extent or degree.

SAMPLE   The girl rang the doorbell twice.
ANSWER   twice—rang; how often

1. The waitress led us slowly to a table in the rear.
2. Mr. Fornas cleaned his basement yesterday.
3. The treehouse was totally destroyed by the hurricane.
4. The actress answered the curtain call twice.
5. Angela studied hard the night before the exam.
6. Doesn't your mother work there?
7. Often I lie down in the field to think
8. The mayor's response confused the citizens thoroughly.
9. Marilyn will probably want to join us.
10. Mel ate heartily when his doctor told him to gain weight.

1.5b Adverbs Modifying Adjectives

Adverbs may modify adjectives. The adverb usually comes directly before the adjective that it modifies.

adv. adj.
This bread is **too** *hard*. [*Too* tells the degree of hardness of the bread.]

adv.   adj.
The comedian's jokes were **usually** *funny*. [*Usually* tells how often the jokes were funny.]

Exercise 3 Adverbs Modifying Adjectives *Step 1:*
On your paper, write the following sentences. In place of each
blank, write an adverb that suits the meaning of the sentence.
Step 2: Underline the adverb. *Step 3:* Draw an arrow from the
adverb to the adjective that it modifies.

SAMPLE Sharon looks __?__ serious all the time!

ANSWER Sharon looks so serious all the time!

1. This movie was __?__ unbelievable.
2. The action sequences in the movie seemed __?__ unrealistic.
3. Most of the actors were __?__ unconvincing in their roles.
4. Also, the plot was __?__ complicated for the audience to follow.
5. The dialogue was __?__ dull.
6. Because of these faults, the movie received __?__ poor reviews.
7. Pat Ronson, who has been __?__ good in other films, said he
   was ashamed to be in this one.
8. To nobody's surprise, box office figures for the movie have
   been __?__ terrible.

1.5c Adverbs Modifying Adverbs

Adverbs can modify other adverbs. Such adverbs usually
precede the adverbs that they modify.

adv. adv.
They were driving **rather** *slowly* on the expressway. [*Rather*
tells to what extent they drove slowly.]

adv. adv.
The understudy has performed **quite** *well*. [*Quite* tells to what
extent the understudy performed well.]

Exercise 4 Adverbs Write the two adverbs in each of
the following sentences and underline them. Next to each
adverb, write the word or words that it modifies.

SAMPLE   Beth was speaking very honestly to the convention.

ANSWER   honestly—was speaking; very—honestly

1. Because the team played badly, we lost interest early.
2. We sometimes sleep late on cold mornings.
3. They greatly admired Jan because she sang beautifully.
4. I play handball regularly, and I am a fairly good player.
5. They swim almost daily.
6. Amanda laughed rather loudly.
7. Sam finally saw the point when the teacher explained it again.
8. If you move over, all of us can be seated comfortably.
9. The child was only three, but she had an amazingly large vocabulary.
10. Almost every student did the assignment perfectly.

1.5d   Adjective or Adverb?

You may sometimes find it difficult to distinguish an adjective from an adverb. Many adverbs end in *-ly,* but so do some adjectives.

ADVERB   The actor *performed* **brilliantly** in the play.

ADJECTIVE   The **friendly** *people* welcomed us to the neighborhood. [Even though *friendly* ends in *-ly,* it is an adjective.]

To decide whether a modifier is an adjective or an adverb, figure out the part of speech of the word that it modifies.

If the modified word is a *noun* or a *pronoun,* the modifier is an adjective.

If the modified word is a *verb,* an *adjective,* or an *adverb,* the modifier is an adverb.

Alternatively, if you figure out which question a modifier answers, you can tell whether the modifier is an adjective or an adverb.

ADJECTIVE	ADVERB
1. Which?	1. How or in what manner?
2. What kind?	2. When?
3. How many?	3. Where?
	4. How often?
	5. To what extent or degree?

ADJECTIVE   Is that a **daily** *newspaper*? [**Think:** *Daily* modifies *newspaper*, which is a noun. *Daily* tells what kind. Therefore, *daily* is an adjective.]

ADVERB   We *bake* our bread **daily.** [**Think:** *Daily* modifies *bake,* which is a verb. *Daily* tells how often. Therefore, *daily* is an adverb.]

Exercise 5 Adjective or Adverb?

Step 1: On your paper, list the words in italic type in the following sentences. *Step 2:* Label each word *Adjective* or *Adverb. Step 3:* List the word modified.

SAMPLE   I have become *more* tolerant.

ANSWER   more—Adverb, tolerant

1. Which of you answered *first?*
2. You behaved *bravely,* Rob.
3. The *stately* mansion was beautiful.
4. It was a *costly* present.
5. Mary spoke *highly* of everyone.
6. She sang *sweetly*.
7. We need *only* one more point.
8. He slammed the door *hard*.
9. Calvin had a *lengthy* run to the train.
10. The racers seemed *slow* at the finish.

Using Modifiers Effectively

Write an original paragraph in which you describe one of the following five situations. As you write, you should choose modifiers that are vivid and descriptive.

1. a hungry animal eating
2. a street after a parade
3. a weightlifter lifting a great weight
4. a sunset
5. a committee working on a project

1.6   Prepositions

A **preposition** is a word that expresses a relationship between a noun or a pronoun and another word in a sentence.

A pad is **under** the *carpet*. [The preposition, *under,* tells where the pad is in relation to the carpet.]
Our vacation was **like** a *dream*.

A list of frequently used prepositions follows.

about	behind	during	off	to
above	below	except	on	toward
across	beneath	for	onto	under
after	beside	from	out	underneath
against	besides	in	outside	until
along	between	inside	over	up
among	beyond	into	past	upon
around	by	like	since	with
at	despite	near	through	within
before	down	of	till	without

A **compound preposition** consists of more than one word. A list of frequently used compound prepositions follows.

according to	in place of
as of	in regard to
as well as	in spite of
aside from	on account of
by means of	out of
in addition to	prior to
in front of	

According to the weather *report,* we will have rain.

A preposition is usually followed by a noun or a pronoun, which is called the **object of the preposition.** Together, the preposition, the object, and the modifiers of that object form a **prepositional phrase.**

                      prep.   obj.
The service station is **around the next corner.** [The prepositional phrase includes the preposition, *around,* the modifiers *the* and *next,* and the object, *corner.*]

In some sentences the preposition comes *after* the object. This is often the case in questions.

Whom did you speak **to?** [**Think:** To whom did you speak?]

A prepositional phrase may have more than one object, which is a compound object.

                      prep.   obj.
The Sampsons were gone **during the afternoon and**
obj.
evening.

Prepositional phrases usually act as modifiers. A prepositional phrase functions as an adjective if it modifies a noun or a pronoun. A prepositional phrase functions as an adverb if it modifies a verb, an adjective, or an adverb.

USED AS AN ADJECTIVE	I prefer the clothing *store* **across the street.** [*Across the street* tells which store.]
USED AS AN ADVERB	I just *drove* **over a nail.** [*Over a nail* tells where I drove.]

Most of the prepositions in the list on page 34 function as other parts of speech when they are not followed by objects.

PREPOSITION	The bus went **near** the curb.
ADVERB	The bus *is coming* **near.**
ADJECTIVE	We will see you in the **near** *future.*

Exercise 1   Prepositions   On your paper, list each preposition in the following sentences.

SAMPLE	He left a note on the desk.
ANSWER	on

1. Please put the spatula on the stove.
2. Please don't stand in front of me.
3. No one is above the law.
4. You may choose between them.
5. He panicked during the storm.
6. Patty hid inside the closet.
7. We haven't met since that day.
8. That is beside the point.
9. I survived by means of my wits.
10. We loaded our equipment onto the bus.

Exercise 2   Prepositional Phrases   On your paper, copy the prepositional phrases in the following sentences. Underline the prepositions once and the objects twice.

SAMPLE	Look into my eyes.
ANSWER	<u>into</u> my <u>eyes</u>

1. I found the book underneath those blankets.
2. They have talked about this matter for a long time.
3. Wendy looked at the audience when she stepped onto the stage of the auditorium.
4. You must choose between beans and peas for dinner.
5. Let's keep the information among ourselves until Monday.
6. All schools will be closed on Friday.
7. Our game with Wilson High was postponed until next week.
8. Ronnie made gifts for his sister and brothers.
9. They won in spite of the absence of their star player.
10. No new construction is planned within the city limits.

Exercise 3 Writing Prepositional Phrases On your paper, rewrite each of the following sentences, and supply a preposition and an object for the two blank spaces. Underline the prepositions and objects in your sentences.

SAMPLE	Just _?_ the _?_, let's go over the facts again.
ANSWER	Just <u>for</u> the <u>record</u>, let's go over the facts again.

1. The lifeguard dived _?_ the _?_.
2. We did this _?_ the _?_.
3. The band practiced _?_ the _?_.
4. Henrietta waited _?_ the _?_.
5. _?_ a _?_ the squirrel leaped.
6. The ball sailed _?_ the _?_.
7. _?_ the _?_, we heard the owl.
8. The cat jumped _?_ the _?_.
9. There's no use going _?_ the _?_.
10. I waited _?_ the _?_.

Assignment Prepositional Phrases In a newspaper or a magazine, find an article that contains prepositional phrases. Clip the article and attach it to a piece of paper. Then underline all the prepositional phrases in the article.

1.7   Conjunctions

A **conjunction** is a word that connects individual words or groups of words. In fact, the word *conjunction* literally means "the act of joining" or "combination."

INDIVIDUAL WORDS
> Dawn likes *mystery, adventure,* **and** *suspense* in what she reads. [The conjunction, *and,* connects the three words *mystery, adventure,* and *suspense.*]

GROUPS OF WORDS
> I was going to write to you, **but** I decided to call instead. [The conjunction, *but,* connects the two groups of words *I was going to write to you* and *I decided to call instead.*]

There are three kinds of conjunctions: coordinating, correlative, and subordinating.

1.7a   Kinds of Conjunctions

Coordinating Conjunctions

A **coordinating conjunction** connects words or groups of words that perform the same function in a sentence. The coordinating conjunctions are in the following list.

and	for	or
but	nor	yet

A coordinating conjunction may connect individual nouns.

I saw a *bucket* **and** a *ladder* on the sidewalk. [The coordinating conjunction, *and,* connects *bucket* and *ladder*.]

A coordinating conjunction may connect two or more **independent clauses** (*Unit 3*), which are groups of words that can stand by themselves as complete sentences.

Janet will meet you at the airport, **or** you can take a bus. [The coordinating conjunction, *or,* connects two independent clauses: *Janet will meet you at the airport* and *you can take a bus*.]

Coordinating conjunctions also connect verbs, verb phrases, adjectives, adverbs, prepositional phrases, and other sentence elements. Each coordinating conjunction shows a different relationship between the words that it connects.

Sabrina was *tiny* **yet** *strong*. [*Yet* shows the contrast between *tiny* and *strong*.]
The shampoo is in the hallway **or** under the sink. [*Or* shows choice.]
Brad cannot mow the lawn, **for** the lawn mower is broken. [*For* shows a cause-and-effect relationship.]

Conjunctions help you to avoid repetition by bringing separate items together into one sentence.

Carol is a sophomore. Sid is a sophomore.
Carol **and** Sid are sophomores.

Exercise 1 Coordinating Conjunctions On your paper, list the coordinating conjunctions in the following sentences.

SAMPLE   Aluminum is light yet sturdy.
ANSWER   yet

1. Do you need a ride to the game tonight, or are you going to walk?
2. I will stay here and wait for Jacqueline.

3. We must hurry inside, for the play is about to start.
4. Father wants to visit his sister in Des Moines, but he also wants to vacation in Florida.
5. The circus will have to be postponed, for the tent needs too many repairs.
6. Mrs. Roberts raises chickens, ducks, and geese for her poultry market.
7. The material must be heavy enough to keep me warm yet light enough to be comfortable.
8. Sharon is older, but Robin is taller.

Correlative Conjunctions

A **correlative conjunction** consists of two or more words that work together as a set. Correlative conjunctions function like coordinating conjunctions because they connect words that perform equal functions in a sentence. The correlative conjunctions are in the following list.

either . . . or . . .	whether . . . or . . .
neither . . . nor . . .	not only . . . but (also) . . .
both . . . and . . .	

We had **both** wind **and** rain. [*Both . . . and* connect *wind* and *rain.*]

You should **neither** spoil your pet **nor** be too strict with it. [*Neither . . . nor* connect *spoil your pet* and *be too strict with it.*]

Not only were we lost, **but** we were **also** without supplies. [*Not only . . . but . . . also* connect *were we lost* and *we were without supplies.*]

Exercise 2   Coordinating Conjunctions and Correlative Conjunctions   On your paper, write the conjunctions in the following sentences.

SAMPLE   We brought neither rain gear nor boots when
we went camping.

ANSWER   neither, nor

1. The building emptied quickly, for a fire alarm had sounded.
2. Mother said that she will neither buy me a new bicycle nor lend me the money for one.
3. This type of plant needs both sun and water.
4. Evelyn can't decide whether to run for class president or to edit the school newspaper.
5. Calvin not only repaired the toaster but also made breakfast by the time the rest of the family got up.
6. Cindy raised the prize-winning calf, and Makita raised the prize-winning pig.
7. The whole class was eager to go on the field trip, but the bus simply would not start.
8. Either Rosa or Sonny painted that mural.
9. Mrs. Woodley is the basketball coach, yet she is substituting for the math teacher.
10. Both Pauline and Louis won scholarships.

Subordinating Conjunctions

Subordinating conjunctions introduce **subordinate clauses** (*Unit 3*), which are clauses that cannot stand by themselves as complete sentences. Subordinating conjunctions connect subordinate clauses to independent clauses, which *can* stand by themselves as complete sentences.

┌—indep. clause—┐ ┌———— sub. clause————┐
Jenny got the role **because** she can sing well.

In the preceding sentence, the subordinating conjunction, *because,* introduces the subordinate clause, *she can sing well. Because* connects the subordinate clause to the independent clause, *Jenny got the role.*

Subordinating conjunctions usually express relationships of time, manner, cause, condition, comparison, or purpose.

TIME	after, as, as long as, as soon as, before, since, until, when, whenever, while
MANNER	as, as if, as though
CAUSE	because
CONDITION	although, as long as, even if, even though, if, provided that, though, unless, while
COMPARISON	as, than
PURPOSE	in order that, so that, that

I ate dinner **after** the show was over. [*After* expresses a time relationship.]

If you want to, we will go to the carnival. [*If* expresses condition.]

We were late for the meeting **because** our car broke down. [*Because* expresses cause.]

Exercise 3 Subordinating Conjunctions On your paper, write the subordinating conjunction in each of the following sentences, and underline it. Then tell whether the subordinating conjunction indicates time, manner, cause, condition, comparison, or purpose.

SAMPLE	Although I enjoy music, I have never attended a concert at the symphony hall.
ANSWER	Although—condition

1. They left the beach as the day drew to a close.
2. Although Paul had never seen his cousin, he wrote her long letters.
3. The glue will hold the pieces together if it is given enough time to set.
4. The bus was late getting to school because the creek rose over the bridge.

5. Let's eat lunch when we return from the grocery.
6. Carl refuses to participate unless he can get credit for his work.
7. We arrived before the heavy snow started.
8. You can play your records provided that you keep the volume down.

1.7b   Conjunction or Preposition?

Certain words can function as either conjunctions or prepositions. However, there are two important differences between a word used as a preposition and one used as a conjunction. First, a preposition is always followed by an object, but a conjunction is not.

PREPOSITION   We should leave **before** *noon*. [The noun, *noon,* is the object of the preposition, *before.*]

CONJUNCTION   **Before** you leave, tell me the story. [*Before* is not followed by an object. Instead, it intro duces the subordinate clause, *before you leave.*]

Second, a preposition introduces a prepositional phrase. A conjunction, on the other hand, connects words or groups of words.

PREPOSITION   He went jogging **after** work. [*After* introduc- es the prepositional phrase, *after work.*]

CONJUNCTION   Meet me **after** the game is over. [*After* con- nects two groups of words: *meet me* and *the game is over.*]

Exercise 4   Conjunction or Preposition? On your paper, write the word in italic type in each sentence that follows, and underline it. Then label each word *Conjunction* or *Preposition*.

SAMPLE   What did you do *during* our absence?

ANSWER   <u>during</u>—Preposition

1. We haven't heard from Nancy *since* the holidays ended.
2. Let's get all this homework done *before* our friends arrive from the ballgame.
3. I had no idea that we came *from* the same city.
4. It's too late to go shopping *across* town.
5. Mr. Johnson wants to talk to you *after* you are done with that job.

1.7c   Conjunctive Adverbs

A **conjunctive adverb** is an adverb that functions similarly to a coordinating conjunction. Conjunctive adverbs usually connect independent clauses (*Unit 3*), which can stand by themselves as complete sentences. A semicolon precedes the conjunctive adverb, and a comma usually follows it.

CONJUNCTIVE ADVERB
I had the engine repaired; **also,** I bought new tires.

COORDINATING CONJUNCTION
I had the engine repaired, **and** I bought some new tires.

The following list contains frequently used conjunctive adverbs.

accordingly	finally	instead	otherwise
also	furthermore	later	still
besides	however	moreover	therefore
consequently	indeed	nevertheless	thus

Exercise 5 Conjunctions On your paper, list the conjunctions and conjunctive adverbs in the following sentences, and label them *Conjunction* or *Conjunctive adverb*. Some sentences have more than one conjunction or conjunctive adverb.

> **SAMPLE**   You should brush your teeth and wash your face.
>
> **ANSWER**   and—Conjunction

1. Talk to Ralph or Connie before you make a decision.
2. We will stay here and work until we finish our project.
3. Basketball isn't my favorite sport; however, I enjoy it now and then.
4. The crowds cheered as the Prime Minister and her husband walked by.
5. If you act now, you will save not only time but money.
6. Our new tenants are quiet; furthermore, they help with the yard work.
7. Sharon must be ready to leave, for her bags are standing at the bottom of the stairs.
8. Both the money and the diamonds were found.
9. I should have spoken up, but I lacked the courage.
10. You have watered neither the lawn nor the plants today.

Exercise 6 Using Conjunctions On your paper, combine each of the following pairs of sentences by using the conjunction or conjunctive adverb in parentheses.

> **SAMPLE**   Last night I didn't do anything. There were too many distractions. (*because*)
>
> **ANSWER**   Last night I didn't do anything because there were too many distractions.

1. My family had gone to the movies. I was alone at home. (*but*)
2. I was becoming rather bored. I decided to read a book. (*because*)

3. I selected John Steinbeck's *The Pearl*. My sister had recommended it to me. (*for*)
4. I started to read it. I soon felt a bit hungry. (*however*)
5. There was nothing appealing in the refrigerator. I sat back down and continued reading. (*because*)

Assignment   Using Conjunctions in Sentences   On your paper, write sentences of your own in which you use the following conjunctions or conjunctive adverbs.

> **SAMPLE**   but
>
> **ANSWER**   It's snowing, but I feel warm.

1. yet   3. or   5. both . . . and
2. however   4. therefore   6. until

1.8   Interjections

An **interjection** is an exclamatory word or phrase that can stand by itself, although it may also appear in sentences. Many interjections express strong emotions. They are followed by exclamation points.

> **My goodness!**
> **Wow!** That was the greatest hook shot I've ever seen!

When an interjection appears within a sentence, you should set it off with commas.

> **Oh,** I beg your pardon.
> **Well,** I knew I was right.

You use interjections often in speech, but you should use them only occasionally in writing. You will find them most often in dialogue.

Exercise 1   Interjections   On your paper, write the interjections in the following sentences.

SAMPLE   Ouch! A bee stung me!

ANSWER   Ouch!

1. Oh, I just don't believe that.
2. Hooray! I knew we could do it.
3. Becky tried her best, but, alas, it wasn't quite enough.
4. It was still a good try. Congratulations!
5. Boy, that was a great movie!
6. Whew! It's really hot outside.
7. Hey, that's nice!
8. Okay! See you later.
9. Ouch! I just banged my thumb.
10. Look out! The train is right behind you.

Unit Practice

Practice 1

A. Nouns *(pages 3–6)* On your paper, list the nouns in each of the following sentences.

1. The Purple Heart, the first medal awarded by the United States for bravery, was created by George Washington.
2. Standing in Grandpa's pasture, Liz saw a dazzling rainbow form above a flock of grazing sheep.
3. When the group arrives from New Zealand, show them the International Peace Garden in North Dakota.
4. My family expressed admiration when they viewed the four figures carved into the side of Mt. Rushmore.
5. Will the graduates perform the fox trot or the waltz at the celebration held at the Fernhill Dance Academy?

B. Pronouns *(pages 6–14)* On your paper, list the pronouns in each of the following sentences.

6. The pigeons helped themselves to crumbs that she threw to them.
7. Everything in the homes near us was ruined in the storm, but nothing across the street was touched.
8. Who did David and Cecilia say could not attend the party that they were planning?
9. Few will believe she is my sister, although everyone who knows us well will confirm this.
10. Of the two quilts, did Aunt Nellie make this or that?

C. Verbs *(pages 14–21)* On your paper, list the verbs and verb phrases in each of the following sentences.

11. They would have been early if they had noticed the clock that hangs on the gallery wall.
12. Why are you so stubborn about the chores that your uncle has given to you?

13. The sky seems brilliant when a meteor shower occurs and flying sparks fill the air.
14. Give my regards to the visitors who will be touring this city while I am away.
15. She may do whatever she wishes if she behaves well.

D. Adjectives and Adverbs *(pages 21–34)* On your paper, list the adjectives and adverbs in the following sentences, and label each *Adjective* or *Adverb*. Do not include articles.

16. Some members of the team practiced consistently for the upcoming tennis match.
17. Will you kindly repeat those lengthy instructions for the difficult drive that I will make tomorrow?
18. A long line is forming rapidly at Hammond's hardware store for the spring sale.
19. Angela's watch suddenly stopped, but she found a local repair shop to fix it.
20. Mara has never walked through one of the rather beautiful gardens.

E. Prepositions *(pages 34–38)* On your paper, list the prepositional phrases in the following sentences, and underline each preposition.

21. Do you often shop at that store across the street?
22. Before the concert, Nora will meet us near the entrance beside the fountain.
23. From that perspective, Doriana saw very little of the play, and she complained about her assigned seat.
24. His quarter fell from his pocket and rolled onto the slippery floor underneath an armchair.
25. Herschel looked through the telescope on Mount Wilson, and like a true scientist he took notes about his experience.

(Continue on the next page.)

F. Conjunctions *(pages 38–46)* On your paper, list the conjunctions in each of the following sentences. The sentences contain coordinating, correlative, and subordinating conjunctions.

26. Both Daniel and his brother will explore the town or the beach.
27. Tomorrow will be the first day of spring, yet the threat of frost or cold still exists.
28. They talk as if they were sure of their plans, but they still must wait until their luggage arrives.
29. Not only were you late, but you went to the wrong event.
30. Tourists adore this town when there is a lively market, but in winter the market is closed.

G. Interjections *(pages 46–47)* On your paper, list the interjections in each of the following sentences.

31. Wow! You nearly missed the deadline.
32. Ben attempted a new record, but, alas, he just missed it.
33. Oh, will you be able to carry all those books?
34. Well, I know you will return for our next reunion.
35. Hey, the sprinklers are turning this way!

Practice 2

On your paper, list the words and phrases in italics in the following passage. Label each word or phrase *Noun, Pronoun, Verb, Adjective, Adverb, Preposition, Conjunction,* or *Interjection*.

The (1) *art* of pyrotechnics, (2) *or* fireworks, (3) *has been practiced* since the (4) *fourteenth* century. These (5) *brilliantly* glowing displays, (6) *which* were created (7) *from* gunpowder, rockets, and hydrogen balloons, helped celebrate important and festive events. Some (8) *early* fireworks   (9) *were* intricate designs or portraits   (10) *of* famous people.   (11) *These* were created   (12) *with* set pieces mounted on   (13) *stationary* frames. Other fireworks were not set upon frames   (14) *but* were propelled across the sky. (15) *Pyrotechnic* shows   (16) *were coordinated* by a firemaster and assistants, who were called   (17) *Green Men* or Wild Men. These assistants did the work, and   (18) *they*   (19) *constantly* risked danger.   (20) *In addition to* being exciting to watch, the spectacles were   (21) *potentially* harmful.   (22) *Alas,* accidents frequently   (23) *occurred* on account of inexperience, overexcited   (24) *crowds,*   (25) *and* the (26) *unpredictable* nature of the materials that were used. (27) *Well,* obviously these hazards   (28) *never* stopped the displays,   (29) *which* are still thrilling   (30) *us* today.

Unit Tests

Test 1

A. Nouns *(pages 3–6)* On your paper, list the nouns in each of the following sentences.

1. Sharks can be found even in the northern waters of the Atlantic Ocean.
2. On Independence Day Mrs. Louis walked past the park on Magnolia Street to hear the band.
3. Her brother-in-law built his own greenhouse on the road to Southbury Farm.
4. The people felt amazement after they found gold near a river not far from the Grand Canyon.
5. One responsibility of Luke and his friend is to collect notebooks from the class.

B. Pronouns *(pages 6–14)* On your paper, list the pronouns in each of the following sentences.

6. Of the two tennis rackets, do you prefer that with the wood frame or this with the aluminum frame?
7. Someone played a funny trick on us, and it made the counselor laugh.
8. Everyone who saw the actor play Othello called it one of the best performances he has ever given.
9. What did they do when they found themselves on the wrong highway?
10. I asked Carl to move the shelves that he built for himself.

C. Verbs *(pages 14–21)* On your paper, list the verbs and verb phrases in each of the following sentences.

11. Before Rachel changes her job, she should consider all her options and then select the best one.
12. He appeared restless before he left on the trip that he had won in the contest.
13. Anna will be swimming as soon as the weather grows warmer and she feels stronger.

14. You could have hurt yourself when you fell from the branch that you climbed.
15. We were lazy and let the frog hop away, but we should have caught it.

D. Adjectives and Adverbs *(pages 21–34)* On your paper, list the adjectives and adverbs in the following sentences, and label each *Adjective* or *Adverb*. Do not include articles.

16. Marcie's skin slowly became tan as she sat in the strong sun at her brother's home.
17. Which two jazz albums did you frequently play at the birthday celebration?
18. I bravely bargained for a few yards of blue and white fabric at the noisy market.
19. Some radio programs in the city are always informative, some usually have entertainment, and some feature an interesting combination of both.
20. Hal expertly prepared a tangy, spicy meal for the family reunion at the old house.

E. Prepositions *(pages 34–38)* On your paper, list the prepositional phrases in the following sentences, and underline each preposition.

21. The applications for jobs had directions printed above the blanks.
22. Upon her return from vacation, Charlotte felt completely exhausted from her long journey through the mountains.
23. Doug likes to walk beyond those elms, along the hedge, and near the main house.
24. This graduation is like previous graduations, but the students will march outside the gates toward the bleachers.
25. How can you laugh at the comedian with such old jokes?

(Continue on the next page.)

F. Conjunctions *(pages 38–46)* On your paper, list the conjunctions in each of the following sentences. The sentences contain coordinating, correlative, and subordinating conjunctions.

26. Neither Lena nor Calvin liked roller skating, but they enjoy it now because they have improved.
27. Whether you drive or ride a bus, you cannot avoid the traffic in rush hour.
28. Folding fans made of lace or feathers were once popular, but electric fans and air conditioners have replaced them.
29. Not only were the election results wrong, but we must recount them.
30. A garden thrives when there is enough rain, but not if there is a drought.

G. Interjections *(pages 46–47)* On your paper, list the interjections in each of the following sentences.

31. Hooray! You made it just in time.
32. Yes, I suppose that you can take your turn first.
33. Oh, no! Frederick won't be able to go with us.
34. Good heavens! I didn't realize it was so late.
35. Greetings! We're glad that you came over to visit for a while.

Test 2

On your paper, list the words and phrases in italics in the following passage. Label each word or phrase *Noun, Pronoun, Verb, Adjective, Adverb, Preposition, Conjunction,* or *Interjection.*

The apple is a (1) *popular* fruit today. However, modern (2) *scientists* have found evidence that apples (3) *were grown* in (4) *ancient* times. Carved representations of the apple (5) *appeared* on tombs (6) *and* buildings. The remains (7) *of* apples (8) *that* had been reduced to charcoal were found in villages of the (9) *Stone Age*. Indeed, the apple's long history accounts for the many myths about (10) *it*. In folklore it (11) *was thought* that certain apples kept people young (12) *forever*. Dunking for (13) *them* was (14) *originally* believed to be a way to foretell the future. (15) *According to* another tale, the destruction of Troy was caused when gods (16) *violently* quarreled over a (17) *golden* apple. Everyone (18) *has heard* about a mysterious man (19) *who* distributed apple seeds (20) *during* the 1800s. John Chapman, who was known as Johnny Appleseed, wore a tin pot for a hat (21) *and* carried a pouch of (22) *those* seeds that early American settlers had brought for (23) *themselves* (24) *so that* they could grow trees. His act of (25) *generosity* spread trees across the country. (26) *Well,* apples (27) *still* exist after more than two million years of cultivation. (28) *Yes,* we certainly (29) *enjoy* the twenty-five varieties that are grown for eating or for cider and (30) *applesauce*.

Sentence Structure

Unit Preview

In order to communicate clearly, we put words together in certain ways to make sentences. As you read the following paragraph, ask yourself what is wrong with the sentences.

> To is fast-paced, highly organized football today's viewer a game. Was the sport so not, however, always. By kicking it the ball advanced players at first, and had as they do today no set plays they. Of carrying the ball from Canadian players the idea got American players in 1874.

The paragraph is difficult to understand because the sentences are not structured in recognizable ways. For instance, reread the first sentence: *To is fast-paced, highly organized football today's viewer a game*. It is incomprehensible because the words do not appear in an order that communicates meaning to us.

For Analysis In the following paragraph, the sentences have been rewritten. Read it, and answer the questions that follow.

> To today's viewer, football is a fast-paced, highly organized game. However, the sport was not always so. At first players advanced the ball by kicking it, and they had no set plays as they do today. In 1874 American players got the idea from Canadian players of carrying the ball.

1. What is the entire paragraph about?
2. How does the first sentence of the rewritten version differ from the first sentence of the original version?
3. In what other way could you rewrite the first sentence so that it makes sense?
4. Why does the rewritten paragraph make more sense than the first?

In this unit you will learn that sentences have certain structures, that is, ways in which they are organized. As you gain understanding of sentence structure, you will develop your ability to write clear sentences.

2.1   Sentences Classified by Purpose

A **sentence** is a group of words that expresses a complete thought. The purpose of a sentence is to describe an action or state a condition of a person, a place, a thing, or an idea. To be a sentence, a group of words must make complete sense by itself.

NOT A SENTENCE   The cat in the garden [This group of words is not a sentence because it does not express a complete thought.]

SENTENCE   The cat in the garden belongs to me.

You can classify sentences into four categories: declarative, interrogative, imperative, and exclamatory. In a **declarative sentence,** you make a statement. The sentence always ends with a period.

Raisins are made from grapes.
Nick read the newspaper and left for the hockey game.

In an **interrogative sentence,** you ask a question. The sentence ends with a question mark.

Whatever became of Agnes?
Do you want eggs or cereal for breakfast?

In an **imperative sentence,** you give an order or make a request. If the command or request is mild, the sentence ends with a period. If the command or request is strong, the sentence ends with an exclamation point.

Sarah, please empty the trash.
Look out behind you!

In an **exclamatory sentence,** you show strong feeling. The sentence always ends with an exclamation point.

Wow, there's Niagara Falls!
I won first prize in the tournament!

Exercise 1   Sentence Purpose   Copy the following sentences on your paper. Label them *Declarative, Interrogative, Imperative,* or *Exclamatory.* Supply the proper punctuation.

SAMPLE   Where did you put my boots
ANSWER   Where did you put my boots?—Interrogative

1. The general signed the treaty
2. Somebody save me
3. Where will the banquet be held
4. What a surprise this is
5. Take the afternoon off, Paul
6. Marie doubted Rob's claim
7. Who's in charge here
8. Shirley just broke the school record for the mile
9. That's a lovely bunch of flowers
10. All good things must come to an end

Assignment   Writing Sentences   On your paper, write four sentences for each of the following word groups. Make the first sentence in each group declarative, the second interrogative, the third imperative, and the fourth exclamatory.

1. that flea-bitten dog
2. save a life
3. the noise of the sirens

2.2   Simple Subjects and Simple Predicates

Simple Subjects

Every sentence has a subject and a predicate. The **simple subject** is the noun or pronoun that states whom or what the sentence is about. The simple subject does not include the modifiers of that noun or pronoun. The complete subject (*page 64*) consists of the simple subject plus all of the modifiers of that subject. In this book the term *subject* refers to the simple subject.

Usually the simple subject is a single word. However, in some cases, such as names (Ellie Farnsworth) and titles (*The Grapes of Wrath*), the subject contains more than one word. In the following sentences, the simple subject is in boldface type.

Margaret Riley has a cottage in Nova Scotia.
The **girls** on the volleyball team have been excused.
That **one** is more expensive.
New London, Connecticut, is known for its shipyards.

The simple subject of an imperative sentence is always *you*. Often, *you* is understood rather than stated.

Stroke the kittens gently. [**Think:** *you* stroke . . .]

Simple Predicates

The **simple predicate** is the verb or verb phrase that describes the action or states the condition of the subject. The simple predicate does not include modifiers and words that complete the meaning of the verb. The complete predicate (*page 65*) consists of the simple predicate plus all of the modifiers and words that complete the meaning of the verb. In this book the term *predicate* refers to the simple predicate.

> subj.   pred.
> Most *Europeans* **drive** small cars.

> subj.   pred.
> The shortest *member* of the team **was** six feet tall.

The simple predicate in the following example consists of a verb phrase.

> subj. ┌───pred.───┐
> *Jesse* **will be stationed** in England. [*Will* and *be* are auxiliary verbs. *Stationed* is the main verb.]

Exercise 1   Subjects and Predicates   Copy the following pairs of sentences on your paper. In each sentence, underline the simple subject once and the simple predicate twice. If the subject is the understood *you,* write *you* in parentheses and underline it once.

> SAMPLE   Don Holt, the football star, is across the street.
>   I just saw him.
>
> ANSWER   <u>Don Holt</u>, the football star, <u>is</u> across the street.
>   <u>I</u> just <u>saw</u> him.

1. Olivia's dog was by her side. Its name was Buster.
2. The pen on the desk is leaking. I will fix it.
3. Mr. Wong was very generous. He often gave to charities.
4. Is that bag of beets yours? Nobody else has claimed it.
5. Those berries are not good. Do not eat them!

6. We are planning a vacation. However, we are not sure where to go.
7. Have you heard the news? Tom bought a car.
8. The Jacksons have begun construction on their house. It will be finished by August.
9. The green platter is in the kitchen. We will need it for the appetizers.
10. Please join us. We are going to the movies.

Exercise 2 Subjects and Predicates *Step 1:* Number your paper from 1 to 10. *Step 2:* Next to each number, write the simple subject and the simple predicate of the corresponding sentence in the following passage. *Step 3:* Underline simple subjects once and simple predicates twice.

SAMPLE   Fog has various origins.

ANSWER   <u>Fog</u> <u>has</u>

(1) Fog is actually a low-lying cloud.   (2) It forms near the surface of a body of water.   (3) Usually, warm air condenses over cooler water.   (4) In addition, warm air may condense over cooler land surfaces.   (5) Air has a saturation temperature or dew temperature.   (6) Fog forms at this temperature.   (7) Fogs over large ocean currents are called advection fogs.   (8) Radiation fogs can be seen in some parts of California.   (9) In radiation fog, warm air quickly turns cold.   (10) Steam fog, common in polar regions, is caused by cold air over warm water.

2.3   Compound Subjects and Compound Predicates

A **compound subject** is a simple subject that consists of two or more nouns or pronouns. The term *compound subject* refers to a compound *simple* subject.

Tall **trees,** large **plants,** and exotic **fruit** grow in the jungle. [*Trees, plants,* and *fruit* form the compound subject.]

A **compound predicate** is a simple predicate that consists of two or more verbs or verb phrases. The term *compound predicate* refers to a compound *simple* predicate.

We suddenly **stopped, looked** closely, and **listened** for a long time. [*Stopped, looked,* and *listened* form the compound predicate.]

A sentence may have both a compound subject and a compound predicate.

        subj.   subj. pred.   pred.
Yellow *daisies* and purple *violets* **swayed** and **nodded** in the gentle spring breeze. [*Daisies* and *violets* form the compound subject. *Swayed* and *nodded* form the compound predicate.]

Exercise 1   Subjects and Predicates   On your paper, write the following sentences. Underline the simple subjects once and the simple predicates twice.

> SAMPLE   Jogging and tennis may keep you fit and provide relaxation.
>
> ANSWER   Jogging and tennis may keep you fit and provide relaxation.

1. Jody or Sam will meet you at the airport and drive you home.
2. Betty and Stewart always do their homework and rarely miss a day of class.
3. Dolphins and porpoises look alike and are sometimes mistaken for each other.
4. Ted and Sally awoke early, fixed breakfast, and brought it to their parents.
5. Tourists and permanent residents take their trash to the dump or hire a company to do so.

6. Grace and Sarah did their warm-up exercises, shot a few baskets, and waited for the rest of the team.
7. Carnivals and amusement parks offer fun and provide excitement for the entire family.
8. Priscilla and Alan looked for coins in the sand but found none.

Exercise 2 Writing Compound Subjects On your paper, copy the following sentences. In place of each blank, write a suitable compound subject. Underline the compound subjects that you write.

SAMPLE __?__ will help keep you physically fit.

ANSWER Vitamins and exercise will keep you physically fit.

1. In our town __?__ are rare occurrences.
2. __?__ look like twins.
3. __?__ told us the good news.
4. __?__ keep the camp counselors busy.
5. Beneath the old elm tree, __?__ were seated.

Exercise 3 Writing Compound Predicates On your paper, copy the following sentences. In place of each blank, write a suitable compound predicate. Underline the compound predicates that you write.

SAMPLE We __?__ during the pollen season.

ANSWER We coughed and sneezed during the pollen season.

1. The normally quiet volcano __?__.
2. One of the searchers __?__.
3. The gorilla in the zoo __?__.
4. Two knights in armor __?__.
5. The Andersons' first child __?__.

Writing a Comparison

Write a paragraph in which you compare two people. In your paragraph use examples that demonstrate how the people are similar. Try to use sentences that have compound subjects and compound predicates so that your writing is smooth rather than choppy.

2.4   Complete Subjects and Complete Predicates

2.4a   Complete Subjects

The **complete subject** consists of the simple subject and all of the words that modify it or identify it.

⌐——— complete subject ———⌐
The *girl* in the burgundy dress sang a lullaby. [*The* and *in the burgundy dress* modify *girl,* which is the simple subject.]

⌐———complete subject———⌐
Our *street*, Lincoln Avenue, runs north and south. [*Lincoln Avenue* identifies *street,* which is the simple subject.]

⌐——— complete subject ———⌐
The *canary* that Mrs. Jefferson owns flew from its cage. [*That Mrs. Jefferson owns* modifies *canary. Canary* is the simple subject.]

⌐——— complete subject ———⌐
A small red *fox* and a brown *raccoon* walked by. [The complete subject includes a compound simple subject: *fox* and *raccoon.*]

Exercise 1 Complete Subjects On your paper, write the complete subjects of the following sentences. Then underline the simple subjects.

> SAMPLE The beautiful white horse galloped across the plain.
>
> ANSWER The beautiful white <u>horse</u>

1. The milk in the back of the refrigerator is probably spoiled by now.
2. The family that lives in the brown house moved in just a month ago.
3. Tony's science project was interesting and informative.
4. Jackie, Gwen's cousin, is visiting in town for a few days.
5. The book that you saw lying on the table was written by one of my favorite authors.
6. The door at the end of the hall leads to the conference room.
7. Mr. Patterson's tenth-grade class went to the auditorium for an assembly.
8. The tall woman leading the parade is a friend of mine.
9. Thunder, the stallion in the corner of the corral, is constantly getting loose.
10. The broken fence around the Coopers' yard needed mending.

2.4b Complete Predicates

The **complete predicate** consists of the simple predicate and all of the modifiers and words that complete the meaning of the verb.

> ┌──── complete predicate ────┐
> The weary soldiers *trudged* **through a dense forest.** [*Through a dense forest* modifies *trudged,* which is the simple predicate.]
>
> ┌──────── complete predicate ────────┐
> The child *molded* **the clay pot quickly and carefully.** [*Quickly* and *carefully* modify *molded. The clay pot* completes the meaning of *molded.*]

```
                          ┌───────────── complete predicate ─────────────┐
```
The outfielder *caught* **the ball and** *threw* **it back to the infield.**
[Included in the complete predicate is the compound simple
predicate: *caught* and *threw*.]

Exercise 2   Complete Predicates   On your paper,
write the complete predicates of the following sentences. Then
underline the simple predicates.

> **SAMPLE**   The parachutist jumped from the plane.
>
> **ANSWER**   <u>jumped</u> from the plane

1. Charlene and her brother Bill have quite a bit of homework
   tonight.
2. The startled pheasant raced across the field.
3. Bridget handled the situation calmly and effectively.
4. The tail of Timothy's kite fluttered in the breeze.
5. I found the missing puzzle piece under the table.
6. Al completed all the necessary forms for a summer job at the
   amusement park.
7. The teacher always graded our test papers as fairly as possible.
8. We watched the ship sail toward the horizon.
9. The marathon began with the shuffle of hundreds of feet.
10. The members of the volleyball team practice four nights a
    week.

2.4c   Placement of Subjects and Predicates

You will find subjects and predicates arranged in a variety
of ways in sentences. The placement of the subject and
predicate often depends on the purpose of the sentence.

Declarative Sentences

In a declarative sentence, the subject usually precedes the
predicate. In the examples one line indicates the complete
subject, and two lines indicate the complete predicate.

The cow grazed in the field. [The subject precedes the predicate.]

However, in some declarative sentences the predicate precedes the subject. Such sentences have inverted word order.

Just above the trees flew the helicopter.
There is a cardinal!

In other declarative sentences, the subject appears between two parts of the complete predicate.

Loudly and enthusiastically, the audience applauded the actors. [The adverbs, *loudly* and *enthusiastically,* are part of the complete predicate because they modify the simple predicate, *applauded.*]

Interrogative Sentences

In an interrogative sentence, the subject usually appears between two parts of the predicate.

Are you the new president of the company?

To find the subject and predicate of a question, turn the question into a statement.

QUESTION   Have the two actors agreed to exchange costumes?

STATEMENT   The two actors have agreed to exchange costumes.

Imperative Sentences

In an imperative sentence, the subject, *you,* is usually understood but not stated. Therefore, the entire sentence is the complete predicate.

Please move out of the way. [**Think:** *you* please move . . .]

Exclamatory Sentences

In an exclamatory sentence, the subject often precedes the predicate.

I really won first prize!

Sometimes, however, the subject appears between two parts of the complete predicate.

What a great show the singer gave!

Exercise 3   Subjects and Predicates   *Step 1:* On your paper, write the following sentences. *Step 2:* Underline the complete subjects once and the complete predicates twice. *Step 3:* Write *sub.* over the simple subjects and *pred.* over the simple predicates.

SAMPLE   Up, up, up went the brightly colored balloon.

                          pred.   subj.
ANSWER   Up, up, up went the brightly colored balloon.

1. What have you been doing in physical education class this week?
2. The steady ticking of the clock made me drowsy.
3. On the night in question, June was studying at home.
4. Will you lend me a pencil?
5. Behind the garage was a beautiful patio.
6. Is Sylvia's new car parked across the street?
7. At sunset the fireworks display will start.
8. Did I make the finals in the contest?
9. Ernie's music teacher showed great patience with him.
10. My cousin Alex has won blue ribbons at several fairs.

Exercise 4   Completing Sentences   *Step 1:* On your paper, copy each word group. *Step 2:* Add a subject or a predicate to form a complete sentence. *Step 3:* Underline the complete subject in each sentence.

SAMPLE   In the willows _?_ whistled.

ANSWER   In the willows <u>a whippoorwill</u> whistled.

1. _?_ chased our boat.
2. Did _?_ say that?
3. The entire island _?_.
4. On the highest peak perched _?_.
5. The motorcycle, a Spencer, _?_.

2.5   Complements

A **complement** is a word or a group of words that completes the meaning of the predicate. Complements are always part of the complete predicate.

Belinda's performance amazed **everyone.** [Amazed *whom?* Amazed *everyone. Everyone* is a complement.]

These peaches taste **sour.** [Taste *how?* Taste *sour. Sour* is a complement.]

If the preceding sentences did not have complements, their meaning would be incomplete.

Belinda's performance amazed

These peaches taste

There are two categories of complements: objects and subject complements.

2.5a   Objects

Objects are nouns or pronouns that follow action verbs in the active voice (*Unit 4*). There are two kinds of objects: direct and indirect.

Direct Objects

A direct object is a noun or a pronoun that follows an action verb in the active voice and answers the question *What?* or *Whom?* It receives the action of a verb. Verbs that take direct objects are called **transitive verbs** (*page 19*). Modifiers do not form part of the object.

The ocean liner *struck* an **iceberg.** [**Think:** struck what? Struck an iceberg.]

D.O.
Have you *thanked* **Aunt Millie** for the present? [**Think:** have thanked whom? Have thanked Aunt Millie.]

Exercise 1   Direct Objects   On your paper, list the predicate and the direct object in each sentence. Draw an arrow from each predicate to its direct object.

SAMPLE   Did you read that article on trout fishing?

ANSWER   Did read; article

1. Donald bought a book.
2. Susan carefully planned the menu.
3. Please carry this package for me.
4. I received a postcard from her on Tuesday.
5. Did you see that program yesterday?
6. Does James understand the question?
7. This library serves the entire community.
8. Pam and Roger have new water skis.
9. Take your little sister to the movies with you.
10. The comedian told a very funny story.

Indirect Objects

An indirect object is a noun or a pronoun that names the person or thing *to* whom or *for* whom an action is done. An indirect object follows an action verb in the active voice. In most cases an indirect object is used with a direct object. The indirect object comes immediately after the verb and before the direct object.

verb   I.O. ←   D.O.
The track team awarded **Margarita** a *trophy*. [**Think:** The team awarded a trophy *to* Margarita.]

To tell whether a word is an indirect object, insert the word *to* or *for* before that word as you read the sentence. If the sentence makes sense, the word is an indirect object.

verb   I.O. ←   D.O.
The audience gave **Peter** a standing *ovation*. [**Think:** The audience gave (*to*) Peter a standing ovation.]

verb   I.O. ←   D.O.
Uncle Maxwell built **us** a soapbox *racer*. [**Think:** Uncle Maxwell built (*for*) us a soapbox racer.]

However, if the word *to* or *for* actually appears in the sentence, the noun or pronoun that follows it is not an indirect object. It is an object of the preposition *to* or *for*.

INDIRECT OBJECT   She sang **me** a song.

OBJECT OF A PREPOSITION   She sang a song *to* **me**.

Compound Objects.   Like subjects and verbs, objects may be compound. A **compound object** consists of two or more objects that complete the same predicate.

COMPOUND
DIRECT OBJECT   The workers picked **grapes** and **peaches.**

COMPOUND
INDIRECT OBJECT   Dad gave **Ella** and **me** a dollar.

Exercise 2   Direct and Indirect Objects   On your paper, list the direct objects and the indirect objects in the following sentences. Label the direct objects *D.O.* and the indirect objects *I.O.* Some objects are compound.

> **SAMPLE**   Give them the details.
>
> **ANSWER**   them—I.O.; details—D.O.

1. The tourists boarded the train to Kyoto.
2. Celia showed us the way to the library.
3. I lent Chris my raincoat.
4. Aunt Connie sent me a sweater and a hat.
5. Tell me no lies.
6. Give us the key to the front door.
7. My friend sold Sandra and Leslie her car.
8. Explain the situation to them.
9. Did you show Ken and Elizabeth the sights?
10. I changed my mind about the Saturday job.

Exercise 3   Subjects, Predicates, Objects   *Step 1:* Copy the following ten sentences on your paper. *Step 2:* Underline the simple subjects once and the simple predicates twice. *Step 3:* Write *D.O.* over the direct objects and *I.O.* over the indirect objects.

> **SAMPLE**   Zoos have a fascinating history.
>
> **ANSWER**   <u>Zoos</u> <u><u>have</u></u> a fascinating history.
>   D.O.

1. Around 1500 B.C., Queen Hatshepsut of Egypt built the earliest known zoo.
2. The Greeks used their zoos as living classrooms.
3. The zoos gave the Greeks the opportunity to study plants and animals.
4. In Rome wealthy citizens gave the people huge animal collections for the Colosseum fights.
5. The Middle Ages marked the decline of zoos in Europe.
6. The Aztecs maintained a huge zoo with exhibits of native animals.

7. After A.D. 1500, people in Europe constructed exhibits of animals.

8. However, these exhibits showed the animals in unnatural settings.

9. Later menageries offered visitors a view of animals in more natural environments.

10. In 1752 the Austrians opened the world's first modern zoo, in Vienna.

Exercise 4   Direct and Indirect Objects   Rewrite the following sentences so that each contains at least one direct object and one indirect object. Do not change the meaning of the sentences. Write *D.O.* over the direct objects and *I.O.* over the indirect objects.

> **SAMPLE**   Alice was lent four dollars by Carrie.
>
>   I.O.   D.O.
> **ANSWER**   Carrie lent Alice four dollars.

1. The baby goat was fed corn and milk by the farmer.

2. Susan was given a special award by her classmates.

3. Rudy and Eric were left the entire estate by Mr. Price.

4. Clothes and food were given to the victims by a great many people.

5. The students were taught the fundamentals of oil painting by Mr. Winston, the teacher.

2.5b   Subject Complements

A **subject complement** is a word that comes after a linking verb and identifies or describes the subject. Subject complements often follow forms of the verb *be*. Other verbs may also function as linking verbs and take subject complements. The most common of these linking verbs are in the following list.

appear	look	sound
become	remain	stay
feel	seem	taste
grow	smell	

There are two kinds of subject complements: predicate nominatives and predicate adjectives.

Predicate Nominatives

A **predicate nominative** is a noun or a pronoun that follows a linking verb and identifies the subject of the sentence. The root of the word *nominative* is *nominate,* which means "to name." In a sense, the predicate nominative *renames* the subject.

P.N.
Connie is a **dentist.** [The predicate nominative, *dentist,* identifies the subject, *Connie.*]

P.N.
Their first *choice* had been that **one.** [*One* identifies the subject, *choice.*]

A sentence may have a compound predicate nominative.

P.N.   P.N.   P.N.
The three *choices* were **Angela, Nick,** and **Julio.** [*Angela, Nick,* and *Julio* identify the subject, *choices.*]

Exercise 5   Predicate Nominatives   On your paper, write the predicate nominatives in the following sentences. Some sentences have compound predicate nominatives.

SAMPLE   Sylvia is not just anyone.

ANSWER   anyone

1. Judy became the group leader.
2. The best part of the trip was Yosemite National Park.
3. Two new products of technology are computers and calculators.

4. Your brother will be a fine teacher.
5. After the election Mark remained an adviser to the president.
6. Peggy became one of the corporate heads of the company.
7. My favorite ride is definitely the Ferris wheel.
8. The contest winners were Jennifer and Ted.

Predicate Adjectives

A **predicate adjective** is an adjective that follows a linking verb and modifies the subject of the sentence.

Your *suggestion* was **clever.** [*Clever* modifies the subject, *suggestion.*]

The entire *incident* seemed **ridiculous.** [*Ridiculous* modifies the subject, *incident.*]

A sentence may have a compound predicate adjective.

The *book* was **long** but **suspenseful.** [*Long* and *suspenseful* modify the subject, *book.*]

Exercise 6 Predicate Adjectives On your paper, write the predicate adjectives in the following sentences. Some sentences may have compound predicate adjectives.

> **SAMPLE** The fog was so thick that we could not see a thing.
>
> **ANSWER** thick

1. The kitchen smells marvelous when you are baking bread.
2. Anna sounded happy and healthy on the telephone.
3. Our dog became so listless that we called the veterinarian.

4. The tourists remained calm and alert while they listened for directions.
5. Greg looked proud as he examined his report card.
6. The garage looked great after we finished painting it.
7. She appears confident and capable of doing the job.
8. Jerry's leg grew stronger every day after the doctor took off the cast.

Exercise 7   Subject Complements   On your paper, list the subject complements in the following sentences. Label each complement *P.N.* (predicate nominative) or *P.A.* (predicate adjective).

> **SAMPLE**   That soup looks delicious.
>
> **ANSWER**   delicious—P.A.

1. The clerk at the department store was courteous to everyone.
2. Her daughter eventually became an admiral.
3. You are an extremely lucky person!
4. Actually, I am rather doubtful about the situation.
5. Could that be it over there?
6. Our soccer team's offense was explosive this year.
7. That woman in the limousine must be a celebrity.
8. Fortunately, the case was not serious.
9. We are still unsure about the candidates.
10. Is my answer, by any chance, the right one?

Assignment   Complements   On your paper, write six sentences, one for each of the following kinds of complements. Underline the complement in each sentence that you write.

1. direct object
2. indirect object
3. predicate nominative
4. predicate adjective
5. compound predicate nominative
6. compound indirect object

Predicate Adjectives in Writing

When you write descriptions, you can often use predicate adjectives to express the mood or feeling of a setting. In the following sentences, the predicate adjectives in italics express a mood of optimism.

The wind suddenly seemed *fresher* than it had been in months, and the air was *warm.*

Write a descriptive paragraph, using predicate adjectives to express the mood of the place that you are describing. Select one of the following settings:

1. a lake surrounded by mountains
2. a football stadium
3. the desert under the midday sun
4. the shore of an ocean or a lake
5. the downtown area of a city

2.6 Sentence Diagrams

Every sentence consists of words from different parts of speech that work together to form a complete thought. One good way to see the relationship between these words is to diagram them. A **sentence diagram** is a picture of the structure of a sentence. For instance, a diagram shows whether a noun is the subject of a sentence, the object of a preposition, a direct object, an indirect object, or a predicate nominative. To diagram correctly, you must follow certain rules.

2.6a   Diagraming Subjects and Predicates

The basic design for a sentence diagram consists of two parts that indicate the subject and the predicate. You form these parts by crossing a horizontal base line with a vertical bar. The vertical bar should extend an equal distance above and below the base line. Always use a ruler in drawing the lines of a diagram.

BASIC DIAGRAM DESIGN

Write the simple subject of a sentence on the base line to the left of the bar. Put the simple predicate to the right of the bar. Use this placement even if the predicate precedes the subject in the sentence, as in interrogative sentences. Put all the words in a verb phrase together. A name consisting of more than one word is a single compound noun. Always capitalize the first word in the sentence, and do not include punctuation marks.

DECLARATIVE   Lucy Anderson sang.

| Lucy Anderson | sang |

INTERROGATIVE   Was Lucy singing?

| Lucy | Was singing |

In many imperative and exclamatory sentences, the subject *you* is understood but not stated. When you diagram such sentences, write the understood subject in the appropriate place in the diagram. Put the understood word in parentheses.

Sing!

| (you) | Sing |

Exercise 1 Diagraming Sentences On your paper, diagram the following sentences. Remember to use a ruler and to allow enough space for each diagram.

SAMPLE   Are you joking?

ANSWER

| you | Are joking |

1. Help!
2. Did Mr. Ames leave?
3. Did you walk?

4. Everyone smiled.
5. Were you calling?

2.6b   Diagraming Modifiers

Diagram each adjective and adverb on a slanted line just below the word that it modifies. If an adverb modifies an adjective or another adverb, write the adverb on an L-shaped line extending from the adjective or adverb that it modifies. Diagram *not* and *never* as adverbs modifying the verb with which they are used.

The young soloist sang quite beautifully. [*Quite* is an adverb modifying *beautifully*.]

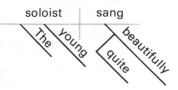

Exercise 2   Diagraming Modifiers   On your paper, diagram the following sentences. Remember to use a ruler and to allow enough space for each diagram.

SAMPLE   Is each student working hard?

ANSWER

1. We have met only recently.
2. Those flowers are wilting quickly.
3. A very kind teacher retired early.
4. Rex proceeded carefully.
5. My older brother bowls extremely well.
6. Have the bus riders been waiting patiently?
7. The silver blimp circled very slowly.
8. Those carefree monkeys played delightfully.

2.6c   Diagraming Complements

Direct objects, indirect objects, and subject complements are all diagramed in different ways.

Diagraming a Direct Object

The direct object appears on the base line and to the right of the predicate. To separate the direct object from the predicate, extend the base line to the right of the verb and draw a vertical bar above it but not below it. Write the direct object on the base line, and place the modifiers of the direct object on slanted lines below it.

Henrietta purchased an extremely old bicycle. [*Bicycle* is the direct object.]

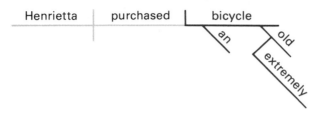

Diagraming an Indirect Object

To diagram a sentence with an indirect object, draw a slanted line below the verb. From the bottom of that line, draw a line parallel to the base. Write the indirect object on the parallel line.

I.O.   D.O.
The incident taught Reggie a lesson. [**Think:** The incident taught a lesson *to* Reggie.]

Diagraming Predicate Nominatives and Predicate Adjectives

To diagram a sentence with a predicate nominative or a predicate adjective, extend the base line to the right of the verb. From the base line, draw a line that extends upward and toward the subject. Write the predicate nominative or the predicate adjective on the extended base line. Place any

modifiers of the predicate nominative or predicate adjective on
slanted lines below it.

Charlene is an artist. [*Artist* is a predicate nominative.]

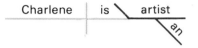

He was much too quiet. [*Quiet* is a predicate adjective.]

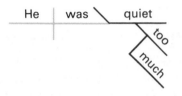

Exercise 3 Diagraming Complements Diagram the
following sentences on your paper.

SAMPLE   The cat quickly grew curious.

ANSWER

1. Did you see Beth yesterday?
2. His name was David Diaz.
3. She made us some tea.
4. We were not wealthy.
5. Can you lend me your car?
6. Sharon is Mrs. Carlson's good friend.
7. Do not miss this chance.
8. Sandy seemed rather timid.

9. I showed Loni another route.

10. Will this be the last one?

2.6d   Diagraming Compound Elements

Compound elements, which consist of two or more items, are diagramed similarly to single elements in a sentence.

Diagraming Compound Subjects and Compound Predicates

Write the parts of a compound subject or a compound predicate on parallel base lines. Then connect them with a vertical line of dashes. On that line, write the conjunction that joins the parts. Connect the compound elements to the rest of the sentence with solid diagonal lines.

Tom, Ed, and I fished.

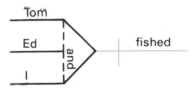

If a compound element has a modifier or a complement, diagram the modifier or complement as you normally would.

Tom, Ed, and I fished first and then played tennis.

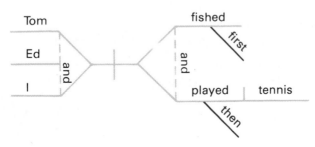

Diagraming Compound Modifiers

When two or more modifiers are connected by a conjunction, write the modifiers on slanted lines below the word that they modify. Then draw a line of dashes between the slanted lines, and write the conjunction on the line of dashes.

The young but talented soloist sang beautifully and movingly.

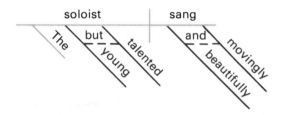

Diagraming Compound Complements

To diagram a compound complement, write the complements on parallel lines and connect the lines with a line of dashes. Write the conjunction on the line of dashes.

COMPOUND DIRECT OBJECT
I have not seen Milly, Rudy, or Wendy.

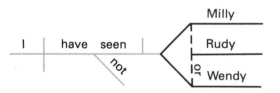

COMPOUND INDIRECT OBJECT
Mrs. Wilson gave him and her their presents.

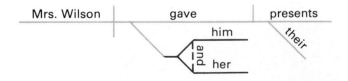

COMPOUND PREDICATE NOMINATIVE
My two sons are Phil and Ron.

Compound predicate adjectives are diagramed in the same way as compound predicate nominatives.

Exercise 4 Diagraming Compound Elements Diagram the following sentences on your paper.

1. Jody and Larry walked quickly.
2. Betty drove downtown, worked, and came home.
3. We spoke slowly and very clearly.
4. We could see their eager and happy faces.
5. She watched David and Wilma closely.

Assignment Diagraming Sentences On your paper, write and diagram five sentences.

Unit Practice

Practice 1

A. Sentence Purpose *(pages 57–59)* On your paper, label each of the following sentences *Declarative, Interrogative, Imperative,* or *Exclamatory*.

1. An angry Siamese fighting fish turns blue, red, purple, and green.
2. Return this reference book to the appropriate shelf.
3. Here is the coin that you lost!
4. Take a photograph of the erupting volcano!
5. Mr. Gelb, does your piano need tuning?

B. Simple Subjects and Simple Predicates *(pages 59–61)* On your paper, list the simple subject and the simple predicate in each of the following sentences. Underline the simple subjects once and the simple predicates twice.

6. Jean-Claude Killy won three skiing medals in the 1968 Olympic Games.
7. Our mathematics class will meet in the lobby this morning.
8. Has *Little Women* been ordered yet?
9. That table had been polished with a soft cloth.
10. Her legs were sore after the long hike.

C. Compound Subjects and Compound Predicates *(pages 61–64)* On your paper, list the compound subject and compound predicate in each of the following sentences. Underline the compound subjects once and the compound predicates twice.

11. Shirts and sheets are flapping and flying off your clothesline!
12. Al's cousin and Susan's friend bicycled to the pond and raced back.
13. You or Jane should wrap these bundles and packages and then mail them.

14. On a farm, tractors and combines pull heavy equipment, thresh grain, and harvest crops.
15. Did the mayor and the council discuss the issue or vote on it?

D. Complete Subjects and Complete Predicates

(pages 64–69) On your paper, write the following sentences, and underline the complete subjects once and the complete predicates twice. If the subject is the understood *you,* write *you* in parentheses and underline it.

16. Was the stranger wearing a gray felt hat?
17. Geraldine and her cousin Beth opened the front door and stepped quietly inside.
18. Send your typed application to this office.
19. That is a gorgeous cabinet standing against the wall.
20. Over the mantel hung an original oil painting.

E. Complements *(pages 69–77)* On your paper, list the complements in each of the following sentences. Label each complement *Direct object, Indirect object, Predicate nominative,* or *Predicate adjective.*

21. Did Marcia lend Judy her world map?
22. Sandy, show us your paper birds and drawings of mammals.
23. Platinum feels heavier than most precious metals.
24. Dorothy quickly handed Beth the baton, and they pulled ahead.
25. The flowers in our garden are tiger lilies and daisies.

F. Sentence Diagrams *(pages 77–85)* On your paper, diagram each of the following sentences. Be sure to use a ruler.

26. Did the chess fans seem especially knowledgeable?
27. Give Claude your address.

(Continue on the next page.)

28. Those bright red cardinals nested and stayed there.
29. You nearly told us the correct answer!
30. Glass blowing and weaving have become popular crafts.

Practice 2

On your paper, write the words and phrases in italics in the following passage. Label each *Simple subject, Simple predicate, Complete subject, Complete predicate, Direct object, Indirect object, Predicate nominative,* or *Predicate adjective.*

Was   (1) *Robin Hood* merely a legend, or did he actually exist? Some historians   (2) *give us certain evidence that he existed.* For example, a man   (3) *was born* at Wakefield in 1285. His name was   (4) *Robin Hood.*   (5) *Another possible candidate* was Robert Fitzooth, Earl of Huntingdon. Either man   (6) *may have been the real Robin Hood.* The legend of Robin Hood is quite   (7) *old.* In 1849 the oldest surviving (8) *ballad* about Robin Hood was printed. These and other ballads describe his skilled   (9) *archery,* his loyal outlaw band, and his generosity. Robin Hood   (10) *stole* from the rich. He gave poor   (11) *people* his plunder. Was Robin Hood   (12) *real?* History will probably never give   (13) *us* a final   (14) *answer.* In spite of that, Robin Hood remains a heroic   (15) *symbol.*

Unit Tests

Test 1

A. Sentence Purpose *(pages 57–59)* On your paper, label each of the following sentences *Declarative, Interrogative, Imperative,* or *Exclamatory.*

1. A barometer measures the pressure of the air.
2. Tell me what that road sign says.
3. How close you came to falling!
4. Leave this arena at once!
5. Do you know the reason for the cancellation?

B. Simple Subjects and Simple Predicates *(pages 59–61)* On your paper, list the simple subject and the simple predicate in each of the following sentences. Underline the simple subjects once and the simple predicates twice.

6. Abraham Gesner invented the lamp oil called kerosene.
7. Most of my family will attend the ceremony.
8. *The Jungle Book* appeared on the summer reading list.
9. Which game can be located easily?
10. A bowl of apples fell from her hands into the sink.

C. Compound Subjects and Compound Predicates *(pages 61–64)* On your paper, list the compound subject and the compound predicate in each of the following sentences. Underline the compound subjects once and the compound predicates twice.

11. Serena and Tim picked and ate all the strawberries.
12. Brushes, crayons, and paint are stored in the studio and should stay there.
13. Will you and your sister stay or move from this city?
14. An old barn and a fence fell during the storm and were destroyed.
15. Ducks and geese flew over us and headed south.

(Continue on the next page.)

D. Complete Subjects and Complete Predicates

(pages 64–69) On your paper, write the following sentences, and underline the complete subjects once and the complete predicates twice. If the subject is the understood *you,* write *you* in parentheses and underline it.

16. Who built the giant pyramids and the Egyptian temples?
17. Gently and safely, the hot-air balloon landed in a large field.
18. Go to the front of the registration line.
19. The audience showed its appreciation with applause and cheers.
20. Above the valley loomed a lush courtyard and a medieval castle.

E. Complements *(pages 69–77)* On your paper, list the complements in each of the following sentences. Label each complement *Direct object, Indirect object, Predicate nominative,* or *Predicate adjective.*

21. Please buy me brass candlesticks at the fair.
22. Did I send Cora her birthday card and presents in time?
23. The youngest scouts were adventurous explorers.
24. Mr. Hess's lectures about archaeology always seem popular.
25. Thomas Edison created the electric light and the phonograph and became one of the world's greatest inventors.

F. Sentence Diagrams *(pages 77–85)* On your paper, diagram each of the following sentences. Be sure to use a ruler.

26. Will Wendy seriously study biology or chemistry?
27. Leave the busy entrance now.
28. Our helpful neighbor gave us our mail.
29. Those mountaineers were quite courageous.
30. Arabian camels are valuable desert animals.

Test 2

On your paper, write the words and phrases in italics in the following passage. Label each *Simple subject, Simple predicate, Complete subject, Complete predicate, Direct object, Indirect object, Predicate nominative,* or *Predicate adjective.*

What (1) *are* sponges? They are fascinating (2) *animals.* They (3) *resemble bushes, branches, cones, or vases.* Their brilliant colors are (4) *red,* blue, pink, yellow, or purple. (5) *Those* in tropical waters are the most colorful sponges. Food and oxygen enter the (6) *sponge* through tiny pores. (7) *Thirty gallons of water* are pumped and filtered through its chambers each day. These sea creatures are (8) *helpful* as well as interesting. Sponges give (9) *crabs,* fish, and sea urchins both (10) *shelter* and camouflage. Humans (11) *harvest, dry, and sell them for commercial use.* They (12) *are* excellent for cleaning just about anything. Also, this primitive animal gives (13) *scientists* valuable clues about adaptation and cell life. Scientists (14) *tell us that sponges have existed and adapted for 550 million years.* The sponge is definitely a (15) *survivor.*

Phrases
and Clauses

Unit Preview

If you read a typical newspaper article, you will notice that most of the sentences are straightforward and easy to understand. If you read a college textbook, you will see that the sentences are longer and more complex. As you read the following paragraph, what do you notice about the structure of the sentences?

> The Panama Canal was a tremendous feat of engineering. It took ten years of hard work to complete. It shortened the distance from New York to San Francisco. The distance became approximately eight thousand miles less. The canal was difficult to build. Workers dug earth from the canal. The earth was soft. It slid back into the canal. The engineers worked hard. They solved this problem. They completed the canal in 1914.

The paragraph is rather monotonous because every sentence has the same structure. In every sentence the simple predicate immediately follows the simple subject: "Panama Canal was"; "it took"; "it shortened."

For Analysis   Read the rewritten version of the paragraph and answer the questions that follow.

> The Panama Canal was a tremendous feat of engineering. When the canal was completed after ten years of hard work, it shortened the distance from New York to San Francisco by

approximately eight thousand miles. However, the canal was difficult to build. When workers dug earth from the canal, the earth, which was soft, slid back into the canal. After the engineers had worked hard to solve this problem, they completed the canal in 1914.

1. In your opinion, what is the major difference between the first paragraph and the second?
2. Which paragraph has fewer sentences?
3. How are the sentences in the second paragraph different from those in the first?
4. Which paragraph reads more smoothly? Why?

In the second paragraph, the sentences are longer and have more variety because they contain a greater mixture of phrases and clauses. Phrases and clauses give the writer much greater flexibility in sentence structure. In this unit you will learn how phrases and clauses function in sentences.

3.1   Phrases

A **phrase** is a group of related words used as a single part of speech. A phrase lacks a subject, a predicate, or both. Consequently, a phrase cannot be a sentence. This unit will deal with three common kinds of phrases: prepositional phrases, appositive phrases, and verbal phrases.

3.1a   Prepositional Phrases

A **prepositional phrase** consists of a preposition, its object, and any modifiers of that object. In most prepositional phrases, the preposition precedes the object. In the following sentences, the prepositional phrases are in boldface.

$$\overset{\text{prep.}}{} \qquad \overset{\text{obj.}}{}$$

We questioned the scientist repeatedly **about her discovery.**

$$\overset{\text{prep.}}{} \qquad \overset{\text{obj.}}{}$$

Please place these towels **in the linen closet**.

In some sentences, especially questions, the preposition follows its object.

$$\overset{\text{obj.}}{} \qquad\qquad\qquad\qquad \overset{\text{prep.}}{}$$

Which building did the man point **to**? [**Think:** *To which building* did the man point?]

A prepositional phrase may have more than one object.

$$\overset{\text{prep.}}{} \qquad\qquad \overset{\text{obj.}}{} \qquad \overset{\text{obj.}}{}$$

I have not heard **from my favorite aunt and uncle**.

Prepositional Phrases Used as Adjectives

A prepositional phrase functions as an adjective if it modifies a noun or a pronoun. Such prepositional phrases are sometimes called **adjective phrases.**

MODIFIES NOUN   The *cargo* on the ship was unloaded.
[Which cargo? The cargo on the ship.]

MODIFIES PRONOUN   Rosalie is *someone* with great talent.
[What kind of person? Someone with great talent.]

A prepositional phrase can modify the object in another prepositional phrase.

She went skating at the **rink** on Mulberry Street.
[Which rink? The rink on Mulberry Street.]

Prepositional Phrases Used as Adverbs

A prepositional phrase functions as an adverb if it modifies a verb, an adjective, or another adverb. Such prepositional phrases are sometimes called **adverb phrases.**

MODIFIES VERB
The scouts *marched* over the hill. [*Over the hill* tells where the scouts marched.]

MODIFIES ADJECTIVE
The child is *skillful* with a paint brush. [*With a paint brush* tells how the child is skillful.]

MODIFIES ADVERB
We should meet *late* in the day. [*In the day* modifies *late*. *Late* is an adverb modifying *should meet*.]

Exercise 1 Prepositional Phrases *Step 1:* On your paper, write the prepositional phrases in each sentence. *Step 2:* Next to each phrase, write the word that it modifies. *Step 3:* Label each phrase *Adjective phrase* or *Adverb phrase*.

SAMPLE   The portrait of the governor was sold.

ANSWER   of the governor, portrait—Adjective phrase

1. The deer struggled up the side of the mountain.
2. Our team traveled to Toronto for the soccer tournament.
3. The children dug roads in the sand for the toy cars.
4. The head of the committee scheduled the bill without delay.
5. I purchased this radio from the store on the corner.
6. With some hesitation, Rhoda agreed to the plan.
7. The snake slithered under the boxes against the wall.
8. I was bored during the movie but stayed until the end.
9. All except Bernie climbed the tower on the hill.
10. Balloons glided over the meadow into the sunset.

3.1b Appositives and Appositive Phrases

An **appositive** is a noun or a pronoun placed near another noun or pronoun to explain or identify it.

The *surgeon*, **Dr. Alfred Thornton,** arrived late. [*Dr. Alfred Thornton* identifies the surgeon.]

On vacation, I enjoy two *activities*, **swimming** and **surfing.** [*Swimming* and *surfing* identify the activities.]

Appositive Phrases

An **appositive phrase** includes all the words or phrases that modify the appositive. The appositive phrase identifies a noun or a pronoun.

Mrs. Hartwell, **my mother's friend from St. Louis,** is visiting us. [*Friend* is the appositive. *My, mother's,* and *from St. Louis* modify *friend.*]

In some sentences the appositive precedes the word that it modifies.

A person of many talents, *Caroline* sings and dances.

Essential and Nonessential Appositives.   An essential appositive or an essential appositive phrase is necessary to the meaning of the sentence. Do not set it off from the rest of the sentence with commas.

I have been talking to my *sister* **Eileen.** [The appositive, *Eileen,* is essential to the sentence. Without it, the reader would not know which sister the writer has been talking to. Therefore, the appositive is not set off with commas.]

A nonessential appositive or a nonessential appositive phrase is not necessary to the meaning of the sentence. Therefore, you must set it off with commas.

John won first *prize, a trip to London.* [The appositive phrase, *a trip to London*, is nonessential. The appositive is not necessary in identifying the prize, for there is only one first prize. Therefore, the appositive phrase is set off with commas.]

Exercise 2 Appositives On your paper, list the appositive or appositive phrase in each sentence. Beside it write the noun or pronoun that it identifies.

SAMPLE   My brother Louis is a plumber.
ANSWER   Louis—brother

1. Mr. Hopkins, the man for whom I work, is opposed to billboard advertising.
2. Stories about Sherlock Holmes, the famous detective, can keep me in suspense for hours.
3. An efficient organizer, Mrs. Wing is always elected chairperson of a committee.
4. The keynote speaker, Brad Bartlett, received an ovation.
5. The homophones *there, their,* and *they're* cause spelling problems for many people.

Exercise 3 Prepositional and Appositive Phrases
In the following passage, prepositional phrases and appositive phrases are in italics. Number your paper from 1 to 18, and write each italicized phrase beside the appropriate number. Label each phrase *Prepositional phrase* or *Appositive phrase*.

SAMPLE   Amelia Earhart disappeared mysteriously *in 1937.*
ANSWER   in 1937—Prepositional phrase

(1) *On the morning* of July 3, 1937, Amelia Earhart piloted her airplane, (2) *a Lockheed Electra,* (3) *down a runway* in Lee, New Guinea. The famed American flyer was accompanied (4) *by Lieutenant Commander Fred Noonan,* (5) *her navigator.* Earhart's destination, (6) *the tiny coral reef named Howland Island,* lay more than twenty-five hundred miles (7) *across the ocean.* Some weeks earlier, she had flown from Florida (8) *on the first leg* of her flight, (9) *an attempt to circle the globe.* It was a journey no woman pilot had ever accomplished (10) *on her own.* Weather conditions were poor and the plane developed problems, but no one knows exactly what happened (11) *aboard the Electra.* Earhart and Noonan could not find the location (12) *of Howland Island.* They had been (13) *in partial contact* with a Coast Guard cutter, and (14) *at one point* Earhart informed the cutter, "Gas is running low." Although numerous signals were sent (15) *by the cutter,* the Electra disappeared (16) *without a trace.* Amelia Earhart, (17) *a truly courageous aviator,* disappeared (18) *with it.*

3.1c   Verbals and Verbal Phrases

Verbals are forms of verbs that function as nouns, adjectives, or adverbs. For instance, a verbal may be the subject of a sentence, or it may be a predicate nominative. Even though verbals function as other parts of speech, they have some of the properties of verbs. For example, they express actions, and they may take direct objects, indirect objects, predicate nominatives, or predicate adjectives. When you use a modifier or a complement with a verbal, you form a **verbal phrase.** There are three kinds of verbals: participles, gerunds, and infinitives.

Participles

A **participle** is a verb form that can function as an adjective. Even when it functions as an adjective, a participle retains some of the properties of verbs. It expresses action or condition, and it may be followed by a complement.

The **cheering** *sailors* stood on deck.

In the preceding sentence, *cheering* is a participle. The word has the properties of a verb because it expresses an action. *Cheering* functions as an adjective because it modifies the noun *sailors*.

There are two kinds of participles: present and past. The present participle and the past participle are two of the four principal parts of a verb. The other two principal parts are the infinitive and the past. For an explanation of principal parts, see Unit 4.

Present Participles. A **present participle** is formed by adding the suffix *-ing* to the infinitive form of a verb.

It was a **frightening** *experience*. [*Frightening* is a present participle that consists of the verb *frighten* and the suffix *-ing*. *Frightening* modifies *experience*.]

Past Participles. How you form a **past participle** depends on whether the verb is regular or irregular (*Unit 4*).

1. To form the past participle of a **regular verb,** add the suffix *-d* or *-ed* to the infinitive form of the verb. Most verbs are regular.

VERB	PAST PARTICIPLE
play	played
move	moved

2. To form the past participle of an **irregular verb,** you use a special form of the verb. You must memorize the past participles of irregular verbs. See Unit 4 for a list of the past participles of many irregular verbs.

VERB	PAST PARTICIPLE
know	known
shrink	shrunk

REGULAR   The **inspired** *workers* tried even harder. [*Inspired* is a past participle that tells what kind of workers.]

IRREGULAR   Clint took a **frozen** *dinner* out of the refrigerator. [*Frozen* is the past participle of *freeze* and modifies *dinner*.]

A participle is sometimes set off from the word that it modifies by commas.

Rescued, the *boy* vowed not to walk on thin ice again.

Present participles and past participles do not always function as adjectives. They can also form part of a verb phrase. When participles are part of a verb phrase, they are not verbals.

The older children *have been* **frightening** the younger ones. [The participle, *frightening,* is the main verb. *Have* and *been* are the auxiliary verbs.]

In this unit the emphasis is on present and past participles that function as adjectives. For a complete explanation of participles used as verbs, see Unit 4.

Exercise 4   Participles   On your paper, list the participles that function as adjectives in the following sentences. Beside each participle, write the word that it modifies. Some sentences may contain more than one participle.

SAMPLE   This has been a most exhausting day.

ANSWER   exhausting—day

1. Everyone enjoys Arturo's wry humor and smiling face.
2. The captivated audience laughed at every joke.
3. I was as quiet as a stalking cat.
4. Charlie made a diving catch to end the exciting game.
5. "I have a flooded basement," my neighbor told me.
6. We set the table with the cleaned and polished silver.
7. The crowded bus sped right by us.
8. The snarling dogs behind the gate frightened us.

Participial Phrases

A **participial phrase** consists of a participle and its modifiers and complements. The entire participial phrase functions as an adjective to modify a noun or a pronoun. Both present participles and past participles may form participial phrases.

Suspecting the butler, *Detective Conroy* set a trap. [The participial phrase consists of the present participle, *suspecting,* and its direct object, *butler.*]

The *child* **lost in the store** began to cry. [The participial phrase consists of the past participle, *lost,* and the prepositional phrase, *in the store.*]

Suddenly remembering the rolls in the oven, *Burt* ran to the kitchen. [The participial phrase consists of the present participle, *remembering;* the adverb, *suddenly,* which modifies *remembering; rolls,* the direct object of *remembering; the,* which modifies *rolls;* and *in the oven,* which modifies *rolls.*]

Exercise 5 Participial Phrases On your paper, list the participial phrases in the following sentences. Next to each phrase, write the word that it modifies.

> SAMPLE   Driving carefully, Harry avoided patches of ice.
>
> ANSWER   Driving carefully—Harry

1. Sitting on the beach, Stacey got a slight sunburn.
2. Thelma found her little sister hiding in the closet.
3. Granted another chance, I could do a better job.
4. Feeling confident, Regina approached the speaker.
5. There were six people standing in line.
6. We could hear the leaves fluttering in the gentle breeze.
7. Determined to earn some money, Margie took two jobs.
8. The wagons, creaking under their loads, moved slowly.
9. The scales used in the earlier experiment were inaccurate.
10. I watched a rooster pecking at a few grains of corn.

Gerunds

A **gerund** is a verbal that ends in *ing* and functions only as a noun. Although it performs the same functions as a noun, a gerund has some of the properties of a verb. It expresses action or condition and may be followed by a direct object, an indirect object, a predicate nominative, or a predicate adjective.

He stopped his **singing** abruptly.

I get exercise by **riding** a bicycle.

SUBJECT	**Jogging** has become very popular.
PREDICATE NOMINATIVE	My favorite pastime is **camping.**
DIRECT OBJECT	They enjoyed your **singing.**
OBJECT OF A PREPOSITION	You can help us by **cooperating.**
INDIRECT OBJECT	Julia gave **fishing** a try.
APPOSITIVE	My favorite exercise, **swimming,** keeps me in great shape.

Gerund or Participle?

Do not confuse gerunds with participles. Remember that a participle can function as an adjective, but a gerund always functions as a noun.

PARTICIPLE   Have you seen my **talking** *bird*? [*Talking* is used as an adjective to tell what kind of bird.]

GERUND   **Talking** is one of my favorite activities. [*Talking* is used as a noun that functions as the subject of the sentence.]

Exercise 6 Gerunds On your paper, list the gerunds in the following sentences. Tell whether each gerund functions as a subject, a predicate nominative, a direct object, an object of a preposition, an indirect object, or an appositive.

SAMPLE   After studying, relax for a while.

ANSWER   studying—object of a preposition

1. You can learn a great deal from reading.
2. Seeing is believing.
3. You can improve your writing with this course.
4. Mountaineering and skydiving are sports for hearty souls.
5. His singing has improved greatly.
6. We could hear the sound of laughing in the distance.
7. The photography instructor said that we would probably need her help with the first step, developing, and the last step, enlarging.
8. Yesterday, a sports network gave curling its first national exposure in the United States.

Gerund Phrases

A **gerund phrase** consists of a gerund and its modifiers and complements.

┌─gerund phrase─┐
The sudden ringing startled me. [*The* and *sudden* are adjectives that modify the gerund, *ringing*.]

┌─gerund phrase─┐
Ringing the bell is Mark's job. [*Bell* is the direct object of the gerund, *ringing*. Remember that a gerund retains the properties of a verb and may take a complement.]

103

┌──────gerund phrase──────┐
Greg's worst habit is **being late for meetings.** [*Late* is a predicate adjective that modifies the gerund, *being. For meetings* is
a prepositional phrase that modifies *late*.]

Like the gerund, a gerund phrase may perform all the
functions of a noun.

SUBJECT	**Playing the drums** is Karl's hobby.
PREDICATE NOMINATIVE	Chester's job was **feeding the lions.**
DIRECT OBJECT	The committee opposed **raising taxes.**
OBJECT OF A PREPOSITION	We should proceed by **moving slowly.**
INDIRECT OBJECT	He gave **television sportscasting** new respectability.
APPOSITIVE	Her task, **reading ten books in two days,** seemed impossible.

Exercise 7   Gerund Phrases   On your paper, list the
gerund phrases in the following sentences. Tell whether each
phrase functions as a subject, a predicate nominative, a direct
object, an indirect object, an object of a preposition, or an
appositive.

SAMPLE	Sally enjoys going to the Indianapolis 500.
ANSWER	going to the Indianapolis 500—direct object

1. Rowing a boat requires agility and strength.
2. Laura enjoyed vacationing in Michigan last summer.
3. Lenore got a sore throat from yelling during the game.
4. I could not stop the ringing in my ears.
5. Passing the course was actually rather easy.
6. What do you hope to gain by exaggerating your grievances?
7. Building a dam requires spending millions of dollars.
8. Their first task was locating the reference books.

Infinitives

An **infinitive** is a verbal that consists of the first principal part (*Unit 4*), or basic form, of the verb. It is usually preceded by the word *to*. An infinitive may function as a noun, an adjective, or an adverb. The infinitive has some of the characteristics of verbs. It expresses action or condition, and it may be followed by a complement.

NOUN   **To travel** is exciting. [subject]

                       Mrs. Palmer loves **to travel.** [direct object]

                       Her plan was **to travel.** [predicate nominative]

ADJECTIVE   The *person* **to see** is Mr. Crosby. [Which person? The person to see.]

ADVERB   I *lowered* my arm **to signal.** [Why did I lower my arm? To signal.]

                       This game is *easy* **to play.** [How is the game easy? It is easy to play.]

Sometimes the infinitive is used without the word *to*.

Do you dare **go** scuba diving? [Think: Do you dare *to* go scuba diving?]

Infinitive or Preposition?

Do not confuse infinitives with prepositional phrases. Remember that *to* plus a verb is an infinitive, and *to* plus a noun or a pronoun is a prepositional phrase.

INFINITIVE   verb
                            I plan **to graduate** next year.

PREPOSITIONAL   noun
PHRASES   You should go **to the hospital.**

                                   pro.
                        She told the truth **to me.**

Exercise 8   Infinitives   On your paper, list the infinitives in the following sentences. Tell whether each infinitive functions as a noun, an adjective, or an adverb.

SAMPLE   The window to paint is in the basement.

ANSWER   to paint—adjective

1. My dog loves to swim.
2. To some people, a foreign language is difficult to learn.
3. I have so much homework to do before we go to the movie!
4. To disagree may not be wise.
5. Carole's goal is to excel so that she can go to college.
6. Your next novel to read is *The Old Man and the Sea.*
7. The scout rode ahead of the wagon train to explore.
8. Jo went to her room, where she planned to study.

Infinitive Phrases

An **infinitive phrase** consists of an infinitive and its modifiers and complements.

MODIFIERS   I want you **to drive slowly.** [The adverb, *slowly,* modifies the infinitive, *drive.*]

COMPLEMENTS   Doreen's mother told her **to look surprised.** [*Surprised* is a predicate adjective following the infinitive, *look.*]

I decided **to give my sister a game.** [*Game* is the direct object of the infinitive, *give,* and *sister* is the indirect object.]

The infinitive phrase can function as a noun, an adjective, or an adverb.

NOUN   **To return the gift** would be impossible. [subject]

She tried **to break the record.** [direct object]

The team's plan is **to use trick plays.** [predicate nominative]

ADJECTIVE	It was a *time* to pull together. [What kind of time? A time to pull together.]
ADVERB	He *braked* to go around the corner. [Why did he brake? To go around the corner.]

Exercise 9   Infinitive Phrases   On your paper, write the infinitive phrases in the following sentences. Tell whether each infinitive phrase functions as a noun, an adjective, or an adverb. In some infinitive phrases, the word *to* is implied rather than stated.

SAMPLE   To own my own car is my dream.
ANSWER   To own my own car—noun

1. We are glad to see you again.
2. He appears to be mistaken.
3. I prefer to listen to classical music.
4. The president made the decision to bring in an expert.
5. I applaud Trudy's ambition to write poetry.
6. The speaker raised her hand to quiet the applause.
7. I would not dare climb the mountain alone.
8. To surrender without a fight would be unthinkable.

Exercise 10   Verbal Phrases   Copy the following sentences on your paper, and replace each blank with the kind of verbal phrase named in parentheses. Underline the verbal phrase that you write.

SAMPLE   Judy's job was __?__. (infinitive phrase)
ANSWER   Judy's job was to watch for everyone's arrival.

1. The rake __?__ belongs to Mr. Wilson. (participial phrase)
2. The Andersons celebrated their granddaughter's graduation by __?__. (gerund phrase)
3. __?__ is Gloria's ambition. (infinitive phrase)

4. __?__, Andrea rose to speak to the city council. (participial phrase)
5. Thomas Edison is most famous for __?__. (gerund phrase)
6. __?__, Peter looked at the stars for more than an hour. (participial phrase)
7. Marilyn fixed the bike __?__. (participial phrase)
8. It's great __?__ when you go to the ballpark. (infinitive phrase)

3.2   Clauses

A **clause** is a group of related words that contains both a subject and a predicate. There are two kinds of clauses: independent and subordinate.

3.2a   Independent Clauses

An **independent clause** can stand by itself as a sentence. The following sentence contains two independent clauses.

We were going to a movie last night, but **the car wouldn't start.**

Both clauses can stand alone as separate sentences.

We were going to a movie last night.
The car wouldn't start.

Like all clauses, an independent clause has a subject and a predicate. In the following example, the simple subject is underlined once, and the simple predicate is underlined twice.

```
       ┌──────indep. clause─────────┐   ┌───────indep. clause─────────┐
       The wind was blowing hard, and the drifts were six feet high.
```

Exercise 1 Independent Clauses On your paper, write the following sentences, replacing the blanks with independent clauses. In each new clause, underline the simple subject once and the simple predicate twice.

SAMPLE   While everyone was sleeping, _?_.

ANSWER   While everyone was sleeping, I prepared breakfast.

1. Either Rick went skating, or _?_.
2. _?_, and she bought three of them.
3. _?_, but it's not funny.
4. You will make the basketball team, for _?_.
5. You were absent; therefore, _?_.

3.2b   Subordinate Clauses

A **subordinate clause** is a group of words that has a subject and a predicate but cannot stand by itself as a complete sentence because it does not express a complete thought. Subordinate clauses are sometimes called dependent clauses. Two subordinate clauses follow. The simple subject of the clause is underlined once, and the simple predicate is underlined twice.

When we asked for one
Because the store had no white paint

When you combine subordinate clauses with independent clauses, you form complete sentences.

————indep. clause———— ——— sub. clause———
Mrs. Dimas gave us a ride home when we asked for one.

————sub. clause———— ———indep. clause———
Because the store had no white paint, Ivy bought green paint.

109

A sentence may have more than one subordinate clause. In the following example, the two subordinate clauses are in boldface.

While I was walking home, I saw a tree **that had beautiful leaves.**

To tell whether a clause is subordinate or independent, read only the clause to yourself. If it can stand alone as a sentence, it is an independent clause. If it cannot stand alone, it is a subordinate clause.

SENTENCE   The mail carrier emptied the mailbox before I could get there.

INDEPENDENT CLAUSE   The mail carrier emptied the mailbox. [**Think:** The clause can stand alone. It is an independent clause.]

SUBORDINATE CLAUSE   before I could get there [**Think:** The clause cannot stand by itself. It is a subordinate clause.]

Exercise 2   Subordinate Clauses   On your paper, write the subordinate clauses in the following sentences.

SAMPLE   If Charles calls, please ask him to call back.
ANSWER   If Charles calls

1. He couldn't remember when you were going to arrive.
2. Is it certain that graduation ceremonies will be held?
3. Someone who could answer that question is Dr. Wakeman.
4. I don't know whether you and Emily will agree.
5. After you finish this work, let's discuss the plans for your next project.
6. Notify Aunt Kate before you leave Portland.
7. Because our house is close to the beach, we expect company each summer.

8. The house, which was built in the 1840s, was renovated five years ago.

9. While he typed, she proofread.

10. We cannot pay a group rate unless five or more persons want tickets.

Exercise 3   Independent and Subordinate Clauses

On your paper, label the following clauses *Independent* or *Subordinate.*

> **SAMPLE** My bicycle is in the repair shop.
>
> **ANSWER** Independent

1. Although we were first in line.
2. Your uncle visited us yesterday.
3. Because Sue lives in Indiana.
4. Whenever you decide which one to buy.
5. As soon as Marie and Alex are ready to leave.
6. He will.
7. That result is certain.
8. Which you promised to do.
9. Unless our luggage arrives late.
10. Call for operator assistance.

3.2c   Kinds of Subordinate Clauses

A subordinate clause may function as an adjective, an adverb, or a noun.

Clauses Used as Adjectives

A subordinate clause functions as an adjective if it modifies a noun or a pronoun. Such clauses are sometimes called **adjective clauses.** In the following sentences, the subjects of the subordinate clauses are underlined once, and the predicates are underlined twice.

The *novel* that you recommended to me was good. [Which novel? The one that you recommended to me.]

A *doctor* who takes care of children is a pediatrician. [What kind of doctor? A doctor who takes care of children.]

Most adjective clauses begin with a relative pronoun:

that   which   who   whom   whose

The **relative pronoun** relates the clause to the word or phrase that the clause modifies. In the following sentences, the relative pronoun is in boldface.

Is she *someone* **whom** you worked for?

Seth missed his home *town,* **which** was near Auburn.

You may also introduce adjective clauses with **relative adverbs.** The relative adverbs include *after, before, since, when, where,* and *why.*

It was a *place* **where** crowds gathered on weekends.

Sometimes the introductory word in an adjective clause is implied rather than stated.

It was a *decision* I do not regret making. [**Think:** It was a decision *that* I do not regret making.]

Essential and Nonessential Clauses. An **essential clause** is an adjective clause that is necessary to the meaning of a sentence. Essential clauses are *not* set off from the rest of the sentence with commas.

ESSENTIAL CLAUSE   I feel sorry for *people* who have hay fever. [The subordinate clause, *who have hay fever,* is essential because without it, the reader would not know which people the writer feels sorry for. The clause is not set off with a comma.]

A **nonessential clause** is an adjective clause that is not necessary to the meaning of a sentence. Nonessential clauses *are* set off from the rest of the sentence with commas.

NONESSENTIAL CLAUSE   *Mary Lee,* who was in Florida, brought us grapefruit. [The subordinate clause, *who was in Florida,* is nonessential because without it the reader would still know who brought the grapefruit. The clause is set off with a comma.]

Exercise 4   Adjective Clauses   *Step 1:* On your paper, write the adjective clauses in the following sentences. *Step 2:* Circle the relative pronoun or relative adverb that introduces each clause. *Step 3:* Write the word or phrase that the clause modifies.

SAMPLE   Is that the man who is having the garage sale?
ANSWER   (who) is having the garage sale—man

1. The church that is on the hill is over two hundred years old.
2. Peg, whose sister is a star, prefers a quiet life.
3. Ricardo wanted someone who would walk to the store.

4. The supermarket, which my uncle owns, stocks everything.
5. Isn't Mary Ellen the girl whose sister won first prize?
6. He is someone whom you would enjoy meeting.
7. My clock, which I used for eight years, is broken.
8. The paint that we chose for the living room is a subtle color.
9. Evening is the time when I enjoy reading novels.
10. Sue, who plans to start her own business, is a skillful artist.

Clauses Used as Adverbs

A subordinate clause functions as an adverb if it modifies a verb, an adjective, or an adverb. Such clauses are sometimes called **adverb clauses.**

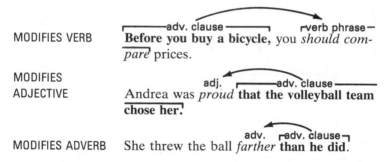

MODIFIES VERB
╭──────adv. clause──────╮ ╭verb phrase─
Before you buy a bicycle, you *should compare* prices.

MODIFIES
ADJECTIVE
adj. ╭──────adv. clause──────
Andrea was *proud* **that the volleyball team chose her.**

MODIFIES ADVERB
adv. ╭adv. clause╮
She threw the ball *farther* **than he did**.

Like adverbs, adverb clauses tell *how, when, where,* and *to what extent*. They may also explain *why*.

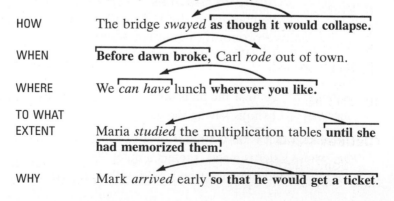

HOW
The bridge *swayed* **as though it would collapse.**

WHEN
Before dawn broke, Carl *rode* out of town.

WHERE
We *can have* lunch **wherever you like.**

TO WHAT
EXTENT
Maria *studied* the multiplication tables **until she had memorized them.**

WHY
Mark *arrived* early **so that he would get a ticket.**

An adverb clause always begins with a **subordinating conjunction**, which is a word that shows the relationship between the subordinate clause and the independent clause. Here is a list of frequently used subordinating conjunctions.

after	before	since	until
although	even if	so that	when
as	even though	than	whenever
as soon as	if	that	where
as though	in order that	though	wherever
because	provided that	unless	while

Exercise 5   Adverb Clauses   *Step 1:* On your paper, write the adverb clauses in the following sentences. *Step 2:* Circle the subordinating conjunction that introduces each clause. *Step 3:* Beside each clause write the word or phrase that it modifies.

SAMPLE   I will pay the bill when you send it.

ANSWER   (when) you send it—will pay

1. Carla gives autographs wherever she goes.
2. The ambassador studied notes before she answered questions.
3. We will stay here until you develop a new plan.
4. Peter looks much older than he did two years ago.
5. I waited until Eric showed me a new approach.
6. Everyone screamed when the lights went out.
7. Kim was glad that you liked the present.
8. After you left our office, we continued the discussion.
9. Randy spoke his lines humorously so that even the director laughed.
10. They helped us even though they were somewhat disorganized.

Clauses Used as Nouns

Some subordinate clauses function as nouns in sentences. Such clauses can be referred to as **noun clauses.** A noun

115

clause may function as a subject, a predicate nominative, a direct object, an indirect object, an object of a preposition, or an appositive.

SUBJECT
> **That he is sincere** is evident.

PREDICATE NOMINATIVE
> That is **what we decided.**

DIRECT OBJECT
> I don't know **where Rick is.**

INDIRECT OBJECT
> Give **whoever is calling** a message.

OBJECT OF A PREPOSITION
> I was praised for **what I did.**

APPOSITIVE
> The subject of my address, **that taxes should be lowered,** was well received.

You may introduce a noun clause with either an interrogative pronoun or a subordinating conjunction.

INTERROGATIVE PRONOUNS
> who, whom, whose, which, what, whoever, whomever, whatever

SUBORDINATING CONJUNCTIONS
> how, that, when, where, whether, why

Exercise 6 Noun Clauses *Step 1:* On your paper, copy the noun clauses in the following sentences. *Step 2:* Circle the interrogative pronoun or subordinating conjunction that introduces each clause. *Step 3:* Tell whether the noun clause functions as a subject, a predicate nominative, a direct object, an indirect object, an object of a preposition, or an appositive.

> SAMPLE What you paid was too much.
>
> ANSWER (What) you paid—subject

116

1. The school will present whoever sells the most tickets a special award.
2. Tell me how you did on your test.
3. What Heather and I discussed is unimportant.
4. Jane couldn't understand why Robert was so confused.
5. You can become whatever you wish.
6. Harold wondered who had left a coat in the closet.
7. Give whomever you see at the party my best regards.
8. The official report disagrees with what you told us.
9. Joe's mother asked where the dog came from.
10. The fact is that you tried your best.

Exercise 7   Clauses   *Step 1:* On your paper, number from 1 to 20, and list the clauses in italics. *Step 2:* Label each clause *Independent clause* or *Subordinate clause.*

> **SAMPLE**   The following excerpt is from Charles Dickens's story "A Christmas Carol," *which is about Ebenezer Scrooge, the famous miser.*
>
> **ANSWER**   which is about Ebenezer Scrooge, the famous miser—Subordinate clause

The phantom slowly, gravely, silently approached. (1) *When it came near him,*   (2) *Scrooge bent down upon his knee,* for in the very air   (3) *through which this Spirit moved* it seemed to scatter gloom and mystery.

It was shrouded in a deep black garment,   (4) *which concealed its head, its face, its form, and left nothing of it visible save one outstretched hand.* But for this   (5) *it would have been difficult to detach its figure from the night, and separate it from the darkness*   (6) *by which it was surrounded.*

He felt   (7) *that it was tall and stately*   (8) *when it came beside him,* and   (9) *that its mysterious presence filled him with a solemn dread.* He knew no more, for   (10) *the Spirit neither spoke nor moved.*

"I am in the presence of the Ghost of Christmas Yet to Come?" said Scrooge.

(11) *The Spirit answered not, but pointed onward with its hand.*

"You are about to show me shadows of the things (12) *that have not happened, but will happen in the time before us,*" Scrooge pursued.   (13) *"Is that so, Spirit?"*

The upper portion of the garment was contracted for an instant in its folds,   (14) *as if the Spirit had inclined its head.* (15) *That was the only answer*   (16) *he received.*

Although well used to ghostly company by this time, Scrooge feared the silent shape so much   (17) *that his legs trembled beneath him,* and he found   (18) *that he could hardly stand*   (19) *when he prepared to follow it.*   (20) *The Spirit paused a moment,* as if observing his condition, and giving him time to recover.

3.3   Sentences Classified by Structure

Sentences are classified according to the number and kinds of clauses they contain. The four kinds of sentences are simple, compound, complex, and compound-complex.

3.3a   Simple and Compound Sentences

A **simple sentence** contains one independent clause and no subordinate clauses. It may have any number of phrases. It may have a compound subject and a compound predicate. However, it has no more than one clause.

Jose *fixed* dinner at home.
Wind and **rain** *lashed* the tiny island. [compound subject]
Isabel **referred** to her notes and then **answered** the question. [compound predicate]

A **compound sentence** consists of two or more independent clauses that are joined together. You usually join the independent clauses with a comma and one of the coordinating conjunctions: *and, but, nor, or, for,* or *yet.*

┌──────indep. clause──────┐ ┌──────indep. clause──────
Elaine graduated last June, **and** now she works as an accountant.

You can also join the independent clauses by using a semicolon.

┌──────indep. clause──────┐ ┌──────indep. clause──────┐
It was a good day for fishing; I caught thirty trout.

In some compound sentences, the independent clauses are joined by a semicolon and a conjunctive adverb, such as *however, therefore,* or *consequently* (*page 44*).

┌────────── indep. clause──────────┐
Both the star and the understudy were ill;

┌──────indep. clause──────┐
consequently, the play was canceled.

Exercise 1   Simple and Compound Sentences Copy the following sentences on your paper. Underline the simple subject of each clause once and the simple predicate of each clause twice. Then label the sentence *Simple* or *Compound.*

SAMPLE   Sally and Sue are sisters.

ANSWER   <u>Sally</u> and <u>Sue</u> <u><u>are</u></u> sisters.—Simple

1. Bert laughs a great deal; he has quite a sense of humor.
2. Some cats were fighting in the alley behind my house last night; therefore, I didn't get much sleep.
3. The coaches and the umpires got into a dispute.
4. Has our special order from Harry's Blue Danube Restaurant arrived yet, or must we still wait?
5. Alice led the orchestra; Herb played the drums.
6. Perhaps that law is unfair and should be changed.
7. Abby and Lena mowed and raked the front and back lawns.

8. My grandmother was born in Poland, but she was raised in Chicago.

3.3b   Complex Sentences

A **complex sentence** consists of one independent clause and one or more subordinate clauses.

```
      ┌──────────sub. clause──────────┐ ┌indep. clause┐
      While we drove along the coast, fog rolled in.

      ┌──────────sub. clause──────────┐ ┌──indep. clause──
      As Coach Luski has often said, we cannot win a

      ──────────────────┐ ┌──────────sub. clause──────────────
      championship unless we have more disciplined players.

                    ┌──────────────indep. clause──────────────┐
      ┌─────────┌──────────sub. clause──────────┐──┐
      The man who just walked into the garden is my grandfather.
```

Exercise 2   Sentences Classified   *Step 1:* Copy the following sentences on your paper. *Step 2:* Underline the simple subject of each clause once and the simple predicate twice. *Step 3:* Label the sentence *Simple, Compound,* or *Complex.*

SAMPLE   After we ate dinner, we went out.

ANSWER   After <u>we</u> <u>ate</u> dinner, <u>we</u> <u>went</u> out.—Complex

1. Stu seems to be cautious, for he always hesitates.
2. John, who is only thirteen, is too young to play in the men's tournament.
3. We all went hiking together.
4. Will you turn off the lights and lock the doors?
5. Kate dances gracefully because she has practiced lately.
6. Ben does not like Frank very well; consequently, they try to avoid each other.
7. It was pouring rain; still, Denise insisted on taking a walk.
8. The person who will fix the washing machine just rang the front doorbell.

3.3c Compound-Complex Sentences

A **compound-complex sentence** has two or more independent clauses and one or more subordinate clauses.

```
┌────────────indep. clause───────────┐┌─sub. clause─
I will give you the name of a company that installs
```
```
┌────────────────────indep. clause────────────────┐
air conditioners, but you must call the company yourself.
```
[The sentence is compound-complex because it has two independent clauses and one subordinate clause.]

In a compound-complex sentence, a subordinate clause may interrupt an independent clause.

```
┌───────indep. clause───────┐
┌─┐┌────────sub. clause────────┐┌───┐
Bud, who wanted to cut firewood, stayed out all
```
```
┌─────────┐┌────indep. clause────┐┌────sub. clause─────
afternoon, but his feet stayed warm because he wore fleece-
lined boots. [The sentence is compound-complex because it
```
has two independent clauses and two subordinate clauses. The subordinate clause *who wanted to cut firewood* interrupts the independent clause *Bud stayed out all afternoon.*]

Exercise 3 Sentences Classified *Step 1:* Copy the following sentences on your paper. *Step 2:* Underline each independent clause. *Step 3:* Put brackets around each subordinate clause. *Step 4:* Label each sentence *Complex* or *Compound-complex*.

SAMPLE   The expert who examined the vase said that it was more than one thousand years old.

ANSWER   The expert [who examined the vase] said [that it was more than one thousand years old.]— Complex

1. Terri worked for the circus before she went to college; it was an unforgettable experience for her.

2. When I called, I had no idea that you would be so busy.

3. While I was routinely pedaling my bike, something glittery caught my eye, and I put on my brakes.

4. As Leonora walked across the pasture, she heard a cow mooing in the distance.

5. Although the day was clear and sunny, it was also extremely hot, and I decided to stay indoors.

6. Arnie's parents left the front light on so that he could find his way.

7. Although she's only four years old, my sister can already read.

8. Even though the storm raged, the travelers pushed onward, for they wanted to reach shelter by nightfall.

9. Before we left for the picnic, we turned on the radio, and the weather report predicted rain.

10. Corinne's roses were on display at the flower show, which was held at the botanical garden.

Writers Workshop

Sentence Variety

When people write summaries of books, films, dramas, or television shows, they sometimes use too many simple sentences. To be interesting, a piece of writing should contain a variety of simple, compound, complex, and compound-complex sentences. Select a novel, a film, a drama, or a television episode with which you are familiar. Write a summary of the plot of the fictional work. In your summary, use a variety of sentence types: simple, compound, complex, and compound-complex.

3.4 Writing Complete Sentences

A **complete sentence** is a group of words that has at least one subject and one predicate and that expresses a complete thought. In writing, you should use complete sentences. Two common errors in writing sentences are the use of sentence fragments and run-on sentences, which are not complete sentences. In this section you will learn how to recognize both kinds of errors and how to turn them into complete sentences.

3.4a Avoiding Sentence Fragments

A **sentence fragment** is a group of words that either lacks a subject or a predicate or does not express a complete thought.

LACKS SUBJECT	I noticed a jet. **Flew overhead.** [The second word group does not tell what flew overhead.]
LACKS PREDICATE	**The blue and silver jet.** [The word group does not tell what the jet did.]
NOT A COMPLETE THOUGHT	**As the jet flew away from me.** [The word group does not tell what happened as the jet flew away.]

A common kind of sentence fragment is a phrase. You can often correct this kind of fragment by including the phrase in a related sentence.

PREPOSITIONAL PHRASE	I noticed a caterpillar. **On my foot.**
COMPLETE SENTENCE	I noticed a caterpillar **on my foot.**

APPOSITIVE PHRASE	I casually observed the caterpillar. **An orange and black one.**
COMPLETE SENTENCE	I casually observed the **orange and black caterpillar.**
INFINITIVE PHRASE	A tiny caterpillar ventured. **To crawl over my foot.**
COMPLETE SENTENCE	A tiny caterpillar ventured **to crawl over my foot.**
PARTICIPIAL PHRASE	I noticed a caterpillar. **Crawling on my foot.**
COMPLETE SENTENCE	I noticed a caterpillar **crawling on my foot.**

Another common type of sentence fragment is the subordinate clause. You can often correct this type of fragment by combining the clause with a related sentence.

SUBORDINATE CLAUSE	We received a postcard from our neighbors. **Who are on vacation.**
COMPLETE SENTENCE	We received a postcard from our neighbors **who are on vacation.**
SUBORDINATE CLAUSE	**As I waited.** Three other people entered the office.
COMPLETE SENTENCE	**As I waited,** three other people entered the office.

In order to correct some sentence fragments, you must add to them or reword them to make complete sentences.

SENTENCE FRAGMENT	Mt. Washington, the highest peak in the Northeast.
COMPLETE SENTENCE	Mt. Washington is the highest peak in the Northeast.

SENTENCE FRAGMENT   Forgetting to be cautious.

COMPLETE SENTENCE   Jill forgot to be cautious.

Exercise 1 Eliminating Sentence Fragments On your paper, rewrite the following word groups to eliminate all sentence fragments.

SAMPLE   Before it is too late. We must all use energy more efficiently.

ANSWER   We must all use energy more efficiently before it is too late.

1. Jason decided to improve the insulation in his house. While he was paying his heating bills one evening.
2. Putting fiber glass insulation in the attic. He hoped to cut heat loss through the roof.
3. He bought materials the next day. Two rolls of fiber glass. And window panes.
4. With the fiber glass. He insulated the attic.
5. He installed windows with thick panes of glass. To keep the harsh winter air outside.
6. Around the doorways he put weather stripping. A thin piece of rubber to prevent drafts.
7. Out of energy himself when the job was finished. Jason went to bed.
8. A month later, when his heating bill was 25 percent lower. He could hardly believe it.

3.4b   Avoiding Run-on Sentences

A **run-on sentence** consists of two or more complete sentences written as if they were one sentence. In some run-ons the two sentences are separated by only a comma. In other run-ons, the sentences are not separated at all.

RUN-ON   Ira fell asleep, his sister drove him home. [A comma alone cannot connect two independent clauses.]

RUN-ON   Ira fell asleep and his sister drove him home. [There is no comma before the coordinating conjunction, *and*.]

CORRECT   Ira fell asleep**, and** his sister drove him home. [A comma and the conjunction, *and,* connect the two clauses.]

There are several ways to correct run-on sentences.

1. Form two or more separate sentences from the run-on sentence.

   RUN-ON   Daryl left hurriedly we caught him.

   CORRECT   Daryl left hurriedly**. W**e caught him.

2. Join the independent clauses with a comma and a coordinating conjunction. The coordinating conjunctions are *and, but, or, for, nor,* and *yet*.

   RUN-ON   Jan waved at me, I waved back.

   CORRECT   Jan waved at me**, and** I waved back.

3. Join the independent clauses with a semicolon.

   RUN-ON   My paper blew away, I caught it.

   CORRECT   My paper blew away**;** I caught it.

4. Turn one of the independent clauses into a subordinate clause, and add a subordinating conjunction (*page 41*) or a relative pronoun (*page 10*).

   RUN-ON   Carol called her aunt's house there was no answer.

   CORRECT   **When** Carol called her aunt's house, there was no answer.

5. Join the independent clauses with a semicolon and a conjunctive adverb like *then* or *consequently* (*page 44*). Put a semicolon before the conjunctive adverb.

   RUN-ON Fifteen inches of snow fell, then the temperature plummeted.

   CORRECT Fifteen inches of snow fell**; then** the temperature plummeted.

Exercise 2   Run-on Sentences   On your paper, rewrite and correct each of the following run-on sentences. You may rephrase the sentences.

   SAMPLE   Ships are sturdy structures this is because they must protect their crews and cargoes.

   ANSWER   Ships are sturdy structures because they must protect their crews and cargoes.

1. The doors on a ship are watertight, therefore, the ship floats for a while even if there is a hole in its side.
2. The propeller turns around like a screw going through the water this action makes the ship go forward.
3. All ships carry ballast, ballast is extra water that helps a ship remain stable.
4. Shipbuilding is an old art but it has changed in the last several years.
5. Years ago, ships were built piece by piece in the shipyard, however, large sections are now put together in factories, these sections are then transported to the shipyard.
6. A ship is launched with its stern first for the bow would dig into the mud if it were launched first.
7. The most awesome modern ships are the supertankers, they may be longer than four football fields and they are extremely difficult to steer because of their size.
8. Even bringing a supertanker to a halt is difficult, in fact, a ship may keep moving for three nautical miles after the engines are turned off.

Assignment   Fragments   and   Run-on   Sentences
On your paper, rewrite the following paragraph, eliminating all fragments and run-on sentences.

> People have many misunderstandings. About snakes. Although snakes are related to other reptiles, like turtles and crocodiles. They bear no relationship to worms and eels, except in shape. Worms and eels are slimy, snakes are dry and covered with scales. Snakes don't sting with their tongues they use their tongues for touching. As we use our hands. Although many people fear snakes. Snakes can be helpful. Snakes eating rodents that harm valuable crops. Snakes are also important because they are used for food by some people also they make fine pets for some people.

3.5   Diagraming Phrases and Clauses

This section will show you how to diagram the phrases and clauses that you studied in this unit. First, though, you may want to review "Sentence Diagrams," which you will find on pages 77-85.

3.5a   Diagraming Phrases

Diagraming Prepositional Phrases

To diagram a prepositional phrase, draw a slanted line below the word that the phrase modifies. From the bottom of that line, draw a line parallel to the base line. Write the preposition on the slanted line and its object on the horizontal line. Write any words that modify the object of the preposition on slanted lines below the object.

Our stay in Europe lasted for two months.

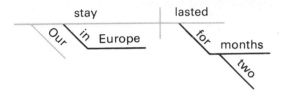

Diagraming Appositive Phrases

To diagram an appositive phrase, place the appositive in parentheses next to the word that it explains and the modifiers on slanted lines directly below the appositive.

That is Mrs. Freeman, our science teacher.

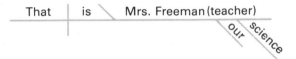

Diagraming Participial Phrases

To diagram a participial phrase, draw a slanted line and a horizontal line below the word that the participial phrase modifies. Write the participle so that it starts on the slanted line and curves onto the horizontal line. If a direct object follows the participle, separate the two elements with a vertical bar. If a predicate nominative follows the participle, separate the two elements with a slanted line.

The smiling couple walked down the aisle.

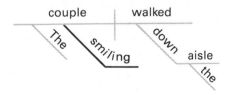

Raising his hand, Elbert signaled to the waiter.
[*Hand* is the direct object of *raising*.]

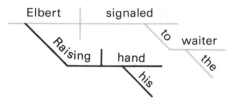

Looking relaxed, the President stepped from the plane.

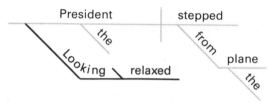

Diagraming Gerund Phrases

To diagram a gerund phrase, place the gerund on a step and place the step on a standard. If the phrase has modifiers or complements, diagram them on the line extending from the step.

Typing the final report is Tina's job.

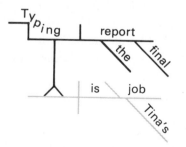

[The gerund phrase, *Typing the final report,* is the subject of the sentence. *Typing* is the gerund, *report* is the direct object, and *the* and *final* are the modifiers.]

Diagraming Infinitive Phrases

To diagram an infinitive phrase, place the entire phrase on a standard. Put the word *to* on a slanted line and the verb on a horizontal line. Diagram modifiers and complements as you would in a sentence.

I wanted to see that movie.

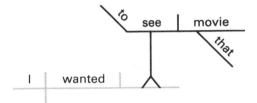

[The infinitive phrase, *to see that movie*, is the direct object in the sentence. *That* modifies *movie*.]

If the infinitive phrase functions as a modifier, place the standard containing the infinitive phrase on a horizontal line below the modified word.

Karl has gone to visit his cousins.

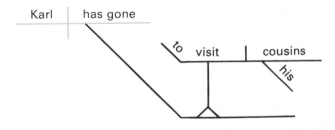

[The infinitive phrase, *to visit his cousins*, functions as an adverb modifying *has gone*.]

Exercise 1   Diagraming Phrases   On your paper, diagram the following sentences. Be sure to use a ruler. The sentences contain prepositional phrases, participial phrases, appositive phrases, gerund phrases, and infinitive phrases.

SAMPLE   The confused cat ran in circles around the yard.
ANSWER

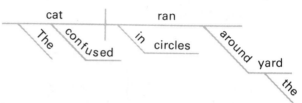

1. My piano teacher, Mr. Franklin, is also an organist and a choir director.
2. Appearing tired, the runners were crossing the finish line.
3. The thunder broke the stillness of the night.
4. Writing term papers is an important skill.
5. Pitching a tent correctly takes practice.
6. Our goal in this course is to write three paragraphs.
7. The mechanics decided to inspect the jet closely.
8. Cheering loudly, the crowd gave the players confidence.

3.5b   Diagraming Clauses

Diagraming Adjective Clauses

To diagram an adjective clause, place the clause below the independent clause and diagram it as if it were a separate sentence. Use a line of dashes to connect the relative pronoun in the adjective clause with the word that the clause modifies.

We are passing the house that the Petersons restored.

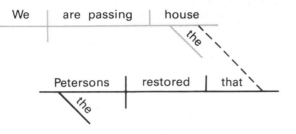

[The clause *that the Petersons restored* modifies *house*. *That* is the direct object in the clause and is diagramed in that position.]

The man who is standing there is my cousin.

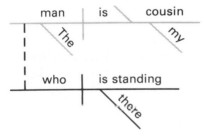

[*Who is standing there* modifies *man*. *Who* is the subject of the clause.]

Diagraming Adverb Clauses

To diagram an adverb clause, place the clause below the word or words that it modifies in the independent clause. Diagram the subordinate clause as if it were a separate sentence. Use a line of dashes to connect the verb in the adverb clause with the modified word or words in the independent clause. Write the subordinating conjunction on the dotted line.

Whenever I open the kitchen door, my dog walks outside.

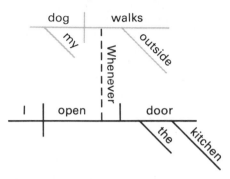

[The adverb clause, *whenever I open the kitchen door*, modifies *walks*.]

Diagraming Noun Clauses

Diagram a noun clause according to its function in the sentence. If the noun clause is the subject, place the clause on a standard located in the subject position. Diagram the word introducing the noun clause according to its function in the noun clause.

SUBJECT   Whatever you want for dinner is fine with me.

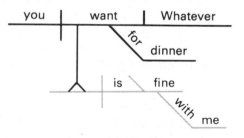

[*Whatever you want for dinner* is the subject of the sentence. *Whatever* is the direct object in the subordinate clause.]

If the noun clause is the complement, place it on a standard that is in the position of the complement.

DIRECT OBJECT   The audience will applaud whoever draws the winning number.

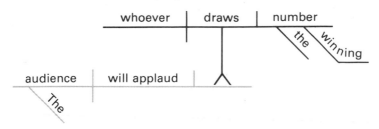

[*Whoever draws the winning number* is the direct object. *Whoever* is the subject in the noun clause.]

Exercise 2 Diagraming Clauses On your paper, diagram the following sentences. The sentences contain adjective clauses, adverb clauses, and noun clauses.

SAMPLE   The apples, which we bought at Olson's Orchard, are delicious.

ANSWER

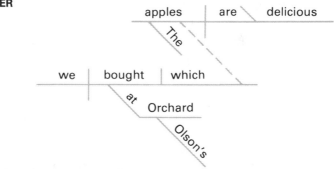

1. Two years have passed since we sailed on Lake Michigan.
2. Sarah ran quickly when she saw the rain.
3. I should decide what I will do.
4. Deborah brought her pet, which is a baby python.

5. Because they had lost their flashlight, the three campers stumbled ahead.
6. The sweater that Jack bought is too small.
7. The guard checked whoever entered the hall.
8. The two sides will meet when the attorneys arrive.

3.5c   Diagraming Sentences

In this section you will learn how to diagram compound and complex sentences.

Diagraming Compound Sentences

To diagram a compound sentence, place the independent clauses on separate parallel lines, and connect the two clauses with a line of dashes between the verb of one clause and the verb of the other. The line should have a step. On the step write the conjunction that connects the two clauses. If the independent clauses are joined by a semicolon, do not write a word on the step.

You take the high road, and I will take the low road.

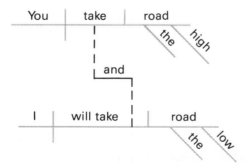

Diagraming Complex Sentences

To diagram a complex sentence, first determine the kind of subordinate clause or clauses that the sentence contains. Then follow the rule for diagraming that kind of clause. The sentence below contains an adverb clause modifying the verb.

ADVERB CLAUSE   The meeting went as they had expected.

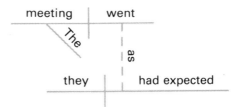

[*As they had expected* modifies *went*.]

Exercise 3   Diagraming Sentences   On your paper, diagram the following sentences.

1. Jack must have left; I could not find him.
2. The rabbit that ran under the hedge has escaped.
3. We moved slowly so that we would not lose our way.
4. Bill has left his desk, for he has a lunch appointment.
5. Will you repeat what you said?
6. We can go to the beach, but I would prefer the carnival.
7. Will Rogers, the humorist, liked whomever he met.
8. Jim wants to start a business, but he lacks the money.

Unit Practice

Practice 1

A. Phrases (*pages 93–108*) On your paper, list the phrases in italics in the following sentences. Label each phrase *Prepositional phrase, Appositive phrase, Participial phrase, Gerund Phrase,* or *Infinitive phrase.*

1. Which candidate *from the list* did you campaign for?
2. *Sailing a raft to Polynesia* was Thor Heyerdahl's way of proving a theory.
3. The hourglass, *a device that measures time,* uses sand to record the passing minutes.
4. Corinne's act in the variety show will be *to juggle hoops and clubs.*
5. *Crashing against the rocks,* the surf kept me awake all night long.
6. The alarm *clanging loudly above us* warned us of a fire.
7. Downhill skiing, *her favorite winter sport,* will be impossible to do unless this warming trend stops.
8. Go to see the seals do their balancing act *at the aquarium.*
9. *Nearly exhausted,* the people in the bog stopped berry picking.
10. *To buy a new racing bicycle* is quite expensive.

B. Subordinate Clauses (*pages 109–118*) On your paper, write the subordinate clauses in the following sentences. Next to each subordinate clause, write the label *Adjective clause, Adverb clause,* or *Noun clause.*

11. When we helped Jake move, he was grateful.
12. You should keep using whatever made your flowers grow so well.
13. Did you see the coins and utensils that the archaeologists found?
14. The outdoor festivities ended when the fireworks display was over.
15. Tess lives in that cabin, which is made of stone.

16. Iris needs the film that you brought, but she requires extra rolls.
17. He lives where he dreamed of moving, and he will not consider leaving.
18. The judges decided whether entries were valid after the deadline.
19. A cliff dwelling that Indians built can be seen in Arizona.
20. Whatever is mailed to this company must be forwarded.

C. Sentences Classified (*pages 118–122*) On your paper, label each of the following sentences *Simple, Compound, Complex,* or *Compound-complex.*

21. Did Vikings who sailed to America build this strange tower?
22. My uncle is staying in town because he has an important meeting, but he will attend our family reunion.
23. Charlotte studied ballet for ten years; her technique is superb.
24. In the United States the population is more than two hundred million.
25. Caroline Herschel, who was the sister of Sir William Herschel, was the first woman to discover a comet.

D. Writing Complete Sentences (*pages 123–128*) On your paper, rewrite each of the following word groups to eliminate sentence fragments and to correct run-on sentences.

26. Teachers and parents at the meeting in the new auditorium.
27. The final countdown has begun the rocket launch will take place.
28. This zoo features a snow leopard. A rare mountain animal.
29. During the experiment chemicals bubbled up. From test tubes.
30. Rob read those two novels he preferred *The Great Gatsby.*
31. Found a clear passageway from the mysterious cavern.

(Continue on the next page.)

32. Candles were lit in the great hall. To welcome the guests.
33. Until the pink paint is completely dried.
34. Willie plays skilled badminton he is on a team.
35. Will the citizens object to skyscrapers? Blocking the view.

E. Diagraming Phrases and Clauses (*pages 128–137*)
On your paper, diagram each of the following sentences. Be sure to use a ruler.

36. The speeding motorboat raced through the water.
37. My cousin Anita is trying to learn golf.
38. Chestnut trees that grew in North America were damaged by blight.
39. Because I worked steadily, I completed my report on time.
40. Lars wore whatever was warm, and he remained comfortable.

Practice 2

The following paragraph contains many sentence fragments and run-on sentences. Rewrite the paragraph by eliminating sentence fragments and correcting run-on sentences.

Ships use canal locks. When moving between bodies of water that are different heights. A lock is an enclosed space. In which the water levels can be raised or lowered. Canal locks have stone or concrete walls. As long as 1200 feet and as wide as 110 feet. A ship may have to pass through a succession of locks. The New York State Barge Canal System, for instance. It has at least fifty-seven. First the ship enters a lock chamber heavy doors close behind the ship. Then water rushes in or is pumped out of the chamber. Until the water level is equal to that of the next lock. The doors in front of the ship open the ship passes through. And continues its journey.

Unit Tests

Test 1

A. Phrases (*pages 93–108*)   On your paper, list the phrases in italics in the following sentences. Label each phrase *Prepositional phrase, Appositive phrase, Participial phrase, Gerund phrase,* or *Infinitive phrase.*

1. Which route will the truck *piled high with produce* take?
2. Her new drawing was shown and we went *to see it.*
3. Jeannette Rankin, *the first woman elected to Congress,* began her term in 1917.
4. *Collecting signatures* was assigned to Anita Diaz.
5. Two galloping colts raced *across the winding stream.*
6. *To begin the hobby of photography,* Roger requested a list of related books at the library.
7. Mr. Gurley, *our neighbor,* wished to test his skill at amateur bowling.
8. *Feeling tired,* the commuters filed onto the train.
9. Martha followed the chicken recipe *borrowed from Uncle Martin*
10. Anthony plans *to fish for trout next week.*

B. Subordinate Clauses (*pages 109–118*)   On your paper, write the subordinate clauses in the following sentences. Next to each subordinate clause, write the label *Adjective clause, Adverb clause,* or *Noun clause.*

11. While dinner was cooking, the children set the table.
12. Do not swim there if the lifeguard has left.
13. A rebus is a riddle that is made of pictures.
14. We will require flashlights because it is so dark.
15. Is Gretchen, who once lived in Canada, our new candidate?

(Continue on the next page.)

16. Before you call directory assistance, you should use a directory that might list the number.
17. We don't know who pushed over the vendor's cart, but the vendor has an idea.
18. Dina will not tell where she hid the documents.
19. Is April your friend who trains young gymnasts?
20. When you tell the story, please speak softly or whisper.

C. Sentences Classified (*pages 118–122*) On your paper, label each of the following sentences *Simple, Compound, Complex,* or *Compound-complex.*

21. Will Rod rake and pile the leaves that fell from the maple trees in his back yard?
22. Although these exhibits are fascinating, the museum is closing now, and we must leave.
23. Her main interest is astronomy; therefore, her brother gave her a book about the stars.
24. By the 1850s indoor roller skating was popular.
25. He paddled the canoe, and we watched him glide away.

D. Writing Complete Sentences (*pages 123–128*) On your paper, rewrite each of the following word groups to eliminate sentence fragments and to correct run-on sentences.

26. Carpets, clothing, and jewelry at a bazaar in Istanbul.
27. Do not ask your question he lacks the current data.
28. Did they find the right exit? The one for Mammoth Cave.
29. People and animals seek shade. When the sun is hot.
30. The rug took months to finish the weaver was proud.
31. Fluttered and chirped before landing on a fence.
32. Hoping to improve his physical fitness. Fred played platform tennis.
33. Because twilight was earlier than we expected.
34. Take the straw hat leave the woolen one for me.
35. Growing up our trellis. Have you seen the morning-glories?

E. Diagraming Phrases and Clauses (*pages 128–137*)
On your paper, diagram each of the following sentences. Be sure to use a ruler.

36. Seeing the ball, the soccer player raced toward it.
37. The author Lewis Carroll wrote *Alice in Wonderland* to amuse a friend.
38. Chris will meet the person who manages the fair.
39. While the rain continued, the campers stayed dry under a shelter.
40. She asked when the concert began, but she had missed the start.

Test 2

The following paragraph contains many sentence fragments and run-on sentences. Rewrite the paragraph by eliminating sentence fragments and correcting run-on sentences.

I went to Florida. With my parents. We planned to swim, sunbathe, and gather shells, one day we explored a beach. One on the Gulf of Mexico. I hunted for unusual shells. That washed up on shore. However, I found the unexpected I wandered over a sandy hill. And stood near the shallow water. I spotted seaweed, eels, many kinds of fish, and a shark. Floating lifelessly in the water. Immediately, I knew that I was seeing the results of a red tide this kind of tide occurs. When tiny plants multiply quickly. These plants use up oxygen in the water and they produce harmful substances. Scientists believe. That these plants grow. As the result of certain amounts of food, sunlight, or salt in the water. The plants red. Is why the condition called a red tide. Those unfortunate animals floating in the water. They were the victims of a red tide.

Unit 4

Usage

Unit Preview

When you speak and write, your purpose is to convey a message to someone else. If you follow the standards of English usage, others will understand you and be prepared to respect what you say.

In addition to the types of usage problems covered in this unit, you should develop a sense of the appropriateness of the five categories of English words that are considered here.

First, **idioms** are combinations of words that have a special meaning when used as a unit: *to be on pins and needles, to make a face.* Be careful to use idioms correctly. Some writers create incorrect idioms instead of using a single word. For example, *where at* and *off of* are always incorrect in place of the correct forms *where* and *off.*

Second, be aware of—and avoid—the pompous, confusing language sometimes known as **jargon.** A user of jargon might say "gives the appearance of being functionally impaired" instead of "looks broken." Note, however, that the word *jargon* may also be used to mean language associated with an occupation, such as computer programming. Special language of this sort is appropriate only for an audience of specialists.

Third, be aware of levels of language. **Colloquial** language is informal, appropriate in most speaking situations but not in formal writing and speaking. *Awfully,* with the meaning of "very," is a **colloquialism**—a colloquial term.

Fourth, watch for **slang,** language that is even more colloquial. Slang is lively, but it is suitable only in casual speech, not in most writing. *Split,* meaning "to leave," is slang.

The fifth category is **nonstandard** language: word choices and combinations that are incorrect for any speaking or writing situation. *Brung* and *to him and I* are nonstandard.

For Analysis The following paragraph contains examples of all five of the types of language discussed on the previous page. Read the paragraph; then answer the questions.

(1) Me and my sister become interested in model railroads only when our father started working on them. (2) At first we thought model trains were a drag, and we used to make fun of Dad for enjoying what we thought of as a child's hobby. (3) Anyways, after we started working on model railroads ourselves, we decided that miniature trains are sort of neat. (4) One day Dad brung home a kit with parts for building a locomotive, cars, tracks, and other equipment. (5) United in productive employment, we constructed the trains with due solicitude, and after finalizing our mutual task, we experienced the satisfaction of observing them in full operation.

1. Which sentence is an example of jargon?
2. What is the idiom in Sentence 2?
3. What are the two slang words In Sentences 2 and 3?
4. What is the colloquial expression in Sentence 3?
5. Identify the instances of nonstandard language in the passage.

Now revise the entire passage to make it suitable for a formal situation. Responding to the questions has made you aware of the language that you use; in this unit you will review all the important details of correct usage.

4.1   Correct Use of Verbs

A verb shows tense, voice, and the number and person of its subject through changes in its form. By knowing how to make these changes, you can use verbs correctly in sentences.

4.1a   Principal Parts of Verbs

Every verb has four basic forms, called its **principal parts.** They are the infinitive, the present participle, the past, and the past participle. You use thc principal parts to form the tenses of a verb.

All verbs follow the same rules for the infinitive and the present participle. The infinitive is the verb in its most basic form, the form given in the dictionary. In sentences, the word *to* usually precedes the infinitive, although sometimes *to* is understood. The present participle consists of the infinitive plus *-ing* and takes a form of the verb *be* as an auxiliary verb.

INFINITIVE

Alice loved *to* **laugh** at the clowns. `[inf.]`

The clowns made Alice **laugh**. `[inf.]`

PRESENT
PARTICIPLE

Alice *is* happily **laughing** at the clowns. `[aux.]` `[pres. part.]`

A verb is either a regular verb or an irregular verb, depending on how its past and its past participle are formed.

Regular Verbs

Verbs that form the past and the past participle according to standard rules are **regular verbs.** The past of a regular verb consists of the infinitive plus *-d* or *-ed*. The past participle of a regular verb also consists of the infinitive plus *-d* or *-ed,* and it takes a form of the verb *have* as an auxiliary verb.

PAST

Alice **laughed** at the clowns.

PAST
PARTICIPLE

Alice *has* always **laughed** at clowns. `[aux.]` `[past. part.]`

The following list shows the principal parts of three regular verbs. The auxiliary verbs in parentheses remind you always to use a form of the verb *be* (*am, is, are,* and so forth) with the present participle and a form of the verb *have* (*has, have, had,* and so forth) with the past participle.

INFINITIVE	PRESENT PARTICIPLE	PAST	PAST PARTICIPLE
invite	(is) inviting	invited	(has) invited
try	(is) trying	tried	(has) tried
plan	(is) planning	planned	(has) planned

Irregular Verbs

Verbs that do not form the past and the past participle according to standard rules are **irregular verbs.** As with regular verbs, you must use auxiliary verbs with both the present participle and the past participle of irregular verbs. The following sentences show the correct use of the irregular verb *fall*.

INFINITIVE	The leaves begin to **fall** early in the autumn.
PRESENT PARTICIPLE	Many leaves are **falling** today.
PAST	Even more **fell** during the night.
PAST PARTICIPLE	All the leaves have **fallen.**

Because no rules govern the formation of the past and the past participle of irregular verbs, you should simply memorize the principal parts. You have probably been using most of these verbs correctly since childhood, and you may have developed a good sense of what sounds correct. Many common irregular verbs are listed on the next two pages. Study this list, and refer to it while doing the exercise that follows.

INFINITIVE	PRESENT PARTICIPLE	PAST	PAST PARTICIPLE
be	(is) being	was, were	(has) been
begin	(is) beginning	began	(has) begun
blow	(is) blowing	blew	(has) blown
break	(is) breaking	broke	(has) broken
bring	(is) bringing	brought	(has) brought
burst	(is) bursting	burst	(has) burst
catch	(is) catching	caught	(has) caught
choose	(is) choosing	chose	(has) chosen
come	(is) coming	came	(has) come
do	(is) doing	did	(has) done
drink	(is) drinking	drank	(has) drunk
drive	(is) driving	drove	(has) driven
eat	(is) eating	ate	(has) eaten
fall	(is) falling	fell	(has) fallen
fly	(is) flying	flew	(has) flown
freeze	(is) freezing	froze	(has) frozen
get	(is) getting	got	(has) gotten
give	(is) giving	gave	(has) given
go	(is) going	went	(has) gone
grow	(is) growing	grew	(has) grown
have	(is) having	had	(has) had
know	(is) knowing	knew	(has) known
lay (put)	(is) laying	laid	(has) laid
lead	(is) leading	led	(has) led
leave	(is) leaving	left	(has) left
lie (recline)	(is) lying	lay	(has) lain
make	(is) making	made	(has) made
put	(is) putting	put	(has) put
ride	(is) riding	rode	(has) ridden
ring	(is) ringing	rang	(has) rung
rise	(is) rising	rose	(has) risen
run	(is) running	ran	(has) run
see	(is) seeing	saw	(has) seen
set	(is) setting	set	(has) set
shrink	(is) shrinking	shrank	(has) shrunk

sing	(is) singing	sang	(has) sung
sit	(is) sitting	sat	(has) sat
speak	(is) speaking	spoke	(has) spoken
spring	(is) springing	sprang	(has) sprung
steal	(is) stealing	stole	(has) stolen
strike	(is) striking	struck	(has) struck, (has) stricken
swim	(is) swimming	swam	(has) swum
take	(is) taking	took	(has) taken
throw	(is) throwing	threw	(has) thrown
wear	(is) wearing	wore	(has) worn
write	(is) writing	wrote	(has) written

Exercise 1 Principal Parts of Verbs On your paper, write the correct form of each verb in parentheses in the following sentences.

SAMPLE   Last summer we (*take*) a week off and (*drive*) to the lake.

ANSWER   took, drove

1. We tried to (*go*) canoeing and swimming every day.
2. One morning my cousin and I (*leave*) the cabin early.
3. The sun had just (*rise*) when we crept from our bunks.
4. The others (*be*) still asleep when we (*set*) out for the dock.
5. We had (*talk*) for days about early morning canoeing, and this (*be*) the day.
6. We (*want*) to pick some blueberries for breakfast from the bushes that (*grow*) all around the lake.
7. Halfway across the lake, Jerry remembered that he had not (*bring*) a bowl for the berries.
8. Luckily, though, I had (*wear*) my straw hat, and it (*make*) a perfect basket.
9. Finally we (*finish*) picking berries and (*begin*) to paddle home.
10. Everyone (*enjoy*) eating blueberries for breakfast, but my hat has never (*be*) the same since.

4.1b   Verb Tense

A verb expresses the time of an action or of a condition through **tense.** By changing the form of a verb, you can show whether something is happening now, has happened in the past, or will happen in the future. Verbs in English have six tenses: present, past, future, present perfect, past perfect, and future perfect. You form the tenses by using the principal parts and auxiliary verbs.

A **conjugation of a verb** is a list of all the forms for the six tenses of a verb. It also shows how the form of the verb changes in the first, second, and third persons and in the singular and plural.

Conjugation of the Verb *Laugh*

Singular	Plural
Present Tense	
I laugh	we laugh
you laugh	you laugh
he/she/it laughs	they laugh
Past Tense	
I laughed	we laughed
you laughed	you laughed
he/she/it laughed	they laughed
Future Tense	
I will (shall) laugh	we will (shall) laugh
you will laugh	you will laugh
he/she/it will laugh	they will laugh
Present Perfect Tense	
I have laughed	we have laughed
you have laughed	you have laughed
he/she/it has laughed	they have laughed

Past Perfect Tense

> I had laughed
> you had laughed
> he/she/it had laughed

> we had laughed
> you had laughed
> thcy had laughed

Future Perfect Tense

> I will (shall) have laughed
> you will have laughed
> he/she/it will have laughed

> we will (shall) have laughed
> you will have laughed
> they will have laughed

Present and Present Perfect Tenses

Rule   Use verbs in the *present tense* to show an action that takes place in the present, or an action that is repeated regularly, or a condition that is true at any time. You should also use the present tense for statements about literary works and other works of art.

To form the present tense of a verb, use thc infinitive form or add -*s* or -*es* to the infinitive.

> PRESENT   I **miss** the freeway exit often.
>
> He **misses** the freeway exit often.

Rule   Use verbs in the *present perfect tense* to describe action completed either in the recent past or at an indefinite time in the past.

To form the present perfect tense of a verb, use *has* or *have* as an auxiliary verb with the past participle of the main verb.

> PRESENT PERFECT
> He **has missed** the freeway exit.
>
> We **have missed** the freeway exit.

Past and Past Perfect Tenses

Rule   Use the *past tense* to describe an action that was completed entirely in the past.

151

To form the past tense of a regular verb, add *-d* or *-ed* to the infinitive.

PAST   He **missed** the freeway exit.

Rule   Use the *past perfect tense* to describe an action that was finished by a certain time in the past or before some other action was completed.

To form the past perfect tense, use *had* as an auxiliary verb with the past participle of the main verb.

PAST   past perfect
PERFECT   He **had missed** the freeway exit before he

                    past
                    realized where he was.

Future and Future Perfect Tenses

Rule   Use the *future tense* to describe action that will occur in the future.

To form the future tense, use *will* or *shall* with the infinitive form of the main verb.

FUTURE   He **will miss** the freeway exit.

                     We **shall miss** the freeway exit.

Rule   Use the *future perfect tense* to describe action that will be concluded at a specific time in the future.

To form the future perfect tense, use *will have* or *shall have* with the past participle of the main verb.

FUTURE PERFECT
        The family **will have arrived** by four o'clock.

Exercise 2   Verb Tense   On your paper, write the required tense of the verb in parentheses for each of the following sentences.

SAMPLE	Len _?_ the article. (*write*—future)
ANSWER	will write

1. Our team _?_ well this year. (*play*—present perfect)
2. I _?_ you that I would be on time. (*promise*—past)
3. We _?_ for student council reform. (*campaign*—future)
4. Lisette _?_ to buy a car last week. (*decide*—past)
5. We _?_ ourselves hoarse by the end of the game. (*cheer* —future perfect)
6. They _?_ by the time the storm began. (*arrive*—past perfect)
7. Peg _?_ the flag in the parade. (*carry*—future)
8. I _?_ working out at the gym. (*enjoy*—present)
9. Tim _?_ in England by evening. (*land*—future perfect)
10. Renee _?_ onto the field before her teammates even arrived. (*start*—past perfect)

The Progressive Forms of Verbs

Each of the six tenses has a **progressive form,** which you use to describe a continuing action. To make the progressive form, use the appropriate tense of the verb *be* plus the present participle of the main verb.

PRESENT PROGRESSIVE
They **are talking** now.

PRESENT PERFECT PROGRESSIVE
They **have been talking** for an hour.

PAST PROGRESSIVE
They **were talking** yesterday.

PAST PERFECT PROGRESSIVE
They **had been talking** since noon.

FUTURE PROGRESSIVE
They **will be talking** until five o'clock.

FUTURE PERFECT PROGRESSIVE
They **will have been talking** all day.

Exercise 3 Progressive Forms of Verbs On your paper, write the required form of the verb in parentheses for each sentence.

> SAMPLE   We _?_ the all-day concert. (*attend*—future progressive)
>
> ANSWER   will be attending

1. We _?_ for the bus. (*wait*—past progressive)
2. Sam _?_ across the country. (*drive*—present progressive)
3. Sue _?_ about the economy. (*speak*—past perfect progressive)
4. We _?_ all afternoon. (*walk*—future progressive)
5. I _?_ about the situation. (*think*—present perfect progressive)
6. By the end of our flight, we _?_ for nine hours. (*travel* —future perfect progressive)
7. Arlene _?_ in the garden since daybreak. (*work*—past perfect progressive)
8. I _?_ to convince him that he should join us. (*try*— present perfect progressive)

Consistency of Tenses

Rule Use verbs in the same tense to express events occurring at the same time.

When two actions occur at the same time, you should be careful to use verbs in the same tense. In compound sentences (*page 118*) and in sentences with compound predicates (*page 62*), you will usually use a single tense for the verbs.

> INCORRECT   Jeremy **reads** and **studied** all evening.
>   present   past
>
> CORRECT   Jeremy **read** and **studied** all evening.
>   past   past
>
> INCORRECT   Marshall **went** to the fish market, and Sam **goes** to the florist.
>   past
>   present

CORRECT
past

Marshall **went** to the fish market, and Sam
past

went to the florist.

Rule Use verbs in different tenses for events occurring at different times.

Use the past perfect tense for the earlier of two past actions. Use the present perfect tense for the earlier action if two actions are occurring in the present but one began in the past and continues. Use the future perfect tense for the earlier of two future actions.

| 1st event | 2nd event |
| past perf. | past |

The bell **had rung** when we **arrived** at school.

| 1st event | 2nd event |
| pres. perf. | pres. |

Simon **has painted** all morning, and now he **wants** to rest.

| 2nd event | 1st event |
| future | future perf. |

Although we **will be** on time, Tom **will have left** already.

Exercise 4 Consistency of Tenses On your paper, rewrite the following sentences, correcting errors in verb tense. If a sentence contains no errors, write *Correct* on your paper.

SAMPLE   The principal spoke to me briefly and tells me to return to class.

ANSWER   The principal spoke to me briefly and told me to return to class.

1. When Jake called, I am mowing the lawn.
2. Every morning she does twenty sit-ups and ran around the block.
3. I will finish my essay tonight, and then I type it.
4. When Lynn got to her car, she discovered a flat tire.
5. By the time I had received Lucille's letter, I had made other plans.

6. Maria finished taking notes, and then she begins to make an outline.

7. When she gets ready to take pictures, the photographer arranged the lights.

8. We will be meeting Hal after your bus came in.

9. You visit Banff before you will drive to Jasper.

10. Lydia built a fire while Frank unpacks the supplies.

4.1c   Active and Passive Voice

Verbs have active and passive voices to tell whether the subject of the sentence is the performer or the receiver of the action. If the subject performs the action, the verb is in the **active voice.** If the subject receives the action, the verb is in the **passive voice.** The passive voice consists of the past participle of the main verb added to a form of the verb *be.*

ACTIVE   Pat **hit** the ball.

              Olga **gives** ballet lessons.

PASSIVE   The ball **was hit** by Pat.

              Ballet lessons **are given** by Olga.

Intransitive verbs *(page 19)* and linking verbs *(page 15)* cannot be in the passive voice because they do not take objects. Only transitive verbs *(page 19)* can be in either the active or the passive voice, because only transitive verbs have receivers of action. Notice that the verbs in the preceding examples are transitive verbs.

Whenever possible, use verbs in the active voice rather than in the passive voice. The active voice is more direct and more concise than the passive voice. Choose the passive voice only when you want to show that the receiver of the action is more important than the person or thing performing the action.

156

Exercise 5   Active and Passive Voice   On your paper, rewrite each of the following sentences. *Step 1:* Change verbs in the active voice to passive, and change verbs in the passive voice to active. Make any other necessary changes in the sentences. *Step 2:* Tell whether the verb in the rewritten sentence is in the active voice or the passive voice.

SAMPLE   My account was checked by the bank teller.

ANSWER   The bank teller checked my account.—Active

1. The clerk is wrapping your gift.
2. My car was moved by someone.
3. The judges have chosen Fred's essay.
4. Mice are chased by our cat.
5. The teams' schedules are being planned by the coaches.
6. Johnson caught the ball.

Assignment   Active and Passive Voice   Rewrite a short article from a newspaper, changing all verbs in the active voice to the passive voice. Then write a sentence or two explaining which version is more effective and why.

Writing Workshop

Verb Tense

Step 1: Write a paragraph describing something that you plan to do over the coming weekend. Use verbs in the future tense. *Step 2:* Rewrite your paragraph as if the weekend were past and you had already completed the activity. Use appropriate verbs in the past and past perfect tenses. You may have to make other changes so that your paragraph will be logical.

4.2   Subject-Verb Agreement

4.2a   Singular and Plural Subjects and Verbs

Rule   A subject and its verb must agree in number.

Number means singular (one) or plural (more than one). Nouns and pronouns that are singular refer to one person, place, or thing. *She, direction, city,* and *success* are all singular. Plural nouns and pronouns refer to more than one person, place, or thing. *They, directions, cities,* and *successes* are all plural. Use singular verb forms with singular subjects, and use plural verb forms with plural subjects. Although nouns ending in *s* are usually plural, verb forms ending in *s* are usually singular.

SINGULAR
subj.   verb
Juanita **enjoys** swimming.

subj.   verb
Alexander **shares** his lunch.

PLURAL
subj.   verb
The *players* **enjoy** winning.

subj.   verb
We usually **share** the work.

Verb Phrases.   In a verb phrase, use an auxiliary verb that agrees in number with its subject.

SINGULAR
subj.   verb phrase
The *doctor* **was discussing** the case.

subj.   verb phrase
Maria recently **has gone** on vacation.

PLURAL
subj.   verb phrase
The *doctors* **were discussing** the case.

subj.   verb phrase
Maria and her mother **have gone** on vacation.

Intervening Words and Phrases. Sometimes words or phrases come between a subject and its verb. For instance, a prepositional phrase that modifies the subject usually follows the subject and separates it from the verb. A prepositional phrase does *not* determine whether the subject is singular or plural.

SINGULAR	The *color* of the walls **was** unusual. [**Think:** color **was.**] The *alternate,* along with two representatives, **is** to attend the meeting. [**Think:** alternate **is.**]
PLURAL	The *students* in this school **are** friendly. [**Think:** students **are.**] The *chapters* at the beginning of the book **are** the shortest. [**Think:** chapters **are.**]

Exercise 1 Subject-Verb Agreement On your paper, write the verb form that agrees in number with the subject of each sentence. Then write whether the verb form is singular or plural.

SAMPLE	Timothy, like the rest of his family, (has, have) red hair.
ANSWER	has—Singular

1. They (was, were) not sure of the soloist's name.
2. The cup next to the glasses (look, looks) clean.
3. Even the youngest children (was showing, were showing) some genuine interest in books.
4. The paintings by Georgia O'Keeffe (is, are) on exhibit until the end of the month.
5. Her main responsibility (was, were) mowing the lawn.
6. The decision of the judges (is, are) final.
7. Many people (seems, seem) to be surprised at the outcome of the school elections.
8. The storms of last winter (is, are) hard to forget.

9. The backpackers (seems, seem) tired and hungry.
10. My grandmother, along with two of her friends, (is, are) planning a trip to Mexico.
11. Your plans to camp in the desert (does, do) not appeal to me.
12. The classes on refinishing furniture (has, have) been canceled.
13. The summary, plus all these reports, (needs, need) to be typed by tomorrow.
14. The witnesses for the prosecution (has, have) been well prepared to testify.
15. The radio towers on the highest hill south of town (transmits, transmit) signals throughout the region.

4.2b Determining the Number of the Subject

You must determine whether the subject of a sentence is singular or plural to be sure that the verb form agrees with it in number. Some subjects, such as compounds and indefinite pronouns, require that you pay special attention in order to use correct verb forms with them.

Compound Subjects

A **compound subject** is made up of two or more words or groups of words connected by one of the following conjunctions: *and, or, nor, either . . . or,* or *neither . . . nor.* Two factors determine the number of the verb to use with a compound subject: (1) the conjunction and (2) whether the words in the compound subject are singular or plural.

Rule Use a plural verb with most compound subjects connected by *and.*

PLURAL   *Sally and* her *grandfather* **play** chess on Tuesdays.

Ralph and his younger *brother* **have been** in Florida for a week.

160

Rule   Use a singular verb with a compound subject that refers to one person or thing or that generally conveys the idea of a unit.

> My *neighbor and* closest *friend* **is** Susan. [one person]
> *Macaroni and cheese* **is** on the lunch menu. [one dish]
> *Wear and tear* often **results** from long use. [one condition]

Rule   Use a singular verb with a compound subject made up of singular nouns or pronouns connected by *or* or *nor*. Use a plural verb with a compound subject formed from plural nouns or pronouns.

SINGULAR   Either the *cat or* the *dog* **has eaten** my lunch.
             Neither *Phil nor Al* **is** here today.

PLURAL   Either *baseballs or softballs* **are** on sale.
             Neither the *children nor* their *parents* **are** here.

Rule   When a compound subject consists of a singular subject and a plural subject connected by *or* or *nor,* use a verb that agrees in number with the subject that is closer to it in the sentence.

> sing.   ⌐pl.⌐
> Either *Ralph* or the *twins* **are** at home this evening.
>
> pl.   ⌐sing.⌐
> Neither the *students* nor the *teacher* **was** in study hall.

Although correct, the sentences sound awkward. If you object to the awkwardness, you can eliminate it by rephrasing the sentences.

> ⌐sing.⌐   ⌐pl.⌐
> Either *Ralph* **is** at home this evening, or the *twins* **are.**
>
> ⌐pl.⌐
> The *students* **were** not in the study hall, and neither
> ⌐sing.⌐
> **was** the *teacher.*

Indefinite Pronouns as Subjects

Indefinite pronouns are pronouns that refer to people or things in general. Some indefinite pronouns are always singular and therefore always take singular verbs. The following are examples of *singular indefinite pronouns*:

anybody	everybody	nobody	somebody
anyone	everyone	no one	someone
anything	everything	nothing	something
each	much	one	
either	neither	other	

SINGULAR   *No one* **was** able to answer the question.

Everyone **likes** a good story.

Some indefinite pronouns are always plural and always take plural verbs. The most common *plural indefinite pronouns* are *several, both, few,* and *many.*

PLURAL   *Many* **are called,** but *few* **are chosen.**

Both **are** at the top of their class.

The following indefinite pronouns can be *either singular or plural,* depending on their use in sentences:

all	enough	most	plenty
any	more	none	some

These indefinite pronouns are singular when they refer to a portion or to a single person, place, or thing. They are plural when they refer to a number of individual persons, places, or things. Sometimes an indefinite pronoun refers to a word that is not in the sentence but is understood.

SINGULAR   *Most* of the weekend **was** enjoyable. [*Most* refers to a portion of the *weekend.*]

Some of the garden **was** weeded. [*Some* refers to a portion of the *garden.*]

The storm has passed, and *all* **is** calm. [*All* refers to *everything,* which is understood.]

PLURAL   *Most* of my homework assignments **are** done. [*Most* refers to several *assignments*.]

Some of the speakers **were** interesting. [*Some* refers to several *speakers*.]

All **are** welcome at the meeting. [*All* refers to *people,* which is understood.]

Exercise 2   Agreement in Number   On your paper, write the form of the verb that agrees in number with the subject. Then state whether the verb form is singular or plural.

SAMPLE   Neither Jorge nor Elena (likes, like) to roller skate.

ANSWER   likes—Singular

1. Kimberly, Chris, and my brother Ed (thinks, think) that the Steelers will win.
2. Nobody in our class (wants, want) to be the moderator of the meeting.
3. Few of my friends (has, have) read this fascinating book about planets.
4. Ham and eggs (was, were) all I wanted for breakfast.
5. Either Frank or Sarah (wins, win) every race.
6. All of the play, except for the second act, (was, were) predictable.
7. Everyone (seems, seem) to be enjoying the band concert.
8. Neither Marvin nor his parents (cares, care) very much for musical comedies.
9. I wanted to borrow a mystery, but most of them (was, were) already checked out.
10. The boys and their father (is, are) hiking this weekend.

Collective Nouns as Subjects

A **collective noun** is a noun that names a group or collection of people or objects, such as *team, crowd, fleet, class,* and *jury.* Although these nouns are singular in form, they may take a singular or a plural verb, depending on their use in a sentence.

Rule   If a collective noun refers to a group as a single unit, use a singular verb. If a collective noun refers to the individual members or parts of a group, use a plural verb.

SINGULAR   The *team* **plays** well. [The team is a unit.]

PLURAL   The *team* **go** their separate ways after the game. [The team members are acting individually.]

SINGULAR   The *jury* **finds** the accused not guilty. [The jury is acting as a body.]

PLURAL   The *jury* **are** staying in different hotels so that they won't discuss the trial. [The members of the jury are acting as individuals.]

Nouns Ending in *s*

Most nouns that end in *s* are plural, but others present agreement problems. Some nouns are plural in form but singular in meaning because they refer to a single thing or a unit. Examples include *news, measles, physics, mathematics,* and *economics*. (Notice that removing the *s* does not leave a singular noun.) Use singular verbs with these nouns.

SINGULAR   The *news* **seems** good.

Mumps **is** not just a childhood disease.

Physics **was** my most difficult subject.

Other nouns ending in *s* take a plural verb even though they refer to one thing or one pair. Examples include *scissors, pliers, trousers, pants, spectacles, clothes,* and *thanks*.

PLURAL   The *pliers* **are** in the tool box.

His *pants* **look** too long.

The *clothes* **have been sent** to the cleaners.

A few nouns ending in *s* may be either singular or plural, depending on the meaning of the sentence. Examples include *politics, athletics,* and *headquarters.*

SINGULAR   *Politics* **has been** a major influence on her plans.

PLURAL   My *politics* **result** from years of study.

Exercise 3   Subject-Verb Agreement   On your paper, write the verb that correctly completes each of the following sentences.

SAMPLE   Thanks (was, were) due everyone who helped.

ANSWER   were

1. My glasses (was, were) broken during the football game.
2. Measles (was, were) once a common childhood disease.
3. These pants (costs, cost) more than I want to pay.
4. The news we heard today (was, were) encouraging.
5. The orchestra (gives, give) two free concerts a year.
6. The herd (huddles, huddle) close to one another.
7. These pliers (doesn't, don't) seem to work.
8. Economics (is, are) a fascinating subject.
9. The committee (doesn't, don't) always see eye to eye with one another.
10. The audience (applauds, applaud) after each song.

Titles and Names as Subjects

The title of a book, story, play, movie, television program, musical composition, or magazine refers to an individual work. It is singular, even though it may include plural words. The name of a country or of an organization is also singular when it refers to an entire country or group.

Rule   Use a singular verb with a subject that is a title or is the name of a country or of an organization.

165

Twelve Angry Men **is** a powerful drama.

The Times **presents** more features than other newspapers.

The Philippine Islands **is** a group of about seven thousand islands.

Words of Amount and Time

Rule   Use a singular verb with a subject that expresses a fraction, a measurement, an amount of money, a distance, or a specific interval of time when it refers to a single unit.

> SINGULAR *Ten centimeters* **is** less than five inches.
>
> *Forty-eight hours* **was** not time enough to get there and back.
>
> *Five dollars* **is** too much to spend for that plant.

Rule   Use a plural verb when the subject expresses a length of time or an amount that is considered as a number of separate units.

> PLURAL *Five years* **have passed** since I've seen my cousins in Florida.
>
> *Two dimes* **were left** in the phone booth.

Exercise 4   Titles, Names, Amounts, and Time   On your paper, write the form of the verb that agrees in number with the subject of the sentence.

> SAMPLE Twenty-six miles (is, are) the approximate length of a marathon.
>
> ANSWER is

1. *TV Facts* (contains, contain) informative articles.
2. Two quarters (was, were) found between the sofa cushions.
3. Fifty dollars (is, are) the amount Aunt Judith sent me.
4. "The Three Little Pigs" (is, are) my favorite childhood story.
5. The *Wilston Star News* usually (includes, include) thought-provoking editorials.

6. Five kilometers (is, are) the distance from here to the town.

7. *Science Fiction Annals* occasionally (has, have) stories that make me skeptical.

8. "The Bulldogs" (seems, seem) to be a popular name for high-school football teams.

9. According to the Gregorian calendar, 366 days (is, are) in a leap year.

10. The United States (maintains, maintain) a complex system of interstate highways.

4.2c   Problems with Agreement

Some kinds of sentences can make subject-verb agreement difficult. Inverted word order (*page 67*) can make the subject of a sentence difficult to determine, for instance. You may confuse other words with the subject of the sentence. If you can recognize these situations, you can avoid many agreement problems.

Inverted Word Order

In some sentences the verb appears before the subject, especially in questions and in sentences beginning with *Here* or *There*. For a sentence with inverted word order, you should first identify the subject and then make the verb agree with it in number. Saying the sentence to yourself in normal word order often helps.

Under the sofa **was** a frightened *mouse*. [**Think:** mouse **was.**]

There **are** many *things* that I don't know. [**Think:** things **are.**]

Here **is** my *plan* for the project. [**Think:** plan **is.**]

Where **are** the *instructions* for this game? [**Think:** instructions **are.**]

When a compound subject follows the verb, determine whether it is singular or plural in the same way that you would if the sentence were in normal order. Then follow the rules for making verbs agree with compound subjects (*page 160*).

There **are** two *restaurants and* a *motel* on that block. [**Think:** restaurants and motel **are.**]

Here **comes** *Samantha or Sue.* [**Think:** Samantha or Sue **comes.**]

Sentences with Predicate Nominatives

A **predicate nominative** (*page 74*) is a complement that follows a linking verb and renames the subject of a sentence. The number of the predicate nominative has no effect on the number of the verb. Even when the number of the predicate nominative is different from the number of the subject, the verb agrees with the subject.

Rule   Use a verb that agrees in number with the subject, not with the predicate nominative.

His favorite *gift* of all **was** the *stamps* from Egypt.

The *stamps* from Egypt **were** his favorite *gift.*

Every and *Many a*

When the adjectives *every* and *many a* precede single or compound subjects, they emphasize that the subjects are individuals rather than groups. *Every boy* means "every single boy" (not "all boys"). *Many a boy* refers to many boys as separate individuals. In these cases the subject (*boy*) is singular and requires a singular verb.

Rule Use a singular verb with a single or compound subject modified by *every* or *many a*.

> *Every actor, chorus member,* and *stagehand* in this room **deserves** praise.
>
> *Many a* good *sailor* **has fallen** into the water.

Exercise 5 Problems with Agreement *Step 1:* On your paper, rewrite the following sentences, correcting all errors in subject-verb agreement by changing the form of the verb. If a sentence contains no error, write *Correct* on your paper. *Step 2:* Underline the correct verb form in each new sentence.

SAMPLE	Here is the magazines that you requested by phone.
ANSWER	Here <u>are</u> the magazines that you requested by phone.

1. Is there too many people in line?
2. Dad's present to Mother were pearls from Japan.
3. Many a student looks forward to vacation.
4. There go either Frank or Paul.
5. Every student, teacher, and administrator are to leave the building in the event of a fire drill.
6. My first choice were the purple sunglasses.
7. Many a wild deer wander into the open fields along country roads.
8. Beneath the calendar was a list of chores to be done.
9. The best act in the show were the trained monkeys.
10. Every chapter need to be read carefully.

Assignment Subject-Verb Agreement Some of the following phrases are singular, and some are plural. *Step 1:* Write five interesting sentences, using one of the phrases in each one. *Step 2:* Change each phrase from singular to plural or from plural to singular, and write five new sentences.

1. spot seems
2. countries are
3. either Rachel or Sam has mentioned
4. attitudes concern
5. people speak

4.3   Correct Use of Pronouns

4.3a   Pronoun Antecedents

An **antecedent** is the word that a pronoun refers to or replaces in a sentence. A pronoun must agree with its antecedent in number, gender, and person (*page 7*).

Agreement in Number

Rule   Use a singular pronoun to refer to a singular antecedent. Use a plural pronoun to refer to a plural antecedent.

SINGULAR	PLURAL
I, me, my, mine	we, us, our, ours
you, your, yours	you, your, yours
she, her, hers	they, them, their, theirs
he, him, his	
it, its	

SINGULAR   When *Stephanie* went home, **she** turned on her radio.

PLURAL   The *boys* left **their** hockey puck at school.

Rule   Use a plural pronoun to refer to two or more singular antecedents joined by *and*.

Larry and Bill are planning **their** schedules for next term.

Rule Use a singular pronoun to refer to two or more singular antecedents joined by *or* or *nor*.

———— sing. ————
Neither *Betty nor Andrea* likes **her** toast buttered.

Indefinite Pronouns as Antecedents. The indefinite pronouns listed here are usually singular in meaning. When they are antecedents, use singular pronouns to refer to them.

anybody	everybody	nobody	somebody
anyone	everyone	no one	someone
anything	everything	nothing	something
each	much	one	
either	neither	other	

SINGULAR   *Someone* left **her** pocketbook in the bleachers.

Everything must be in **its** place before you leave.

Some indefinite pronouns are plural in meaning, such as *several, both, few,* and *many*. When they are antecedents, use plural pronouns to refer to them.

PLURAL   *Many* gave **their** best efforts in the marathon.

The following indefinite pronouns can be either singular or plural antecedents.

all	enough	most	plenty
any	more	none	some

Refer to these indefinite pronouns with either singular or plural pronouns, depending on the meaning of the sentence.

SINGULAR   **Some** of this old *jewelry* has lost **its** shine. [*Some* refers to *jewelry,* which is singular; *its* refers to *Some.*]

PLURAL   **Some** of these *people* have not paid **their** dues.
[*Some* refers to *people,* which is plural; *their* refers to *Some.*]

Collective Nouns as Antecedents.   When the antecedent is a collective noun, you must make sure that the pronouns that refer to it agree in number with the collective noun itself (*page 163–164*).

The *class* are sharpening **their** pencils. [The members of the class are acting as individuals.]

The *committee* were arguing among **themselves.** [The committee *members* were arguing.]

Agreement in Gender

Rule   Use a pronoun that agrees in gender with its antecedent.

The **gender** of a noun or pronoun is masculine, feminine, or neuter. When the gender of the antecedent is masculine, refer to it with *he, him,* or *his.* When the antecedent is feminine, refer to it by using *she, her,* or *hers.* Use *it* or *its* to refer to a neuter antecedent, one that is neither masculine nor feminine.

Nicky whistled as **he** gathered the firewood.

Janet was pleased with **her** new job.

A *diamond* is precious because of **its** brilliance and hardness.

When it is not clear whether a singular antecedent is masculine or feminine, the pronoun should show that it could be either. You can often use *his or her* for that purpose.

Somebody forgot **his or her** homework.

A good diamond *cutter* is known for **his or her** ability to shape the diamond.

Using two pronouns to refer to the same antecedent is sometimes awkward, however. If possible, rephrase the sentence and make the antecedent and the words that refer to it plural.

AWKWARD   A *leader* depends on the people **he or she** leads.

BETTER   *Leaders* depend on the people **they** lead.

Agreement in Person

Rule   Use a pronoun that agrees in person with its antecedent.

Pronouns are in the first person, the second person, or the third person (*page 7*). First-person pronouns refer to the person(s) who are speaking. Second-person pronouns refer to the person(s) being spoken to. Third-person pronouns refer to any person(s) or thing(s) being spoken about.

FIRST PERSON   *I* may read this in **my** spare time.

SECOND PERSON   Thank *you* for **your** invitation.

THIRD PERSON   *Peter and Lily* have brought **their** cameras.

The indefinite pronoun *one* is in the third person. When *one* is an antecedent, use a third-person pronoun to refer to it.

One can learn from **his or her** mistakes.

Exercise 1 Pronoun Antecedents
On your paper, write a pronoun that agrees with the antecedent to complete the sentence correctly.

SAMPLE   Each student recited __?__ favorite poem.

ANSWER   his or her

1. Either Sheila or Ellen will bring __?__ camera to the picnic.
2. Each of the boys paid for __?__ own uniform.
3. Someone left __?__ lunch tray on the table.
4. One should take time to do __?__ work properly.
5. The tree had a bird's nest in __?__ branches.
6. My family and I plan to spend __?__ vacation canoeing.
7. Either Bill or Sam has promised to lend us __?__ projector.
8. Neither Linda nor Diane remembered __?__ umbrella.
9. Some of the students forgot to bring __?__ homework.
10. Larry has already finished his report, but I haven't had time to complete __?__ .

4.3b   Pronoun Case

Personal pronouns change form to specify number, gender, person, and case. **Pronoun case** is the change in form that shows the grammatical use of the pronoun in the sentence. Pronouns have three cases: nominative, objective, and possessive.

	SINGULAR	PLURAL
NOMINATIVE CASE	I	we
	you	you
	he, she, it	they
OBJECTIVE CASE	me	us
	you	you
	him, her, it	them
POSSESSIVE CASE*	my, mine	our, ours
	your, yours	your, yours
	his, her, hers, its	their, theirs

* The words *my, your, his, her, its, our,* and *their* are sometimes called pronominal adjectives (*page 26*).

Pronouns in the Nominative Case

Rule   When a pronoun is a subject or a predicate nominative, use the nominative case.

SUBJECT **They** used to live across the street.
Did **she** ring the doorbell?

PREDICATE
NOMINATIVE The man on the phone was **he.**
The winners of the contest were Roland and **I.**

Rule   When a pronoun is an appositive to a subject or a predicate nominative, use the nominative case.

APPOSITIVE Two *students*, **she** and Frankie, tied for first place. [**Think: She** and Frankie tied.]

The finalists were my *cousins*, **he** and Paul. [**Think:** The finalists were **he** and Paul.]

Pronouns in the Objective Case

Rule   When a pronoun is a direct object, an indirect object, or an object of a preposition, use the objective case.

DIRECT OBJECT James thanked **us** for raking the lawn.
Did Ted ask **them** to the party?

INDIRECT OBJECT Dad bought **me** a new bicycle.
Will Sam give **her** a birthday present?

OBJECT OF A
PREPOSITION The reward was given to **him.**
The children made dinner for **them.**

Rule   When a pronoun is an appositive to a direct or indirect object or to the object of a preposition, use the objective case.

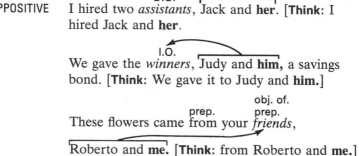

APPOSITIVE   I hired two *assistants*, Jack and **her**. [**Think**: I hired Jack and **her**.

We gave the *winners*, Judy and **him**, a savings bond. [**Think**: We gave it to Judy and **him**.]

These flowers came from your *friends*,

Roberto and **me**. [**Think**: from Roberto and **me**.]

Compound Constructions with Pronouns

Sometimes pronouns are used in a compound subject or in a compound direct or indirect object. To determine which case of the pronoun to use, say the sentence to yourself without the conjunction and the noun or other pronoun. Then decide whether the nominative case or the objective case is correct.

Ben and **I** went to the movies last night. [**Think**: **I** went.]

Dad showed Kathy and **me** how to do a swan dive. [**Think**: Dad showed **me**.]

Everyone saw Terry and **him** leave early. [**Think**: Everyone saw **him**.]

Brad will send a taxi for you and **me**. [**Think**: for **me**.]

Exercise 2   The Nominative and Objective Cases

On your paper, write the pronoun that is correct in each of the following sentences.

> **SAMPLE**   Come with Carl and (I, me) to the circus.
> **ANSWER**   me

1. The coaches, (he, him) and Mr. Warren, called a meeting.

2. I saw all of the neighbors at the store except the Henshaws and (they, them).

3. Send the notice to everyone, the teachers and (we, us).

4. The hosts, Herman and (he, him), greeted their guests.

5. You and (I, me) are going to be late.

6. It is a secret between the two of (they, them).

7. Just between you and (I, me), I think she's wrong.

8. Can you have lunch with Richard and (I, me)?

9. Give (he, him) back his fishing rod.

10. Did you and (she, her) fall asleep during the movie?

11. Let Ronald and (I, me) help you.

12. Martha will save seats for you and (I, me).

Pronouns in the Possessive Case

Possessive pronouns show to whom or to what something belongs.

Rule Use the following possessive pronouns to replace and refer to nouns: *mine, yours, his, hers, its, ours,* and *theirs.*

The preceding possessive pronouns can replace nouns as subjects, predicate nominatives, direct or indirect objects, objects of prepositions, or appositives. They can refer to singular and plural antecedents without changing form. (Only *mine* does not end in *s*.) Remember that none of the possessive pronouns has an apostrophe.

SUBJECT	**Yours** are the green mittens.
PREDICATE NOMINATIVE	That uniform is **hers.**
DIRECT OBJECT	I may borrow **his.**
INDIRECT OBJECT	Phil sent his mother perfume, but Evelyn sent **hers** a bouquet.
OBJECT OF A PREPOSITION	Your plans sound intriguing, but let me tell you about **mine.**

Rule   Use the following possessive pronouns* to modify nouns: *my, your, his, her, its, our,* and *their*.

Your new *sweater* fell onto the floor.

Her *ambition* is to be a doctor.

Rule   Use possessive pronouns to modify gerunds as well as nouns.

Gerunds are *-ing* forms of verbs and are used as nouns (*page 102*). Because they serve as nouns, they require possessive forms of nouns or pronouns to modify them.

Their *talking* disturbed the speaker. [*Their* is used instead of *them* because it is the *talking* that disturbed the speaker, not *them. Whose* talking? *Their* talking.]

He objected to **my** *borrowing* his records. [*My* is used instead of *me* because it is the *borrowing* to which he objected, not *me. Whose* borrowing? *My* borrowing.]

Exercise 3   Possessive Pronouns   On your paper, write the pronoun that is correct in each of the following sentences.

> **SAMPLE**   I heard about (you, your) winning first place.
>
> **ANSWER**   your

1. These skates are (their, theirs).
2. (You, Your) arriving early was fortunate.
3. (Our, Ours) are the prettiest roses.
4. (Her, She) being sick caused a postponement.
5. I don't mind (him, his) playing the trumpet at night.
6. Ralph's books are on the table beneath (your's, yours).
7. The prompter helped me quickly, and no one noticed (me, my) forgetting my lines.

---

*These possessive pronouns are sometimes called pronominal adjectives (*page 26*).

8. The decision will have to be (hers, her's) alone.
9. (You, Your) jogging every morning should put you in good shape for the race.
10. Monroe has always respected (them, their) opinions.

Who and *Whom*

You can use the forms of the word *who* as either interrogative pronouns or relative pronouns. As with other pronouns, your choice of case depends on how you are using the pronoun in the sentence. *Who* and *whoever* are in the nominative case. *Whom* and *whomever* are in the objective case. *Whose* is in the possessive case. Usage of *whose* rarely causes any problem, because the need for a possessive form is usually clear from the meaning of the sentence. Choosing between *who* and *whom*, however, requires special attention.

Who and Whom as Interrogative Pronouns. When you use *who* or *whom* to introduce a question, it is an interrogative pronoun. To determine whether to use the nominative form (*who*) or the objective form (*whom*), mentally rearrange the question to make it a statement.

Rule If an interrogative pronoun serves as a subject or as a predicate nominative, use *who*. If it serves as an object, use *whom*.

SUBJECT   **Who** washed the dishes?
               Who will buy these lovely strawberries?

OBJECT   **Whom** did you see at the party? [**Think:** You did see **whom**. *Whom* is the direct object.]
           To **whom** does the book belong? [**Think:** The book does belong to **whom**. *Whom* is the object of the preposition *to*.]

Sometimes an interrupting phrase such as *does she think, did he say,* or *do you suppose* follows the interrogative pronoun *who* or *whom*. To decide which case of the interrogative pronoun to use, say the sentence to yourself without the phrase, and rearrange the inverted word order, if necessary. Then you can tell whether to use the nominative or the objective form in the sentence.

Who *did you say* is on the phone? [**Think**: Who is on the phone?]

Whom *do you suppose* she was calling? [**Think**: She was calling whom?]

In informal usage, such as in casual conversation, people often use *who* to ask a question, regardless of whether it is the subject or the object. In formal usage, as in most serious conversation and writing, you should follow the rules for using the nominative form, *who,* and the objective form, *whom.*

INFORMAL   **Who** did you invite to the game?

FORMAL   **Whom** did they nominate for secretary?

Who and Whom as Relative Pronouns. *Who* and *whom,* as well as *whoever* and *whomever,* are also relative pronouns used to introduce subordinate clauses (*page 109*). To determine which pronoun to use, first find the subordinate clause. Then decide how the relative pronoun is used in the clause.

Rule If a relative pronoun serves as the subject of the subordinate clause, use *who* or *whoever.* If it serves as an object within the subordinate clause, use *whom* or *whomever.*

```
          ┌────── sub. clause──────┐
          │subj.   verb            │
```
The person **who** answered the phone was very polite.

```
              ┌────── sub. clause──────┐
              │ subj.    verb          │
```
Give the package to **whoever** answers the door. [*Whoever* is the subject of the subordinate clause, not the object of the preposition *to.* The entire subordinate clause is the object of the preposition.]

```
              ┌─────────sub. clause─────────┐
        ┌prep. obj.                          │
```
The teacher to **whom** you are referring has retired. [**Think:** You are referring to **whom**.]

```
                    ┌──────────sub. clause──────────┐
        │    D.O.      subj.  verb                    │
```
I would welcome **whomever** you invite to the party. [**Think:** You invite **whomever**.]

Exercise 4 *Who* **and** *Whom*   On your paper, write *who, whom, whoever,* or *whomever* to complete each of the following sentences correctly.

> **SAMPLE**   To _?_ should I send my letter?
>
> **ANSWER**   whom

1. _?_ did you see at the movies last week?
2. I wanted to know _?_ came over to visit today.
3. Rhonda, _?_ has been my best friend since first grade, just moved to St. Louis.
4. Sally will not tell me _?_ she called.
5. To _?_ are you speaking, him or me?
6. Besides Peter, _?_ do you think will receive an award?
7. You may forward this report to _?_ you wish.
8. All the people to _?_ I sent invitations came to the party.
9. _?_ is chosen will be required to make a presentation to the Board of Education.
10. The man _?_ I met at the game last Saturday was from Toronto.

We and Us Used with Appositives

In a phrase containing an appositive such as *we students* and *us girls,* the function of the noun in the sentence determines which case of the pronoun to use. If the noun is the subject, use a pronoun in the nominative case with it. If the noun is an object, use a pronoun in the objective case with it. To find out which pronoun form to use, say the sentence to yourself without the noun.

We students want to produce the play. [**Think:** We want. *We* and *students* are subjects. Use the nominative case.]

All the responsibility was given to **us** girls. [**Think:** to us. *Us* and *girls* are objects of the preposition *to*. Use the objective case.]

Pronouns in Comparisons

In some comparisons using *than* or *as,* one or more words are implied rather than stated. If you mentally supply the missing words, you can easily select the pronoun form to use.

She is much taller than **I**. [**Think:** taller than **I** *am*.]

They are not as clever as **we**. [**Think:** as clever as **we** are.]

I find these maps clearer than **them**. [**Think:** clearer than *I find* **them**.]

Sometimes the choice of a pronoun for a comparison depends on your intention. In the following example, the change in pronoun case changes the meaning of the sentence.

NOMINATIVE   I don't know Claudia as well as **she**. [**Think:** as well as **she** does. *She* is the subject of the verb *does,* which is implied. Someone else knows Claudia better than I do.]

OBJECTIVE   I don't know Claudia as well as **her**. [**Think:** as well as *I know* her. *Her* is the direct object. I know Claudia less well than I know someone else.]

Exercise 5   Other Uses of Pronoun Case   On your paper, write the pronoun that is correct in each of the following sentences.

SAMPLE   Sandra drove farther than (he, him).

ANSWER   he

1. Ruby plays the piano much better than (he, him).
2. Mom sent (we, us) boys to the supermarket.
3. They didn't score as well on the test as (we, us).

4. (We, Us) students raised the money ourselves.
5. Katy dances better than (I, me).
6. I guess I dream more often than (he, him).
7. Don't you think (we, us) boys can cook dinner?
8. We consider you a better ventriloquist than (she, her).

4.3c   Correct Pronoun Reference

A pronoun must refer clearly to an antecedent. If the antecedent is missing or unclear, your reader or listener may misunderstand what you are trying to say.

Rule Avoid using a pronoun that could refer to more than one antecedent.

Your reader should not have to guess which word is the antecedent. You can avoid an unclear reference by rephrasing the sentence.

UNCLEAR   Peg told Sheila that **she** had been accepted at the University of Arizona. [Who had been accepted—Peg or Sheila? The antecedent of *she* is not clear.]

CLEAR   Peg said to Sheila, "**I**'ve been accepted at the University of Arizona." [Changed to a direct quotation.]

Peg had been accepted at the University of Arizona, and **she** told Sheila. [Changed to a compound sentence.]

UNCLEAR   When I put the vase on the shelf, **it** broke. [What broke—the vase or the shelf? The antecedent of *it* is not clear.]

CLEAR   The vase broke when I put **it** on the shelf.

183

Rule   In formal speaking and writing, avoid using the pronoun *it, they, you,* or *your* without a clear antecedent.

The following examples show how to avoid an indefinite reference by rephrasing the sentence. Usually you can replace the pronoun with a noun.

INDEFINITE   In this article **it** says that Alfred Nobel invented dynamite. [What says? The pronoun *it* has no antecedent.]

CLEAR   This article says that Alfred Nobel invented dynamite.

According to this article, Alfred Nobel invented dynamite.

INDEFINITE   Last week **they** tore down the old Fairmont Hotel. [Who are *they*? The pronoun has no antecedent.]

CLEAR   Last week Ace Wrecking tore down the old Fairmont Hotel.

Last week the old Fairmont Hotel was torn down.

INDEFINITE   In some countries **you** can't travel without government permission. [*You* refers to people in general and has no definite antecedent.]

CLEAR   In some countries *people* [or *a person* or *one*] can't travel without government permission.

Avoid using *your* in place of an article (*a, an,* or *the*) when no possession is really involved.

AVOID   Your Perseid meteor showers occur in August.

USE   The Perseid meteor showers occur in August.

Exercise 6   Pronoun Reference   On your paper, rewrite the following sentences, making sure that all pronoun references are clear and accurate.

SAMPLE   In this book it has a picture of the Bridge of Sighs in Venice.

ANSWER   This book has a picture of the Bridge of Sighs in Venice.

1. Tommy talked to his brother about his plans.
2. We tried to put those curtains at these windows, but they were too long.
3. Why don't they plan buildings with windows that will open?
4. Dr. Davidson bowed to Professor Wolfe when he was introduced to him.
5. As a finale they played "America, the Beautiful."
6. In this book it tells how Lewis and Clark opened a new trail to the Pacific Ocean.
7. Karen told Ethel that she should learn to swim.
8. In colonial times you often didn't permit children to eat at the table with adults.

Assignment   Pronoun Usage   Collect examples of misused pronouns from newspapers, magazines, television, and radio. Look for errors in agreement, case, and reference. Consider usage of indefinite, relative, and interrogative pronouns as well as personal pronouns. Make the necessary corrections, and bring your examples to class.

Writing Without Pronouns

Your cousin is moving to your community from another state and will be attending your school. You want to write a letter telling her what to expect when she arrives and helping her to look forward to coming. In your letter you plan to

---

include a paragraph describing your favorite teacher. (You may create a fictitious teacher, if you wish.)

Suppose, however, that you have never learned about the existence of pronouns. Describe your teacher in a paragraph that contains no pronouns at all. (You need not write the entire letter.) Then rewrite your paragraph, using pronouns correctly.

4.4   Correct Use of Modifiers

4.4a   Comparison of Modifiers

Adjectives and adverbs can be used to compare two or more things. Modifiers have three forms to show three degrees of comparison: positive, comparative, and superlative.

In the **positive degree,** a modifier assigns some quality to a person, a thing, an action, or an idea. No comparison is made.

POSITIVE   Lake Michigan is a **large** lake.

In the **comparative degree,** a modifier compares one person, thing, action, or idea with another one.

COMPARATIVE   Lake Huron is larger than Lake Michigan.

In the **superlative degree,** a modifier compares one person, thing, action, or idea with at least two others.

SUPERLATIVE   Lake Superior is the **largest** of the Great Lakes.

One-Syllable Modifiers.   If a modifier has only one syllable, add *-er* to form the comparative and *-est* to form the superlative. In some cases you must drop a final *e* or double a final consonant before adding the suffix (*Unit 16*).

low   lower   lowest
sad   sadder   saddest
fine   finer   finest
near   nearer   nearest

Two-Syllable Modifiers.   For most two-syllable modifiers, add -*er* to form the comparative and -*est* to form the superlative. Change a final *y* to *i* before adding the suffix.

shallow   shallower   shallowest
heavy   heavier   heaviest

If a two-syllable modifier is difficult to pronounce when -*er* and -*est* are added, form the comparative and superlative by using *more* and *most* before the positive form. For all adverbs ending in -*ly,* form the comparative and superlative degrees by using *more* and *most.*

careful   more careful   most careful
vivid   more vivid   most vivid
briskly   more briskly   most briskly

Modifiers of Three or More Syllables.   If a modifier has three or more syllables, always form its comparative and superlative degrees by using *more* and *most* before the positive form.

athletic   more athletic   most athletic
extraordinary   more extraordinary   most extraordinary
awkwardly   more awkwardly   most awkwardly

Comparisons Using *Less* and *Least*.   For comparisons showing less, form the comparative and superlative degrees by using *less* and *least* before the positive form.

likely   less likely   least likely
important   less important   least important

Irregular Comparisons. Some modifiers do not form comparisons according to the preceding guidelines. The best way to learn the correct forms of irregular comparisons is to memorize them.

good	better	best
well	better	best
many	more	most
much	more	most
little	less	least
bad	worse	worst
ill	worse	worst
far	farther,	farthest,
	further	furthest

Exercise 1   Degrees of Comparison   On your paper, list each modifier in the following sentences and write its degree of comparison.

> SAMPLE   Read more carefully, Luke.
>
> ANSWER   more carefully—Comparative

1. Doug is the finest artist in our class.
2. According to Stan, that movie is sad.
3. Who is the better athlete, you or your sister?
4. I secretly planned a surprise.
5. Because of the service, it was the least enjoyable meal that I've had on the trip.
6. Which window is dirtier?
7. Patience was her greatest virtue.
8. That was courageously said.

Exercise 2   Using Comparisons   On your paper, write the form of the modifier named in parentheses to complete the sentence correctly.

> SAMPLE   Joseph is the __?__ boy in the class. (*tall* —superlative)
>
> ANSWER   tallest

1. It was __?__ than I had expected. (*bad*—comparative)
2. The final scene was __?__. (*dramatic*—positive)
3. Are you feeling __?__? (*well*—comparative)
4. The audience laughed __?__. (*loudly*—positive)
5. The fanfare heralded the __?__ moment in the festivities. (*triumphant*—superlative)
6. This path is __?__ than the one along the creek. (*rough* —comparative)
7. Of all the speakers, she was the __?__ one to understand. (*easy*—superlative)
8. I hope your room is __?__ than it was yesterday. (*tidy* —comparative)
9. I didn't expect you to buy the __?__ umbrella available. (*expensive*—superlative)
10. My grandmother's college graduation last week was her __?__ moment in decades. (*proud*—superlative)

4.4b   Using Comparisons Correctly

Rule   Avoid double comparisons.

Use either the suffixes *-er* and *-est* or the words *more* and *most* to form the comparative and superlative degrees of adjectives and adverbs. Do not use a suffix when you use *more* or *most*. Such a combination is a **double comparison** because it states the comparison twice.

INCORRECT   That was the **most funniest** movie I ever saw.

CORRECT   That was the **funniest** movie I ever saw.

Rule   Avoid incomplete comparisons.

When you compare one member of a group with the rest of the group, use the comparative degree and the word *other* or *else*. An incomplete comparison is often unclear or misleading.

UNCLEAR	Manny is *cheerier* **than** anyone in the room. [The sentence does not tell whether Manny is in the room.]
CLEAR	Manny is *cheerier* **than** *anyone* **else** in the room. [Manny is in the room. He is cheerier than any *other* person there.]

Rule In a compound comparison, use the words *as . . . as* or *as . . . as . . . than* to complete the comparison.

A **compound comparison** includes both the positive and the comparative degrees of a modifier and really makes two statements. The positive degree says that the things compared are at least equal or similar. The comparative degree says that they may, in fact, be different.

That pine is *as* **tall** as the oak, if not **taller.**

Use commas to set off the second part of a compound comparison from the rest of the sentence. If you mentally remove the second part of the comparison, you should still have a complete sentence.

INCORRECT	We worked **as** *hard* if not *harder* **than** they did.
CORRECT	We worked **as** *hard* **as,** if not *harder* **than,** they did.
	We worked **as** *hard* **as** they did, if not *harder.*

Rule Avoid making comparisons that are illogical because of missing or faulty elements.

An **illogical comparison** expresses a comparison between things that you cannot logically compare. It says something other than what you really mean.

ILLOGICAL	*Michele's time* for the hundred-meter dash is **as fast as** *Martin*. [Time compared with a person.]
CLEAR	Michele*'s time* for the hundred-meter dash is **as fast as** *Martin's*. [**Think:** as fast as Martin's time.]

ILLOGICAL	Your *photos* of the desert are **sharper than** the *mountains*. [Photos compared with mountains.]
CLEAR	Your *photos* of the desert are **sharper than** *those* of the mountains. [**Think:** sharper than photos of the mountains.]

Exercise 3 Correct Use of Comparisons On your paper, rewrite the following sentences to make clear and complete comparisons or to eliminate double comparisons.

SAMPLE	Chris is taller than anyone on the team.
ANSWER	Chris is taller than anyone else on the team.

1. Tony likes Ann more than Maureen.
2. This has been the most happiest day of my life.
3. Lisa speaks French as well if not better than Charles.
4. Winters in Los Angeles are warmer than New York.
5. I think Julie is feeling more better today.
6. Our goalie is stronger than anyone on the team.
7. I like the symphony better than Bart.
8. The cheetah can run faster than any animal.
9. Strawberries are the most cheapest fruit at the market now.
10. He is as old if not older than Ray.

4.4c Placement of Phrases and Clauses

Rule Avoid using misplaced modifiers.

You should always place modifying phrases and clauses as close as possible to the words that they modify; otherwise, your sentence may be absurd or unclear.

UNCLEAR	A bird landed on the roof of the house **with red wings.** [What has red wings—the house, the roof, or the bird?]

CLEAR   A **bird** with red wings landed on the roof of the house. [*With red wings* clearly modifies *bird*.]

To revise a sentence containing a misplaced modifier, you must first identify the word being modified. Then place the modifying phrase or clause as close as possible to the word that it modifies. Do so without changing the meaning.

UNCLEAR   **Lying on the sidewalk,** Marcia found a wallet. [Who or what was lying on the sidewalk —Marcia or the wallet?]

CLEAR   Marcia found a **wallet** lying on the sidewalk. [The wallet, not Marcia, was on the sidewalk.]

In the following example, the misplaced adverb clause makes the meaning of the sentence unclear. Notice that the two revisions have quite different meanings.

UNCLEAR   Al asked me **as soon as I got home** to call Ted. [What happened when?]

CLEAR   Al asked me to **call** Ted as soon as I got home. [Meaning: I was to call as soon as I got home.]

As soon as I got home, Al **asked** me to call Ted. [Meaning: Al asked me as soon as I got home.]

Rule   Avoid using dangling modifiers.

A dangling modifier is a modifying word or phrase that does not clearly or sensibly modify any word in the sentence. To correct the problem, provide a word for the word or phrase to modify.

DANGLING   **Noticing that Tex was shedding,** my dog got a good brushing. [Who was noticing—my dog?]

CLEAR   Noticing that Tex was shedding, I gave my dog a good brushing.

DANGLING   **Finishing my homework,** all the lights went out. [Were the lights finishing the homework?]

CLEAR   Finishing my homework, I was interrupted when all the lights went out.

              While I was finishing my homework, all the lights went out. [Participial phrase changed to a subordinate clause.]

When the dangling modifier is a prepositional phrase, the best remedy is to change the phrase to a subordinate clause.

DANGLING   **At the age of twelve,** Aaron's mother taught him how to use a potter's wheel.

CLEAR   **When Aaron was twelve,** his mother taught him how to use a potter's wheel.

Exercise 4   Placement of Modifiers   On your paper, rewrite the following sentences to eliminate misplaced or dangling modifiers.

SAMPLE   While on vacation, the weather was fine.

ANSWER   While I was on vacation, the weather was fine.

1. Tim had a dog with black and brown spots named Rufus.
2. At age eleven, my father retired from the army.
3. After working in the garden all day, a hot bath was just what I needed.
4. To become a doctor, years of study are required.
5. We boarded the plane with great sadness.
6. Sitting down at last to Thanksgiving dinner, the telephone suddenly rang.
7. Tell me what you just read with your books closed.

8. After canceling my favorite program, I wrote a letter of protest to the network.
9. I saw many squirrels eating my lunch in the park.
10. Waiting for the bus to arrive, my mind wandered.

Assignment   Dangling   and   Misplaced   Modifiers
Find and bring to class examples of dangling and misplaced modifiers. Look for them in newspapers and magazines. Write down those that you hear on radio and television. Exchange examples with your classmates and correct the examples.

4.5   Usage Notes

The following pages contain an alphabetical list of words and phrases that often present usage problems. Each entry describes correct usage, and most entries include examples. Cross-references help you to locate related information.

a lot, alot   *A lot* means "a great number or amount" and is always two words. Because it is imprecise, you should avoid it except in informal usage. *Alot* is not a word.

> I will need a lot of time to finish the project.

a while, awhile   *Awhile* is an adverb. *While* is a noun and can be preceded by *for a* or *in a* to make a prepositional phrase. Do not use *for* or *in* before *awhile*.

> The Bowlers lived in France *for* **a while.** [not *for awhile*]
> I will see you *in* **a while.** [not *in awhile*]
> Judith wanted to rest **awhile.** [adverb]

accept, except   *Accept* is a verb that means "to agree" or "to receive." *Except* is a preposition that means "leaving out" or "but."

> She was happy to **accept** the award.
> I have finished all of my homework **except** math.

affect, effect   *Affect* is a verb that means "to influence." *Effect* is sometimes a verb that means "to bring about" or "to achieve." It is also a noun that means "result."

> Changes in the weather do not **affect** my moods. [verb meaning *influence*]
> This year's student senate has **effected** several policy changes. [verb meaning *brought about*]
> The **effects** of poor nutrition will soon become obvious. [noun meaning *results*]

ain't   *Ain't* is nonstandard. Do not use it.

all ready, already   *All ready* means "entirely ready or prepared." *Already* means "previously."

> I was **all ready** to enjoy the movie.
> When we arrived, the movie had **already** started.

all right, alright   *All right* means "satisfactory," "unhurt," "correct," or "yes, very well." *Alright* is an incorrect spelling. Do not use it.

> I am sure that everything will be **all right.**

all together, altogether   *All together* means "in a group" or "collectively." *Altogether* means "completely" or "thoroughly."

> We wanted to sit **all together** in the bleachers.
> They are not **altogether** certain how many people are coming to the party.

almost, most   Do not confuse the adverb *almost* with the adjective *most*.

> adv.
> We go camping **almost** every weekend in the summer and the fall. [not *most*]

> adj.
> **Most** people don't get enough exercise.

although, though   Both of these words are conjunctions meaning "in spite of the fact that." In conversation you can also use *though* as an adverb meaning "however." You should avoid this usage in written English.

> We worked in the garden today **although** [or though] the sky was overcast. [conjunction]

> We went inside, **though,** when the rain started. [Adverb meaning "however." Use in conversation only.]

among, between   Use *among* when you are discussing three or more persons or things and are considering them collectively. Use *between* with two persons or things.

> She divided the apples **among** the three children.

> She divided the apple **between** Kristen and Mandy.

angry, mad   In formal English the adjective *mad* means "insane" or "very foolish." In informal usage, *mad* can also mean "angry."

> Was he **angry** because the date was changed? [formal]

> Was he **mad** because the date was changed? [informal]

any more, anymore   These terms are not interchangeable. The phrase *any more* describes quantity; *any* is an adverb modifying the adjective *more*. *Anymore* is an adverb meaning "at present" or "from now on."

> I don't have **any more** change.

> They don't live here **anymore**.

as, like   *As* is most often used as a conjunction; it introduces a subordinate clause. *Like* is often used as a preposition, followed by an object. Do not use *like* as a conjunction.

> ┌────sub. clause────┐
> Nancy sings **as** a professional would. [*As* is a subordinating conjunction.]

> ┌───prep. phrase───┐
> Nancy sings **like** a professional. [*Like* is a preposition.]

bad, badly   *Bad* is always an adjective, and *badly* is always an adverb. Use *bad* after linking verbs (*page 15*).

> Jerome has had a **bad** day. [adjective]
> Alice has a severe cold and feels very **bad.** [adjective]
> He behaved **badly** when he was upset. [adverb]

because, on account of   Do not use *on account of* instead of *because* to introduce a subordinate clause. *On account of* means "because *of*" or "due *to*." It serves as a preposition and should be followed by an object.

> ┌────sub. clause────┐
> Trudy stayed at home **because** it was raining.

> ┌───prep.───┐   obj.
> Trudy stayed at home **on account of** the *rain*.

being as, being as how, being that   Do not use these expressions in place of *because*.

> **Because** Ted wasn't ready on time, we were all late for school this morning. [not *being as, being as how*, or *being that*]

beside, besides   *Beside* means "next to." *Besides* means "in addition to."

> I sat **beside** Wanda on the subway.
> **Besides** his schoolwork, Billy has chores to do.

between, among   See *among, between*.

between you and me   Never use the nominative case *I* as the object of a preposition (*page 175*). *Between* is usually a preposition.

>   Divide it *between you and* **me**. [not *between you and I*]

borrow, lend, loan   A person *borrows from* another person and *lends to* another person. *Loan* is a noun meaning "that which is lent" or "the act of lending." You can also use *loan* as a verb, but *lend* is preferred.

>   Sean **borrowed** a notebook from Ramona. [verb]
>   Please **lend** me a notebook. [verb]
>   He was grateful for the **loan**. [noun]

bring, take   Use *bring* when you mean "to carry to." Use *take* when you mean "to carry away."

>   When you come over to study, **bring** your dictionary.
>   When you go home, **take** your dictionary with you.

bust, busted   Do not use these words as verbs to mean "break" or "burst." Such forms are nonstandard.

>   Don't **burst** the child's balloon. [not *bust*]
>   Ken fell and **broke** his arm. [not *busted*]

can, may   *Can* refers to ability; *may* refers to permission.

>   I **can** sing very well; **may** I sing for you now?

can't hardly, can't scarcely   *Hardly* and *scarcely* are negative words. Do not form double negatives (*page 199*) by using them with other negative words, such as *not, never,* or contractions with *-n't*.

>   Mike **can hardly** speak above a whisper; he has a sore throat. [not *can't hardly*]
>   I **can scarcely** hear him. [not *can't scarcely*]

could of, might of, should of, would of Do not use these nonstandard phrases. Use *could have, might have, should have,* and *would have* in your writing. In conversation you may use the contractions *could've, might've, should've,* and *would've.*

differ from, differ with Things (or persons) *differ from* each other if they look dissimilar. When persons *differ with* each other, they disagree. These phrases are idioms.

> Tom **differs from** his brother in both height and weight.
>
> Joan **differs with** Mitchell on the issue of library fees.

different from, different than Use *different from* only. One thing differs *from* another; it docs not "differ than" something.

> My opinion is **different from** Eddie's.

dived, dove Either word is correct as the past tense of the verb *dive*. The past participle, however, is always *dived*.

> He **dived** off the rock.
>
> He **dove** off the rock.
>
> He **had dived** off the rock.

double negative A double negative is the use of two negative words when one is sufficient. Do not use *not* or contractions with *-n't* with words such as *no, none, never,* or *nothing.* (See also *can't hardly, can't scarcely.*)

> I have **no** pencils.
>
> I do**n't** have any pencils.
>
> I can find **nothing** wrong in this picture.
>
> I ca**n't** find anything wrong in this picture.

double subject Do not use a noun and a pronoun together as a single subject. Use one or the other, but not both.

INCORRECT	My **mother she** called me.
CORRECT	My mother **called** me.
CORRECT	**She** called me.

dove, dived   See *dived, dove.*

effect, affect   See *affect, effect.*

emigrate, immigrate   *Emigrate* means "to move *from* one country to another to live." *Immigrate* means "to come *to* a country to live."

> The Joneses **emigrated** from Wales.
> They **immigrated** to Canada.

etc.   The Latin abbreviation for *et cetera* means "and other things, and so forth." Do not use *and* before *etc.* Avoid using *etc.* in formal writing.

every day, everyday   *Everyday* is an adjective meaning "ordinary." Do not confuse it with *every day*, which means "each day."

> I swim **every day** in the summer.
> These clothes are good enough for **everyday** wear.

every one, everyone   *Every one* refers to each individual in a group. It is usually followed by *of. Everyone* means "everybody, every person."

> **Every one** of these cups is cracked or chipped.
> **Everyone** came to my party.

except, accept   See *accept, except.*

farther, further   Use *farther* to refer to physical distance. Use *further* to refer to greater extent in time or degree, or to mean "additional."

Chris jogged **farther** than Mike.

The **further** I read in this book, the more exciting the mystery becomes.

She will give **further** instruction next week.

fewer, less   Use *fewer* to refer to things that you can count individually. Use *less* to refer to quantities that you cannot count. Use *less* to refer also to amounts of time, money, or distance when the amount is a single quantity.

There were **fewer** children in school today than there were yesterday.

I have **less** spare time than he.

I have **less** than two hours to finish my project.

first, firstly; second, secondly   Do not use *firstly* or *secondly* to mean "in the first (or second) place."

First, assemble the necessary ingredients and utensils.

formally, formerly   *Formally* means "in a formal manner." *Formerly* means "previously or at an earlier time."

We dressed **formally** for the dinner party.

Formerly, the Watsons lived in Memphis.

former, latter   Use *former* to refer to the first of two previously mentioned persons or things and *latter* to refer to the second of the two persons or things.

Erin and Denise both went to college. The **former** (Erin) studied history, and the **latter** (Denise) studied geology.

further, farther   See *farther, further*.

good, well   Always use *good* as an adjective. You can use *well* as an adverb to mean "ably, capably," or as a predicate adjective to mean "satisfactory" or "in good health." The opposite of feeling sick is feeling *well*.

> He is a **good** cook. [adjective]
> He cooks **well**. [adverb]
> She now feels **well**. [predicate adjective]

got, have   *Got* is the past tense of the verb *to get;* it means "obtained." Avoid using *got* with *have* or in place of *have*.

> I **have** the flu. [not *have got* or *got*]
> I **got** some skates at the garage sale. [*obtained*]

hanged, hung   *Hanged* and *hung* are alternate forms of the past tense and past participle of the verb *to hang*. Use *hanged* when referring to death by hanging. Use *hung* in all other cases.

> After the law was changed, criminals were no longer **hanged**.
> The medallion was **hung** around the victor's neck.

have, got   See *got, have*.

hisself, theirselves   *Hisself* and *theirselves* are both nonstandard. Do not use them. Use *himself* and *themselves*.

hung, hanged   See *hanged, hung*.

immigrate, emigrate   See *emigrate, immigrate*.

in, into   Use *in* to mean "within" or "inside." Use *into* to suggest movement toward the inside from the outside.

> Estelle was **in** the kitchen.
> Estelle walked **into** the kitchen. [not *in*]

irregardless, regardless   Do not use *irregardless;* it is nonstandard. Use *regardless* instead.

> Jack is leaving **regardless** of the storm. [not *irregardless*]

its, it's   *Its* is a possessive pronoun. *It's* is the contraction for *it is*.

> The cat was licking **its** fur.
>
> **It's** ten minutes past six.

just exactly   Use either *just* or *exactly*, not both together.

> I have **just** ninety-seven cents. [not *just exactly*]
>
> I have **exactly** ninety-seven cents.

kind, sort, type   See *this kind, these kinds*.

kind of, sort of   In most writing do not use these colloquial terms to mean "rather."

> Sara felt **rather** tired after play rehearsal. [not *kind of* or *sort of*]

latter, former   See *former, latter*.

lay, lie   *Lay* is a transitive verb meaning "to put or place something somewhere." It always takes a direct object. *Lie* is an intransitive verb meaning "to rest or recline." It does not take a direct object. See page 148 for the principal parts of these irregular verbs. The verbs in the following sentences are all forms of the verb *lay*.

> Let's **lay** our cards on the table. [*Cards* is the direct object of *lay*.]
>
> The builders **are laying** the foundation now. [*Foundation* is the direct object of *are laying*.]
>
> Martin **laid** his glasses down. [*Glasses* is the direct object of *laid*.]
>
> We **have laid** our jackets on the chair. [*Jackets* is the direct object of *have laid*.]

The verbs in the sentences on the next page are all forms

of the verb *lie*. They do not have direct objects.

> I **lie** down for a nap every afternoon.
> The books **were lying** underneath the sofa.
> The dog **lay** down on command.
> My homework **has lain** on my desk all day.

learn, teach *Learn* means "to gain knowledge." *Teach* means "to give knowledge." Do not use them interchangeably.

> My parents **taught** me how to skate. [not *learned*]

leave, let *Leave* means "to go away from" or "to abandon." *Let* means "to allow."

> Please **leave** the room in an orderly manner.
> The train **left** on schedule.
> My parents **let** me stay up for the late movie. [not *left*]
> **Let** us not quarrel over such a minor matter. [not *leave*]

lend See *borrow, lend, loan*.

less, fewer See *fewer, less*.

let, leave See *leave, let*.

lie, lay See *lay, lie*.

like, as See *as, like*.

loan See *borrow, lend, loan*.

loose, lose *Loose* is an adjective that means "not tight," "not bound," or "free." *Lose* is a verb that means "to fail to find" or "to be deprived of."

> This button is **loose**; try not to **lose** it.

mad, angry   See *angry, mad.*

many, much   Use the adjective *many* to describe things that you can count (*books, persons*). Use the adjective *much* to describe things that you cannot count (*water, work, strength*). When used as indefinite pronouns, *much* is singular and *many* is plural.

> Not **much** ink is left, but we do have **many** pencils.
> **Much** of my time **is** spent in studying. [singular]
> **Many are** waiting in line despite the rain. [plural]

may, can   See *can, may.*

may be, maybe   In the verb phrase *may be*, *may* is an auxiliary that indicates possibility. The adverb *maybe* means "perhaps."

> Calvin **may be** able to play the lead.
> **Maybe** Calvin will play the lead.

might of   See *could of.*

most, almost   See *almost, most.*

much, many   See *many, much.*

myself, yourself   Do not use a reflexive pronoun in place of a single personal pronoun, such as *I, me,* or *you.*

> INCORRECT   Amanda and **myself** take gymnastics.
>
> CORRECT   Amanda and **I** take gymnastics.

nohow, noway   *Nohow* and *noway* are nonstandard English. Do not use them. You can use *no way* correctly as two words, however.

> INCORRECT   **Noway** can we get there on time.
>
> CORRECT   There is **no way** to get there on time.

off, off of   *Of* is unnecessary. Do not use *off* or *off of* in place of *from*.

> The salt shaker fell **off** the counter. [not *off of*]
> Teresa got that gift **from** her cousin. [not *off*]

on account of, because   See *because, on account of*.

ourself, ourselves   *Ourself* is not a word. Do not use it. *Ourselves* is a reflexive pronoun.

> We found **ourselves** without enough money.

outside, outside of   Use *outside of* only when *outside* is a noun and *of* is a preposition.

> prep.   obj.
> We stepped **outside** the subway *station*. [not *outside of*]

> noun prep.   obj.
> The **outside** of the subway *car* was covered with dust.

passed, past   *Passed* is the past tense of the verb *to pass*. *Past* can be a noun, an adjective, an adverb, or a preposition.

> Jonathan **passed** the school on his way to work this morning. [verb]
> That is all in the **past.** [noun]
> This **past** summer, Jonathan took the express bus to work. [adjective]
> The school bell rang as Jonathan rode **past.** [adverb]
> He rode his bicycle **past** the elementary school this morning. [preposition]

perfect, unique   Do not use *more, most, less,* or *least* with *perfect* or *unique*. Both of these words refer to qualities that do not vary in degree. A thing is either perfect or not; it is unique or not. Other adjectives and adverbs that should not be compared are *fatal, dead, round,* and *empty*.

precede, proceed *Precede* means "to go or come before." *Proceed* means "to go forward."

> We **proceeded** toward the house, hoping that our friends, who had **preceded** us, had lunch ready.

raise, rise *Raise* is a transitive verb that means "to lift or make something go upward." It always takes a direct object. *Rise* is an intransitive verb that means "to move upward." It does not take a direct object. *Raise* is a regular verb. *Rise* is irregular. See page 148 for its principal parts.

> They **raised** the flag at the graduation ceremonies. [*Flag* is the direct object of *raised*.]
>
> They **rose** from their seats at the signal. [*Rose* has no direct object].

real, really *Real* is an adjective; *really* is an adverb.

> That is a **real** diamond.
>
> The weather was **really** miserable last week. [not *real*]

reason is because, reason is that *Reason is because* is redundant. Use *reason is that* or simply *because*.

> INCORRECT   The **reason** we are late **is because** traffic was heavy.
>
> CORRECT   The **reason** we are late **is that** traffic was heavy.
>
> CORRECT   We are late **because** traffic was heavy.

regardless, irregardless See *irregardless, regardless*.

rise, raise See *raise, rise*.

said, says, goes, went   *Said* is the past tense of the verb *to say; says* is a present tense form. Do not substitute *says* (present tense) for *said* (past tense). Do not use *goes* or *went* instead of *said*.

> Michael looked up and **said,** "I didn't hear you." [not *says, goes,* or *went*]

second, secondly   See *first, firstly; second, secondly.*

-self, -selves   The suffix *-self* is singular; *-selves* is plural. Be sure to use the correct suffix for a reflexive pronoun.

> SINGULAR   my**self,** your**self,** him**self,** her**self,** it**self**
>
> PLURAL   our**selves,** your**selves,** them**selves**

set, sit   *Set* is a transitive verb meaning "to place something." It always takes a direct object. *Sit* is an intransitive verb meaning "to rest in an upright position." It does not take a direct object.

>   D.O.
> We **set** the *candlesticks* in the center of the table.
>   D.O.
> Terry **had set** one *cup* on top of another.
> Please **sit** here. [no direct object]
> They **sat** on the floor. [no direct object]

should of   See *could of.*

sit, set   See *set, sit.*

slow, slowly   *Slow* is an adjective, but you may use it as an adverb in informal speech, especially in commands or for emphasis. *Slowly,* which is an adverb, is preferred in writing.

> The train is **slow** today. [adjective]
> Walk **slow.** [adverb, informal]
> You should drive **slowly** in the rain. [adverb]

sometime, sometimes, some time   *Sometime* can be an adverb meaning "at an indefinite time," or it can be an adjective meaning "occasional." *Sometimes* is an adverb meaning "occasionally, now and then." When you use two words, *some* is an adjective modifying *time*.

> adv.
> They promised to visit **sometime.**

> adj.
> Letty is a **sometime** musician.

> adv.
> **Sometimes** I forget to set the alarm.

> adj. noun
> I need **some time** to finish this job.

sort of, kind of   See *kind of, sort of.*

supposed to, used to   Be sure to spell *supposed* and *used* with a *d*. Both are past participles.

> Weren't you **supposed to** finish your homework first? [not *suppose*]
> We were **used to** our old apartment, but we had to move. [not *use*]
> I **used to** like crossword puzzles. [not *use*]

sure, surely   In most writing do not use the adjective *sure* to mean "certainly." Such usage is colloquial.

> adj.
> Are you **sure** you told Maggie to meet us here?

> adv.
> She will **surely** arrive soon.

take, bring   See *bring, take.*

teach, learn   See *learn, teach*.

than, then   Use *than* as a conjunction in a comparison. Use *then* as an adverb to show a sequence of events.

> This year's team is better **than** last year's.
> I wish I had known **then** what I know now.

that, which, who   Use *that* to introduce essential clauses (*page 113*) that refer to things or groups of persons. Do not use a comma before *that* when it introduces an essential clause.

> The book **that** *you sent me* was delightful.
> A committee **that** *cannot make decisions* is useless.

Use *which* to introduce nonessential clauses (*page 113*) that refer to things or to groups of persons. Always use a comma before *which* when it introduces a nonessential clause.

> The Oakhurst game, **which** *had been postponed twice,* was finally played last Saturday.
> My service club, **which** *meets on Thursdays,* has raised money for three charities.

Use *who* or *whom* to introduce essential and nonessential clauses that refer to persons. Use a comma before *who* or *whom* only when it introduces a nonessential clause.

> The person **who** *leaves last* should lock the door.
> Dr. Hart, **whom** *I greatly admire,* has been made a full professor.

their, there, they're   *Their* is the possessive form of *they*. *There* points out a place or introduces an independent clause. *They're* is the contracted form of *they are*.

The children waited for **their** parents outside the gym.
On the table, **there** are several magazines.
If you'll wait in the foyer, I'll meet you **there.**
My parents said that **they're** sending us oranges from
Florida.

theirselves, hisself   See *hisself, theirselves.*

this kind, these kinds   Use *this* or *that* to modify the singular
nouns *kind, sort,* and *type.* Use *these* and *those* to modify
the plural nouns *kinds, sorts,* and *types. Kind* should be
singular when the object of the preposition following it is
singular. It should be plural (*kinds*) when the object of the
preposition is plural.

> **This kind** of story is my favorite. [singular]
> **These kinds** of stories interest me. [plural]

this here, that there   Do not use. Simply say *this* or *that.*

> **This** typewriter works well. [not *this here*]
> I would choose **that** picture. [not *that there*]

though, although   See *although, though.*

till, until   Both words are acceptable. *Until* is preferred as the
first word in a sentence. Do not use *til* or *'til.*

> It didn't stop raining **till** past midnight. [or *until*]
> **Until** we find my keys, we can't leave.

toward, towards   Both mean "in the direction of" or "approaching," but *toward* is preferred in American usage.
Towards is the British form.

> Jacob started running **toward** his sister.

try and, try to   Use *try to* instead of *try and*.

> Please **try to** close the door gently. [not *try and*]

unique, perfect   See *perfect, unique*.

until, till   See *till, until*.

used to, supposed to   See *supposed to, used to*.

way, ways   Do not use *ways* for *way* when referring to distance.

> It was only a short **way** from our house to the school. [not *ways*]

well, good   See *good, well*.

where . . . at   Do not use *at* after *where*.

> I don't know **where** that building *is*. [not *where that building is at*]

which, who, that   See *that, which, who*.

who, whom   See pages 179–181.

who's, whose   *Who's* is the contraction for *who is* or *who has*. *Whose* is the possessive form of *who*.

> **Who's** in the kitchen?
> **Whose** sweater is this?

-wise   Do not use *-wise* at the end of a word to mean "with reference to" or "concerning."

> AVOID   It has been a nice spring **weatherwise.**
>
> USE   The weather has been nice this spring.

would of   See *could of*.

your, you're   *Your* is the second person possessive pronoun. *You're* is a contraction for the words *you are*.

> **Your** books were in my locker.
> **You're** too late; the sale is over.

Unit Practice

Practice 1

A. Correct Use of Verbs (*pages 145–157*) On your paper, write the verb form that correctly completes each of the following sentences.

1. Felice had added a title before she (turns, turned) in the paper.
2. Street noise (disturbs, is disturbed) my sleep.
3. This bridge (cross, crosses) the Delaware River.
4. Mason had planned to (leaving, leave) earlier.
5. If we hurry, we (will see, saw) the first act.
6. The clerk (will be delivering, has been delivering) books next week.
7. Betsy will volunteer and (donates, will donate) her time.
8. Juliette has (swum, swam) the length of the pool twice.
9. The experiment (is being conducted, conducts) by botanists.
10. By mid-afternoon three candidates had (spoke, spoken).

B. Subject-Verb Agreement (*pages 158–170*) On your paper, write the verb form that correctly completes each of the following sentences.

11. Six dollars (is, are) all that you need for the poster.
12. Every member of their family (catches, catch) cold easily.
13. Physics (involves, involve) matter and energy.
14. Neither my brother nor his friends (drives, drive).
15. Chinese checkers (is, are) her favorite game.
16. Heavy snow, along with high winds, (is, are) expected.
17. A herd of elephants (is, are) approaching the camp!
18. Either a suitcase or a knapsack (is, are) needed for the trip.
19. *A Tale of Two Cities* (is, are) a captivating novel.
20. Circus performers (was, were) always a welcome sight.

C. Correct Use of Pronouns (*pages 170–186*)   On your paper, write the pronoun that correctly completes each of the following sentences. Make sure the pronoun that you use makes sense and agrees with the antecedent.

21. One gives a speech with __?__ notes already prepared.
22. Aunt Edna wore __?__ corsage to the reunion party.
23. With __?__ will you drive to the Blue Ridge Mountains?
24. Few brought __?__ sneakers to the bowling alley.
25. Our favorite mystery novel gives my friend and __?__ shivers.
26. When will you show us __?__ antique hat collection?
27. Some of this scenery has kept __?__ appeal for us.
28. A challenge faces __?__ you hire for this position.
29. Before this exam, I completed __?__ studying.
30. Most Sierra redwoods can be dated by __?__ growth rings.

D. Correct Use of Modifiers (*pages 186–194*)   On your paper, rewrite each of the following sentences, correcting all errors in the use of modifiers.

31. Cheryl sang as much if not more than Bernard.
32. Put those cartons into the closet overflowing with albums.
33. His last attempt was the goodest that he could manage.
34. The prices downtown are as reasonable as the corner store.
35. The logrolling event was harder than any of the events at the competition.
36. Sitting on a branch, we saw a robin.
37. We chose the smaller kitten of the entire litter.
38. After the glass fell, the floor was more wet than the table.
39. This day was as clear if not clearer than yesterday.
40. Our lifeguard gave lessons in the shallowest end of the pool.

(Continue on the next page.)

Practice 2

Rewrite the following passage, correcting all usage errors. Make sure that you use all verbs, pronouns, and modifiers correctly.

Imagine seeing a man more taller and more heavier than any man that you have saw. In the spring of 1869 George Hull will uncover a giant body while one were digging on their brother-in-law's farm in Cardiff, New York. Him discovery maked a greatest sensation. No one had saw a figure most unusually preserved. It seemed that the Cardiff giant is petrified. Whom was this giant? Hull believes that your most strange discovery were a prehistoric man. Eventually spectators bringed its families and gived fifty cents to viewing the larger man whom were ten feet in height and weighs three thousand pounds. By December, however, the public begun to realizing its mistake. The hoax were seen most clearly. The figure were a gypsum block that had been carving by Chicago stonecutters resembling a human being. Hull had bury it and had springed this hoax on the public. Despite Hull's trick, him Cardiff giant was displayed today at the Farmer's Museum in Cooperstown, New York. Crowds of people still enjoys itself when it saw one of the most strangest giants.

Unit Tests

Test 1

A. Correct Use of Verbs (*pages 145–157*) On your paper, write the verb form that correctly completes each of the following sentences.

1. Mary had darted away before the scooter (backs, backed) up.
2. Frederico (strikes, is struck) the dulcimer strings.
3. My mother (pass, passes) that cathedral each day.
4. This winter we will try to (return, returning) to Dallas.
5. If Greg continues to practice, he (will win, won) the tournament in Edmonton.
6. The street mimes (have been, will be) performing tomorrow.
7. Kay will write and (tells, will tell) me all of her news.
8. All spring the dam has (caught, catched) the flow of water.
9. The tugboat (blowed, blew) its whistle mournfully.
10. By 1700 the Industrial Revolution had (begun, began).

B. Subject-Verb Agreement (*pages 158–170*) On your paper, write the verb form that correctly completes each of the following sentences.

11. Everyone (is, are) willing to complete the survey.
12. Twelve feet of carpet (covers, cover) the wood floor.
13. Every dish, glass, and pan in the kitchen (rattles, rattle) during an earthquake.
14. Either Chopin or Liszt (is, are) his favorite composer.
15. Mathematics (challenges, challenge) Dara.
16. Neither our moving van nor our helpers (arrives, arrive) on time.
17. Behind the lilacs (stands, stand) an abandoned factory.
18. Overhead a flock of starlings (was, were) flying.
19. *Drums Along the Mohawk* (belongs, belong) on my shelf.
20. Bart's dried flowers (was, were) a thoughtful gift.

(Continue on the next page.)

C. Correct Use of Pronouns (*pages 170–186*)   On your paper, write the pronoun that correctly completes each of the following sentences. Make sure the pronoun that you use makes sense and agrees with the antecedent.

21. Mr. Solomita forgot to bring __?__ slide rule.
22. To __?__ should I mail this contribution?
23. __?__ held our annual picnic on Friday.
24. The pale woman wearing a plumed hat is __?__.
25. Few planned __?__ projects at the last minute.
26. Our Aunt Violet visited my sister and __?__ after we returned.
27. Amanda will ride __?__ Arabian horse along the trail.
28. Some of these boats had __?__ hulls painted.
29. The debate club will accept __?__ you choose as your partner.
30. Most of this old city has retained __?__ character.

D. Correct Use of Modifiers (*pages 186–194*)   On your paper, rewrite each of the following sentences, correcting all errors in the use of modifiers.

31. Mark splits logs as fast if not faster than his helper.
32. A commuter dashed after the train holding a briefcase.
33. Manuel's pole beans climb higher than his neighbors.
34. The star Deneb is brighter than any of the stars in its constellation, Cygnus.
35. The young rescuer received the most greatest praise.
36. Of all her books, this science fiction story is unusual.
37. Realizing that the concert was starting, the applause began.
38. After the election, our senator felt more sad than his opponent.
39. Her lavender mittens are as warm if not warmer than her blue ones.
40. He described a supernova as a rarer event in the sky.

Test 2

Rewrite the following passage, correcting all usage errors. Make sure that you use all verbs, pronouns, and modifiers correctly.

In 1894 women was least likely to participating in sports than men. For they, athletics was rarer except for occasional games of lawn tennis and croquet. Yet many women mountain climbers whom belong to the Pacific Northwest club called the Mazamas will achieve amazing heights. The Mazamas (which are the Aztec Indian word for deer) taked chances in its climb up Mount Hood, Oregon. Although mountaineering were perceived to be dangerous for women, Mazama members tackle most difficult peaks than Mt. Hood. Club members complete its more difficult ascent up the ice wall of Mount Baker, Washington, in 1906. A report was maked by a survey group that the journey will be too hazardous and the climb was maked in secret. Seventy-one men and forty-seven women for the climb roped together is risking his or her lives. Them made their way up more than 10,000 feet of ice, dense forests, and cliffs. The women was pioneers to attempt such a courageous expedition. The club motto were chose well by they—"We Go Up."

Mechanics

Unit Preview

doyouhavetroublereadingthesesentencesifyoudoitsbecause
therulesofcapitalizationspacingandpunctuationwerentobserved
whenthesentenceswerewritten

The preceding passage should help you understand why there are rules about **mechanics,** the rules that we must follow when we put our thoughts on paper to communicate with others. These rules are simply ways of doing things that most people have agreed to use in order to make writing easier to read. For example, we leave space between words that we print or write. The space makes it easier for someone else to read what we write.

There is no special reason why a little dot should mean "end of a sentence," yet people generally accept the rule that a period signals the end of a sentence. In the same way, we agree that a capital letter signals the beginning of the next sentence.

For Analysis   On a separate sheet of paper, copy the passage shown at the beginning of this preview. As you copy it, try to use correct capitalization, spacing, and punctuation. Then answer the following questions.

1. What should you do to the first word in a sentence?
2. What mark should you put at the end of a sentence?
3. What marks do you put within a sentence to show that the reader should pause?
4. What mark do you use to show that something has been left out of a word?

In this unit you will learn the rules of mechanics—the rules for putting your words down on paper in such a way that your readers will understand what you mean.

5.1 Capitalization

Capital letters are used for two main purposes in English: to show the beginning of a sentence and to show that a noun is a proper noun (*page 4*).

5.1a Capitalization in Sentences

Rule Capitalize the first word of a sentence.

Our team's colors are blue and orange.

Rule Capitalize the first word of a direct quotation that is a complete sentence. A **direct quotation** contains the exact words that a person said, wrote, or thought.

The vendor cried, "**Get** your tickets while they last!"
Marsha thought, "**Why** am I doing this?"

Interrupted Quotation. When a quoted sentence is interrupted by an expression such as *I asked* or *Father replied,* begin the second part of the quotation with a lower-case letter.

"You will find the answers," I said, "**on** page nine."

New Sentence in a Quotation. If the second part of the quotation is a new sentence, put a period after the interrupting expression, and begin the second part with a capital letter.

"Is this your wallet?" asked Inspector Chu. "**It** has your initials on it."

Rule Capitalize the first word of each line in a poem unless the word is not capitalized in the original.

> **By** the rude bridge that arched the flood,
>> **Their** flag to April's breeze unfurled,
> **Here** once the embattled farmers stood
>> **And** fired the shot heard round the world.

Ralph Waldo Emerson, "Concord Hymn"

Exercise 1   Capitalization in Sentences

On your paper, write each sentence correctly, using appropriate capitalization. If no added capitalization is needed, write *None* on your paper.

SAMPLE   "we should walk home," Nan said, "especially in weather like this."

ANSWER   "We should walk home," Nan said, "especially in weather like this."

1. one day Neal remarked to his sister, "do you enjoy Robert Frost's work as much as I do?"
2. "what made you think of that?" asked Angie. "were you studying poetry in class today?"
3. "no," Neal replied, "but I bought a book of his poetry."
4. Angie observed that this was a new interest for Neal.
5. then Neal told her the stanza that he had learned from Robert Frost's "Stopping by Woods on a Snowy Evening":
>> the woods are lovely, dark, and deep,
>> but I have promises to keep,
>> and miles to go before I sleep,
>> and miles to go before I sleep.
6. he said, "the poem describes such a peaceful scene that I wish I could be there."
7. Neal recited another stanza:
>> he gives his harness bells a shake
>> to ask if there is some mistake.
>> the only other sound's the sweep
>> of easy wind and downy flake.

8. "also," he added, "the lively horse reminds the man that this peace cannot last forever."
9. Angie offered another thought to the discussion: "do you suppose that you and I would have stayed to watch the snow?"
10. "I can tell you for sure," Neal said, "that I would have."

5.1b   Proper Nouns

Rule   Capitalize the names and initials of people. If a person's last name begins with *Mc, O',* or *St.,* capitalize the next letter as well.

Ellen Brodsley   Martin McDevitt
Grace T. Whelan   Harriet O'Rourke

If the last name begins with *Mac, de, D', la, le, van,* or *von,* capitalization varies. In such cases, capitalize the name the way its owner does.

Family-Relationship Words. Capitalize words that show family relationship when they are used as part of a person's name or as a substitute for a person's name.

Today is **Grandmother's** birthday.
Where are we going, **Dad**?
Is **Uncle Gene** coming with us?

Do not capitalize a family-relationship word if it is used as a general term. Usually if the word is preceded by a possessive pronoun (*page 25*), it should not be capitalized. If the person's name follows the relationship word, and if that phrase is the name by which you call the person, capitalize both words. Otherwise, capitalize only the person's name.

Is your **uncle** coming, too?
My **aunt Sarah** lives in Phoenix. [I call her *Sarah*.]

BUT   My **Aunt Sarah** lives in Phoenix. [I call her *Aunt Sarah*.]

Personal and Official Titles. Capitalize a personal or official title or its abbreviation when it is used as a name in direct address (*page 236*) or precedes a person's name. Do not capitalize a preposition, a conjunction, or an article that is part of a title unless it is the first word in a sentence.

> What do you think of our plan, **Senator**?

BUT   The **senator** was unhappy with our plan.

Mr. Brown   **Mayor** Denise Homer
Senator White   **Secretary of State** Hurley
Dr. Sanchez   **the Reverend Doctor** Johnson

Do not capitalize a title that follows or is a substitute for a person's name unless it is the title of a head of national government.

TITLE BEFORE NAME   TITLE FOLLOWING NAME

Rabbi David Spiegel   David Spiegel, **rabbi**
Governor Helen Krohn   Helen Krohn, **governor**
President James Madison   James Madison, **President**
Prime Minister Golda Meir   Golda Meir, **Prime Minister**

The **Prime Minister** met with labor leaders today.
The **governor** announced that she would resign.

Capitalize the names and abbreviations of academic degrees or honors that follow a person's name. Capitalize the abbreviations *Sr.* and *Jr.*

Bryan Massey, **Doctor of Laws**   Terence Lem, **D.D.S.**
Elizabeth Blackstone, **Ph.D.**   James Dillon, **Sr.**

Gods of Mythology. Capitalize the names of gods of mythology, but do not capitalize the word *god* when it refers to gods of mythology.

The Greeks believed that the **god Apollo** used his chariot to pull the sun across the sky.

Rule Capitalize the names of particular places, such as countries, cities, mountains, streets, oceans, and so on.

Chile	Everglades National Park
New England	the Nile River

Compass Points. Capitalize compass points that refer to specific geographic areas or that form part of a place name. Do not capitalize a compass point that merely indicates direction or a general region.

When she left **South** Dakota, Sue moved to the **East**.

I was born on a military base near the **North** Pole.

Have you ever visited the **Southwest**?

We live on a farm **west** of town.

Heavenly Bodies. Capitalize the names of heavenly bodies, such as stars and planets. Do not capitalize *sun* and *moon*. Capitalize *Earth* if the word is referring to this planet and if it does not have *the* before it.

Jupiter	the Milky Way
the Big Dipper	Alpha Centauri

The satellite took photographs of **Earth**.

BUT **The earth** travels around the sun.

Rule Capitalize words that name nationalities, peoples, and languages.

Canadian	Israeli	Korean	Russian
Asian	Caucasian	Mayan	French

Rule Capitalize the names of days, months, holidays, and special events. Do not capitalize the name of a season unless it is part of a proper noun.

Tuesday	Thanksgiving	summer
March	Winter Carnival	winter

Rule Capitalize the names of historical events and periods, awards, and documents.

World War II   the Pulitzer Prize
the Middle Ages   the Bill of Rights

Rule Capitalize the first and last words and all other important words in titles of books, movies, paintings, and so forth. (See also pages 244, 253.)

The Waltons   "Battle Hymn of the Republic"

Conjunctions, Articles, and Prepositions in Titles. Capitalize a conjunction, an article, or a preposition if it is the first or last word in a title. Also capitalize in a title any preposition that has five or more letters.

"**If** Ever I Would Leave You"
"**The** Man **Without** a Country"

Rule Capitalize the name of a school subject that is a language, a proper adjective (*page 24*), or is followed by a course number.

Spanish   Typing II   European history
Chemistry I   typing   history

Rule Capitalize the names of structures and the names of organizations, such as religions, businesses, government bodies, clubs, and schools. Capitalize a word such as *college, university, high school, club, society,* or *store* only when it is part of a proper noun.

Islam   Department of the Interior
Lutheran   the Circle Club
Family Service Association   Hollywood High School
Main Street Sporting Goods   the Taj Mahal

Howard **University**   BUT   a local **university**
the James Joyce **Society**   BUT   a literary **society**

Rule Capitalize trade names. Do not capitalize a common noun that follows a trade name.

Lightning floor cleaner   Best-Look shirts

Rule Capitalize the names of trains, ships, rockets, planes, and spacecraft. (See also page 253.)

the *Super Chief*   the *Gossamer Albatross*
H.M.S. *Bounty*   *Mariner IV*
the *Titan* rocket

Exercise 2   Capitalization of Proper Nouns   On your paper, write each sentence correctly, adding capital letters as needed.

SAMPLE   I read *the golden bowl* by henry james.

ANSWER   I read *The Golden Bowl* by Henry James.

1. We will board uncle mel's boat for a cruise along the southern california coastline.
2. White polar caps are visible at the north pole and the south pole of both mars and earth.
3. The capital of morocco, rabat, is located on the northwest coast of africa.
4. Mayor p. henry braxton and colonel drew davis, jr., will lead the parade.
5. Her cousin, muriel ziggler, m.d., wrote an exercise book called *the way to stay fit and healthy.*
6. According to greek mythology, demeter was the goddess of agriculture.
7. I saw *it's a wonderful life* and *you can't take it with you* at the frank capra film festival.
8. Yesterday grandfather, jacqueline, and mr. h. b. o'brien enjoyed the sun at sherwood beach and wildlife reserve.
9. The mississippi river is long, but the nile is the longest river in the world.
10. Usually captain barnett uses the north star to guide his ship while e. charles putney, first mate, studies the moon.

11. The international red cross won the nobel peace prize in 1917.
12. The italian renaissance brought an end to the middle ages.
13. Each thursday mr. osumi teaches japanese to his language students at the university.
14. I purchased brilliance pottery glaze and hardy's glue at slade's art supplies.
15. The american author herman melville frequently wrote about the polynesian people.
16. Our community center will offer spanish, european history, algebra II, and business law.
17. My favorite exhibit in the national museum of anthropology in mexico city is the aztec sculpture.
18. The *zephyr* was one of the first passenger trains powered by a diesel-electric locomotive.
19. The centerville citizens' council will sponsor career day at centerville senior high school this friday.
20. One danish custom is to send pressed white flowers to friends on valentine's day.

5.1c   Other Uses of Capitalization

Rule   Capitalize most proper adjectives (*page 24*).

Capitalize these	*But not these*
Geiger counter	**bowie** knife
Gothic novel	**cashmere** sweater
Irish stew	**herculean** task

If you are not sure whether a particular word should be capitalized, look it up in your dictionary.

Rule   Capitalize the pronoun *I*.

They won't start the game until **I** arrive.

Rule   Capitalize both letters in the following abbreviations: *A.D., B.C., A.M., P.M.,* and Postal Service abbreviations.

Note: Use Postal Service abbreviations only with ZIP codes in addresses. Do not use them in formal writing.

    Massachusetts **MA**   Iowa **IA**   Wyoming **WY**

Exercise 3 Other Uses of Capitalization On your paper, write each sentence correctly, using appropriate capitalization. If no added capitals are needed, write *None*. Use your dictionary if you need help.

> **SAMPLE**   They arrived at 6:00 p.m. to hang the chinese lanterns.
>
> **ANSWER**   They arrived at 6:00 P.M. to hang the Chinese lanterns.

1. I received the green shetland sweater for my birthday.
2. When i feel tired, i often fall asleep before 9:00 p.m.
3. Alexander the Great conquered Egypt in 332 b.c.
4. The banquet table was set with antique china.
5. At 1:00 p.m. the sun gets too hot, and i must close the venetian blinds.
6. Regina Cutter
   135 Court Street
   Louisville, ky 40200
7. Leif Ericson discovered Vinland about a.d. 1000.
8. Blair Stevens
   21220 S.W. 140 St.
   Vancouver, wa 98666
9. This belgian linen is the finest that i could purchase.
10. Darren spilled india ink on his mother's favorite cashmere scarf.

Assignment Capitalization Number your paper from 1 to 10. For each item listed below, write the name of someone or something that is your favorite. Be sure to use capital letters correctly.

SAMPLE	musician
ANSWER	Yehudi Menuhin

1. musician
2. relative
3. name for a pet
4. movie
5. song

6. city
7. river, lake, or ocean
8. book
9. school subject
10. building

Using Capital Letters

Write a brief autobiographical sketch of yourself. Tell where and when you were born, give the names of all the people in your immediate family (parents, brothers and sisters, grandparents, and so forth), and give the name of the first school you attended.

Then tell about yourself in the present: the address of your home, the names of the people you live with, the name of your school, and the names of your current teachers. When you finish, check your sketch for correct use of capital letters.

5.2   Punctuation

Punctuation marks are the traffic signs and signals of written language. They show you when to slow down or stop, and they tell you when you need to change directions or where you are going. When you use punctuation marks correctly, your readers will have no trouble finding their way through what you have written.

5.2a   The Period

Rule Use a period at the end of a declarative sentence.

Most of the students were well prepared for the test.

The ball sailed over the center-field fence.

Rule Use a period at the end of a sentence that issues a mild command or asks a polite question.

Pass the carrots to Dorothy.

Terry, will you please take out the garbage.

Rule Use a period after an initial that is part of a person's name or title.

R. L. James, **Jr.**   Rochelle **M.** Berger, **D.D.S.**

Rule Use a period after most standard abbreviations. Do not use a period after abbreviations for units of measure. You should, however, use a period after *in.* to show that you are writing the abbreviation of *inch,* not the word *in.* Do not use periods when the abbreviation of a company or an organization is in all capital letters or when you are writing Postal Service abbreviations of state names.

Use periods

Mr.	mister	**Dec.**	December
P.M.	post meridiem	**Wed.**	Wednesday

Do not use periods

oz	ounce	**lb**	pound
min	minute	**kg**	kilogram
NFL	National Football League	**AL**	Alabama
UMW	United Mine Workers	**CA**	California

Do not confuse standard state abbreviations (which require periods) that may have only two letters with Postal Service abbreviations (which require no periods). If the two abbreviations are spelled the same, do not use periods when the ZIP code is given, but do use periods when the ZIP code is not given.

> York, **SC** 29745 [ZIP code]
> Rolla, **MO** 65401 [ZIP code]

BUT   Hilda, **S.C.** [no ZIP code]
> Joplin, **Mo.** [no ZIP code]

Note: Avoid using abbreviations in formal writing. Spell words out instead.

5.2b   The Question Mark

Rule   Use a question mark at the end of an interrogative sentence.

> Do these shoes go with my blue suit?
> Did we win the soccer game?

5.2c   The Exclamation Point

Rule   Use an exclamation point at the end of a sentence that expresses strong feeling.

> That was a wonderful show!
> I was never so surprised in all my life!

Rule   Use an exclamation point after a forceful command.

> Go home immediately!
> Come here right now!

Rule   Use an exclamation point after a strong interjection or other exclamatory expression.

> Wow! What a game!
> Oh, what a mess!

Exercise 1 End Punctuation The following sentences lack periods, question marks, and exclamation points. On your paper, write the sentences correctly, adding all necessary punctuation.

> SAMPLE   Will you be able to work tomorrow
> ANSWER   Will you be able to work tomorrow?

1. Sarah Updike Goddard was a colonial newspaper publisher
2. Great You found my skate key
3. Did you hear Ralph R Benton, Jr, deliver his address
4. Who won the kayak race
5. What an inventive suggestion
6. I had 1 ft 10 in of ribbon left after completing the project
7. An apple tree once grew on this spot
8. Will Charlene complete her quilting project
9. Mr Santos, will you please come in
10. Turn the pages of the old book gently
11. Watch out for the garden hose
12. Washington, DC, is the site of NASA headquarters

5.2d The Comma

Commas in Series

Rule Use commas to separate three or more items in a series. Put a comma after each item except the last. Do *not* use commas to separate pairs of nouns that are thought of as a unit.

> The Smiths grow **corn, soybeans,** and **alfalfa.**
> **Milan, Rome, Florence**, and **Venice** are in Italy.
>
>   ┌───── unit─────┐
> Brunch included **bacon and eggs**, fruit, sandwiches,
> ┌───── unit─────┐
> **soup and crackers**, salad, and a beverage.

Modifiers. Use commas to separate three or more modifiers in a series.

The dancer was **tall, slender,** and **graceful**.

Phrases. Use commas to separate three or more phrases in a series. Do *not* use commas to separate items or phrases in a series if all of them are joined by conjunctions.

Ours is a government **of the people, by the people,** and **for the people**.
The Linden Street Drug Store sells cosmetics **and** prescriptions **and** assorted magazines.
You can take the crosstown bus **or** the subway **or** the train.

Independent Clauses. Use commas to separate three or more short independent clauses in a series.

I awoke, I ate breakfast, and **I brushed my teeth**.

Subordinate Clauses. Use commas to separate three or more subordinate clauses in a series.

I did not know **who the stranger was, where he had come from,** or **why he was there**.

Commas After
Introductory Expressions

Rule   Use a comma to show a pause after introductory words or phrases.

Prepositional Phrases. Use a comma after a prepositional phrase of four or more words at the beginning of a sentence.

In case of an emergency, the fire crew will be called.
Underneath the new telephone book, you will find a map of New York.

Participial Phrases. Use a comma after a participial phrase (*page 101*) at the beginning of a sentence.

Walking home after work, I tried to decide what I was going to say.

Much encouraged by the latest poll, the senator decided to run for re-election.

Adverb Clauses. Use a comma after an adverb clause (*page 114*) at the beginning of a sentence.

Whenever the doorbell rings, my cat runs to the front door and starts purring.

Yes, No, and Interjections. Use a comma to separate *yes, no,* and interjections, such as *oh* and *well,* from the rest of the sentence.

Yes, the circus will be here on the fourteenth.

Well, I think the brown slacks fit better.

Confusing Sentence Parts. Use a comma to separate a short introductory phrase from the next part of the sentence if it would be confusing to read them together. If possible, you should try to rewrite the sentence to separate the confusing parts.

Six days before, Lillian had reported the problem.

Rather than five, ten volunteers helped at the show.

Exercise 2 Commas In the following sentences, commas have been left out. On your paper, write each sentence correctly, using commas where necessary. If no commas are needed, write *None* on your paper.

SAMPLE   I knitted mittens scarves gloves and sweaters.
ANSWER   I knitted mittens, scarves, gloves, and sweaters.

1. Ms. Redding told the movers to put her bed bureau and rocker in the blue bedroom.
2. Yes Richard and Kim will represent us in the debate.
3. A pigeon suddenly flew in the window and knocked a picture off the wall a vase off the mantel and a hat off the hat rack.
4. She served the ball she cleared the net and she won the point.
5. Fredrika will take the one o'clock train and will arrive at six o'clock or seven o'clock.
6. When had the storm started what damage had it done and where was it going?
7. Playing in the first college football game Rutgers defeated Princeton in 1869.
8. Instead of apples oranges were delivered.
9. In the late 1800s metal weather vanes were a part of folk sculpture.
10. Before morning our boat left the harbor.

Commas to Separate Sentence Parts

Rule   Use a comma before a coordinating conjunction (*page 38*) that joins the independent clauses of a compound sentence (*pages 118–119*).

> We have suffered a major setback, but we are by no means prepared to give up the struggle.
> Pat will arrive tonight at 9:00 P.M., **and** she is bringing her guitar.

Rule   Use commas to set off certain words or phrases within a sentence.

Direct Address. Use a comma or a pair of commas to set off words of **direct address**, words that name the person(s) being spoken to.

> **Mr. Schneider,** how do you keep your lawn so green?
> Gather around, **everyone,** and listen to Pearl's story.

Parenthetical Expressions. Use a comma or a pair of commas to set off **parenthetical expressions,** which add information or opinions that are not essential to the meaning of the sentence. (See also page 251).

Helen was planning to go skating tonight, **I believe**.

She could, **of course,** have changed her mind.

Everyone will be on time, **we hope,** and class will start promptly at two.

Ed finishes work at six-thirty, **not six o'clock.** We are meeting, **therefore,** at the movies.

That movie, **besides being four hours long,** was boring!

Nonessential Appositives. Use a comma or a pair of commas to set off nonessential appositives (*page 97*). An abbreviated title or degree following a name is one kind of nonessential appositive. Do *not* set off essential appositives (*page 96*).

NONESSENTIAL

Chaucer, **the cook,** has studied in Paris.

The owner, **a woman famous for her business success,** had made the restaurant most appealing.

My brother, **David,** was born on December 25. [I have only one brother.]

The first speech was given by Donna Rios, **Ph.D.**

I thought Chris Logan, **Jr.,** was Tom's brother.

ESSENTIAL

My sister **Harriet** got an *A* in Spanish. [I have more than one sister.]

My friend **Daniel** has a terrific sense of humor. [I have more than one friend.]

The painter **Salvador Dali** is famous for his surrealistic style. [There is more than one painter.]

Nonessential Phrases and Nonessential Clauses. Use a comma or a pair of commas to set off a nonessential phrase or a nonessential clause (*page 113*) from the rest of the sentence. Do *not* separate an essential phrase or an essential clause from the rest of the sentence.

NONESSENTIAL

Much to my amazement, Kristen executed a perfect dive off the ten-meter board.

Carol**, who is my cousin,** is a research chemist.

Rod**, not satisfied with his low score,** asked if he could take the math test again.

ESSENTIAL

The man **who is standing beside you** is my brother. [That particular man is my brother.]

The students **who received A's** will be given special recognition at the Awards Assembly. [Only those particular students will receive recognition.]

Dates or Addresses. Use commas to separate the items in a date or an address and to set off a date or an address from words that follow it. Do *not* use a comma if only the month and year are given. Do *not* use a comma between the state and the ZIP code.

The triplets were born on **October 31, 1968,** in Doctors' Hospital.

Muncie**, Indiana,** is my home town.

We lived there from **August 1972** to **September 1982**.

My address is 11 Main Street, Lompoc, **California 93436**.

Rule Use a comma after the salutation and the closing of a friendly letter.

Dear Pablo,   With best regards,

Exercise 3   Commas Some of the following sentences need commas. On your paper, write each sentence correctly, using commas where necessary. If a sentence needs no commas, write *None* on your paper.

SAMPLE   Amelia wants to travel and she will make plans
          soon.

ANSWER   Amelia wants to travel, and she will make plans
          soon.

1. Gail you should enter the American history essay contest.
2. The Battle of Gettysburg began on July 1 1863 and ended on July 3 of the same year.
3. The biologist J. Calvin Williams Ph.D. conducted the research.
4. Glass snakes which are actually lizards can shed their tails.
5. Arthur woke up one hour late and consequently missed his bus.
6. Dear Aunt Sophie
   I had a great time on the farm last weekend!
                                        Yours truly
                                        Richard
7. Martin became a gymnast in May 1980.
8. Take the striped shirt not this one.
9. My mother loves lilacs and this spring I will bring her a bunch.
10. Two of the five campers who were lost were found almost immediately.

5.2e   The Semicolon

The semicolon has two distinct uses: to connect or help connect two independent clauses, and to prevent confusion in sentences that contain commas.

Rule Use a semicolon to connect independent clauses.

Without a Coordinating Conjunction. Use a semicolon in a compound sentence to connect closely related independent clauses that are *not* joined by a coordinating conjunction.

          I flipped the switch; bright light filled the room.
          Lara's clock was broken; she was late for school.

BUT   Lara's clock was broken, **and** she was late for school.

239

Do not connect unrelated independent clauses. They should be left as separate sentences.

Lara's clock was broken. She wore a sweater.

With a Conjunctive Adverb. Use a semicolon to connect independent clauses that are joined by a conjunctive adverb (*page 44*) or an explanatory expression. Use a comma after the conjunctive adverb or the explanatory expression.

Alberto is an excellent athlete**; consequently,** he should be eligible for an athletic scholarship.

Leslie demanded a refund**; after all,** the store had guaranteed complete satisfaction with the product.

Rule   Use a semicolon to help clarify the meaning of a sentence that contains several commas.

Independent Clauses. Use a semicolon to clearly separate independent clauses that have commas within them, even if a coordinating conjunction is used.

Aldo, my youngest nephew, is a good shortstop, catcher, and outfielder**; and** I think he deserves to be named captain.

Items in a Series. Use semicolons to separate items in a series if those items have internal commas. The semicolons make clear how many things are in the series.

UNCLEAR   Lydia's guests were Angel Carrasco, a diplomat, Larry Young, Meg Putnam, a designer, and Yolanda Wyatt, a photographer. [six guests?]

CLEAR   Lydia's guests were Angel Carrasco, a diplomat; Larry Young; Meg Putnam, a designer; and Yolanda Wyatt, a photographer. [four guests]

Exercise 4   Semicolons   Some of the sentences that follow need semicolons. On your paper, write each sentence correctly, using appropriate punctuation. If a sentence needs no semicolon, write *None* on your paper.

SAMPLE   Dinner was late all of us were hungry.

ANSWER   Dinner was late; all of us were hungry.

1. Mr. Emery, the lecturer, spoke to Mrs. Rodriguez, the chairperson and her message to him was that the film had not arrived.
2. The tryouts start on Tuesday the decisions will be posted by Friday.
3. Cedric collected a few acorns, leaves, and pine cones for his project.
4. Synthetic dyes are available therefore, indigo plants are no longer cultivated.
5. For dinner we had peas, a green vegetable carrots, a yellow vegetable potatoes, a starch and chicken, a protein.
6. Althea tried the new stilts and nearly fell.
7. The weather report mentioned rain instead, thick fog rolled in.
8. I tossed the stone the pond's surface rippled.

5.2f   The Colon

Rule Use a colon to introduce an explanatory phrase or a statement or a list of items that completes a sentence. The statement before the list may contain a demonstrative word (*these, those*) or an expression such as *the following* or *as follows*.

She told us what she likes best: **reading science-fiction novels.**

The sign read as follows: **Register Here.**

The following students should report immediately to the main office: **Dee Collins, Tina de Veronne, Jacob Reinhardt, and Becky Anderson.**

You will need these materials: **a yard of denim, a zipper, five blue buttons, and some dark thread.**

Do *not* use a colon between a verb and its complements or a preposition and its objects. In other words, do not use a colon to introduce a compound complement or a compound object of a preposition (a list that follows a verb or a preposition).

> Loretta made lists of her favorite movies, her favorite books, and her favorite records. [not *made lists of:*]
>
> For her birthday Mom received a potted plant, a pair of bowling shoes, and a toaster. [not *Mom received:*]

Rule   Use a colon to separate the hour and minutes in an expression of time, and the chapter and verse of a Biblical reference.

> Melba gets up every day at **6:30** A.M.
>
> We discussed the meaning of Proverbs **16:18**.

Rule   Use a colon after the salutation of a business letter.

> Dear Mr. Spiegel: Dear Sir or Madam:

Exercise 5   Colons   Some of the following sentences need colons. On your paper, write each sentence correctly, using appropriate punctuation. If a sentence needs no colon, write *None* on your paper.

> SAMPLE   The florist used these flowers violets, roses, and daisies.
>
> ANSWER   The florist used these flowers: violets, roses, and daisies.

1. The evening's program is as follows the choir at 800 P.M., the madrigal singers at 830 P.M., and the finale at 900 P.M.
2. At the amusement park, we rode the giant roller coaster, the parachute ride, and the ferris wheel.
3. Anita Louise walks two miles each Tuesday and three miles each Thursday.
4. The host of the awards banquet called these students O'Hara, Tattaglia, Murphy, and Woodley.

5. The service began with a reading from Genesis 822.

6. They journeyed to the last frontier Alaska.

7. Dear Senator Cole
Please consider my proposal.
Sincerely,
Jerome Lieu

8. Our poetry course includes the following poets
Emily Dickinson, Walt Whitman, and Anne Sexton.

5.2g   Quotation Marks

Rule Use quotation marks to show that you are quoting someone directly (*page 221*) or that you are copying words that someone else wrote. Use quotation marks at the beginning and the end of the quotation.

> **"I didn't know you could dance, Charlie,"** Anita said.
> Jack ended his theme with a line by Charles Kingsley:
> **"Do noble things, not dream them, all day long."**

Do not use quotation marks with an **indirect quotation**: a retelling, in the writer's words, of what some other person said, thought, or wrote.

> Tom announced that he could not find the path.
> Kit said something strange was going on.

BUT   Kit said, **"Something strange is going on."** [the exact words that Kit used]

Rule Each time there is a different speaker, begin a new paragraph and use a separate set of quotation marks.

> **"Can I get you anything, Cass?"** Lee asked as he started toward the kitchen.
> **"No, thank you, I don't need anything more,"** Cass replied.

Rule Use quotation marks to set off the title of a short story, a short poem, or a song. Use them also to set off the title of a piece that is part of a longer work, such as a chapter of a book, a section of a newspaper, an article in a magazine, or a single television show that is part of a series. (See also page 253.)

> My favorite Sherlock Holmes short stories are **"The Red-Headed League"** and **"The Adventure of the Speckled Band."**
> I always read **"Technifacts"** in *Skin Diver* magazine.

Rule Use quotation marks to set off words used in unexpected ways, such as nicknames, slang, technical terms, or unusual expressions.

> Kenneth **"King"** Mallory wore size 22 shoes!
> The **"author"** made a lot of money on that book, but he didn't write it; someone else wrote it for him.

Note: The preceding rule is for informal usage only. Avoid using quotation marks for such purposes unless it is absolutely necessary.

Other Punctuation with Quotation Marks. In order to use punctuation marks properly with quotations, there are some rules you should remember about where to put those other marks.

Rule Use single quotation marks to set off quoted material or a title within a longer quoted passage.

> "I heard him plead, **'Give me back my ring!'**" Julie told us.

Rule Use a comma or commas to separate an explanatory phrase, such as *Kit asked* or *she said,* from the quotation itself. Place the commas outside the opening quotation marks but inside the closing quotation marks.

> Kit asked, "Are you sure this is the path to the pond?"
> "It's the only one I know," Tom replied.

Rule Place a period inside closing quotation marks.

Alicia told us she would read Frost's poem "Fire and Ice."

Rule Place a semicolon or a colon outside closing quotation marks.

For the costume party, Liz came as "Tweedle Dee"; she had the most original costume.

Several people are reading excerpts from the short story "The Gift of the Magi": Larry, Tony, Dora, and Estelle.

Rule Place a question mark or an exclamation point inside the quotation marks if it applies only to the material quoted. If it applies to the entire sentence, place it outside the quotation marks. If both the quotation and the sentence require a question mark or an exclamation point, put it inside the quotation marks.

"Who's your new neighbor?" Sherry asked Cindy.

Did you say, "The meeting will come to order"?

Who asked, "Where are my shoes?"

Exercise 6 Quotation Marks Some of the following sentences need quotation marks. On your paper, write each sentence correctly, using quotation marks where they are needed. Make new paragraphs if necessary. If a sentence needs no quotation marks, write *None* on your paper. Remember to place other punctuation marks correctly in relation to the quotation marks.

SAMPLE   Please pass me the cookbook, said Dawn.

ANSWER   "Please pass me the cookbook," said Dawn.

1. Mr. Morgan said, Today we will read the short story A Worn Path by Eudora Welty.
2. His mother exclaimed, What has happened? Robby quickly replied, I can explain!
3. Yolanda finished the chapter called The Pioneer Woman's Story in *My Ántonia*.

4. At the recital, Paul will sing Lift Every Voice and Sing; Lee will read Robert Hayden's poem Middle Passage; and Joyce will read Raymond's Run, a short story by Toni Cade Bambara.
5. Randi thought that the rain made the field too soggy for soccer.
6. I heard Seth whisper, When will the bikes be delivered? as I passed the stairs, she revealed.
7. Ms. Horowitz, said Dalia, tell me about William Count Basie.
8. Tania told Mike that his colorful new sweater was too bright for her eyes.
9. When Mrs. Wilson saw the painter's work did she exclaim, That's not the correct color?
10. There are five main characters in Ray Bradbury's story Dark They Were and Golden-Eyed: Mr. and Mrs. Bittering, Dan, Laura, and David.

5.2h   The Apostrophe

Rule   Use an apostrophe to show possession.

Singular Nouns. Use an apostrophe and an *s* (*'s*) to form the possessive of a singular noun, even if it ends in *s, x,* or *z.*

the pet that belongs to Herbert	**Herbert's** pet
the voice of the operator	the **operator's** voice
the shirt that Charlene has	**Charlene's** shirt
the poetry that Bess wrote	**Bess's** poetry
the mustache Max is growing	**Max's** mustache

Plural Nouns. Use an apostrophe and an *s* (*'s*) to form the possessive of a plural noun that does not end in *s.*

the speeches the women wrote	the **women's** speeches
the toys that belong to the children	the **children's** toys

Plural Nouns Ending in s. Use an apostrophe alone to form the possessive of a plural noun that ends in *s.*

the stable the horses are in	the **horses'** stable
the club the boys shared	the **boys'** club
the house the Wrights own	the **Wrights'** house
the cheers of the spectators	the **spectators'** cheers

Do *not* add an apostrophe or *'s* to **possessive personal pronouns:** *mine, yours, his, hers, its, ours, theirs.* They already show ownership.

Irene has Joe's books; I will lend you **mine.**

Here is my clock; where is **yours**?

Joint Ownership. Use the possessive form of only the name mentioned last when one thing is owned by two or more persons.

Ted and Elena's house is on Warren Street.

George and Marguerite's apartment is being repainted.

Separate Ownership. Use the possessive form of each name when two or more persons possess separate things.

Howard's and Darrell's families will arrive tonight.

Mia's, Ginny's, and Bob's drawings all won prizes.

Rule Use an apostrophe to replace letters or numbers that have been left out in a contraction.

it is	**it's**	1940s	**'40s**
do not	**don't**	1981	**'81**

Rule Use an apostrophe and *s* (*'s*) to form the plural of letters, numbers, symbols, and words when you are talking about them (*page 253*). Be sure to use italics (underlining) correctly in such instances. Do not underline the *'s.*

He forgets to dot his *i***'s.**

The stencils for the *3***'s** and *5***'s** are worn out.

She used *$*'s as a border on her paper.

Many people use too many *and*'s when they speak.

Although names of years look like numerals, they usually function as words and should be treated as such.

Those laws were made in the **1800s**.

Everyone expects the **1990s** to be years of change.

BUT   Laurie wrote three *1986*'s on her notebook to show her graduation year.

Exercise 7   Apostrophe The following sentences lack apostrophes. On your paper, write each sentence correctly, using appropriate punctuation.

SAMPLE   Isnt that Carls wallet?

ANSWER   Isn't that Carl's wallet?

1. The expression "Mind your *p*s and *q*s" derives from early typesetting.
2. Wesleys annual sale will save us money on mens coats.
3. I dont think thats the way its supposed to look.
4. What happened on Rosss hike to Jed Saltters cabin?
5. This letter couldnt be delivered because your *7*s look like *1*s.
6. When will Jack and Lorettas vacation be over?
7. Brandons and Charless books were left in the boys locker room; I left mine in my desk.
8. Yvonnes photographs were taken in the 1920s; when were yours taken?
9. The mechanics tools fell from their boxes onto the bosss floor.
10. They tapped their feet as they listened to Maxs music.

5.2i   The Hyphen

Rule Use a hyphen to divide a word at the end of a line. Do not divide any word so that one letter stands by itself. Do not divide a word of one syllable, such as *through* or *groaned.* Always divide a word between its syllables and in such a way that the reader will not be confused about its meaning or pronunciation.

> He said he would not work under such **miserable** conditions. [miserable]
>
> Bill has already taken the spelling and **vocabulary** parts of the test. [vocabulary]

UNCLEAR   After he fixed the tire, Sal had to **readjust** the chain on his bike. [Word looks like *read* and *just*.]

CLEAR   After he fixed the tire, Sal had to **readjust** the chain on his bike. [Clear that the word is the prefix *re-* plus *adjust*.]

Prefixes and Suffixes. Divide a word with a prefix after the prefix. Divide a word with a suffix before the suffix.

> When we heard that our class had been **discontinued**, we were all upset. [discontinued]
>
> Color Graphics International has made a **remarkable** contribution to our yearbook. [remarkable]

Compound Words. Divide a compound word between the base words if the compound is written as one word. Divide a hyphenated compound word at the hyphen.

> The principal congratulated us on our **businesslike** handling of the ticket sales. [businesslike]
>
> We are exploring the possibility of using a **solar-powered** water heater on the farm. [solar-powered]

Rule   Use a hyphen after the prefixes *all-, ex-,* and *self-.* Use a hyphen to separate any prefix from a proper noun or a proper adjective.

all-powerful	**non**-Asian	BUT	**non**scheduled
ex-governor	**inter**-American	BUT	**inter**scholastic
self-improvement	**post**-Civil War	BUT	**post**war

249

Rule Hyphenate a compound modifier when it precedes the word that it modifies. Do not hyphenate a compound modifier when it follows the word it modifies. Do not hyphenate a compound modifier when its first part is an adverb ending in -*ly*.

> The **well-organized** meeting was a success.
>
> BUT The meeting was **well organized**.

> The **slow-moving** train finally arrived.
>
> BUT The train was so **slow moving** that we thought it had stopped.

> Our **slowly descending** elevator inched its way to the first floor.
>
> The **crisply cooked** chicken was delicious.

Fractions. Use a hyphen in a fraction that is used as a modifier, but not in a fraction that is used as a noun.

> Jan has a **three-fifths** share of the business.
>
> BUT I did only **three fifths** of my math problems.

Rule Use a hyphen to separate compound numbers from *twenty-one* through *ninety-nine*.

> thirty-three   seventy-nine
>
> BUT one hundred   twenty thousand

5.2j The Dash

Rule Use a dash to show that a thought or a speech was not finished or was interrupted. Use a second dash to mark the end of the interruption if the sentence continues.

> "I wonder if you—**but, no, you weren't here yesterday**," Jerry said.
>
> This show—**one of my favorites**—is on the radio every weekday afternoon.

If you are typing, type two hyphens to represent a dash. Do not type a single hyphen to represent a dash.

Note: Avoid using dashes in formal writing.

5.2k   Parentheses

Rule   Use parentheses to enclose material that is not basic to the meaning of the sentence.

> Franklin Delano Roosevelt **(Democrat, New York)** was the only person to be elected President four times.
> Charles A. Lindbergh made the first solo flight from New York to Paris **(May 20 – 21, 1927).**

Mechanics with Parentheses. The only punctuation that immediately precedes the closing parenthesis is end punctuation: a period, a question mark, or an exclamation mark. If the parenthetical material is not inside another sentence, use capitalization and punctuation within the parentheses just as if the parentheses were not there.

> Nick left me a note telling me when the party would start. **(It** had already started.)

If the parenthetical material is inside another sentence, do not use a capital letter or period inside the parentheses. If a question mark is needed, you may include it.

> Marshall and Jennifer **(what** would we have done without them?) took care of our house while I was sick.

After the closing parenthesis, use the punctuation that would be needed if the parenthetical material were not in the sentence. If the parenthesis ends the sentence, put the period *outside* the parenthesis.

> Maureen's new bike **(a Roll-Right)** is too big for me.
> We never should have planned a picnic so far in advance (but I didn't think it would rain).

Exercise 8   Hyphen, Dash, Parentheses   On your paper, copy the following sentences, adding hyphens, dashes, and parentheses where they are needed.

SAMPLE   Nearly three fifths of the group gained self discipline.

ANSWER   Nearly three fifths of the group gained self-discipline.

1. The guest speaker was the ex governor of Virginia.
2. The half asleep children stumbled out of the sled into the knee deep snow.
3. A two thirds majority is required for passage of this highly important law.
4. I want that drawing the one of the hands for my collection.
5. In July we will climb the highest mountain 13,776 feet in the Teton Range.
6. "I assume correct me if I am wrong that this statue is pre Columbian," said Donald.
7. He listed twenty five of his favorite self portraits by painters.
8. My grandfather's old fashioned ladderback chair was well made.
9. Of the twenty five steps required for the badge a woodworking award, she has completed the first twenty.
10. After Freda's trip to Montreal May 7–10, she said, "I am nearly but not quite certain that I'd like to move there."

Assignment   Punctuation   Choose five items from the following list. On your paper, write a sentence for each, being sure to include the part described in the item. Punctuate correctly, using the rules on pages 221–251 if you need help.

1. A direct quotation with a possessive
2. A question containing a series of four items
3. A statement that begins with a number
4. Two closely related independent clauses joined by a conjunctive adverb or explanatory expression
5. An expression of time without A.M. or P.M.

6. A nonessential phrase or clause and a short-story title that contains an abbreviation
7. An introductory participial phrase including a date or address
8. A quotation within a quotation that includes a contraction
9. A list of titles of books
10. An interrupted speech or thought expressing strong feeling
11. A parenthetical expression including a compound number under *101*
12. Two independent clauses joined by conjunctions, including an expression of time with A.M. or P.M. and a word with the prefix *all-, ex-,* or *self-*

5.3 Italics

Italic type (*slanted letters such as these*) is used for a variety of reasons. When you are writing or typing something that should be italicized, use underlining to represent the italics.

Rule Italicize (underline) the titles of books, book-length poems, newspapers, television series, and other long written materials. Also italicize the names of paintings and other works of art and the names of airplanes, trains, ships, and so forth. Do not capitalize or italicize an article (*a, an,* or *the*) at the beginning of a title unless it is part of the title. (See also page 244.)

The Old Man and the Sea	*Meet the Press*
the *Morristown Eagle*	Rembrandt's *The Night Watch*

Dad thinks the *Consumer Digest* is a helpful magazine.

I've just read *The Elephant Man.* It's fascinating!

Rule Italicize (underline) letters, numbers, symbols, or words when you are talking *about* them specifically rather than simply using them in a sentence.

I forgot to capitalize the *D* in MacDermott.

Different from is correct, not *different than.*

Exercise   Italics   In the following sentences, words that should be in italics are not. On your paper, write each sentence correctly, underlining all the words that should be in italics.

SAMPLE   NASA's first American satellite was Explorer I.

ANSWER   NASA's first American satellite was <u>Explorer I.</u>

1. John Steinbeck's novel The Grapes of Wrath is a classic.
2. The word etymology means "the study of words."
3. Captain Nemo's ship, the Nautilus, was featured in Twenty Thousand Leagues Under the Sea.
4. Last year in English class we read The Song of Hiawatha and Evangeline—two book-length poems by Henry Wadsworth Longfellow.
5. Calligraphy is more than just a fancy way to dot your i's and cross your t's.
6. Dorian found the meanings and roots of genial and ingenious in his dictionary.
7. My drama club will perform Curtain Call, Mr. Aldridge, Sir by Ossie Davis.
8. Our public library has the following: Consumer Reports, Ebony, Omni, and the Chicago Tribune.
9. The space shuttle Columbia made its maiden flight in the summer of 1981.
10. Vincent Van Gogh's painting Sunflowers was reproduced in the magazine article above the words Still Life.

5.4   Using Numbers in Writing

Rule   Spell out numbers of *one hundred* or less and all numbers rounded to hundreds.

Charlene graduated **eighteen** years ago this month.

About **fifteen hundred** people are in the audience.

BUT   About **1550** people are in the audience.

Rule Use Arabic numerals for numbers greater than *one hundred* that are not rounded numbers.

My grandparents live **1749** miles from here.

Rule If a number appears at the beginning of a sentence, spell it out or rewrite the sentence. The word *and* is unnecessary in writing out numbers except between *one hundred* and *one hundred and ten* and so forth.

INCORRECT	**212** people were assigned to Whitman School.
CORRECT	**Two hundred twelve** people were assigned to Whitman School.
CORRECT	There were **212** people assigned to Whitman School.
	Two hundred and two old comic books were sold at the convention.
BUT	**Two hundred thirteen** of the comic books in my collection are old.

Rule Use words to write the time unless you are writing the exact time (including the abbreviation A.M. or P.M.) or writing a technical paper.

We arrived at **four-thirty**.
Class starts at **a quarter after twelve**.

BUT She left the house at **5:00 A.M.**
The bus leaves at **12:32 P.M.**

Rule Use numerals to express dates, street numbers, room numbers, apartment numbers, telephone numbers, page numbers, and percentages. Spell out the word *percent*.

January 4, 1977   555-6061
337 Dupont Avenue   pages 24–36
Apartment 6B   17 percent

Rule   When you write a date, do not add *-st, -nd, -rd,* or *-th* to the numeral.

INCORRECT   June **18th**, 1960   April **4th**

CORRECT   June **18**, 1960   April **4** *or* **fourth** of April

Exercise   Numbers in Writing   On your paper, write the following sentences correctly, using the appropriate forms for numbers in composition. If no corrections are needed, write *None.*

SAMPLE   I will be 20 on February 5th.

ANSWER   I will be twenty on February 5.

1. My grandparents were married on November 26th, 1942, and they moved twenty-one hundred and three miles away.
2. We lived at forty-four 1st Street until three years ago July 2nd.
3. 2 of my classmates will visit Geneva, Switzerland, a city of one hundred fifty-nine thousand two hundred citizens.
4. Less than forty % of the committee are expected to vote in the election at eleven A.M. on December 1st.
5. Our class has planned a trip to the museum on May 17.
6. There are approximately 600 species of gentian.
7. On June 26th I will become 15, and I will celebrate with a visit to my aunt and uncle for 1 week.
8. 2700 miles is the approximate distance from Washington, D.C., to Sacramento, California.
9. Her essay can be found on pages thirty-seven to forty-two.
10. Allison and Marissa live in Apartment two in the Essex Arms, which is near Route eighty.

Assignment   Mechanics   Find an interesting short article in a newspaper or magazine. Copy the article on a separate sheet of paper, leaving out all capitalization, punctuation, and italics (underlining). You may also wish to change the forms of numbers to make them incorrect. Exchange papers with a classmate. Using a colored pen or pencil, add all the missing

punctuation marks and capital letters, and correct other items
of mechanics. Then use the original article to check your work.

5.5   Proofreading Symbols

The following symbols are commonly used to identify and
correct errors in composition. Use them when you revise and
proofread your writing.

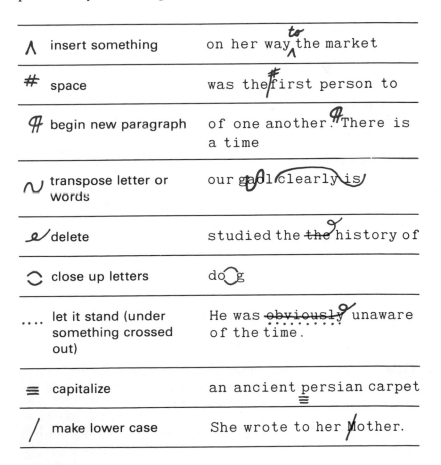

∧	insert something	on her way ᵗᵒ the market
#	space	was the#first person to
¶	begin new paragraph	of one another.¶There is a time
∼	transpose letter or words	our gaol clearly is
℮	delete	studied the the history of
◡	close up letters	dog
....	let it stand (under something crossed out)	He was obviously unaware of the time.
≡	capitalize	an ancient persian carpet
/	make lower case	She wrote to her Mother.

5.6   Manuscript Form

Suggestions for Handwritten Manuscripts

Paper.   Write compositions on standard paper (8½ by 10 inches or 8½ by 11 inches). Write on one side only.

Ink.   Use black or blue ink.

Margins.   Leave margins of 1½ inches at the left side and 1 inch at the right side. The left margin must be even.

Title.   Write the title of the composition in the center of the top line. Skip at least one line between the title and the first paragraph. Do not put quotation marks around the title.

Indentation.   Indent the first line of every paragraph about 1 inch.

Suggestions for Typewritten Manuscripts

Paper.   Use standard-size white typewriter paper (8½ by 11 inches). Double space and use only one side of the paper.

Ribbon.   Use a black ribbon.

Margins.   Leave margins of 1½ inches at the left side and 1 inch at the right side. The left margin must be even. On all pages except the page with the title on it, place the first line at least 1 inch below the top of the page. Leave a margin of 1 inch at the bottom of all pages.

Title.   Center the title about 2 inches below the top of the page. Do not put quotation marks around the title. Begin the first paragraph four lines below the title.

Indentation.   Indent the first line of every paragraph five spaces.

Labeling and Numbering Pages

Write your name, the subject, and the date (in that order) in the upper right-hand corner of the first page. On every page except the first page, put the page number in the upper-right corner unless your teacher gives you other instructions. Use Arabic numerals.

If your paper consists of more than one page, attach the pages at the upper-left corner with a staple or a paper clip.

Unit Practice

Practice 1

A. Capitalization (*pages 220–230*)   On your paper, write each sentence correctly. Make sure that you use appropriate capitalization.

1. The *great republic,* the largest wooden ship ever constructed, was built by the canadian donald mckay.
2. principal vieira will cancel journalism, geometry II, and spanish so that we may attend the band concert at bethune high school on tuesday.
3. our mother said, "thank you for this copy of dickens's *oliver twist* and for the african violet."
4. ms. staw, president of the mayville astronomy club, showed us orion.
5. "hurricane carla struck the texas coast in 1961," said uncle jake. "luckily we had moved to the east the previous fall."
6. the most distant known planet in the solar system, pluto, was discovered by c.w. tombaugh, ph.d.
7. john cappelletti, a football player from pennsylvania state university, won the heisman memorial trophy in 1973.
8. one greek myth states that the daughter of zeus, helen of troy, caused the trojan war.
9. "last march i went to the st. patrick's day parade," she said, "and at 5:15 p.m. i took the *broadway limited* train to philadelphia."
10. w.h. auden wrote the poems "ballad" and "spain."

B. Punctuation (*pages 230–253*)   On your paper, write each sentence correctly. Make sure that you use appropriate punctuation.

11. Mother asked Will you set the table with knives forks spoons and plates before you begin to read HG Wellss story The Empire of the Ants
12. Herbs recitation of the poem Mr Floods Party was well done however he forgot line twenty one

260

13. We must catch that bus at 830 PM in fact it is the last one or well miss the well known actors speech Merry cried

14. RB Associates
442 Windham St
Baltimore MD 21201

15. The pre dawn departure began wagon trains packed with boxes loaded with pots and pans and stocked with food left Independence Missouri

16. In front of the rose colored dish youll see my well worn copy of Hans Christian Andersens short story The Ugly Duckling said Grandmother

17. Painting on an off white canvas Mr Bennett who is my teacher completed his self portrait on November 12 1984 with these colors orange tan and gray

18. Louiss gifts included the following a ten speed bicycle Japanese an oriental rug Persian and a red fringed poncho Mexican

19. Were those ladies gloves the ones embroidered with *m*s and *n*s on sale

20. Phyllis exclaimed Then the review stated Phylliss calligraphy the art of penmanship is also perfect for invitations posters and announcements

C. Italics (*pages 253–254*) On your paper, write each sentence correctly. Make sure that you underline the words that should be in italics.

21. His photographs appeared in Life, National Geographic, and Time.

22. Was Grandfather the engineer for the Comet or the Super Chief?

23. The uncrossed t's made the document hard to read.

24. Adam saw the painting by Winslow Homer called The Gulf Stream.

25. Have you seen my copy of today's Arkansas Gazette?

(Continue on the next page.)

26. We saw the original of the epic poem Beowulf in the British Museum.
27. Jen wrote, "Miss Noguchi, I forgot to add the last % to my graph."
28. I always check the spelling of onomatopoeia in the dictionary.
29. Please return my copy of Jane Austen's Emma.
30. We added the columns of 3's, 8's, and 9's to get the totals.

D. Using Numbers in Writing (*pages 254–257*)   On your paper, write the number form that correctly completes each of the following sentences.

31. (125, One hundred twenty-five, One hundred 25) years ago, the building was first moved.
32. Almost (two 100, two hundred, 200) cyclists participated in the race.
33. Our van had traveled (3425, three thousand 425, three thousand four hundred twenty-five) miles.
34. How often have you walked the (99, ninety-nine, ninetynine) steps to your house?
35. On the Monday after November (22nd, 22, twenty-two), the new law will go into effect.
36. Inflation in that country was (one hundred seventeen %, 117%, 117 percent) last year.
37. I moved to (twentynine, twenty-nine, 29) Oak Alley, Apartment (2, Two, two) yesterday.
38. The (thirtieth, Thirty, 30) Years' War in Germany began in 1618.
39. (314, Three hundred fourteen, three hundred and fourteen) residents planted small shrubs.
40. (Twenty-eight, twentyeight, 28) pairs of shoes were delivered to the shop at (4:30, 430, four-thirty) P.M. on May (3rd, three, 3).

Practice 2

Rewrite the following passage, making all necessary corrections in capitalization, punctuation, italics (underlining), and the use of numbers.

lavender sandalwood cinnamon and myrrh are unrelated materials yet they have something in common from them these scented substances are produced perfumes soaps sachets and incense 3000 years ago people crushed plants flowers and wood into fragrant powder this powder was often burned the word perfume comes from the latin words per through and fūmus smoke also egyptians soaked certain substances in water and oil to produce a well scented liquid

todays technological methods of removing essential oils from scent producing materials are the following steam distillation used with plants extraction used with flowers and enfleurage also used with flowers these methods yield oils which are then blended with chemical fixatives newly developed synthetics spices and herbs

the uses of perfume have evolved according to the demands of culture and lifestyle for instance greeks used scents in religious ceremonies and during the middle ages perfume disguised disagreeable odors although the uses of perfume have changed perfume creation is still a significant art

Unit Tests

Test 1

A. Capitalization (*pages 220–230*)   On your paper, write each sentence correctly. Use appropriate capitalization.

1. throughout winter the *southern crescent* chugs by each monday morning.

2. phyllis and cheryl will study american history and german in high school.

3. grandmother suggested, "let's take circle line's trip to the northwest islands next april."

4. samuel l. shaw, president, announced awards in french II, asian history, and chemistry.

5. "join us on saturday," said mrs. stein. "our table-tennis tournaments at woodside sports club are challenging."

6. helen sawyer hogg, the first woman president of the royal astronomical society of canada, studied the milky way.

7. *west side story,* a film based on shakespeare's *romeo and juliet,* won an academy award.

8. professor williams explained that the egyptian god atum was often identified with the setting sun.

9. "we just read *the lord of the rings,*" Kevin and I told Catherine, "and you should read this trilogy by j.r.r. tolkien also."

10. at 7:30 p.m. at the rabb art institute, director hong will talk about styles of victorian clothing.

B. Punctuation (*pages 230–253*)   On your paper, write each sentence correctly. Use appropriate punctation.

11. In 1964 Dr. Martin Luther King Jr was awarded the Nobel Peace Prize said Professor Jackson for his civil rights work

12. Kate didnt enjoy the second chapter entitled Over the Hill consequently she stopped at page seventy two

13. Realizing that her light blue sweater was lost she cried Oh no then she searched field bleachers and bus until 700 PM

14. Ms Nancy R Frazier
    14 Poplar Dr
    Sioux Falls SD 57105

15. The well informed reviewer began with this statement The Civil War Period 1861 to 1865 is the setting of Stephen Cranes novel *The Red Badge of Courage*

16. When Liza finished the story she exclaimed Oh how I enjoyed in fact hated to finish Guy de Maupassants The Necklace

17. Casss and Elsas post graduation plans I believe are different later I will ask them about their ideas ambitions and hopes

18. Our travel guide stated in a well organized manner the following Three of the tallest buildings are the Sears Tower Chicago the World Trade Center New York and the Empire State Building New York

19. Lee who is fascinated by baseball wrote Im planning a trip to Cooperstown New York on Sept 15 1987 to visit the National Baseball Hall of Fame and Museum

20. Although thirty five guests were anticipated only twenty one arrived on time for the Carvers celebration however by 830 PM all the guests had finally appeared

C. Italics (*pages 253–254*)   On your paper, write each sentence correctly. Underline the words that should be in italic type.

21. Our company advertises in Fortune, Ebony, and Newsweek.

22. The Constitution was one ship that was active in the War of 1812.

23. Have you included all the s's in Mississippi?

24. Laurel greatly admires Mary Cassatt's painting The Bath.

25. I read the Daily Register nearly every morning.

26. Ned and Olivia recited parts of Homer's epic poem the Odyssey.

27. The & was missing from the sign, so it just said Thompson Sons.

(Continue on the next page.)

28. Will you define the term sepia in your photography report?
29. James Fenimore Cooper's The Pathfinder was found at the sale.
30. We rang up more 2's than 4's on the register.

D. Using Numbers in Writing (*pages 254–257*) On your paper, write the number form that correctly completes each of the following sentences.

31. (1, one, One) dollar will buy your book of admission tickets.
32. Nearly (four hundred, four-hundred, 400) people attended the bazaar.
33. He bicycled (1322, one thousand three hundred 22, one thousand three hundred twenty-two) miles.
34. Her nephew will be (Twelve, twelve, 12) years old next month.
35. The geese were sighted on October (20th, twenty, 20).
36. Farmers lost (25 percent, twenty-five percent, 25%) of their crops in the drought.
37. Our invitation to (Seven, seven, 7) Mill Street is for (nine, 9, 9:00) o'clock May (10th, 10, ten).
38. Nellie Bly made a trip around the world in (Seventy-two, seventy-two, 72) days.
39. The train is due to leave at (422, 4:22, four twenty-two) P.M.
40. (One hundred and one, One hundred one, 101) lanterns lighted their party on July (4th, 4, four).

Test 2

Rewrite the following passage, making corrections in capitalization, punctuation, and number usage.

payse weston received universal praise during his long distance walking career however he was not a characteristic athlete weston performed dressed in the following silk hat tan gloves high work shoes and black pants and jacket at age 70 he broke yet another record and hiked from san francisco to los angeles in 10 days this distance five hundred and twelve miles helped to prove his belief in the many values of walking beginning in eighteen sixty one payse weston started his career on a bet westons achievements included winning the astley belt for what was called pedestrian excellence for himself payse westons interest in walking was as a sport yet he recommended long distance hiking for everyone was westons view correct he believed these three things walking improves health teaches patience and gives self discipline indeed because he was a long time competitor and he lived to be 90 he may have been right

Part Two

Composition

Have you ever wondered why writing seems difficult, while talking seems so easy? Both speaking and writing require you to state your ideas clearly in order to communicate with others. Writing requires special skills, however. In Part Two you will learn ways to write more easily and more effectively.

Units 6 through 9 teach you the process of writing as a series of steps: prewriting, writing, and revising. By taking one step at a time, you will develop skills that you can use whenever you write. Units 10 through 13 teach you various purposes to which you can apply the writing process: to explain, to describe, to tell a story, and to state an opinion. Units 14 and 15 introduce you to two special forms of writing: formal reports and business correspondence.

Prewriting

Unit Preview

Learning to write well is a difficult task. But the task can be simplified if you approach it one step at a time. The writing process has three steps: prewriting, writing a draft, and revising. No matter what you are writing, the process is the same.

Prewriting ──────▶ Writing ──────▶ Revising
(Finding ideas   (First draft)   (Rewriting
Listing ideas   Proofreading)
Selecting topics
Organizing)

Prewriting is the planning and preparation that you do before you write. If you do a thorough job of prewriting, writing the first draft will not be difficult. During the prewriting stage, you determine what you will write about, what your purpose is, and for whom you are writing. You gather and develop ideas, sort them out, and focus them.

The following notes are a writer's prewriting material on the subject of beliefs and sayings about weather.

Red sky at night, sailors' delight.
Red sky at morning, sailors take warning.

Lightning never strikes twice in the same place.

A white ring around the moon means snow; a colored ring means rain.

When a groundhog sees its shadow on February 2, there will be six more weeks of winter.

It's raining cats and dogs.

This is the calm before the storm.

You can tell how hard the winter will be when you look at a woolly caterpillar.

What sayings about weather have a basis in fact?
—A red morning sky indicates warm, moist air;
rain or snow likely
—Halo around moon caused by ice crystals in clouds

Why are these sayings useful?
—Help forecast weather
—Help you plan your daily activities

How did these weather beliefs originate?
—Observation of certain signs coincided with
weather patterns.
—Importance of good harvests for survival and need
to "read" signs in nature

For Analysis On your paper, answer the following questions about the prewriting notes.

1. What are two methods that the writer used to collect ideas for this subject?
   a. Made a list of ideas about weather
   b. Wrote a paragraph
   c. Asked and answered questions about weather sayings
2. Which two of the following possible writing ideas do these notes suggest?
   a. How to predict weather
   b. Truth of weather beliefs
   c. Origins of weather beliefs
   d. Weather satellites

In answering these questions, you observed the process of prewriting. In this unit you will learn effective ways to do prewriting. You will discover that you have subjects to write about, you will gather and develop ideas, and you will learn to focus your prewriting notes for specific assignments.

6.1   Finding Ideas for Writing

Often the most difficult part of writing is getting started, that is, knowing what to write about. Prewriting helps you to discover the ideas that you have and to develop your ideas into specific topics. You can find ideas for writing from many sources—interests, experiences, and your observations of the world around you. Three ways to find subjects are to take an inventory of your interests, to draw upon your experience and that of others, and to keep a writer's notebook. Your goal at this point is simply to identify and record possible subjects and to keep them on file to develop later.

6.1a   Taking an Interest Inventory

An **interest inventory** is an itemized list or summary of your interests. It can include subjects that you would like to learn about as well as those that you are already familiar with. Your inventory is one source of ideas for writing assignments. Keep a special section in your notebook for your interest inventory.

An interest inventory might look like this:

WHAT I KNOW ABOUT	WHAT I'D LIKE TO LEARN ABOUT
folk dancing	candle making
baseball history	careers in theater
horses	photography
MY HOBBIES	MY FAVORITE SPORTS
drawing	baseball
listening to music	hockey
woodworking	track

Exercise 1   Prewriting: Interest Inventory   On your paper, write an inventory of your interests. Use the following questions to get started.

1. What are three subjects that I know about?
2. What are three subjects that I would like to learn about?
3. What are my hobbies?
4. What do I enjoy doing with friends? with family?

5. What kind of music do I like?
6. What sports do I like?
7. What books and magazines do I enjoy?
8. What school activities do I like?
9. What clubs or organizations do I belong to?
10. Where did my ancestors come from?

Exercise 2 Prewriting: Interest Inventory On your paper, write the following sentences, completing them with your own interests. Save your paper as part of your interest inventory.

> **SAMPLE**   I am glad to be . . .
> **ANSWER**   I am glad to be living in the twentieth century.

1. Someone I know and admire is . . . because . . . .
2. Three changes I would like to make are . . . .
3. I would like to invent a better way to . . . .
4. The best book I ever read is . . . .
5. I am concerned about . . . .
6. I would like to be able to . . . .
7. One talent that I have is . . . .
8. I would like to travel to . . . .
9. In ten years I would like to . . . .
10. My ambition is . . . .

Exercise 3 Prewriting: Interest Inventory On your paper, list five of the following subjects in which you have some interest. Next to each subject that you list, write specific aspects or examples of it that you would like to know about. Add your paper to your interest inventory.

> **SAMPLE**   Animals
> **ANSWER**   Animals: dolphins, communication among animals, training dogs

1. Art	9. Dance	17. Music
2. Astronomy	10. Explorers	18. Photography
3. Athletes	11. Farm life	19. Poisonous snakes
4. Computers	12. Fashion	20. Science
5. Conservation	13. Heroes, heroines	21. Ships
6. Crafts	14. History	22. Sports
7. Crime detection	15. Literature	23. Theater
8. The Crusades	16. Machines	24. Transportation

6.1b   Drawing Upon Your Experiences

Experiences are a valuable source of ideas for writing. For example, many possible writing subjects could come from the following experiences: riding a train across Canada, losing a locket that had been handed down in your family, or being in a tornado. Draw up a list of your own memorable experiences. The following exercises will help you to recall them.

Exercise 4   Prewriting: Experiences   On your paper, complete six of the following sentences with examples from your own experience.

> SAMPLE   I laughed so hard when . . .
>
> ANSWER   I laughed so hard when my father dressed up as Tarzan for a costume party.

1. One of my earliest memories is . . . .
2. The happiest day of my life was . . . .
3. I was very much surprised when . . . .
4. An experience that helped me was . . . .
5. I was sorry when I learned that . . . .
6. I will never forget the time when . . . .
7. A sensible decision that I made was . . . .
8. It was difficult to learn to . . . .
9. A teacher once showed me how to . . . .

10. The best opportunity I ever had was . . . .
11. I was really challenged when . . . .
12. The most rewarding experience I ever had was . . . .

Exercise 5 Prewriting: Experiences On your paper, make a list of specific examples of three of the following experiences.

SAMPLE Outdoor adventures

ANSWER Last year we camped out during a storm.
I once bicycled up a two-mile hill.
A friend and I got lost in a cave.

1. Feeling proud of myself
2. Trying to make a good impression
3. Meeting new people
4. Being a good friend
5. Doing or saying something that I regretted
6. Mastering a new subject or skill

6.1c Keeping a Writer's Notebook

Keep a notebook in which you record information and ideas that interest you. Your writer's notebook will be another valuable source of writing ideas. You need not record your ideas in complete sentences. Use the following strategies to collect ideas in your notebook.

Strategies

1. *Take notes on whatever you observe, think, hear, or do that you want to remember.* Your notes might resemble these, for example:

Saw bird building a nest
Heard crowd cheering loudly at baseball game
Do bees find flowers by sight or by smell?

2. *Record interesting bits of conversation or remarks that you hear and your observations or questions about them.* You might have notes similar to these:
   Mr. Richardson to a group of students: "When I was your age, no one played soccer."
   When did soccer become popular in this country?

3. *Include articles, advertisements, and letters to editors* from magazines and newspapers on subjects that interest you. For example, you might include an article on a ten-year-old stock market genius or an advertisement for a build-it-yourself grandfather clock.

4. *Clip pictures and cartoons from newspapers or magazines* because they inspire you or say something that you agree or disagree with. For example, you might include a picture of a family with seven adopted children or a cartoon of a political figure.

You can keep your interest inventory and your lists of experiences in your writer's notebook. Your notebook will then become a file of possible writing ideas.

Exercise 6   Prewriting: Writer's Notebook   Make at least one entry in your notebook for five of the items that follow.

SAMPLE	An item of interest that you have read recently
ANSWER	Scientists have recently discovered that for many years they have been putting the wrong head on fossil skeletons of the brontosaurus.

1. Something of interest that you have seen recently
2. Something interesting that you have heard recently
3. Something you have wondered about in the last few days
4. A stimulating conversation you have participated in or heard during the past week

5. Something of interest that you have read recently
6. A funny or clever advertisement that you have seen
7. A new fact that you have learned in the past week
8. An interesting picture that you have seen
9. A cartoon that you like
10. An unusual or pleasant event that has happened to you or to someone you know

Assignment 1 Prewriting Ask a friend or a family member to complete Exercise 4 on page 274. Ask the person for more information on any response that particularly interests you. Add the completed exercise and your notes to your writer's notebook.

Assignment 2 Prewriting Read a newspaper every day for a week. In your notebook, put clippings of items that interest you. Include your comments about them.

Assignment 3 Prewriting As you go through a day, jot down the things that you do, observe, or hear. Include your comments about these events. Add this information to your writer's notebook.

Continuing Assignment Prewriting Select one item that you would like to develop from your interest inventory, one from your list of experiences, and one from your writer's notebook. Write each item on a separate piece of paper. Save your papers.

Assignment Checklist

Check your assignments for the following points:

  ✔1. In Assignment 1, did you add a list of another person's significant experiences to your notebook?

✔ 2. In Assignment 2, did you put into your writer's notebook news stories, features, editorials, or cartoons that interest you?

✔ 3. In Assignment 3, did you keep an accurate record of your actions and observations for a day?

✔ 4. In your Continuing Assignment, did you select one item to develop from your interest inventory, one from your experience list, and one from your writer's notebook?

6.2 Gathering and Developing Ideas

You can find a great number of writing subjects in your interest inventory, your list of experiences, and your writer's notebook. Each item that you have listed or recorded is a subject that you can develop for writing. Whether your subject is one that you will learn about through research or one that you know well, you can gather and develop your ideas by making lists, asking questions, and doing free-flow writing. You will produce a large amount of material from which you can select specific topics and support for those topics.

6.2a Making Lists and Associations

To start, write down all your ideas or information gathered about the subject that you are developing. Do not reject any ideas or try to organize the list. Next, expand your list by letting your mind wander and writing down any associations, or related ideas, that your imagination connects with your subject. Add these to your list. Suppose that an item on your interest inventory is kites. Your list of ideas and associations for kites might look like the following:

Making kites, materials needed to make kites
Open fields, windy days
Kite tournaments

Box kites, carp kites
Flying techniques
Kites' Day in China
Kites used in scientific research on weather
Franklin used kite in discovery of electricity

Exercise 1 Prewriting: Making Lists Choose five of the following subjects. On your paper, list at least ten ideas and associations for each subject that you choose.

SAMPLE	Mountain climbing
ANSWER	Boots, backpack, equipment
	High altitudes, tree line
	Cliffs, rock climbing
	Avalanches, glaciers
	Mt. Everest, expeditions
	Formation of mountains during Ice Age

1. California Gold Rush
2. Circus
3. Cities
4. Electronic games
5. Health
6. Movies
7. Neighbors
8. Restaurants
9. Sharks
10. Television
11. Wild animals
12. Volcanoes

6.2b Asking Questions

Asking and answering questions about a subject will help you to gather information about that subject. If you do not have answers for some of your questions, ask someone who might know, or do research yourself to find the answers. Your answer to a particular question may suggest other questions. The continuing questioning process will help you to develop your subject.

Start with questions that begin with *who, what, when, where, why,* and *how.* The answers to those questions will give you information. The following is a preliminary list of questions and answers on the subject of rodeos.

1. Who rides in rodeos?   —Men, women, boys, and girls
2. What is a rodeo?   —Entertainment featuring lasso throwing, cattle roping, bronco riding
3. When did rodeos begin?   —In the mid-1800s
4. Where do rodeos take place?   —In arenas all over country, particularly in western states and provinces
5. Why do people participate in rodeos? —Challenge, prize money
6. How are rodeo events scored?   —I don't know.

Next, ask questions that will help you to explore aspects of the subject. Not all of the following questions will apply to any subject that you are developing, but you can use those that do.

1. What are the characteristics of the subject? —Competition, riding and roping skills, timed events
2. What are examples of the subject? —The Calgary Stampede, Alberta, Canada —Texas Cowboy Reunion and Rodeo in Stamford
3. What terms need to be defined?   —*Hazer, bronco*
4. What processes (how something is done) are part of the subject?   —How to mount a bronco
5. Can the subject be compared with anything else? —I can't think of anything now.
6. Are any of the following contrasts contained in the subject?

   good / bad   advantages / disadvantages
   past / present / future   problems / solutions
   danger / safety   strengths / weaknesses

   —Past / present: In the past, rodeos were for cowboys' relaxation; now they are a sport.
   —Danger / safety: There is danger of injury in some events; participants need to take care.

7. Do you have any experience with your subject that you can describe?   —I attended the Western Montana Fair and Rodeo Meet in Missoula.

Exercise 2 Prewriting: Asking Questions Choose two of the listed subjects. On your paper, write the two subjects, and answer at least six of the following questions about each.

National park system   Computer programming
Gymnastics   Scuba diving
Sign language   Dancing

1. Who is involved?
2. What are the characteristics of the subject?
3. When did it happen or begin?
4. Where did (does) it exist?
5. How is it used?
6. What are two examples?
7. What can I compare it to?
8. What contrasts are in the subject?
9. What processes within it can I explain?
10. What terms must I define?

6.2c Using Free-Flow Writing

Free-flow writing is a method of gathering ideas by writing continuously, without pausing to think or plan, until you have filled a page or so. Begin with a memory, a subject, a quotation, or any other idea. Write whatever thoughts come to your mind. You may find that you stray far from your subject or that you center your writing around one small detail.

Although no two pages of free-flow writing will ever look alike, the following example shows you what free-flow writing might look like. The writer begins with a well-known proverb.

"A penny saved is a penny earned." Ben Franklin wrote that. Was it in *Poor Richard's Almanac*? In those days a penny was worth more than it is today. Franklin started off as a poor boy (one of seventeen children) and ended up quite rich, so maybe he took his own advice. He had a lot of advice about how to live: Early to bed and early to rise. But he says in his autobiography that he didn't follow all his rules for living. He says that he was not neat and did not keep things in place.

Your page of free-flow writing is not a first draft for a composition but simply another way for you to gather ideas to use. From your free-flow writing, you can later pull out related details or ideas to use in a piece of writing.

Exercise 3 Prewriting: Free-Flow Writing Choose one of the following as a starting point for free-flow writing. Write without stopping until you have filled a page.

1. "Honesty is the best policy."
2. Moving to a new town or school
3. The custom of shaking hands
4. Talking with an older relative
5. "Give me liberty or give me death."
6. A missed opportunity

Assignment 1 Prewriting Choose an item from your writer's notebook. Develop it by listing all the thoughts about it that come to your mind.

Assignment 2 Prewriting Select one of your answers from Exercise 3 on page 273. Look up an article on the subject in an encyclopedia or other reference book and find the answers to *who, what, when, where, why,* and *how* questions.

Assignment 3 Prewriting Select one item from your list of experiences. Using free-flow writing, write in detail about your experience. When you have finished, read through your free-flow writing and underline important ideas or details.

Continuing Assignment Prewriting In the Continuing Assignment on page 277, you selected three items of interest to you. Develop each of these items as much as you can by making lists, asking questions, and using free-flow writing. Do not be concerned if your notes from each method overlap. You can sort out all your material later. Save your papers.

Assignment Checklist

Check your assignments for the following points:

✔ 1. In Assignment 1, did you list all the ideas and associations that came to your mind about your subject?
✔ 2. In Assignment 2, did you explore aspects of your subject by asking and answering basic questions?
✔ 3. In Assignment 3, did you underline the important ideas and details?
✔ 4. In your Continuing Assignment, did you develop each of your three subjects as fully as you could?

6.3 Focusing Your Ideas

When you use the prewriting techniques in this unit, you will develop a great volume of material to use in writing—too much to use at any one time. Your task now is to make your prewriting notes useful to you for specific writing assignments. To do so, you must determine a topic and identify a purpose and an audience for your topic.

Topic

Each subject that you have developed can yield many writing topics. A **topic** is a specific aspect of a subject, one that you can use for a paragraph, an essay, or a report. For example, your notes on a train trip across Canada might suggest the following topics: "Modern railroads," "Meeting people," "Contrasts between Canada and the United States."

Purpose

Your purpose for writing is what you intend or hope to accomplish with your writing. For example, your purpose for a paragraph might be to explain how riders mount broncos, or it might be to entertain by telling about your first attempt to ride a horse.

The following list presents the most common purposes for writing and gives an appropriate topic for each purpose.

PURPOSE	TOPIC
To inform or explain	Regulations for recycling containers at the town dump
To entertain	How you fell off the dock into the lake
To describe	The Canadian Rockies from a train window
To express an opinion	The need for first aid training

Audience

Your **audience** is the reader or group of readers for whom your writing is intended. You decide to whom your writing is directed. If you write about kites, for example, your audience could be readers who have never flown kites or readers who build kites for a hobby. In either case, you should consider what would interest your particular audience and how much or how little they know about the subject. You might, for example, explain how a kite flies to those who have never flown a kite and want to learn how.

Planning the Writing Situation

The following procedure will help you to focus your prewriting ideas and notes for specific writing assignments.

Procedure

1. *Review your prewriting notes on a subject. Jot down topic ideas that emerge.* You may find a topic in one item on a list or in your answer to a question.

2. *Look for ways to sort the information in your notes.* You might find several notes, for instance, that contain examples, descriptions, reasons, or results, or that suggest a comparison between two items. Grouping your notes can suggest further possible topics. Several notes about your success in kite flying might suggest the topic "Ideal conditions for kite flying."

3. *Consider a purpose and an audience for your possible topics.*

4. *Focus on a topic that you want to use for your writing assignment.* Look through your prewriting notes again and find all the details that will be useful for that topic. Select those details that support your topic and are in keeping with your purpose and your audience.

Once you have identified your topic, your purpose, and your audience, you may need to repeat some of the prewriting techniques given in this unit. You may need to make lists, ask questions, or do research to obtain more information for your specific topic. As you work on a particular writing assignment, you will do additional prewriting in the form of organizing your information for your paragraph, essay, or report. Each composition unit in this book will give you further prewriting instruction and practice.

Exercise 1   Prewriting: Purpose and Audience   On your paper, list the following topics. For each topic, write an appropriate purpose and audience from those given.

SAMPLE	Changes in laws about strip mining
ANSWER	To express an opinion to senators

TOPICS

1. Getting stuck in a traffic jam
2. Ways to improve drawing skills
3. Trying to install a wood stove
4. Your need for a new bicycle
5. Finding trails in the forest
6. Planting herbs to eliminate weeds
7. The value of knowing a foreign language
8. The appearance of a moose
9. The need for a new traffic light
10. Your neighborhood in winter

PURPOSES

To inform or explain   To describe
To entertain   To express an opinion

AUDIENCES

Gardeners   A hiker
A new neighbor   Homeowners
Parents   Department of Streets and Parks
Motorists   A traveler
Art students   A ten-year-old child

Exercise 2   Prewriting: Focusing Ideas   On your paper, answer Questions 1-4 following these prewriting notes on the subject of tornadoes.

Looks like dark funnel   Huge oak torn out of ground
Hurricanes   Smashed buildings
Violent winds   Listen to radio announcements
Dust clouds   Newspaper accounts of disasters
Sirens for tornado warning   Hide away from windows
Rumble of thunder   Governor surveyed area
The Wizard of Oz   How weather affects us
Natural disasters

Who can give help?   —Red Cross
Where do you go during a tornado?   —Basement
What causes tornadoes?   —Warm, humid air rises quickly
When do they happen?   —Spring or early summer
How did I feel?   —Frightened, alert

1. What are three possible writing topics in this material?
2. What details would you use if you were writing about the topic "What to do during a tornado"?
3. What could be your purpose for the topic "What to do during a tornado"?
4. Who would be a likely audience for the topic "What to do during a tornado"?

Assignment   Prewriting   Choose a subject from your interest inventory, your experience lists, or your writer's notebook. Develop it by using the prewriting techniques that work best. From your prewriting notes, find three possible writing topics.

Continuing Assignment   Prewriting   In the Continuing Assignment on page 283, you developed three subjects. Now focus your prewriting notes, and identify three possible writing topics. Specify a purpose and an audience for each.

Assignment Checklist

Check your assignments for the following points:

✓ 1. Did you develop your subjects by making lists, by asking and answering questions, and by doing free-flow writing?
✓ 2. Did you find three possible writing topics from the subjects that you developed?

Check your Continuing Assignment for this additional point:

✓ 3. Did you identify a purpose and an audience for each topic?

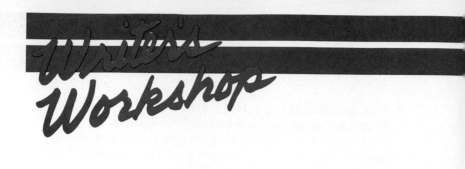

Sports Desk: Ideas for Articles

Situation: You are a writer asked by your editor to come up with ideas for a series of articles on outstanding teen-age athletes or teen-age athletes with unusual skills. Your editor has given you notes on some types of athletes and skills that you may consider. You decide to use your editor's notes and prewriting techniques to develop some ideas for the articles. Keep in mind the following information.

Writer: you as writer of "Sports Desk" column

Audience: editor, readers

Topic: teen-age athletes with outstanding or unusual skills

Purpose: to gather and develop ideas for articles

Directions: To come up with ideas, follow these steps.

Step 1. Write across the top of a paper: "What do I know about teen-age athletes with outstanding or unusual skills?" Look at your editor's notes on page 289, and list whatever information they suggest to you in answer to your question.

Step 2. Write free-flow for at least a page on one of the items on your list from Step 1 or on one of the items in your editor's notes. Underline important ideas and details in your free-flow writing.

Step 3. Write five questions that will help you to gather more ideas about these athletes or their skills. Include questions that will lead to comparisons, contrasts, and other explorations as well as those that will give you information. Answer the questions if you can, or find the answers to the questions.

Step 4. Review all your notes. Make a list of the five athletes and their sports or skills that will be the topics of your articles. Skip a line between each item on your list.

For example: Anthony D'Amato, race walking

Step 5. After each topic on your list, write a possible purpose for an article on that athlete and sport or skill.

For example: to inform readers about Anthony D'Amato's training and strategies for a walking race

Notes to "Sports Desk" writer

Athletes in local junior high and high schools
Other local teenage athletes
Olympic athletes
Teenage athletes whose skills have
    been reported in national publications
Teenage athletes whom you have seen
    on television
Unusual skills: unicycle riding,
    race walking, trick skateboarding
Teenage athletes that you know
Teenage athletes that your friends
    have told you about

Unit Assignments

Assignment 1   You are planning to write about the advantages and disadvantages of neatness. Write down at least ten details and associations, two experiences related to the subject, and three examples.

Assignment 2   You have been assigned by your school newspaper to do an imaginary interview with a famous person from history. Choose the person whom you will interview. Write down ten questions that you think your readers would like to have you ask in your interview.

Assignment 3   Choose a childhood memory. In free-flow writing, describe everything about it that you can remember.

Assignment 4   Imagine that you could write a letter to a student of one hundred years ago. In your prewriting, make notes on the contrasts that you would observe in education, social life, and entertainment.

Assignment 5   Do prewriting on the subject of enduring an exhausting day. After you have developed the subject, sort your notes and find two writing topics.

Unit Tests

Test 1

A. Number your paper from 1 to 5. Next to each number, write *True* if the sentence is true or *False* if it is false.

1. Prewriting involves making a first draft for a composition.
2. Your own interests, experiences, and observations of the world around you are sources of ideas for writing.
3. Each item that you have recorded in your interest inventory, your list of experiences, and your writer's notebook is a subject that you can develop for writing.
4. You can gather and develop your ideas about a subject by making lists, asking and answering questions, and doing free-flow writing.
5. When you write a particular assignment, you will use all of the material that you have gathered with prewriting techniques.

B. Number your paper from 6 to 10. Next to each number, write the letter of the term that correctly completes the sentence. You will not use one of the terms.

    a. writer's notebook   d. interest inventory

    b. prewriting   e. free-flow writing

    c. list   f. topic

6. The planning and preparation that you do before you write is called __?__.
7. A(n) __?__ is an itemized list or a summary of your interests.
8. A method of gathering ideas by writing continuously, without pausing to think or plan, is called __?__.
9. A(n) __?__ contains information, ideas, observations, articles, pictures, and cartoons from which you can find writing subjects.
10. From your prewriting notes, you can focus on a(n) __?__, or specific aspect of a subject for a particular assignment.

(Continue on the next page.)

C. Number your paper from 11 to 15. Read the following prewriting notes about Florida. Next to each number, write the letter of the item that correctly answers the question.

(1) Ponce de Leon

(2) Tourists

(3) Scorching sun

(4) Swimming in Gulf of Mexico

(5) Orange groves

(6) St. Augustine, oldest city

(7) Last summer's trip to the Everglades

(8) Walt Disney World and Marineland

(9) Seminole Indians

(10) Cypress and palm trees

(11) Tallahassee is state capital

(12) Traveled by swamp boat

11. Which one of the following is a purpose you might use for an assignment from the prewriting notes?

    a. To tell a funny story about shell collecting

    b. To explain or inform about the "red tide"

    c. To describe Florida's attractions

    d. To express an opinion about Cape Canaveral, Florida

12. Which one of the following would be the least suitable audience for writing based on the prewriting notes?

    a. A family planning a vacation

    b. A person who enjoys only winter sports

    c. A visitor from Europe

    d. A person interested in Florida's history

13. Which one of the following sets of notes would help develop a topic about the history of Florida?

    a. 3, 5, 12   c. 4, 7, 10

    b. 2, 8, 11   d. 1, 6, 9

14. Which one of the following sets of notes could help develop a topic about a summer vacation trip?

    a. 3, 5, 11   c. 1, 2, 6

    b. 4, 7, 12   d. 8, 9, 10

15. Which one of the following contrasts could *not* be developed from these prewriting notes?

    a. Advantages and disadvantages of a tropical climate

    b. Florida's past and present

    c. Problems and solutions for wildlife conservation

    d. Good and bad aspects of tourism

Test 2

Choose one of the Unit Assignments or one that your teacher suggests. Complete the assignment and hand it in to your teacher.

Unit 7

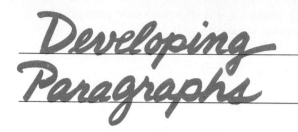

Developing Paragraphs

Unit Preview

A paragraph is the step-by-step development of an idea. In the following paragraph, each sentence is a step that develops the main idea.

STEPS	PARAGRAPH
(1) Main idea: a small town	(1) What is a small town? (2) It sits on four city blocks; its inhabitants are friendly; it oper-
(2) Size, residents, buildings	ates on one grocery store, one gas station, one post office, one beauty shop, one cafe, one bar, one car wash, and four different churches. (3) On
(3) Bands and trains	any given day, the band marches through town, and a three-car train chugs by. (4) Traffic is light;
(4) Driving	you can make a U-turn in the middle of Main Street. (5) Conversation is easy. (6) If you smile at
(5) (6) Friendliness	people, they smile back. (7) The only things more
(7) Kids, pets, caring	abundant than kids are stray animals—and the whole town takes care of both. (8) The folks who
(8) A nice place to live	live here would not live anywhere else.

Lesley Coleman
Grand Valley Community High School
Kellerton, Iowa

The main idea of a well-written paragraph is usually expressed in one sentence. Then the idea is developed sentence by sentence, detail by detail. The final sentence of a paragraph often states a conclusion or summarizes the sentences that precede it.

The following diagram will help you to understand the structure of a paragraph.

MAIN IDEA $\longrightarrow$	DETAILS $\longrightarrow$	CONCLUSION
A small town	Size, residents, buildings Bands, trains Driving Friendliness Kids, pets, caring	A nice place to live

For Analysis   On your paper, follow these instructions about the model paragraph.

1. Write the number of the sentence that expresses the main idea of the paragraph. In your own words, state the main idea.
2. List by sentence number the details that develop the main idea.
3. Write the number of the sentence that summarizes the details in the other sentences. State in your own words how the sentence summarizes the details.

In this unit you will practice writing unified paragraphs. In the prewriting stage, you will select a topic, limit it, and list details for it. Then you will write the sentences: a topic sentence, supporting sentences, and a concluding sentence for each paragraph.

7.1   What Is a Paragraph?

A **paragraph** is a series of sentences that develops a single idea or topic. In paragraph writing, *develops* can have any number of meanings, from "explains" to "argues," but the development always relates to just one topic. Thus, a paragraph is a unit of thought.

Most paragraphs contain a sentence called the topic sentence and several other sentences, called supporting sentences, that provide specific information. A **topic sentence** states the main idea of a paragraph and indicates the purpose of the paragraph. Usually placed at the beginning of a paragraph, it gives readers an overview of what they are about to read. **Supporting sentences** explain or develop what is stated in the topic sentence. They do so by giving specific facts, examples, or reasons related to the topic. A paragraph may also have a **concluding sentence** to bring it to a close.

In the following paragraph, the topic sentence is in italics. Each of the other sentences offers specific information that supports the general idea stated in the topic sentence.

Model

Topic sentence

Supporting sentences

No other inventor has had more impact on modern life than Thomas Alva Edison. You probably know that Edison invented the light bulb. But are you aware that he also gave us the light switch, the light socket, and the three-wire system of electrical wiring? Edison's inventions ranged from ore-crushing machines and underground electric mains to storage batteries and electric pens. If you have ever ridden a train, you are indebted to Edison, for he invented the electric railway car and the electric railroad signal. In fact, the next time you turn on a radio, play a record, watch a movie, copy a paper, or record a message, remember that it was Edison who invented the radio vacuum tube, the phonograph and phonograph record, the motion-picture camera, and the first mimeograph and dictating machines. Furthermore, if you ever take your lunch to school, you can thank you-know-who for inventing wax paper!

A paragraph has **unity** when each sentence in it clearly contributes to the unit by saying something about the topic. To write a unified paragraph, you must know when to include a detail and when to omit it. The preceding paragraph on Edison begins with a clearly stated topic sentence. It then includes only those details that relate to the idea stated in the topic sentence. Notice that the paragraph does not contain sentences such as the following:

> Edison favored the use of direct current (DC) electricity, for he considered alternating current (AC) dangerous.
>
> Thomas Edison never completed grade school.
>
> When Edison publicly stated his intention to devise durable filaments for lamps, gas company stocks fell sharply on the New York Stock Exchange.

Although these sentences are about Thomas Edison, they have little to do with the impact on our lives of Edison's important inventions.

Exercise Prewriting: Unity   On your paper, write the letter of the topic sentence in each of the following lists. Then write the letter of the sentence that is not directly related to the topic.

1. a. Its teeth are quite sharp and are as strong as steel.
   b. The largest carnivorous fish in the ocean, it is driven by its insatiable hunger.
   c. It has very tough skin, is able to scent blood, and can pick up sounds as far as a mile away.
   d. The white shark has features that make it a frightening fish.
   e. It prefers the warm waters of the tropics and the temperate zone.
   f. It is immune to almost every kind of sickness and can function normally even after receiving brain damage.

2. a. George drove to the wrong church and was an hour late getting to the right one.

   b. As he was walking down the aisle with Carla, Carla's father accidentally stepped on the train of her dress, causing Carla to lurch backward just as she reached George.

   c. George and Carla's wedding was not without problems.

   d. The flower girl turned out to be allergic to flowers and kept sneezing throughout the ceremony.

   e. The organist, George's favorite aunt, played quite well.

   f. Near the end, the best man fainted and had to be carried out.

3. a. The little we know of Atlantis comes from a fragment of a dialogue written by Plato, a philosopher in ancient Greece.

   b. According to the dialogue, the island was located west of Gibraltar in the Atlantic Ocean and was destroyed by an earthquake, disappearing without a trace.

   c. The Atlantic Ocean was named after Atlas, the son of the ocean god Poseidon and first king of Atlantis.

   d. Supposedly, Atlantis was an almost perfect society: its people were honest and happy, its cities were beautiful, and its land was lush and fertile.

   e. Throughout history, attempts have been made to find the lost island, but all have failed.

   f. The legendary lost island of Atlantis has fascinated people since ancient times.

4. a. It leaks water, oil, and transmission fluid all at the same time.

   b. In its heyday it got more than thirty miles to the gallon.

   c. The hood and windshield are missing, and so is the door on the passenger's side.

   d. My sister's car is ready for the junkyard.

   e. The upholstery looks as though it's been trampled by a herd of buffalo.

   f. Every time my sister starts it up, a fender or a bumper or something else falls off.

Assignment Prewriting Select two of the following topics that interest you, or think of two topics of your own. On your paper, write the two topics. For each, list eight supporting details. Put a check beside four or five details on each list that would be most useful in writing a unified paragraph. The details that you check should all have something in common.

1. New clothes
2. Listening to music
3. Learning to drive

4. Team sports
5. Summer work
6. New friends

Assignment Checklist

Check your assignment for the following point:

✔ Do all the details that you checked have something in common?

7.2 Selecting and Limiting a Topic

The first step in planning your paragraph is selecting a topic. If you are free to select a topic, choose a subject that you are familiar with or are prepared to study. Chances are you will choose an idea that is somewhat general, like "Discoveries in outer space" or "Dieting." However, in the few sentences that you have to work with in a paragraph, a limited topic is more suitable. A limited topic gives you a focus for your paragraph. It also gives you an opportunity to present specific information that makes interesting reading.

There are a number of ways that you can limit your topic for a paragraph.

Strategies

1. *Select one example of your topic idea.*

   TOPIC IDEA   Architects

   LIMITED TOPIC   Louis Sullivan

2. *Substitute a brief time period for a long one.*

TOPIC IDEA   All-time baseball greats

LIMITED TOPIC   The hero of last year's World Series

3. *Concentrate on part of a subject instead of on the entire subject.*

TOPIC IDEA   Health

LIMITED TOPIC   Aerobic exercise

4. *Limit the topic idea to a specific condition, place, or purpose.*

TOPIC IDEA	Cooking
LIMITED TOPIC (CONDITION)	Cooking for a family
TOPIC IDEA	Traveling
LIMITED TOPIC (PLACE)	Traveling in the Bad Lands
TOPIC IDEA	Bicycles
LIMITED TOPIC (PURPOSE)	Bicycling for recreation

Sometimes you have to set all of your ideas out in front of you before you can limit your paragraph topic. Begin by writing down your topic idea and listing under it as many related details as you can. The following is an example of this kind of list.

TOPIC IDEA: THE BRAIN

1. Weighs only three pounds, yet controls body's entire nervous system
2. Contains fifteen billion nerve units that store millions of memories
3. Protected by skull plate, scalp, and hair
4. Sends and receives more messages than a very large computer

5. Has connections that control all of body's muscles
6. "Floats" in fluid that provides shock-absorber protection
7. Wrapped in tough membrane called dura mater
8. Collects and records information obtained through eyes, ears, skin, and so on
9. Sends and receives tens of thousands of messages in reaction to even a small event, such as stubbed toe
10. Brain of some large dinosaurs smaller than a walnut

When you have listed as many details as you can, determine the most specific thing that the details have in common. Try this with the list about the brain. Of the ten details, all but the final one deal with the human brain. By eliminating this detail, you limit the topic to "The human brain." Of the nine remaining details, three items (3, 6, 7) are concerned with the protection of the brain. The other six items (1, 2, 4, 5, 8, 9) are related to the complexity of the brain. You may omit the three details related to the protection of the brain, further limiting the topic to "The complexity of the human brain."

Exercise 1   Prewriting: Limiting Topics   The follow ing topics are too general for paragraphs. Limit each topic to make it suitable for a paragraph, and write the limited topic on your paper.

> **SAMPLE**   Water sports
>
> **ANSWER**   How to stand up on water skis

1. Famous legends
2. The qualities of a good friend
3. Are humans physically superior to animals?
4. The life and death of Cleopatra, queen of ancient Egypt
5. National flags
6. How to mend clothes
7. City life versus small town or country life

8. Twentieth-century female athletes
9. The first transcontinental railroad in North America
10. Modern music

Exercise 2   Prewriting: Limiting Topics   On your paper, list under each of the following topic ideas the lettered items that are closely related. Discard any detail that is not closely related to any of the others on the list. Then write the limited topic of the group.

1. *Topic Idea:* The United States' Space Program
   a. The United States' space program has created thousands of jobs for scientists, technicians, and engineers.
   b. The space program has produced economic benefits for the United States.
   c. The space program has a rigorous screening program for astronaut candidates.
   d. Another important economic benefit of the space program is the development of space-flight equipment that can also be used in business and industry.
   e. The United States has space-communication stations around the world.
   f. The program has resulted in the development of numerous consumer products.
   Limited Topic: __?__

2. *Topic Idea:* Ballet
   a. A ballet dancer is part athlete and part artist.
   b. Dancing doesn't always involve music.
   c. To perform leaps and other movements effortlessly, a ballet dancer must be strong, well coordinated, and in excellent condition.
   d. Because of the physical demands of dancing, professional ballet dancers must work out daily.
   e. There are many kinds of dancing.

f. Like actors, performers in ballets must study the characters whom they will play, in order to bring them to life on the stage.

g. Besides developing their athletic skills, ballet dancers devote much effort to the art of dance—the ability to communicate feelings through movement.

h. Ruth St. Denis was a pioneer of modern dance.

Limited Topic: __?__

Assignment Prewriting Choose five topics that you are familiar with or are prepared to study. Limit each for a paragraph, and write the limited topic.

Continuing Assignment Prewriting *Step 1:* In a ten-minute period, write down as many topics as you can. Go over the list of topics and select the two that interest you most. *Step 2:* Write those topics side by side on a piece of paper. Under each, list at least eight details that you could use in writing a paragraph. *Step 3:* Put a check beside the four or five details that are most closely related. Write the limited topic of each group of details. Save your paper. You will develop this assignment throughout the unit.

Assignment Checklist

Check your assignment for the following points:

✔ 1. Did you choose five topics?
✔ 2. Did you limit each topic for a paragraph?

Check your Continuing Assignment for these points:

✔ 3. Did you list at least eight details for each of the two topics that you chose?
✔ 4. Did you select the details that are most closely related in each list?
✔ 5. Did you write the limited topic of each group?

7.3 Writing a Topic Sentence

A topic sentence states the idea that unifies the details in the other sentences of the paragraph. Your topic sentence should be neither too general nor too narrow. A topic sentence is too general if it is only partly developed by the details in the other sentences of the paragraph. An example of too general a topic sentence is "There are several reasons why it pays to get a college education" followed by sentences that discuss only one reason. A topic sentence is too narrow if it states only part of what is discussed in the other sentences. An example of too narrow a topic sentence is "High school rallies can be enjoyable" followed by sentences that discuss not only rallies but also sports events.

Your list of details will help you to write a topic sentence. You can more easily see what the details have in common when they are on paper than you can when you have to keep recalling them. The following is the limited topic and list of details for the topic idea "The brain."

LIMITED TOPIC: THE COMPLEXITY OF THE HUMAN BRAIN

1. Weighs only three pounds yet controls body's entire nervous system
2. Contains fifteen billion nerve units that store millions of memories
3. Sends and receives more messages than a very large computer
4. Has connections that control all of body's muscles
5. Collects and records information obtained through eyes, ears, skin, and so on
6. Sends and receives tens of thousands of messages in reaction to even a small event, such as stubbed toe

Consider each of the following statements as a topic sentence for a paragraph written from the details on the list.

A. The human brain is more complex than other parts of the body.

B. The human brain is more complex than a computer many times its size.

C. The human brain is an enormously complex organ.

Sentence A calls for details that are not on the list; that is, you would need information about other parts of the body to prove that the brain is more complex. The first sentence, therefore, is too general. Sentence B is specific, but because it focuses on only one detail (Number 3), it is too narrow. Sentence C, however, covers everything on the list, without calling for other details that are not listed. Therefore, Sentence C would be a suitable topic sentence for a paragraph based on the details listed.

Exercise 1 Prewriting: Topic Sentences Three possible topic sentences are given for each set of details. On your paper, write the one that would be suitable for a paragraph written from the given details.

1. *Details*
   The volcano nearly destroyed the island on which it was located.

   The rumble from its blast reportedly was heard thousands of miles away.

   For hundreds of miles in all directions, Krakatoa filled the sky with its ash, turning day into night.

   Ash from the volcano drifted over many parts of the globe.

   Possible Topic Sentences
   a. The eruption of the Indonesian volcano Krakatoa in 1883 had a severe impact on the atmosphere around the world.
   b. The eruption of the Indonesian volcano Krakatoa in 1883 was awesome.
   c. The Indonesian volcano Krakatoa erupted in 1883.

2. *Details*

He always forgets his homework assignments and has to call me up to find out what they are.

Then he forgets to bring the completed assignments to school.

At school he has to leave his locker open because he can never remember the combination.

He often forgets to bring his lunch to school; fortunately, he just as often forgets that he is hungry.

One day last month, he forgot that he was in high school and took the bus to his old elementary school!

Possible Topic Sentences

a. I have a friend named Sidney.

b. My friend Sidney is an incredibly forgetful person.

c. My friend Sidney has a problem.

3. *Details*

Each of the towers is 110 stories tall and has 102 elevators.

The Center's dozen restaurants serve 20,000 meals a day.

One thousand people are needed each night to clean the offices in the complex.

The Center has its own force of 38 uniformed police officers and 200 private security guards.

Possible Topic Sentences

a. The World Trade Center is located in New York City.

b. The World Trade Center in New York City is big.

c. The World Trade Center in New York City is a building complex that is big in every way.

4. *Details*

Most Romans knew that Nero wanted to rebuild the city and rename it after himself.

When the terrible fire broke out, many people assumed that Nero was responsible.

Historians tell us that, while thousands of terrified people wandered through the streets of Rome, Nero watched the fire from a tower, singing a song about the destruction of the city of Troy centuries before and strumming a stringed instrument called a lyre.

However, Nero did make an effort to control the fire.

Nevertheless, he rejoiced at the opportunity to rebuild the burned city.

Possible Topic Sentences
a. Rome burned during the reign of the emperor Nero.
b. The famous story about the Roman emperor Nero playing his fiddle while Rome burned is partly true.
c. The famous story about the Roman emperor Nero playing his fiddle while Rome burned is entirely true.

Exercise 2 Writing: Topic Sentences Select two of the following topics. On your paper, write a set of three possible topic sentences for each of your two topics. Each topic sentence in a set should have the same subject but a different predicate. Make sure that each topic sentence that you write is specific enough to be developed adequately in a paragraph. If you wish, look up more information on the topics before you write the topic sentences.

SAMPLE   Shopping

ANSWER   Shopping wisely and efficiently requires making comparisons for cost and quality.

Shopping on a Saturday brings out the worst in me.

Shopping by telephone saves time and energy.

1. Rock music
2. The twenty-first century
3. Old movies
4. Television commercials

Assignment Writing List five topics that you are interested in or familiar with. Write a topic sentence for a paragraph on each topic.

Continuing Assignment   Writing   In the Continuing Assignment on page 303, you selected related details and wrote a limited topic for your two groups of details. Now write a suitable topic sentence for each group of details. Save your paper.

Assignment Checklist

Check your assignment for the following point:

> ✔ 1. Is each topic sentence specific enough to be developed adequately in a paragraph?

Check your Continuing Assignment for this point:

> ✔ 2. Does each topic sentence state the limited topic of each group of details?

7.4   Writing Supporting Sentences

The supporting sentences of a paragraph provide the details that explain the topic. The kind of support that you need depends on your topic sentence and the purpose of your paragraph. The basic kinds of support are facts, examples, and reasons. You may develop a paragraph with only one kind of supporting detail, or you may use any combination of the three kinds.

7.4a   Facts

The most common kind of supporting sentence that you can use is the statement of fact. A **fact** is something that you know with certainty. Facts are such things as events, characteristics of something, physical observations, and statistics.

The topic sentence of the following paragraph is in italics. The numerous facts given in the supporting sentences help you to understand the topic sentence.

Model

Topic sentence	*Tenochtitlán, the capital of the ancient Aztec empire, was a remarkable city.* Inhabited
Fact	by nearly 100,000 people when the Spaniards
Fact	arrived in 1519, it was larger than any Spanish city at that time. The truly unusual feature of
Fact	Tenochtitlán is that it was built in Lake Texcoco on an island, which had been enlarged by filling swampland with silt dredged from the bottom of the lake and earth brought from the mainland
Fact	in canoes. Canals crossed the island-city, and
Fact	three causeways connected it with the mainland.
Fact	To feed the large population, the people grew fruit and vegetables in artificially created floating gardens encircling the city. This unusual city was a testimony to the ingenuity of the Aztecs.

Exercise 1   Prewriting: Facts   Some of the sentences that support the following topic sentence state facts. Others state the opinion of the writer. On your paper, write the numbers of the supporting sentences that state facts.

Topic Sentence: Both its history and its subject make Leonardo da Vinci's *Mona Lisa* one of the world's most famous paintings.

1. Leonardo worked on the painting, on and off, for four years, completing it in 1503.
2. I think that no other painting can compare with Leonardo's *Mona Lisa*.
3. The actual title of the painting is *La Giaconda;* the woman portrayed was the wife of a merchant of Florence.
4. In the nineteenth century, the *Mona Lisa* was stolen by an Italian who was determined to return it to his homeland.
5. Today, the painting, protected by bulletproof glass, hangs in the Louvre, in Paris.
6. The face in the painting is basically plain and innocent, but to me its half-smile suggests a sly worldliness.

7. Mona Lisa's smile has inspired numerous poems and songs
   —and even an entire opera.
8. The hands are, I believe, the most perfectly drawn in all
   of art.
9. Everyone who views the painting is moved by it.
10. X-rays have revealed that there are three other versions of the
    portrait underneath the final one.

Exercise 2 Writing: Facts On your paper, write a
paragraph using the topic sentence provided. Use the facts
listed to write the supporting sentences.

Topic Sentence: As the United States has become more industrial-
ized, the average length of a workweek has decreased.
Facts:

1. Before factories and offices, most laborers in United States
   were farmers
2. Farmers worked all daylight hours to provide for selves and
   families
3. After factories established, workers put in six ten-hour or
   twelve-hour days each week
4. In 1868 President Andrew Johnson signed congressional act
   establishing eight-hour day for factory workers
5. Eventually, six-day work week shortened to five-day workweek
6. Now, experiments with four-day weeks and job sharing may
   lead to shorter workweeks

7.4b Examples

Another way to support your topic sentence is to give
examples. An **example** is something that is typical of a whole
group. An example helps readers to understand the characteristics of a group. You will notice that facts can serve as
examples. The writer of the following paragraph offers four

examples. The examples support the topic sentence (in italics), which makes a general statement about a group.

Model

Topic sentence	No insect has a voice. *All the familiar sounds they make are mechanical, like the sounds coming from the instruments in an or-*
Example	*chestra.* Certain beetles burrow into wood and make a tapping sound as their hard heads strike
Example	against the wood. The mosquito's hum comes from the vibration of its wings. The call "Katy
Example	did! She didn't! She did!" is made by a male katydid. To make this sound he hangs high in a tree, head down, rubbing his left wing against
Example	his right wing. Male crickets also make their sounds with their wings, rubbing the right wing over the left. The centers of the wings are clear, making good sounding boards for the rubbed edges.

Frances N. Chrystie
The First Book of Surprising Facts

Exercise 3   Prewriting: Examples On your paper, write the topic sentence of the following paragraph. Then list the examples used to illustrate the topic sentence.

(1) You can get almost anything you want at our local discount store. (2) The store has two long aisles loaded with every game and model assembly kit ever invented. (3) The section called Health and Beauty Aids includes soaps and shampoos, many kinds of perfume, and a lot of inexpensive jewelry. (4) Next to these are the stationery supplies: binders, envelopes, scissors, erasers, paper clips, staples, rulers, glue, and notebook paper that has a cartoon character printed in the corner. (5) At the back of the store is a housewares department; here you can get plastic knives and forks,

plastic dishes and bowls, plastic curtains, and plastic "hardware." (6) There is also a section that sells prints of classical paintings, posters that glow in the dark, and ninety-nine-cent recordings. (7) The store even has a photo booth where you can take pictures of yourself that sometimes come out looking as if you just woke up in the morning.

Exercise 4   Writing: Examples   On your paper, write a paragraph using the topic sentence provided. Use the examples listed to write the supporting sentences.

Topic Sentence: George Washington Carver made significant contributions to increased agricultural production in the South.

Examples:

1. Did agricultural research at Tuskegee Institute in Alabama
2. Left $33,000 to establish fund for agricultural research at Tuskegee Institute
3. Convinced Southern farmers that crops such as sweet potatoes and pecans could be grown and sold as successfully as cotton
4. Made starch and wallboard from cotton stalks
5. Made soap, ink, and more than three hundred other products from peanuts
6. Made flour, shoe polish, and several other products from sweet potatoes

7.4c   Reasons

A third kind of supporting sentence that you can use is one that gives a reason. A **reason** is a statement that explains or justifies another statement. A reason answers the question "Why?" for your reader: Why did that event occur? Why is this the way it is? Why should I believe that remark? Why should I perform that action? Facts can serve also as reasons.

In some paragraphs each supporting sentence offers a different reason that explains what is said in the topic sentence.

In other paragraphs only one or two supporting sentences actually offer reasons; the remaining supporting sentences further explain those reasons.

The topic sentence of the following paragraph is in italics. The supporting sentences of the paragraph give reasons that explain the topic sentence.

Model

Topic Sentence	*In the Northwest Passage, the sea route that threads its way through the Canadian Arctic, danger is never very far away for ships and their*
Reason	*crews.* The weather alone makes the voyage difficult. Temperatures often fall to −50°F (−46°C), strong winds blow off the polar ice cap, and visibility is frequently near zero. Navi-
Reason	gation by compass is not possible because the magnetic North Pole lies along the route, and radio communications are often interrupted by
Reason	Arctic blackouts. The greatest menace, however, is the polar ice pack. This immense mass of ice clogs much of the passage all year long Huge pieces of ice, some of them miles long, often break free from the pack and float into open waters, where they can trap or sink a ship that has overcome the other dangers of the Northwest Passage.

Exercise 5   Prewriting: Reasons   On your paper, write the topic sentence and the two reasons that explain the topic sentence of the following paragraph. Then write the numbers of the supporting sentences that further explain each reason.

(1) The truth about pigs is that their reputation for being dull and dirty is undeserved. (2) The pig is actually a curious and intelligent animal. (3) For instance, a pig will not take anything for granted; it will push, poke, and prod

something until it arrives at a conclusion.   (4) A pig's intelligence is so keen that the animal needs to do something only once—such as turn on an automatic drinking fountain—to know how to do it again.   (5) Furthermore, pigs are basically no dirtier than any other farm animal.   (6) Because pigs don't sweat, they seek out water in order to cool off.   (7) On a farm, the water that a pig finds is usually in a mud puddle.   (8) However, the pig would be just as happy splashing in a bathtub, since it's water, not dirt, that pigs enjoy.

Exercise 6   Writing: Reasons   On your paper, write a paragraph using the topic sentence provided. Use the reasons listed to write supporting sentences.

Topic Sentence: There are several reasons why the germs that people encounter every day do not make them continually sick.
Reasons:

1. Skin is barrier that prevents most germs from entering body
2. Mucous membranes and mucus they produce stop many germs from entering areas not covered by skin
3. Some germs that reach eye washed out by tears or killed by substance in the tears
4. Acid in stomach destroys germs swallowed with food and drink
5. Antitoxins in blood stream fight bacteria or gather them together so that white blood cells can destroy them

Exercise 7   Prewriting: Supporting Details   On your paper, write what kind of supporting details—facts, examples, or reasons—would be most suitable for developing the following topic sentences.

SAMPLE   Seaweed has many uses outside the ocean.
ANSWER   examples

1. The city would save money if school were in session throughout the entire year.

2. Some flowers appear while snow is still on the ground.
3. Preserving food must be done carefully.
4. The first microscopes were developed near the end of the sixteenth century.
5. Monet is only one of several Impressionist painters.
6. The Inca empire in South America was supported by its successful farming.
7. During the Ice Age, glaciers caused many changes in the land.
8. A complex of tunnels underneath Walt Disney World keeps visitors from seeing the collection of garbage, the delivery of goods, and the performance of other chores.
9. In the United States, six different coins are produced for use as money.
10. Whitewater rafting can be a dangerous sport.

Assignment 1 Prewriting Choose one of the following topic sentences and write it on your paper. Below it, list facts that you could use to support it. If necessary, use an encyclopedia or other reference book to find appropriate facts.

1. Geysers are unusual geological formations.
2. The word *twilight* refers to a specific time interval of the day.
3. Blood circulates through the body in a complex system.
4. Roberto Clemente accomplished a great deal in his lifetime.
5. Interesting tree-planting traditions are associated with Arbor Day.

Assignment 2 Prewriting Choose one of the following topic sentences and write it on your paper. Below it, list examples that could be used to support it. If necessary, use a reference book to find appropriate examples.

1. Some cities in North America have trouble with air pollution.
2. Certain sports require a good sense of balance.
3. Many of Mark Twain's books present his own experiences.

4. Some fabrics and clothing are designed to protect people from the sun in the summer.

5. Some mammals live in the ocean.

Assignment 3   Prewriting   Choose one of the following topic sentences and write it on your paper. Below it, list reasons that you could use to support it. If necessary, use a reference book to find appropriate reasons.

1. Animals such as bears hibernate during winter for specific reasons.

2. Exercising regularly contributes to good health.

3. Whirlpools form for several reasons.

4. Some people believe that Shakespeare did not write the plays attributed to him.

5. Farmers grow winter rye for many reasons.

Assignment 4   Writing   Write a paragraph using the list of details that you created for a topic sentence in Assignment 1, Assignment 2, or Assignment 3. Write supporting sentences from your list of details.

Continuing Assignment   Writing   In the Continuing Assignment on page 308, you wrote topic sentences for your two lists of details. Now convert your lists of details to sentences that state facts, examples, or reasons that support your topic sentences. Save your paper.

Assignment Checklist

Check your assignments for the following points:

✔ 1. Do your supporting details that state facts include such information as events, characteristics, observations, and statistics?

316

✔ 2. Do your supporting details that give examples name typical samples of the group identified in the topic sentence?

✔ 3. Do your supporting details that give reasons answer the question "Why?" about another statement?

✔ 4. Did you write supporting sentences from your list of details?

7.5 Writing a Concluding Sentence

After you have composed a topic sentence and supporting sentences, you will sometimes want a concluding sentence that summarizes your thoughts and brings your paragraph to a close. You will often need a concluding sentence when the paragraph stands by itself instead of forming part of a longer piece of writing.

A concluding sentence can restate your topic sentence or can offer a final comment about the topic. By restating the topic sentence, you remind your reader of the main point. Such a restatement, of course, should be worded differently from the topic sentence. The concluding sentence ought to say the same thing but in a fresh way.

In the following paragraph, the concluding sentence restates the topic sentence and strengthens the reader's understanding of the topic of the paragraph.

Model

Topic sentence

Have you thought of weeds as a help in meeting our petroleum needs? According to Dr. Russell Buchanan of the United States Department of Agriculture, "Ragweed, sow thistle, and other common weeds could become a mainstay of the chemical industry because they are

317

Concluding
sentence

high in hydrocarbons, oils, and rubber." Buchanan points out that weeds are easy to grow, despite insects, poor weather, and undernourished soil. *Weeds may be an alternative to crude oil as a source of petroleum.*

Instead of restating the topic sentence, you may offer a final comment about the topic in the concluding sentence. Your final comment may take many forms. You can state a logical conclusion, give a personal impression or feeling, pose a question, recommend a course of action, and so on. However, your final comment must meet one important requirement: it must be based on what has already been said in the paragraph.

The concluding sentences that follow could be used for the paragraph on weeds and petroleum given earlier. Each demonstrates a different method for offering a final comment on the topic.

Concluding sentence stating a logical conclusion:

Clearly, weeds offer us an opportunity we should not pass up to develop a cheap and dependable source of fuel.

Concluding sentence stating a personal impression:

It is ironic that the weeds we have always regarded as a worthless nuisance may someday prove to be a valuable resource.

Concluding sentence asking a question:

Could it be that we have, growing in our own back yards, at least part of the answer to the energy crisis?

Concluding sentence stating a course of action:

The chemical industry should make immediate efforts to develop the technology necessary for converting weeds into petroleum.

Exercise 1 Prewriting: Concluding Sentences On your paper, write the letter of the most appropriate concluding sentence from the three choices given after each of the following paragraphs.

1.   Sunlight passing through a closed window puts heat inside a room. To prevent the room from heating, you can block out the sunlight by lowering shades or drawing curtains. You can also lower an awning outside the window to block the sun's rays.

    a. Sunlight warms cool rooms in winter but makes them hotter in summer.

    b. Either way, you will stay cooler without the direct sunlight.

    c. A hot room can be uncomfortable.

2.   Soccer is a fast and exciting sport. It combines the speed of hockey with the strategy of football. Eleven players, including a goalie, make up a team. The object of the game is to move the ball down the field and into the opposing team's goal. Only the goalies can touch the ball with their hands. With no time-outs allowed except for injuries, the action of the game is nearly continuous.

    a. However, I prefer a slower-moving game.

    b. Soccer, like most sports, provides good exercise.

    c. Because of its speed and excitement, soccer is rapidly growing in popularity.

3.   Many families in the United States have joined food cooperatives to save money on their grocery bills. In a food cooperative, the members buy food collectively. Each week the members of a food cooperative list the food that they want. All of the orders are combined, and the cooperative buys cases of food from warehouses. The food is then distributed to the members according to their orders.

    a. Therefore, many families have joined food cooperatives.

    b. By joining together to buy their food, the families in a cooperative pay much less.

    c. There are other ways to save money too.

Exercise 2 Writing: Concluding Sentences On your paper, write five possible concluding sentences for the paragraph that follows. Write one of each of the following types:

    a. one that restates the topic sentence
    b. one that states a logical conclusion
    c. one that states a personal impression or feeling
    d. one that asks a question
    e. one that states a course of action

      Warts were a puzzle for centuries, but their cause is now well understood. A wart is caused by a virus that enters the body through a cut, a scrape, or some other break in the skin. A cover of cells grows into a small, hard lump over the virus. The lump may be gray or brown, flat or raised, single or part of a cluster. A wart may last for months or years, and then disappear, sometimes to reappear in the same spot. Warts may also spread to other parts of the body if the surface of a wart breaks and contacts healthy skin.

Exercise 3 Writing: Concluding Sentences On your paper, write two paragraphs, one for each of two of the lists of sentences given in the exercise on pages 297-298. Begin each paragraph with the topic sentence and arrange the supporting sentences in a logical order. Be sure to omit the sentence in each list that is not related to the topic. Then write a concluding sentence for each paragraph. One concluding sentence should restate the topic sentence. The other should offer a final comment in any of the ways listed on page 318.

Assignment Writing Write a paragraph on a topic of your choice. You may use facts, examples, or reasons in your supporting sentences. Write two possible concluding sentences for your paragraph. For the first, restate the topic sentence. For the second, state a personal impression or feeling.

Continuing Assignment Writing In the Continuing Assignments in this unit, you selected and narrowed a topic. Then you wrote a topic sentence and supporting sentences for two paragraphs. Now, to complete your Continuing Assignments, write a concluding sentence for each paragraph.

Assignment Checklist

Check your assignments for the following points:

✔ 1. Did you write a concluding sentence that restates your topic sentence?
✔ 2. Did you write a concluding sentence that offers a final comment on the topic?

The Encyclopedia of Everything There Is to Know: Writing an Article

Situation: You are a staff writer for *The Encyclopedia of Everything There Is to Know*, a new encyclopedia for high school students. The publication will be competing against other encyclopedias for readers. Every article, including yours, must deliver a maximum of information in the fewest words possible. As you write, keep the following information in mind.

Writer: you as staff writer for the encyclopedia

Audience: high school students

Topics: samurai, silk

Purpose: to inform fully in one paragraph

Directions: To write your article, follow these directions:

Step 1. Study the sample article on the saber-toothed tiger.

Saber-Toothed Tiger

The Saber-Toothed Tiger was a catlike prehistoric animal. The cat acquired its name because of the two long, fanglike teeth in the front part of its upper jaw. The teeth looked like sabers (curved swords). They were very effective in making the cat the equal of its much larger prey. Fossils of the saber-toothed cat have been found on several continents. The largest find in the United States was at the Rancho La Brea tar pits in California. The cat was a fierce predator, but it disappeared about 12,000 years ago when its prey became extinct.

Step 2. Read the information on either "samurai" or "silk." The information is not necessarily listed in the order in which it should appear in your article.

Step 3. Choose either topic, and organize your article as follows: statement of topic (topic sentence), history or background (supporting sentences), and current status or use (concluding sentence).

INFORMATION SHEET FOR STAFF WRITERS

Topic: samurai   Topic: silk

Facts

Topic: samurai	Topic: silk
Military class in feudal Japan	Strongest of all natural fibers; often called "Queen of Fibers"
Name originally referred to men who guarded the emperor	Strong, shiny fiber (a threadlike substance) of great beauty
Known for obedience and loyalty to their daimyo (war lord)	Fiber produced by the silkworm
Title of samurai inherited	Silkworm spins a cocoon made of silk fibers
Held honor above money or life	Fibers drawn off cocoon, processed, and woven into material
Lost privileges in 1871	
Also served the shogun, the "great general" of Japan	Finished material used to make many items. Examples: designer dresses, high-quality neckties, scarves, furniture upholstery, sheets, and curtains
Wore two swords and an elaborate headdress	
Have inspired many legends and stories. Modern examples: movies, novels, TV specials	

Unit Assignments

Assignment 1   *Step 1:* Select one topic from each of the following groups and use it to write a topic sentence. You will have three topic sentences. *Step 2:* Below the first topic sentence, list at least four facts that you could include in supporting sentences. *Step 3:* Below the second topic sentence, list at least three examples. *Step 4:* Below the third topic sentence, list at least two reasons. If you wish, you may think of your own topic for each category. You may also look up information on a topic before beginning the assignment.

SUPPORT WITH FACTS
The components of air
Changes in the automobile
How fish breathe

SUPPORT WITH EXAMPLES
Situations that require patience
Famous actors
Unusual animals

SUPPORT WITH REASONS
My favorite season
The change to the metric system
Being self-reliant

Assignment 2   Select two of the lists that you wrote in Assignment 1, and write a paragraph from each list. Be sure that each paragraph contains a topic sentence and supporting sentences stating facts, examples, or reasons. End each paragraph with a suitable concluding sentence.

Assignment 3   Write a paragraph about a geographic exploration. You may write about one of the explorations listed in this assignment or some other exploration. Limit your topic, and write a topic sentence. Use facts as supporting details, and end the paragraph with a concluding sentence that restates your topic sentence.

1. Exploration of the North Pole
2. First landing on the moon

3. Exploration of the upper Mississippi River region
4. Search for the Fountain of Youth

Assignment 4   Write a paragraph on the many ways that news of current events is transmitted to people. Use supporting sentences that give examples of at least three different ways. End your paragraph with a concluding sentence that recommends a course of action.

Assignment 5   Write a paragraph to explain why people wear shoes, hats, ties, or some other item of clothing. In your supporting sentences, give at least three reasons. End your paragraph with a concluding sentence that expresses a personal impression.

Revising Your Assignments

For help in revising a paragraph, consult the Checklist for Revision on the last page of this book.

Unit Tests

Test 1

A. Number your paper from 1 to 5. Next to each number, write *True* if the sentence is true or *False* if it is false.

1. You can use reasons in your supporting sentences.
2. A concluding sentence is the same as the topic sentence.
3. The first step in planning is writing a topic sentence.
4. A limited topic gives you a focus for your paragraph.
5. When you choose a topic for your paragraph, choose a subject that you are familiar with or are prepared to study.

B. Number your paper from 6 to 10. Next to each number, write the letter of the term that correctly completes the sentence. You will not use one of the terms.

a. topic sentence
b. concluding sentence
c. unity
d. paragraph
e. supporting details
f. example

6. A(n) _?_ may state a logical conclusion, give a personal impression, ask a question, or suggest a course of action.
7. A paragraph has _?_ when each of its sentences clearly contributes to the unit by saying something about the topic.
8. A(n) _?_ contains a topic sentence, supporting sentences, and, often, a concluding sentence.
9. A(n) _?_ states the main idea of a paragraph.
10. Facts, examples, and reasons are types of _?_.

C. Number your paper from 11 to 15. Read the following paragraph. Next to each number, write the letter that correctly answers each question about the paragraph.

(1) Maria Mitchell had an outstanding career as the first female astronomer. (2) As a child in Nantucket, Massachusetts, she studied the sky from her father's observatory and, when she was just twelve years old, helped record the time of an eclipse. (3) In 1847 Maria Mitchell discovered a new

comet. (4) Because of this discovery, the comet was named for her, and she received a gold medal from the King of Denmark. (5) In later years she was a respected astronomy professor at Vassar College and continued studies of sunspots and satellites. (6) Eventually, because of her contributions to astronomy, Maria Mitchell was the first woman elected to the American Academy of Arts and Sciences.

11. Which of the following describes the topic of the paragraph?

   a. The study of astronomy
   b. The childhood of Maria Mitchell
   c. The career of Maria Mitchell

12. In the paragraph, which of the following is the topic sentence?

   a. Sentence 1   c. Sentence 5
   b. Sentence 2   d. Sentence 6

13. Which sentence does *not* contain a supporting fact?

   a. Sentence 2   c. Sentence 3
   b. Sentence 1   d. Sentence 6

14. Which of the following is *not* a supporting sentence that you might include in the paragraph?

   a. Maria Mitchell was elected to the Hall of Fame in 1905.
   b. Maria Mitchell was largely self-educated.
   c. Maria Mitchell enjoyed teaching astronomy very much.

15. Which of the following would be the best concluding sentence?

   a. Maria Mitchell was also a schoolteacher and librarian.
   b. Astronomy was important to the Nantucket fishermen.
   c. Even today, Maria Mitchell's career in astronomy is inspiring to young women scientists.

Test 2

Choose one of the Unit Assignments. Write the paragraph as directed and hand it in to your teacher.

Organizing
Paragraphs

Unit Preview

Coherence is the clear and orderly presentation of ideas. You make a paragraph coherent by arranging the supporting details logically and by making clear the connection between them. As you read the following paragraph, notice how the details are arranged and connected.

Clear topic sentence

Relevant supporting sentences

(1) So fierce was the Black Death that swept Europe in 1348 that people were driven to try some rather extraordinary remedies. (2) Certain of these **bizarre cures** were aimed at ridding the air of its "badness." (3) *For example,* towns would ring bells all day in hope of scattering any **plague gases** in the air. (4) People would *also* douse the walls of their homes with scent, hoping to offset the **foulness** of the **disease** with the sweetness of perfume. (5) *Other* **unusual treatments** involved animals. (6) Smelling a pig, *for instance,* was thought to **help** a person suffering from the **disease,** and toads were considered useful for extracting the poison from **plague** boils. (7) Perhaps the most **curious** of the home remedies was that of writing the magical term "abracadabra" in exotic shapes on a card and hanging the card from a string worn around the neck.

Concluding sentence

(8) In spite of their **imaginativeness,** *though,* none of these **remedies** proved to be at all effective.

The paragraph is coherent for the following reasons:

It contains a clear topic sentence, relevant supporting sentences, and a suitable concluding sentence.

It contains topic reminders, that is, key words of the topic sentence and synonyms of these words. For example, the word *bizarre* in the second sentence reminds readers of the word *extraordinary* in the topic sentence. The topic reminders are in boldface in the model paragraph.

The paragraph contains transitional words, such as *for example* and *other,* to introduce and connect the ideas. The transitional words are in italics in the model paragraph.

The ideas in the paragraph are arranged in an orderly fashion. Five plague remedies are discussed in the paragraph. The first two are related to the air, the second two involve animals, and the last one deals with magic.

For Analysis On your paper, follow these instructions about the model paragraph.

1. Write the topic sentence.
2. List the topic reminders for each of the following key words: *Black Death, extraordinary, remedies.*
3. List the transitional words and phrases used to introduce or connect ideas.

As you plan a paragraph, ask yourself, "What order will make the most sense to my readers?" Your answer will depend on your purpose and on the information that you wish to present. This unit will give you practice in arranging the details in a paragraph according to different types of order.

8.1 Chronological Order

Chronological order is a way of organizing events according to the time in which they happen. When you use chronological order, you begin with what is oldest or happens first, and you end with what is newest or happens last.

Chronological order is useful for relating historical events, telling a story, or explaining a process.

The writer of the following paragraph has organized events chronologically.

Model

> Fiddling with the amplifier, the stage director asked me to turn off the house lights. I took a deep breath and heard the principal announcing the guest speaker. Feeling strangely like the Wizard of Oz, I pulled down the dimmer levers of the light console and reached for the first of the breaker switches. The amplifier buzzed obnoxiously, underscoring the clicking of the switches as I hit them one by one. I finished the first row and began on the second. The audience murmured and the speaker faltered, and then a hush fell over the auditorium as I continued flicking the breaker switches, undeterred. The stage director whirled to me. Seeing what I had done, he burst into uncontrollable laughter. "You just turned off all the stage lights," he finally managed to gasp, reaching for the innocuous switches. I wanted to crawl into a dark niche somewhere and hide. The stage manager was still chuckling beside the light console as the speaker resumed.
>
> *Rebecca Morgan, Beaver Area High School*
> *Beaver, Pennsylvania*

The chronological arrangement of ideas in the preceding paragraph is made clear by transitional words such as *first, as, then,* and *just.* There are many other transitional words and phrases that you can use to indicate a chronological arrangement of ideas. The following are among the most common:

after	earlier	next
after a while	eventually	now
after that	finally	second
as soon as	first	since
at first	in the end	since then
at the same time	later	soon
before	meanwhile	then

You can also show chronological order with time-related words that specify a particular time, date, or period. Examples are *at five o'clock in the morning, January 12,* and *for five years.*

Exercise 1 Prewriting: Transitional Words Number your paper from 1 to 4. Beside each number, write the appropriate transitional word or phrase for each blank to show the chronological order of the events in the paragraph. Do not use a word or phrase more than once.

after	before	soon
after that	first	then

    The hard shell that protects a lobster from other creatures in the ocean does not grow with the lobster, so the lobster must occasionally shed its shell and grow a new one. The shedding process is simple. __1__, the lobster produces a substance that makes its shell soft. __2__ it flexes its muscles and breaks open the old shell, revealing a newly formed shell. __3__ the old shell is shed, the lobster hides until the new shell is hard enough to protect it. During the first month of its life, the lobster loses its shell four times. __4__, the male changes its shell once a year, and the female changes its shell once every two years. Some lobsters may go through the shedding process eighteen or nineteen times.

Exercise 2 Prewriting: Chronological Order On your paper, arrange the following list of sentences in chronological order to form a paragraph. The first sentence of the paragraph should be the topic sentence. Underline all the transitional and time-related words and phrases.

1. George's daughter Myra rediscovered the gem ten years later in a jewelry store window and immediately purchased it.
2. The magnificent "Starfire" gem was in and out of the Van Buren family's hands for ten generations.

3. It was first acquired at an auction in 1604 by Colonel Marcus Van Buren and was passed to descendants for seventy-five years.

4. Then, in 1680, George Van Buren, a spendthrift and a gambler, lost the "Starfire" in a card game.

5. Rudolf hired an entire detective agency, and soon the friend had been apprehended and the gem recovered.

6. Unfortunately, the Van Buren family suffered financial disaster in the early 1800s, and the gem had to be sold.

7. During the time of Rudolf Van Buren, Myra's great-nephew, the gem was stolen by a so-called family friend.

Exercise 3   Writing: Chronological Order   On your paper, write a paragraph arranged in chronological order. Use the information in the following list. First, write a topic sentence for the paragraph. Then use the dates and other information to write the supporting sentences. Use at least three transitional words or phrases to emphasize the chronological order. Underline the transitional words that you use.

1. New Year's night, 1801: Father Giuseppe Piazzi, Italian astronomer, discovers previously unreported object circling sun between Mars and Jupiter.

2. 1802: Heinrich Olbers, German physician and amateur astronomer, discovers second object in same orbit as Piazzi's.

3. 1804 and 1807: Several astronomers, working independently, spot third and fourth objects in same orbit.

4. 1810: Olbers concludes that objects are remains of a shattered planet that once orbited between Mars and Jupiter.

5. 1810 to present: More than 1700 similar objects are discovered; they are named asteroids and are thought to number 50,000.

6. Present: Many astronomers do not agree with shattered-planet theory; they suggest that asteroids are actually small planets formed in the same way as other planets in the solar system.

Assignment 1 Prewriting List five limited topics for paragraphs that you think would call for chronological order. Explain why you would use chronological order to develop each topic.

Assignment 2 Prewriting/Writing Using chronological order, write a paragraph about yourself. In the paragraph, relate some of the major events that have occurred in your life in the past three years, for instance, entering a new school, moving to a new home, joining a team or club. Use dates and transitional words to emphasize the chronological organization of your paragraph. Underline the transitional words.

Assignment 3 Prewriting/Writing Recall a humorous incident. It may be one in which you were involved or one in which someone you know was involved. List the details of the incident and arrange them in chronological order. Then write a paragraph from your list of details. Include transitional words and phrases in your paragraph to show the chronological development of the incident. Underline the transitional words and phrases that you use.

Assignment Checklist

Check your assignments for the following points:

✔ 1. Did you list topics suitable for development by chronological order?
✔ 2. Did you arrange all the events in your paragraphs in the order of their occurrence?
✔ 3. Did you use transitional words that indicate chronological order?
✔ 4. Did you check your paragraphs for correct grammar, usage, spelling, and punctuation?

8.2   Spatial Order

Spatial order is a way of organizing details according to their location in space. It is useful for description. To use spatial order, you begin at a certain point and direct the reader's attention from one item to the next. The direction in which you move depends on your topic and your desired effect. For instance, if you wish to stress the great height of an object, you could describe it from bottom to top. Similarly, you can stress width by describing from side to side, and stress depth by describing from foreground to background.

The writer of the following paragraph describes a pyramid from bottom to top in order to highlight the huge dimensions of the pyramid.

Model

The Great Pyramid of Cheops in Egypt is the lone survivor of the Seven Wonders of the ancient world. Built approximately 4800 years ago, the monument covers thirteen acres at its base and has a perimeter of 3020 feet. The foundation is almost perfectly level, and the four sides of the base align precisely with the points of the compass. The pyramid's four triangular faces rise at equal angles from the ground and are supported by 2,500,000 limestone and granite blocks that weigh from two to seventy tons apiece. These walls were originally wrapped in a 100-inch-thick mantle of beautifully polished limestone blocks, and atop them, 480 feet above the earth, sat a brilliant capstone made of either gold or silver. Although it has been much scarred through the ages, the Great Pyramid of Cheops remains a true wonder of the world.

Transitional words help to show spatial order. In the preceding paragraph, for example, you can more easily visualize the pyramid because the writer uses such words and phrases as *at its base, rise . . . from the ground, atop,* and *above the earth.* There are hundreds of words and phrases that you can use to show spatial order. The following are among the most common:

above	beneath	on
across	beside	outside
alongside	between	over
among	beyond	to
around	down	to the side of
at	in front of	toward
before	inside	under
behind	in the middle	underneath
below	off	up

Exercise 1   Prewriting: Transitional Words   Number your paper from 1 to 5. Beside each number, write the appropriate transitional word or phrase for each blank to show the details in top-to-bottom spatial order. Do not use a word or phrase more than once.

above	down	over
around	in front of	toward
below	in the middle	underneath

   When I was on an airplane for the first time last summer, I spent several minutes becoming familiar with my surroundings. __1__ my seat was a closed compartment for stowing small luggage, and I put my overnight bag inside it. __2__ that compartment and __3__ my head was a set of controls for a light and a fan. On the back of the seat __4__ me were a fold-down tray to hold food and a pocket for magazines. __5__ my seat was a small space into which I had to put my tote bag until the plane had taken off. Once I had surveyed everything, I sat back to enjoy my flight.

Exercise 2   Prewriting: Spatial Order   On your paper, arrange the following list of sentences in spatial order to form a paragraph. The first sentence of the paragraph should be the topic sentence. Underline all space-related transitional words or phrases.

1. In her left arm, Liberty carries a tablet on which is inscribed "July IV, MDCCLXXVI," the nation's birthdate.
2. The statue itself rises 151 feet above the pedestal and weighs 225 tons.
3. Given to this country by France in 1884, Liberty rests on a 150-foot pedestal, supported by steel underpinnings.
4. On Liberty Island in New York Harbor stands the country's most famous woman, the Statue of Liberty.
5. In her right hand, she holds aloft the torch for which she is named: "Liberty Enlightening the World."
6. Her crowned head is stately, with the face turned toward the ocean that so many immigrants have crossed in hope of a new life.

Exercise 3 Writing: Spatial Order Write a paragraph using the following topic sentence and supporting details. Arrange the details in side-to-side spatial order. Use at least four transitional words or phrases in your paragraph. Underline the transitional words that you use.

TOPIC SENTENCE

    I stood in the doorway, gazing at the messy room.

SUPPORTING DETAILS

Bed unmade for days	Trash can overflowing
Clothes in pile on chair	Dresser drawers open
Desk littered with papers	Record albums on floor
Orange peels on dresser	Milk carton on windowsill

Assignment 1 Prewriting List five topics for paragraphs that you think would call for spatial order. Explain why you would use spatial order for each topic.

Assignment 2   Prewriting/Writing   In a newspaper or a magazine, find a picture that you think would be a good subject for a paragraph written in spatial order. Attach the picture to a sheet of paper. On a separate sheet of paper, compose the paragraph. Select the type of spatial order that you think is most suitable for the subject (for example, bottom to top, side to side, foreground to background). Be sure to include transitional words or phrases in your paragraph. Underline the transitional words that you use.

Assignment 3   Writing   Write a paragraph in which you describe a room in which you feel comfortable. Arrange the descriptive details in the type of spatial order that is most suitable for the room. Use transitional words and phrases to show the spatial order. Underline the transitional words and phrases that you use.

Assignment Checklist

Check your assignments for the following points:

  ✔ 1. Did you list topics suitable for development by spatial order?

  ✔ 2. Did you arrange the details in your paragraph to show a particular direction?

  ✔ 3. Did you use transitional words to indicate spatial order?

  ✔ 4. Did you check your paragraph for correct grammar, usage, spelling, and punctuation?

8.3   Order of Importance

    Order of importance is a way of organizing supporting details according to their importance. When you write a paragraph containing a number of equally important items, you can arrange the items in any order. However, in many paragraphs you will want to present your supporting facts, examples, or reasons according to their importance—to develop interest in them, to emphasize their authority, and so on.

When you arrange items according to their importance, you may start with the least important item and proceed to the most important, or you may start with the most important item and proceed to the least important.

You will probably find the order of least to most important to be the more useful of the two. When you use it, you promise readers increasingly more important, and therefore more interesting, ideas. In other words, you build reader interest in your paragraph. The following paragraph contains four main ideas. The topic sentence is in italics, and the ideas are in boldface. The author begins with the least important idea and builds to the most important.

Model

Of all the creatures that inhabit the earth, I find the mosquito the most loathsome. To begin with, **it has an annoying hum.** This hum is particularly irksome when you hear it in your room at night just before going to sleep. If you listen to it long enough, you continue to hear it even after the pest has gone, and you never get to sleep. Much worse than the hum, of course, is what it signifies: **you are about to be bitten.** The mosquito is equipped with a sharp tubular snout that can penetrate the skin. In just one feeding, the insect can extract one-and-a-half times its weight in blood! As if stabbing you and robbing you were not enough, the mosquito also leaves you with an **unsightly red sore and an itch** that won't go away. Worst of all, **mosquitoes are often disease carriers.** Personally, I would shed no tears if the mosquito became an "endangered species" tomorrow.

The order of most to least important is useful for capturing the immediate attention of readers. This order has the advantage of communicating your main point to your reader immediately. The following paragraph illustrates the order of most important to least important. The topic sentence is in italics, and the main details are in boldface.

Model

> *At least three factors contributed to the disappearance of the great dinosaurs.* First was the fact that the **dinosaur's brain was extremely small.** Some dinosaurs had six-foot-long skulls that housed walnut-sized brains. The dinosaur could not cope with the major environmental changes taking place around it. A second factor in the decline of the dinosaur, at least the plant-eating variety, was the **drying-up of water sources.** Some of the plant-eaters had fifty-ton bodies that could be supported only in water. When changes in the climate caused many lakes and swamps to dry up, these water animals had no means of support. Their water-based food supply also diminished. A third factor, perhaps less important than the other two, was that **other animals would feed on the eggs of dinosaurs,** thus hastening their extinction.

Both of the preceding model paragraphs contain certain words and phrases to indicate the relative importance of different ideas: *to begin with, worst of all, first, a second factor,* and so on. Other expressions that you can use to indicate importance include adjectives in the comparative or superlative degree, such as *better, best, worse,* and *worst.* You can also use such transitional words and phrases as *compared to, furthermore, moreover, least important, most important, in the first place, finally, of major concern,* and *of minor concern.*

Exercise 1   Prewriting: Transitional Words   Number your paper from 1 to 4. Beside each number, write the appropriate transitional word or phrase for each blank to show the arrangement of the items from most to least important. Do not use a word or phrase more than once.

even better	first	third
finally	a third factor	worst of all

> You can easily improve your ability to remember someone's name if you follow this method. __1__, listen carefully to the person's name when you are introduced. Repeat the name to yourself, or, __2__, try to spell it out or write it down. __3__, associate a picture with the name. For example, if you meet Mr. Greenwood, think of a green forest. __4__, associate the picture with the person. Visualize Mr. Greenwood as being as tall as one of the trees in the forest that you pictured.

Exercise 2 Prewriting: Order of Importance On your paper, arrange the following list of sentences in order of importance to form a paragraph. The first sentence of the paragraph should be the topic sentence. Then underline the words, including transitional words and phrases, that indicate relative importance.

1. More frustrating than this inconvenience was the sudden invasion of our campsite by an army of red ants, which got into most of our food.
2. My family went on a picnic yesterday, but the outing proved disastrous.
3. For one thing, no one had remembered to bring forks and spoons.
4. Even more stimulating than the ant raid was the torrent of rain that drenched us as soon as the ants left.
5. Worst of all was the trip home; we took a short cut and got lost.
6. But the rain was refreshing compared to the war we waged against a swarm of angry bees.
7. Apparently, they didn't like our taking shelter from the rain under the tree in which their hive was located.

Exercise 3 Writing: Order of Importance On your paper, write a paragraph using the following topic sentence and supporting details. *Step 1:* Rank the supporting details from least important to most important. *Step 2:* Write a sentence that states each detail. *Step 3:* Combine the sentences into a paragraph. Use at least four transitional words or phrases that indicate degree of importance. *Step 4:* Underline the transitional words that you use.

TOPIC SENTENCE

> The law of the land guarantees United States citizens many vital rights.

SUPPORTING DETAILS

> The right to vote in public elections
>
> The right to life, liberty, and the pursuit of happiness
>
> The right to speak and to worship freely
>
> The right to receive fair payment for property taken for public use
>
> The right to a speedy and public trial

Assignment 1 Prewriting/Writing Jot down the major events reported on the front page of a newspaper. Rank the events from the least to the most important. Use your list to write a paragraph developed in order of importance. Include transitional words that indicate the degree of importance of the various events.

Assignment 2 Prewriting/Writing Select one of the following persons and list at least three of his or her accomplishments. You may use a reference work to help you complete the list. Arrange the person's accomplishments in the order of most to least important. Then write a paragraph that reflects this order. In the paragraph use transitional words and phrases that indicate the decreasing importance of the accomplishments. Underline the transitional words and phrases that you use.

1. Ansel Adams
2. Shirley Chisholm
3. Leonardo da Vinci

4. Agnes De Mille
5. Benjamin Franklin
6. Julia Ward Howe

Assignment 3   Prewriting / Writing   Select one of the following job titles. List and describe the duties of a person who has that job. Arrange the duties in the order of least important to most important. Then write a paragraph about the duties of a person with that job. In your pargraph use transitional words and phrases that indicate order of increasing importance.

1. Telephone operator
2. Receptionist

3. Dietitian
4. Pharmacist

Assignment Checklist

Check your assignments for the following points:

✔ 1. Did you arrange the ideas in the paragraphs from least to most important or from most to least important?
✔ 2. Did you use transitional words to indicate the order of importance?
✔ 3. Did you check your paragraphs for correct grammar, usage, spelling, and punctuation?

8.4   Comparison and Contrast

You can organize a paragraph through comparison, contrast, or a combination of the two.

Comparison

A simple **comparison** shows how two or more items are alike. The following paragraph is an example of development by comparison.

Model

> Perhaps the greatest athletes the United States has ever produced were Jim Thorpe (1888–1953) and Mildred "Babe" Didrikson Zaharias (1914–1956). These two giants of the sports world were alike in many ways. Both achieved All-American status as amateurs, Thorpe for his football exploits in 1911 and 1912 and Didrikson for her performance in basketball in 1930 and 1931. Each was a great Olympic champion. In the 1912 Olympic Games, Thorpe became the first athlete to win both the pentathlon and the decathlon. Didrikson took home two gold medals from the 1932 Olympics and narrowly missed a third. The outstanding similarity between Jim Thorpe and Babe Didrikson was their proficiency in so many sports. Thorpe is remembered for his achievements in track and field, football, and baseball; Didrikson, for her superiority in golf, basketball, and track and field. There was almost no sport in which the two did not excel. In 1950 the Associated Press named Jim Thorpe and Babe Didrikson the outstanding male and female athletes of the first half of the twentieth century.

You can sometimes use comparisons to help readers understand something that may be unfamiliar to them. In the following paragraph, for example, the writer has explained the science of archaeology by comparing it with the more familiar subject of crime detection. As you read the paragraph, note the words and phrases that refer to detective work.

Model

> Of all the sciences archaeology is perhaps the most appealing. For archaeologists are in fact detectives, and we all have something of the detective in us. We like to work out puzzles and solve mysteries—which is what archaeologists do.

They find clues and follow them, then reconstruct what happened and try to interpret its meaning. They try to find out the way our ancestors lived—how they got their food and built their houses and worked and fought. They try to learn about their skills, their trade, their travels, their fun. Above all, they want to get at the mind and spirit of [our ancestors]. What did our dead-and-gone ancestors believe? What did they feel? What did they imagine?

Anne Terry White, *All About Archaeology*

You can use transitional words and phrases such as the following to help you show a comparison:

alike	both	like	similar
also	compared to	the same as	similarly

Contrast

You can develop some paragraphs by **contrast,** which shows how two or more items differ. Therefore, when you develop a paragraph by contrast, you concentrate on the differences between things, not on their similarities. Of course, you can contrast only items that are alike in some way. The writer of the following paragraph contrasts two members of a family.

Model

My sister and I are close in age, but that's about the only way in which we're similar. I love to talk, even to myself. I prefer to go to bed as late as possible and will sleep well past breakfast if our parents don't wake me up. I also tend to have a hot temper, and I can't think of a better thing to do with money than spend it. Julie, on the other hand, is very quiet. Unlike me, she goes to bed early and wouldn't think of sleeping later than 7 A.M. Finally, Julie is slow to anger and even slower at spending money. Although I might not admit it to her, in those last two ways I would like to be similar to, not different from, Julie.

344

You can use transitional words and phrases such as the following to help you show a contrast:

although	in contrast	unlike
but	nevertheless	while
different	on the other hand	yet
however		

Balance in Comparisons and Contrasts

Balance is important in any paragraph developed by comparison, by contrast, or by both methods. For every detail that you present about item A, you should present a corresponding detail about item B.

You may arrange these details in either of two ways:

1. You can follow each point that you make about item A by a corresponding point about item B. The pattern of such a paragraph is AB AB AB, and so on. This alternating pattern is used in the model paragraph on page 343.

2. You can group all of the details about item A in the first half of the paragraph and all of those about item B in the second half. The pattern of this kind of paragraph is AAA BBB. The model paragraph on page 344 uses this pattern.

Whichever approach you choose, you should present the details about item B in the same order that you use for the details about item A.

Exercise 1   Prewriting: Transitional Words   Number your paper from 1 to 6. Beside each number, write the appropriate word or phrase for each blank that makes clear the comparison or contrast between the items in the paragraph. Do not use a word or phrase more than once.

alike	both	on the other hand
also	however	while

Although modern dance and ballet have some similarities, they are really quite different dance forms. The ballet dancer and the modern dancer __1__ wish to entertain an audience. __2__, modern dance and ballet are __3__ because in both arts the dancers move in steps planned by a choreographer. __4__, the dance forms differ considerably in important ways. Ballet requires a courtly bearing, __5__ modern dance makes use of more natural body positions. In ballet the emphasis is on following a tradition. Modern dance, __6__, emphasizes the originality of the individual.

Exercise 2   Prewriting: Comparison and Contrast

The following paragraph compares and contrasts the sports of football and rugby in a disorganized manner. On your paper, make a chart like the one in the sample. On your chart, match the details showing similarities and differences between football and rugby. Save your paper.

SAMPLE

Similarities	Differences	
	Football	Rugby
contact sport	11 players	15 players

The game of football was derived from the British game of rugby, although the sports differ quite a bit today. Football is a contact sport played with an egg-shaped ball. It involves running, kicking, passing, and tackling. The game is played with two teams of eleven players each. In rugby each team has fifteen players. A football field is a little over 53 yards wide and 100 yards long, with goalposts at each end of the field. Rugby, too, is a contact sport involving running, kicking, passing, and tackling. A rugby field is about 75 yards by about 100 yards with a goal at each end. The aim in football is to move the ball across the opponent's goal line. The ball used in rugby is rounder and larger than a football, but the aim of rugby, like that of football, is to move the ball across the goal line of the opponent.

Exercise 3 Writing: Comparison and Contrast On your paper, rewrite the paragraph on football and rugby. Use your chart from Exercise 2. Follow each point about football with a corresponding point of comparison or contrast about rugby so that your paragraph has an AB AB pattern. In rewriting the paragraph, you may change the wording and combine some of the sentences.

Exercise 4 Writing: Comparison From the following list, select three corresponding details that show similarities between directing traffic and conducting an orchestra. Use these details to develop a paragraph by comparison, arranging the facts in AAA BBB order. You may change the wording and combine some of the details. Be sure that your paragraph has a topic sentence and a concluding sentence.

TRAFFIC DIRECTORS	ORCHESTRA CONDUCTORS
Move hands and arms to direct drivers	Poor-sounding music or disappointed audiences may result from their absence or faulty performance
Surrounded by automobiles and by honking horns	Surrounded by orchestra music and often by an audience
Traffic jams or auto accidents may result from their absence or faulty performance	Use batons to direct musicians
Use whistles to gain the attention of drivers	Move hands and arms to direct musicians playing a selection

Exercise 5   Writing: Contrast   From the following list, select three corresponding facts that show differences between the United States Senate and the House of Representatives. Use these facts to develop a paragraph by contrast, arranging the facts in AB AB order. You may change the wording and combine the facts in your sentences. Be sure that your paragraph has a topic sentence and a concluding sentence.

FACTS ABOUT THE SENATE	FACTS ABOUT THE HOUSE
Has 100 members	Begins action on impeachment
Senators serve six-year terms	
Each state has two senators	Legal minimum age for representatives is twenty-five
One senator from each party is floor leader	Passes tax and revenue bills before they go to Senate
Receives tax and revenue bills from the House	Number of representatives depends on population of state
Acts as court for impeachment	Members serve two-year terms
Votes on treaties	One representative from each party is floor leader
Legal minimum age for senators is thirty	Has 435 members

Assignment 1   Prewriting   Choose one of the following topic sentences and write it on your paper. Then list at least three points that you would use to develop a paragraph by comparison.

1. Libraries and museums share some of the same functions.
2. While earthquakes are not fiery like volcanic eruptions, they both share several characteristics.
3. Having either chicken pox or measles will keep you at home, but the two diseases have more in common than their ability to confine you to bed.

Assignment 2   Prewriting   Choose one of the following topic sentences and write it on your paper. Then list at least three points that you would use to develop a paragraph by contrast.

1. Building a doll house and building a real house are different processes.
2. Although both stars and planets shine in the night sky, they differ from one another in many ways.
3. Some people confuse dolphins with porpoises.

Assignment 3   Writing   Write a paragraph of comparison or contrast. Use the list of details that you compiled for either Assignment 1 or Assignment 2.

Assignment 4   Prewriting/Writing   Write a paragraph in which you contrast your elementary school with the school that you now attend. Before you begin writing, make a list of major differences between the two. Then group corresponding details in AAA BBB order, and use them in your paragraph.

Assignment Checklist

Check your assignments for the following points:

 ✔ 1. Did you list at least three corresponding points of comparison or contrast?
 ✔ 2. Did you group the points in AAA BBB order?
 ✔ 3. Did you use transitional words to show either comparison or contrast?
 ✔ 4. Did you check your paragraph for correct grammar, usage, spelling, and punctuation?

Touring the State Capital: An Announcement

Situation: The Travelers' Club has raised enough money to make its annual trip. This year members have voted to go to the state capital. As president of the club, you are writing an announcement of the day's highlights. Keep the following information in mind as you write.

Writer: you as president of the Travelers' Club
Audience: members of the Travelers' Club
Topic: proposed trip to the state capital
Purpose: to generate enthusiasm for the tour

Directions: To write your announcement, follow these steps.

Step 1. Read the attached schedule. Select important and interesting highlights.

Step 2. Arrange these highlights in order of importance, saving the most exciting event for last.

Step 3. Write a paragraph describing highlights of the tour. Be informal and enthusiastic in tone. Be sure to use transitional words and phrases to show the importance of the events.

SCHEDULE FOR ONE—DAY TOUR OF STATE CAPITAL

Date of tour: April 15

Hour of departure: 6 A.M.

Expected hour of return: 10 P.M.

6 A.M.   Meet advisors, and board bus at main entrance to cafeteria.

6:15   Bus departs.

8:30   Breakfast at Capitol Diner opposite courthouse. The Diner's specialty: waffles with an international flair.

10:00   Tour of governor's mansion. Includes Blue Room, West Wing, State Dining Room, art collection, furniture from different periods. Final highlight: walk through the governor's study.

Noon   Picnic lunch on the hillside overlooking the reflecting pool and fountain outside the State Legislature.

1 P.M.   Guided tour of State Legislature. Meet the state representative from our district. Question—and—answer session.

3:00   Visit to the Antiques Museum. Highlights include an original Rumford fireplace, the first telephone in the state, early American furniture and crafts, American Indian artifacts, fossils. A talk on local history, illustrated with slides.

5:00   Dinner in the dining room of the Hotel Diplomat. Guest speaker: Congresswoman McKinnon.

7:30   Board bus for home.

Unit Assignments

Assignment 1   In a paragraph tell a friend how to do something that you know how to do well. For example, explain how to build a kite or how to play table tennis. Use transitional words to show chronological order and to help your friend progress from one step to the next.

Assignment 2   Using spatial order, write a paragraph describing your home as it looks when you stand across the street from it. Help your reader to visualize your home by using transitional words that show spatial order.

Assignment 3   Imagine that you are going to a cabin in the woods for a month. In a paragraph, explain what things other than food and clothing you think would be most important to take with you. Use transitional words to emphasize the greater importance of some objects.

Assignment 4   Write a paragraph in which you compare or contrast the ways two people think about the same subject. For example, you could compare two friends' opinions about playing baseball or about reading mystery stories.

Assignment 5 Write a paragraph about the equipment needed to play a game or to cook your favorite dish. Present the equipment in the order in which each item is needed or in the order of its importance.

Assignment 6   Write a paragraph in which you recount an event. It may be a historical event or one in which you participated. Use transitional words and phrases to show the chronological development of the event.

Assignment 7   Write a paragraph in which you give the reasons why one of the following creatures is generally disliked. Arrange your reasons from the least important to the most important, and use appropriate transitional words and phrases.

1. Spiders
2. Snakes
3. Bats
4. Wolves

Assignment 8 Write a paragraph in which you compare and contrast a book that you have read and a movie that has been made from it. Include the points of comparison first, followed by the points of difference. Arrange the points in AB AB order. Use words and phrases to make clear the comparison and contrast.

Revising Your Assignments

For help in revising a paragraph, consult the Checklist for Revision on the last page of this book.

Unit Tests

Test 1

A. Number your paper from 1 to 5. Next to each number, write *True* if the sentence is true or *False* if it is false.

1. Spatial order is useful for relating historical events, telling a story, or explaining a process.
2. A paragraph developed by contrast shows how two or more similar items differ.
3. Transitional words such as *above, behind,* and *below* can be used to indicate a chronological arrangement of ideas in a paragraph.
4. A paragraph developed by comparison or contrast must have balance, that is, corresponding details for items A and B.
5. When you arrange a paragraph, you can make it coherent by using chronological order, spatial order, or order of importance.

B. Number your paper from 6 to 10. Next to each number, write the letter of the term that correctly completes the sentence. You will not use one of the items.

a. spatial order
b. comparison
c. chronological order
d. coherence
e. balance
f. order of importance

6. __?__ in a paragraph is the arrangement of items according to their location in space.
7. The arrangement of events in a paragraph according to the time in which they happened shows __?__.
8. The development of a paragraph by __?__ shows how two or more items are alike.
9. In a paragraph, __?__ is the clear and orderly presentation of ideas.
10. A paragraph developed by __?__ arranges supporting details according to their importance.

354

C. Number your paper from 11 to 15. Next to each number, write the letter of the item that correctly answers the question.

11. Which of the following would be the best organization for a paragraph describing the Gateway Arch in St. Louis, Missouri?

    a. Spatial order
    b. Chronological order
    c. Order of importance
    d. Comparison

12. Which of the following topics would best be developed by chronological order?

    a. What is a meteor?
    b. A description of the Red River
    c. The first moon landing in 1969
    d. Agriculture in the Middle Ages and today

13. Which group of transitional words would best show the development of a paragraph by comparison?

    a. Also, similarly, alike
    b. First, even better, best of all
    c. Toward, in front of, over
    d. Unlike, however, although

14. Which of the following would best develop a paragraph discussing the differences between wild animals and zoo animals?

    a. Spatial order
    b. Chronological order
    c. Order of importance
    d. Contrast

15. Which group of transitional words would best show the organization of a paragraph in order of importance?

    a. Also, similarly, alike
    b. First, even better, best of all
    c. At first, now, later
    d. Unlike, however, although

Test 2

Choose one of the Unit Assignments. Write the paragraph as directed and hand it in to your teacher.

Unit 9

Unit Preview

Your responsibility to your audience is to make your writing as clear and as smooth as you possibly can. You can improve your writing by revising it. Even the best writers rarely produce effective writing on their first try. When you revise, you reorganize or rewrite your first draft. You must be willing to rearrange words and sentences, add or remove details, and combine or separate sentences to make your writing say exactly what you want it to say—to your reader as well as to yourself.

The following is a writer's first draft. Next to it, the author has made notes for revisions. After you have read the first draft and the notes, compare the draft with the revised version that follows it.

FIRST DRAFT	
Combine sentences.	when was ing ∧ ∧ ∧ visited my cousin in the city, a few years ago, We saw a street musician, and he was stand-
Too many *and*'s. Divide.	ing in the middle of a crowd, and he was bundled up in a heavy coat, It was a warm spring day.
Remove sentence.	even though i There was not a cloud in the sky. He was playing a harmonica. He played the same sad melody
Move adverbs to beginning.	over and over again, Some people dropped money into his battered hat, It was on the ground which
Combine sentences.	in front of him. He never smiled, He never ac- The man nor did h knowledged the money, He just kept playing the that same melancholy tune. I couldn't help wondering what he was thinking.

356

REVISED DRAFT

(1) A few years ago, when I was visiting my cousin in the city, we saw a street musician. (2) He was standing in the middle of a crowd, bundled up in a heavy coat, even though it was a warm spring day. (3) He was playing a harmonica. (4) Over and over again, he played the same sad melody. (5) The man never smiled, nor did he acknowledge the money that people dropped into his battered hat, which was on the ground in front of him. (6) He just kept playing the same melancholy tune. (7) I couldn't help wondering what he was thinking.

For Analysis On your paper, answer the following questions about the writer's revised draft.

1. How did the writer change Sentence 1?
2. What effect is achieved by the revisions in the first sentence?
3. What did the writer do in Sentence 2?
4. What is the effect of shifting the adverbs to the beginning of Sentence 4?
5. The writer removed one sentence. Why?

In answering the questions, you observed how a writer revises. In this unit you will practice techniques for revising your paragraph as a whole and the sentences within it.

9.1 Revising for Unity and Coherence

A good paragraph has unity (*page 297*) and coherence (*page 328*). Therefore, check for them first when you are revising your work.

9.1a Unity

To make your point, your paragraph must have unity. A paragraph has **unity** when all of the supporting sentences are directly related to the idea stated in the topic sentence. Apply the following strategies to revise for unity.

egies

1. *Be certain that your paragraph contains a precise topic sentence and relevant supporting sentences.* Remove any sentence that does not contribute to the topic. Rewrite any supporting sentence that is not clearly related to the topic. If your rewritten sentence still does not fit, discard it.

2. *Add any details still needed to support your topic sentence.* If you lack the necessary information, look it up or ask someone for it.

3. *Check whether your paragraph needs a concluding sentence.* If your paragraph is long, you can probably strengthen it by adding a concluding sentence that restates the topic sentence. If your paragraph seems unfinished, add a final question, conclusion, summary, or personal response that will complete it.

Exercise 1   Revising: Unity   On your paper, revise the following paragraph to give it unity. Remove three unrelated sentences, and add a concluding sentence.

Until the 1700s the practice of using forks was rare. Before then the majority of people considered the use of forks impractical and pretentious. Imagine eating a meal without a fork! Most people used only knives to eat, and, in some instances, spoons. Their manners were unrefined. However, an Italian noblewoman of the twelfth century began using a fork because she preferred not to pick up food with her hands. Two-pronged forks became common in Italy by the 1500s. Much later, a seventeenth-century English traveler to Italy discovered these two-pronged forks. When he brought one to Queen Elizabeth, she was so delighted that she ordered copies of the fork made. Shortly, the use of forks, particularly gold and crystal ones, became fashionable at court. Wealthy aristocrats kept their elaborately decorated forks in special leather cases.

9.1b   Coherence and Clarity

To be clear to your reader, your paragraph must have **coherence.** Make sure that the supporting sentences are organized logically and that you have made clear the connection between the ideas in the sentences. Apply the following strategies to revise for coherence.

Strategies

1. *Be sure that you have introduced your topic before discussing it.* Readers normally should not have to wait until the end of a paragraph to learn what the topic is. The best practice is to begin your paragraph with a topic sentence.

2. *Be sure that you have presented your supporting details in an order that makes sense to your reader.* Use chronological order if the paragraph deals mainly with events; use spatial order if the topic is a physical object or a scene; or use order of importance if you are presenting a series of reasons. If you have developed your paragraph by comparison or contrast, make sure that you have given only corresponding details about the items being compared or contrasted and that you have arranged those details according to a pattern (*page 345*).

3. *Discuss a series of items in the same order in which you introduce them.* If you write a topic sentence in which you identify three or more items to be discussed in your paragraph, arrange your supporting sentences in the same order. For example, if you promise in your topic sentence to explain the variety of nutrients found in apricots, peaches, and pears, do not discuss pears first, then peaches, and finally apricots.

4. *Define an unfamiliar or unusual term the first time that you use it.* Make sure that your readers understand technical terms that you use in writing about such subjects as science, mechanics, sports, crafts, and hobbies.

5. *Be sure that you have included suitable transitional words and phrases* to connect your ideas and to make your paragraphs read more smoothly. You may use words and phrases to show time, direction, importance, or comparison and contrast (*pages 330–345*).

Exercise 2 Revising: Coherence On your paper, complete these steps for each of the following paragraphs. *Step 1:* Tell why the paragraph lacks coherence. *Step 2:* List the numbers of the strategies just described that you should apply to make each paragraph coherent. *Step 3:* Write the paragraphs with the sentences in the correct order.

1. Most serious joggers warm up first, run, and then cool down. By exercising first to warm up slowly, the athletes avoid pulled muscles. By exercising again to cool down gradually, they avoid straining their hearts with a sudden change in activity. Once the joggers are warmed up, they try to run enough to make their hearts beat between 130 and 150 times per minute for fifteen minutes.

2. The Greek computer was discovered in 1900 in a shipwreck off the island of Crete. At first, scientists thought that the machine was a tool to help sailors navigate. After further study the scientists concluded that the machine could be used to determine past or future positions of the sun and moon. Most people think that computers are modern inventions, but the ancient Greeks built a computing instrument in the first century B.C. Therefore, it appears that the ancient Greeks were using computers centuries ago.

3. A sailor must know how to adjust the mainsheet. When the mainsheet is held too loose, the sail will flutter, and the boat will not move quickly. When the mainsheet is pulled too

tight, the sail will not fill with air, and again, the boat will not move quickly. The mainsheet is the rope that controls the tension of the mainsail. With a perfectly adjusted mainsheet, the sailor will enjoy brisk sailing.

4.   After reaching a peak of brightness, novas and supernovas gradually dim. The explosion of a nova sends a small portion of the star's mass into space but increases its brightness many thousands of times. The explosion of a supernova may involve a millionfold increase in brightness. The nova is one of nature's most interesting "light shows." A nova is a star that undergoes a sudden and dramatic increase in brightness. Originally believed to be new stars, novas are actually exploding stars.

Exercise 3 Revising: Coherence On your paper, revise the following paragraphs. Insert transitional words and phrases to connect ideas and to show how they are related. In Paragraph 1 use words to show time. In Paragraph 2 use words to show contrast.

1.   The landing of the space shuttle was a spectacular sight. The shuttle appeared as a dot far away in the bright blue sky. It came closer, and I could see its white tiles reflecting the sun. The shuttle began to look like a large, ordinary airplane. I could hardly believe that it had just returned from outer space. The shuttle came even closer. It banked and turned to the right so that it was heading down the proper runway. The enormous landing gear descended, and the shuttle was on the ground. I was thrilled to have witnessed its return from space.

2.   Sheep farmers in the United States are experimenting with using dogs to protect their sheep. There are two types of sheep dogs: guarding dogs and herding dogs. Guarding dogs are used where there are few attackers and where the sheep graze close together. Herding dogs are used in areas where there are many predators and where the sheep wander over a wide area. Guarding dogs live among the sheep as members of the flock and attack any enemies that threaten the flock. Herding dogs are outsiders that gather the sheep together when an

enemy appears. They gather the sheep by attacking them as an
enemy would. These dogs do not use their teeth on the sheep.
Sheep farmers are finding that both types of dogs can be
efficient shepherds.

Exercise 4   Revising: Unity and Coherence   The following paragraph is a first draft. To the left of the draft are
notes on needed revisions. On your paper, revise the paragraph. Use the notes as a guide.

Make topic sentence more specific.	Baseball is the national pastime in the United States. The first team baseball contest was held on June 19, 1846, in Hoboken, New
Add transitional words throughout.	Jersey. It grew in popularity. Youths played it on sandlots as well as in schools and colleges. Amateur clubs were formed in many cities. The first paid professional team, the Cincinnati Red Stockings, appeared in 1869, winning sixty-four
Remove irrelevant sentence.	games without a loss. This was twenty-six years before the first professional football game was played. By 1901 two major leagues, the National
Correct for chronological order.	and the American, had been organized. The first World Series followed just two years later. By 1893 most of the present rules were in force.
Add a concluding sentence.	Millions of people became fans, not only of major league teams but also of teams in the minor leagues.

Assignment   Revising   On your paper, revise the following paragraph for unity and coherence. The finished paragraph
should be organized in spatial order.

One of the most imposing of all reptiles in the United
States is the diamondback rattlesnake. It should always be
avoided. It has a rather broad head. Darting in and out of its
mouth is the familiar forked tongue that it uses as a combination taste-smell device. The tongue aids the snake in tasting

its food and tracking its prey. The diamondback has razor-sharp fangs with which it administers its deadly venom. It delivers a larger dose of venom than any other rattlesnake. Located on the face between the nostrils and the eyes are two pits that are sensitive to heat and that allow it to detect nearby warm-blooded animals. The famous rattle actually is made up of hollow segments. The snake vibrates them to frighten away enemies. Its strong jaws are capable of stretching open quite wide. Even a short snake can open its jaws wide enough to swallow a full-grown rabbit. The diamondback is one of the biggest and probably the most dangerous of all North American snakes. Little is known about its life span.

Assignment Checklist

Check your assignment for the following points:

✔ 1. Does your revised paragraph have strong, clear topic and concluding sentences?
✔ 2. Did you remove or rewrite sentences that are not related to the main idea?
✔ 3. Did you organize the supporting details in spatial order?
✔ 4. Did you add necessary transitional words?

9.2 Revising Sentences: Coordination

When you are certain that your paragraph is unified and coherent, you are ready to improve your sentences. Keep in mind that effective sentences are those that convey your intended meaning directly and precisely. Furthermore, all sentences in a paragraph should work together smoothly.

One way to show a logical connection between ideas and, at the same time, to eliminate choppy sentences is to combine sentences. You can revise two or more simple sentences (independent clauses) by **coordination,** that is, by combining them in a compound sentence (*page 119*). The sentences that you combine must be related in meaning.

NOT RELATED   We spent hours on the crossword puzzle, and my pencil broke.

RELATED   We spent hours on the crossword puzzle, and we finally finished it.

9.2a   Methods of Coordinating

You can use the following strategies to connect independent clauses to form compound sentences.

Strategies

1. *Use a comma and a coordinating conjunction.* The coordinating conjunctions are *and, but, or, nor, for,* and *yet.*

   The thunderclap frightened us, **and** we ran back to camp.

   Trent gave up the search, **but** Hilda persisted.

2. *Use a semicolon and a conjunctive adverb.* Examples of conjunctive adverbs are *consequently, furthermore, however, nevertheless, otherwise, therefore,* and *thus.* Put a comma after the conjunctive adverb.

   The merchandise in this store is not displayed well; **consequently,** it is difficult to find what you want.

   I like this dress; **however,** it doesn't suit me.

3. *Use a semicolon alone.*

   The first lap around the track was difficult; the second was even harder.

   The male lion has a long, heavy mane; the female lion does not.

Exercise 1   Revising: Coordination If the ideas in each pair of sentences are related, combine them with a comma and a coordinating conjunction. If they are unrelated, write *Unrelated* on your paper.

> **SAMPLE**   Melanie was determined to win the contest.
> She acted accordingly.
>
> **ANSWER**   Melanie was determined to win the contest, and she acted accordingly.

1. A huge crowd was already assembled at the gate. We managed to work our way to the front of it.
2. I have had the most exciting time. Anyone can learn to scuba dive.
3. Plants need a certain amount of sunshine. They will not grow properly.
4. Norman does not polish his shoes. He does not iron his shirts.
5. I have two woolen hats. The snow has stopped.
6. The tickets were not in my pocket. I had put them there that morning.
7. The book was not in the library. I didn't know where else to look for it.
8. Along the road are brilliant wildflowers. The roads are badly in need of repair.
9. Apparently, Joel has a new job. I haven't seen him in two weeks.
10. Little rain falls in the desert. Many types of plants grow there.

Exercise 2   Revising: Coordination If the ideas in each pair of sentences are related, combine them with a semicolon and a conjunctive adverb or with a semicolon alone. If they are unrelated, write *Unrelated* on your paper.

> **SAMPLE**   My grandfather always offers good advice. It sometimes falls on deaf ears.
>
> **ANSWER**   My grandfather always offers good advice; however, it sometimes falls on deaf ears.

365

1. Jill lost her lead in the second set. She did not give up.
2. There was nothing to do after the performance. It was an excellent show.
3. We dressed formally. We would not have been admitted to the restaurant.
4. The rehearsals are going well. Much remains to be done.
5. For a long time, the residents complained about the dangerous intersection. The road needed repaving.
6. Dominic has been practicing faithfully. His technique has improved noticeably.
7. The pond did not freeze that winter. The children could not go skating.
8. This old car runs well. The body needs work.
9. Alison has always loved animals. She wants to become a veterinarian.
10. The judge was firm. She banned photographers from the courtroom.

Exercise 3   Revising: Coordination   On your paper, coordinate each pair of sentences in three ways. First, use a comma and coordinating conjunction. Then, use a semicolon and a conjunctive adverb. Finally, use a semicolon alone.

SAMPLE   The fog had settled over the city. We couldn't see the tops of any tall buildings.

ANSWER   a. We couldn't see the tops of any tall buildings, for the fog had settled over the city.

b. The fog had settled over the city; consequently, we couldn't see the tops of any tall buildings.

c. The fog had settled over the city; we couldn't see the tops of any tall buildings.

1. Captain Ahab lost his leg to Moby Dick, the white whale. Captain Ahab still chased the whale.
2. The bicycle path was rough. LaShawn's deflated tire made her ride even rougher.

3. The mountain roads are covered with snow. The travelers will not reach the town tonight.

4. Nora usually goes to the delicatessen for lunch. Sometimes she goes for a walk.

5. My town's baseball team did not win the final game. It will still compete in the playoffs.

9.2b Coordinating Words

The coordinating word that you use between independent clauses tells exactly how the clauses are related. The most common coordinating words and the relationships that they express are shown in the following chart.

ADDITION	and	Juan has returned, *and* he brought gifts for everyone.
	furthermore, in addition, moreover	Juan has returned; *moreover,* he brought gifts for everyone.
CONTRAST	but, yet	Pat is shy, *but* I like him.
	however, instead, nevertheless, still	Pat is shy; *nevertheless,* I like him.
ALTERNATIVE	or, nor	I will go alone, *or* I won't go at all.
	otherwise	I will go alone; *otherwise,* I won't go at all.
RESULT	therefore, thus, consequently, accordingly	Tina fixed the tire; *consequently,* we can start now.
CAUSE	for	We will surely be late, *for* we just missed the bus.

Each coordinating word has a specific meaning. Choose a coordinating word carefully to convey the relationship that you want between the independent clauses in a sentence. Notice how the meaning of the following sentences changes as the coordinating word changes.

Somebody broke the shell, *and* the chicken hatched. [Addition]

Somebody broke the shell; *nevertheless,* the chicken hatched. [Contrast]

Somebody broke the shell, *or* the chicken hatched. [Alternative]

Somebody broke the shell; *therefore,* the chicken hatched. [Result]

The shell is broken, *for* the chicken has hatched. [Cause]

Exercise 4   Revising: Coordination   On your paper, combine each pair of sentences into a compound sentence. Use a coordinating word that expresses the relationship shown in parentheses.

SAMPLE   Modern canoes are similar to those of early North American Indians. Modern canoes are made of aluminum or fiber glass. (Contrast)

ANSWER   Modern canoes are similar to those of early North American Indians, but modern canoes are made of aluminum or fiber glass.

1. Canoes may be used for a relaxing afternoon on the water. They may also be used for camping and racing. (Addition)

2. There are different kinds of canoes. Canoeists may choose according to their needs. (Result)

3. Most canoe paddles are made of wood. Some are made of aluminum or plastic. (Contrast)

4. The canoeist must learn to enter and leave a canoe properly. A dunking may result. (Alternative)

5. Canoeists can paddle on "flat," or still, water. They may test their skills on "white," or rough, water. (Alternative)

6. A kayak resembles a canoe. The kayak has a covered deck area. (Contrast)

7. The deck of a kayak may have one small opening. It may have as many as four openings. (Alternative)
8. The kayak paddle is similar to a canoe paddle. The kayak paddle has a blade at each end. (Contrast)
9. A kayak is difficult to sink. A waterproof flap keeps it from filling with water. (Cause)
10. The Inuits made kayaks from animal skins. They used their kayaks for hunting and transportation. (Addition)

Exercise 5 Revising: Coordination On your paper, revise the following paragraph. In your revision coordinate Sentence 1 with 2, Sentence 3 with 4, and Sentence 7 with 8.

(1) The dodo was a bird that was unable to protect itself. (2) It became extinct. (3) It had wings. (4) It could not fly. (5) Because dodoes could not fly, they were easy prey for hunters and their dogs. (6) Also, rats and hogs ate the dodoes' eggs. (7) Drawings were made of dodoes before they became extinct in the 1680s. (8) Only from these pictures and from written descriptions do we know what they looked like. (9) We should make an effort to protect animals that are as vulnerable as the dodo.

Assignment Revising On your paper, revise the following paragraph by coordinating some related sentences.

Nellie Bly was one of the country's most daring journalists. Elizabeth Cochrane Seaman was her real name. She used Nellie Bly as her pen name. At eighteen she began to produce the exciting stories for which she later became known. Bly wanted to write about the treatment of women prisoners. She had herself arrested as a thief. When she wanted to know how mentally ill patients were treated, she had herself admitted to an institution. Her biggest assignment began in November of 1889. She wanted to beat the record of Jules Verne's fictional hero by traveling around the world in fewer than eighty days. She did. Traveling by ship, train, cart, and donkey, she made the trip in just over seventy-two days. As she traveled, Bly sent back reports for her newspaper. Certainly, Nellie Bly's readers were entertained.

Assignment Checklist

Check your assignment for the following points:

✔ 1. Did you coordinate some related sentences?
✔ 2. Did you use coordinating words that express the correct relationship between ideas?

9.3   Revising Sentences: Subordination

You can also revise sentences by **subordination,** which is the joining of ideas of unequal importance. *Subordinate* means "less important." To use subordination to combine sentences, place the main idea in an independent clause and the less important idea(s) in the subordinate clause(s) (*page 109*). When you make one clause subordinate to another, you form a complex sentence (*page 120*).

The use of subordinate clauses allows you to avoid the monotony of short, choppy sentences, which make your paragraph less effective.

CHOPPY I became concerned. The conductor shouted something. I couldn't hear it.

REVISED I became concerned when the conductor shouted something that I couldn't hear.

9.3a   Subordinating with Adjective Clauses

One way to subordinate a related idea is to put it in an adjective clause (*page 111*). An adjective clause modifies a noun or a pronoun in an independent clause, which expresses the main idea of a sentence. Adjective clauses are generally introduced by relative pronouns (*that, which, who, whom, whose*) or, sometimes, by subordinating conjunctions (*after, before, when, where*). The adjective clauses are in italics in the following revised sentences:

TWO SENTENCES
> Rafts are the simplest kind of watercraft. They can be made of logs tied together with ropes.

REVISED SENTENCE WITH ADJECTIVE CLAUSE
> Rafts, *which are the simplest kind of watercraft,* can be made of logs tied together with ropes.

TWO SENTENCES
> Thor Heyerdahl made an ocean voyage on a wooden raft. He wrote an exciting account of his adventure in the book *Kon-Tiki*.

REVISED SENTENCE WITH ADJECTIVE CLAUSE
> Thor Heyerdahl, *who made an ocean voyage on a wooden raft,* wrote an exciting account of his adventure in the book *Kon-Tiki*.

(See pages 237–238 for rules about punctuating essential and nonessential adjective clauses.)

Exercise 1   Revising: Subordination   On your paper, rewrite each set of sentences as one complex sentence. Place the subordinate idea in an adjective clause. Use the subordinating word given in parentheses.

> SAMPLE   I have the statistics. Unfortunately, the statistics do not support my theory. (*that*)

> ANSWER   Unfortunately, the statistics that I have do not support my theory.

1. In front of the counter stood the woman. We heard her voice throughout the restaurant. (*whose*)
2. The runner is being interviewed by reporters. He won the marathon. (*who*)

3. *Louis* was the name of many French kings. *Louis* means "famous warrior." (*which*)
4. No one gets letters from Bernie Thompkins. He moved away a few years ago. (*who*)
5. The ferry leaves every half hour. It crosses the channel. (*that*)
6. The painter is going to do a portrait of me. Her work was displayed in the gallery. (*whose*)
7. The lovely meadow is now a housing development. We played there as children. (*where*)
8. For the curtains Roscoe chose a plain blue fabric. It complements the plaid sofa. (*that*)
9. She is a talented woman. I admire her. (*whom*)
10. No one else could recite the poem. It has always been one of my favorites. (*that*)

Exercise 2   Revising: Subordination   On your paper, rewrite each set of sentences as one complex sentence. Place the subordinate idea in an adjective clause.

> **SAMPLE**   Johanna was a child. Everyone loved her.
>
> **ANSWER**   Johanna was a child whom everyone loved.

1. I shivered despite my heavy sweater. My grandmother knitted my sweater.
2. Ms. Barnes is a coach. She inspires us to work hard.
3. He returned to the pond. He had caught his first fish there as a six-year-old child.
4. I have a friend named Nerissa. Her talents include the ability to play the recorder and the flute.
5. Many adventurers try to climb Mount Everest. Mount Everest is the highest mountain in the world.
6. Those long, thin animals are lizards. They are closely related to snakes.
7. The rain fell steadily all afternoon. It kept us from weeding the garden.
8. Huck Finn admired Tom Sawyer. Tom Sawyer was his best friend.

9. The boots fell apart. I bought them on sale.
10. The student was overjoyed. Her science exhibit won first prize.

9.3b Subordinating with Adverb Clauses

You can subordinate ideas of time, manner, cause, condition, comparison, or purpose in adverb clauses (*page 114*). An adverb clause modifies a verb, an adverb, or an adjective in an independent clause. Introduce an adverb clause with a subordinating conjunction, which shows just how the clause is related to the word that it modifies. The following chart reviews the relationships expressed by subordinating conjunctions.

TIME	after, as, as long as, as soon as, before, since, until, when, whenever, while	The game was canceled *when* the storm began.
MANNER	as, as if, as though	The water shimmered *as though* it had been disturbed.
CAUSE	because	Brad joined the chorus *because* he likes to sing.
CONDITION	although, as long as, even if, even though, if, provided that, though, unless, while	*Although* the train left late, it made up time along the way.
COMPARISON	as, than	A cheetah runs faster *than* any other animal.
PURPOSE or RESULT	in order that, so that	They worked hard all week *so that* they could have Saturday free.

When you begin a sentence with an adverb clause, separate it from the rest of the sentence with a comma.

Exercise 3   Revising: Subordination   On your paper, rewrite each set of sentences as one complex sentence. Place the subordinate idea in an adverb clause. Use a subordinating conjunction that expresses the relationship in parentheses.

> SAMPLE   Some plants are considered carnivorous. They trap and digest insects. (Cause)
>
> ANSWER   Some plants are considered carnivorous because they trap and digest insects.

1. Carnivorous plants get few nutrients from the soil. They must obtain nutrients from insects. (Cause)
2. Insects see the flowers on carnivorous plants. They are attracted to the traps in the flowers. (Time)
3. The flower of the pitcher plant is specially shaped. It holds rainwater. (Result)
4. An insect flies into the plant. It drowns in the rainwater. (Time)
5. Some insects avoid the rainwater. They cannot escape through the thick hairs at the top of the plant. (Condition)
6. The plant needs nourishment. It digests the insects. (Time)
7. The two leaves of a Venus's-flytrap are hinged. They can open and close. (Purpose)
8. Its leaves are covered with sensitive hairs. The flytrap can feel the presence of an insect and close around it. (Cause)
9. The insect is consumed. The leaf opens to catch another insect. (Time)
10. Carnivorous plants are not common. You may have to visit a special greenhouse to see one. (Cause)

Exercise 4   Revising: Subordination   On your paper, rewrite each set of sentences as a complex sentence with an adverb clause.

> SAMPLE   Driving is often unpleasant. There are too many cars on the road.
>
> ANSWER   Driving is often unpleasant because there are too many cars on the road.

1. Everyone cheered Kate. She crossed the finish line.
2. Wendy mowed the lawn. Rod trimmed the hedges.
3. Robin could not go to the game. Someone gave her a ride.
4. You sit quietly in the forest. You may see a deer.
5. We walked five more miles. We rested for an hour.
6. The Wilsons had to use candles for light. The electric company restored their power.
7. People and the environment would benefit. People would walk more instead of driving.
8. I have lost five pounds. I started jogging regularly.
9. Hoisting the sail was useless. There was no wind.
10. Gerard had a cold. He did not stay at home.

Exercise 5   Revising: Subordination   On your paper, revise the following paragraph. In your revision, combine Sentence 1 with 2, Sentence 3 with 4, Sentence 5 with 6, and Sentence 8 with 9 to form complex sentences.

(1) Molds have been used to treat skin infections for almost three thousand years. (2) Scientists have studied them only within the past two hundred years. (3) In 1929 Alexander Fleming discovered the germ-killing effects of a substance in mold. (4) Fleming was a bacteriologist at the University of London. (5) He noticed that a piece of mold had killed all the germs around it. (6) This mold accidentally had fallen on a colony of germs. (7) He called the germ-killing substance penicillin. (8) He had trouble extracting penicillin from the mold. (9) He could not conduct many experiments with it. (10) Finally, in 1930, Chain and Florey, two English scientists, discovered how to extract penicillin from the mold, and scientists were able to develop penicillin as an effective medicine.

Assignment   Revising   On your paper, revise the following paragraph. Combine some sentences by subordination, and change words as necessary.

Shoemakers have been able to make left shoes different from right shoes for thousands of years. They did not do so regularly until 1850. It was too difficult. In ancient Rome only patricians had left and right shoes. Patricians were the members of the ruling class. Not even kings and queens in the Middle Ages had two different shoes. In the sixteenth century, right and left shoes were a short-lived fad. Better shoemaking equipment was invented in 1850. Different shoes for left and right feet became popular. Now it would be unthinkable to have identical shoes for both feet.

Assignment Checklist

Check your assignment for the following points:

✔ 1. Did you make some sentences subordinate clauses?

✔ 2. Did you use subordinating words that express correct relationships between the ideas?

9.4   Revising Sentences: Phrases

9.4a   Revising with Participial Phrases

Sometimes you can combine two sentences by making one of them a participial phrase (*page 101*). By doing so, you express your thoughts more directly. The participial phrases are in italics in the following revised sentences.

TWO SENTENCES
I looked at the quiet child. The child was sitting on the steps.

REVISED SENTENCE WITH PARTICIPIAL PHRASE
I looked at the quiet child *sitting on the steps*.

TWO SENTENCES
A solitary tree stood in the meadow. The tree was outlined in the moonlight.

REVISED SENTENCE WITH PARTICIPIAL PHRASE
> A solitary tree, *outlined in the moonlight,* stood in the meadow.

(See pages 237–238 for rules about punctuating essential and nonessential participial phrases.)

Exercise 1 Revising: Participial Phrases On your paper, use one or more participial phrases to combine each group of sentences into one sentence. You will have to change some verbs to *-ing* forms.

> **SAMPLE** Our group carried flags and banners. We paraded through the streets.
>
> **ANSWER** Carrying flags and banners, our group paraded through the streets.

1. Kate tried not to disturb the cat. The cat was sleeping on the work table.
2. The building is a welcome refuge from the heat on summer days. The building is cooled by air conditioning.
3. I was distracted by a shadow. The shadow was moving across the wall. I had difficulty watching the *Creature Feature*.
4. The camel is able to travel extremely long distances. The camel is equipped with a hump. The hump carries fats and fluids.
5. Lorenzo groped along the wall in the darkness. He found the light switch.
6. Trina returned home. She carried some unusual rocks. They were wrapped carefully in paper.
7. Len's shoes were bought just a few days ago. Len's shoes squeaked when he walked.
8. The young man was exhausted from his work. He turned off the light and immediately fell asleep.
9. The watchdog leaped up. He growled at the intruder.
10. Marty looked at the papers on the floor. She groaned and sank into a chair.

9.4b Revising with Appositive Phrases

A descriptive detail of one sentence can be included as an appositive phrase (*page 96*) in another. Appositive phrases are placed just before or just after the words that they identify. The appositive phrases are in italics in the following revised sentences.

TWO SENTENCES
> Samuel Adams had the support of many colonists. He was a prominent Boston patriot.

REVISED SENTENCE WITH APPOSITIVE PHRASE
> Samuel Adams, *a prominent Boston patriot,* had the support of many colonists.

TWO SENTENCES
> The book sold rapidly. It was an updated edition of a beloved classic.

REVISED SENTENCE WITH APPOSITIVE PHRASE
> *An updated edition of a beloved classic,* the book sold rapidly.

Exercise 2 Revising: Appositive Phrases On your paper, use an appositive phrase to combine each pair of sentences into one sentence.

SAMPLE
> The finalists will have their match today. The finalists are Marianna Stevens and Chad Wallace.

ANSWER
> The finalists, Marianna Stevens and Chad Wallace, will have their match today.

1. Aaron is a cheerful person. He is always smiling.
2. James is a close friend of mine. He has started a collection of rare and unusual stamps.

3. Next weekend Carmen will join Rob in a parachute jump. She is a beginning skydiver.

4. Rainbow trout is my favorite fish. I caught a rainbow trout in a quiet stream below the mill.

5. Ruby dived into the heavy surf. She was a fearless swimmer.

6. I loved my birthday present from my grandparents. It was a trip to Mexico City.

7. Mark sells his products at crafts fairs. He is a skilled cabinet-maker.

8. In the Air and Space Museum, we saw the *Spirit of St. Louis.* The *Spirit of St. Louis* is the plane that Charles Lindbergh flew across the Atlantic.

9. Many people are fascinated by rocks and minerals. Rocks and minerals are nature's jewelry.

10. Corine Appleton will speak at our next meeting. She is the author of *Organizing Your Time.*

Exercise 3 Revising: Phrases On your paper, combine each set of sentences into one sentence. Use participial phrases and appositive phrases. Change or omit words as necessary.

> **SAMPLE**   I was trying to leave quietly. I tripped over the cat. The cat was lying in the doorway.
>
> **ANSWER**   Trying to leave quietly, I tripped over the cat lying in the doorway.

1. I was feeling rather excited. I confided in my younger sister. Her name is Magdalena.

2. Cal was shuffling his feet in embarrassment. He admitted that he had eaten the whole basket of strawberries.

3. Braxton yawns all through breakfast. He is a deep sleeper.

4. My right knee stiffens in cold, damp weather. It was injured on a ski slope in the Rocky Mountains.

5. He giggled uncontrollably. He was holding the egg on his spoon. He was trying to keep it from falling.

6. The children eagerly watched the elephants. The elephants were parading in groups of three.

7. Amanda was preparing to run three miles. She did warm-up exercises on the floor.

8. Laura Robinson has had many poems published in the school magazine. Laura is admired by her classmates.

9. We made our way through the back yard with only the dim light of a flashlight. We were bumping into objects in the dark.

10. Daisy is our cow. She likes to lie under the old maple tree at the far end of the field. She is chewing her cud.

Assignment Revising On your paper, revise the following paragraph. Use phrases to combine some sentences.

> We left early for a long hike. Our goal was to hike up and down the peak of Half Dome. Half Dome is a mountain in Yosemite National Park. We hiked for hours along many narrow switchbacks. Switchbacks are zigzagging trails up a steep slope. We finally reached the top. We were feeling exhilarated. The view in front of us was beautiful. On our way down the mountain, darkness began to fall. We decided to take the shortest trail. The shortest trail was the Mist Trail. We were proceeding down the trail. We discovered why it was called the Mist Trail. The whole area was covered with spray from a waterfall, and we hiked in the mist for over an hour. We were at the end of our long hike. We were pleased that we had accomplished our goal.

Assignment Checklist

Check your assignment for the following points:

✔ 1. Did you combine some sentences in which the ideas are related?

✔ 2. Did you use participial phrases and appositive phrases?

9.5 Revising Sentences That Are Not Clear and Coherent

Sentences in which clauses are carelessly joined with *and* and *so* are not clear and often are monotonous. In the following sentence, for example, the relationship between the ideas in the clauses is blurred. The revised version is coherent.

NOT COHERENT

> Many ambulances are staffed by paramedic teams, and paramedics are qualified to give emergency medical care, so they are able to save many lives.

REVISED

> Many ambulances are staffed by paramedic teams. Because paramedics are qualified to give emergency medical care, they are able to save many lives.

Use the following strategies to revise sentences that are not coherent.

Strategies

1. *Rewrite an independent clause as a phrase or a subordinate clause.* The use of an exact subordinating word makes your meaning clear.

   NOT COHERENT

   > The plane came from Chicago, and it was very late because of bad weather.

   REVISED

   > The plane, *which came from Chicago,* was very late because of bad weather. [One independent clause changed to an adjective clause.]

   NOT COHERENT

   > Beth and Jill spent an hour with Ms. Fortini, and she is the new director.

REVISED

> Beth and Jill spent an hour with Ms. Fortini, *the new director.* [One clause reduced to an appositive phrase.]

2. *Divide the sentence into two or more sentences.*

NOT COHERENT

> Petrified forests are found in many states and provinces, and they show the types of trees from different geologic periods.

REVISED

> Petrified forests are found in many states and provinces. They show the types of trees from different geologic periods. [Sentence divided into two sentences.]

3. *Use Strategies 1 and 2 together as necessary.*

NOT COHERENT

> The storm ended, and the trees glistened, and a fresh layer of ice and snow covered the ground.

REVISED

> After the storm ended, the trees glistened. A fresh layer of ice and snow covered the ground. [One clause subordinated and sentence divided.]

Exercise 1   Revising: Coherence   On your paper, revise the following sentences. Make one clause the kind of subordinate clause or phrase indicated in parentheses.

> **SAMPLE**   Obedience training should start when a puppy is eight weeks old, and it will make a dog a more manageable pet. (Adjective clause)

> **ANSWER**   Obedience training, which should start when a puppy is eight weeks old, will make a dog a more manageable pet.

1. Judy Lopez is only an amateur, and she skates as well as a professional. (Adverb clause)

2. He turned and walked quickly away after the incident, and he was blushing furiously. (Participial phrase)
3. The Appalachian Trail extends from Springer Mountain in Georgia to Mount Katahdin in Maine, and it passes through fourteen states. (Adjective clause)
4. Two families were selected as hosts to the foreign students, and they were the Carrs and the Guidos. (Appositive phrase)
5. Albert loves to make people laugh, so he should be a clown. (Adjective clause)
6. The water tank is painted bright orange, so it is visible for miles. (Participial phrase)
7. Last year Shawn read *The Chronicles of Narnia,* and that is a series of seven books about a place called Narnia. (Appositive phrase)
8. Donna invited me to spend a week with her family at Trout Lake, and I eagerly accepted. (Adverb clause)
9. We were alarmed by the noise, so we ran outside to see what was happening. (Participial phrase)
10. Florida has a long shoreline and warm weather all year, so it is a popular vacation spot for beach lovers. (Adverb clause)

Exercise 2   Revising: Coherence   On your paper, revise the following sentences. Divide each sentence, and make one clause a phrase or a subordinate clause as necessary.

SAMPLE	We have some new neighbors, and I would like you to meet them, and they used to live in Toronto.
ANSWER	We have some new neighbors, whom I would like you to meet. They used to live in Toronto.

1. Alaska is the largest state, but it has the smallest population, and it also has a variety of climates.
2. Naomi's jade plant died, and she bought a new one, but the new one didn't live long because her cat chewed its leaves.

3. Jose was running ahead of the other racers, and he heard the steps of the other runners close behind him, so he quickened his pace, and he tried to outrun his competitors.

4. Early in the morning, Clayton put film in his camera, and he started down to the river to take pictures of the rowing races, and he was hoping to enter some of the photos in a contest.

5. Lynette was not paying attention, so she didn't hear the question addressed to her, but it was repeated, and she looked up with a start.

6. Emma Lou wanted to earn money for tuition, so she took a job waiting on tables, and she worked only on weekends, but she saved enough money.

7. The production was extremely successful, and every seat in the auditorium was filled, and the late-comers had to stand in the aisles.

8. The Kleins were filled with awe, and they marveled at the depth and beauty of the canyon, and they knew that they could not capture its beauty on film.

9. Josie was following the calls of the starlings, so she walked out into her garden, and she saw the birds flitting in the branches above her.

10. There is a great need for industrial designers, and they are the people who plan and develop industrial equipment and techniques, and they must be both artists and engineers.

Assignment   Revising   On your paper, revise the following paragraph to eliminate sentences that are not coherent. Divide sentences as necessary, and use phrases and subordinate clauses to make your sentences more precise.

Valentina Tereshkova is a Soviet woman, and she was the first woman to go into outer space. She had never done any test piloting, but she had done some parachuting, and she had been trained as a pilot, so she went into space in 1963. She made forty-five revolutions around the earth, and her parachuting experience was useful because she parachuted from her spaceship after it entered Earth's atmosphere.

Assignment Checklist

Check your assignment for the following points:

✔ 1. Did you divide the long sentences?
✔ 2. Did you make some independent clauses into phrases or subordinate clauses?

9.6   Revising Sentences for Variety

When you revise sentences in a paragraph, check them for variety. Too many of the same kinds of sentences in a paragraph can distract a reader. Compare the following paragraphs.

MONOTONOUS

Janine came into the room. She walked slowly. She looked hot, dusty, and discouraged. She could barely move after spending a day interviewing and filling out forms. Her bones ached and her head pounded. She had been seeking a job in the city from early morning until late afternoon. She had found nothing. She would repeat the process tomorrow. [Each sentence begins with the subject immediately followed by a verb. The sentences are choppy.]

VARIED

Walking slowly, Janine came into the room. Looking hot, dusty, and discouraged, she eased onto the sofa. After spending a day interviewing and filling out forms, she could barely move. Her bones ached and her head pounded. From early morning until late afternoon, she had been seeking a job in the city, but she had found nothing. Tomorrow she would repeat the process. [Sentence beginnings and sentence structures are varied. The paragraph reads smoothly.]

When you revise a paragraph, read it aloud to yourself or to a friend. You will be able to hear whether your sentences

385

read smoothly and fit well together. If they do not, use a variety of sentence beginnings and sentence structures to keep your writing fresh and lively.

9.6a Variety in Sentence Beginnings

Revise your sentences so that they do not all begin with the subject. You have a number of possibilities for different sentence beginnings. These are illustrated in the chart that follows.

ADJECTIVE(S)	*Happy and proud,* Lin walked onto the stage.
ADVERB	*Confidently,* she sat at the piano.
PREPOSITIONAL PHRASE	*In a few seconds,* she would begin to play.
PARTICIPIAL PHRASE	*Smiling to herself,* Lin waited for the murmuring in the audience to cease.
	Impressed by her stillness, the audience became silent.
ADVERB CLAUSE	*When she finished the sonata,* the audience gave a standing ovation.
	Although the cheering seemed to overwhelm the small concert hall, this noise did not bother Lin.
APPOSITIVE PHRASE	*A confident pianist,* Lin experienced little anxiety.

Be careful also to avoid a succession of sentences with the same kind of beginning, whatever it may be. That pattern can be as monotonous as a series of sentences that begin with the subject.

Another way to vary sentence beginnings is to invert the normal sentence order (*page 67*). Instead of beginning with the subject, begin with the predicate or a part of the predicate.

NORMAL ORDER	Several gold coins were buried under the rock.
INVERTED ORDER	Buried under the rock were several gold coins.

Not every phrase, adverb, or adverb clause can be moved to the beginning of a sentence. For example, the modifier in the following sentence cannot be shifted to the beginning, because making the change causes a misplaced modifier (*page 191*).

CORRECT	Sam saw the spider crawling up the wall.
INCORRECT	Crawling up the wall, Sam saw the spider. [The spider, not Sam, is crawling up the wall.]

Exercise 1   Revising: Variety   On your paper, revise the following sentences by shifting a part of the sentence to the beginning. If no part can be moved, write *No change*.

SAMPLE	*The Odyssey,* composed by the poet Homer, tells the adventures of Odysseus, king of Ithaca.
ANSWER	Composed by the poet Homer, *The Odyssey* tells the adventures of Odysseus, king of Ithaca.

1. *The Odyssey,* an epic poem, is one of the greatest adventure stories in literature.
2. Odysseus sets out to return to Ithaca after he has fought in the Trojan War.
3. His return, unexpectedly, takes ten years.
4. Odysseus has many terrifying adventures, in which he loses all of his men.
5. He and his crew sail to the island of the one-eyed giants, where they are imprisoned by the Cyclops Polyphemus.
6. Circe, an evil enchanter, turns Odysseus's men into pigs.
7. The Sirens, using their beautiful singing, lure sailors to their death on a magic island.

387

8. Odysseus is the prisoner of Calypso for seven years, but she finally helps him to return home.
9. Odysseus, clever and quick, outwits all of his captors.
10. Odysseus, disguised as a beggar, finally returns to his own palace and sets everything right.

9.6b   Variety in Sentence Structure

Another way to achieve sentence variety is to use different sentence structures. In a paragraph try to use sentences that are simple, compound, and complex. You can often say essentially the same thing in sentences having different structures. Compare the following sentences:

Hoping for a promotion, Angelo worked late every night. [Simple sentence with participial phrase]

Angelo hoped for a promotion; therefore, he worked late every night. [Compound sentence]

Angelo, who hoped for a promotion, worked late every night. [Complex sentence with adjective clause]

Because Angelo hoped for a promotion, he worked late every night. [Complex sentence with adverb clause]

Choose a way of stating your ideas that fits well with the surrounding sentences. Make certain that your wording is in keeping with your purpose.

Exercise 2   Revising: Variety   On your paper, revise each sentence. Change the structure, but keep the meaning the same.

> **SAMPLE**   Hearing the good news, I was elated.
> **ANSWER**   I was elated when I heard the good news.

1. The actor smiled and waved as he returned to the stage.
2. Edith put on roller skates for the first time last week, but already she is quite a good skater.
3. The heavy traffic delayed us; consequently, we were late for the show.
4. Jessie takes her responsibilities very seriously, yet she still manages to have fun.
5. Manny is a charming child, who wins the hearts of all who meet him.
6. On damp mornings the mist rises over the river, obscuring the distant mountains.
7. The car screeched to a stop, and two reporters jumped out and ran into the building.
8. Hoping to be noticed, Imogene talked loudly.
9. Alberto fished all day, but he did not catch anything.
10. The basketball player, catching the ball on the run, raced down the court toward the basket.

Assignment Revising On your paper, revise the following paragraph. Provide sentence variety by combining some sentences and changing the beginnings.

Artists in the 1500s wanted to make exact copies of scenic views. There was no way to do that. Someone invented the *camera obscura. Camera obscura* means "dark chamber." The *camera obscura* was a dark room with only one small hole for light. The room was just large enough for the artist to stand inside it. The light coming through the hole projected on the opposite wall an inverted picture of the view outside. The artist traced the picture. The artist made an exact copy of the view. The box became smaller later. A mirror projected the image from inside the box onto a piece of paper. The artist traced the image. That led to the invention of photography.

Assignment Checklist

Check your assignment for the following points:

✔ 1. Did you move at least one modifier to the beginning of a sentence?

✔ 2. Did you combine some sentences so that the paragraph contains simple, compound, and complex sentences?

✔ 3. Did you use phrases to combine some sentences?

9.7   Revising and Proofreading

Completing Your Revision

The final step in revising is proofreading. **Proofreading** is the checking for correct grammar, usage, spelling, capitalization, and punctuation. If you proofread your work carefully, you will do a better job of conveying your ideas. Language rules serve the purpose of making communication clear and easy.

When you proofread a piece of writing, examine each word and sentence individually. In this way, you can be sure of spotting errors. Use the following guidelines for proofreading:

1. Are all of your sentences complete?
2. Do all verbs agree with their subjects?
3. Did you use correct pronouns?
4. Did you spell words correctly?
5. Did you punctuate your sentences correctly?
6. Did you use correct capitalization?

If you are unsure about something, assume that it is incorrect. Then either look up the information in this book or ask your teacher about it. You may use the proofreading symbols shown on page 257.

When you have completed revising and proofreading a piece of your writing, you can make a finished copy according to your teacher's instructions or the guidelines on page 258.

An Example of Revising and Proofreading

The following is a draft of a paragraph about weathervanes. The paragraph has unity, but the sentences need revision, and the entire paragraph must be proofread. To the left of the draft are notes on desirable revisions and corrections. After you have read the first draft and the notes, compare the draft with the revised version that follows it.

FIRST DRAFT

Correct sentence fragment.

Make into appositive.

Remove.

Coordinate sentences.

Subordinate in adj. clause.

Divide long sentence.

Make into part. phrase.

Shift phrase to beginning.

Make into appositive.

Subordinate in adverb clause.

In these days of computerized equipment for weather recording and prediction. The oldest weather instrument is still the most common one. The oldest weather instrument is the weathervane. The newest weather instrument is the weather satellite. A weathervane is a wind-direction instrument. It is also an ornament. The pioneer farmers, whittling their weathervanes out of wood, made them in the shape of simple animals and arrows. Later generations of farmers obtained their weathervanes from local blacksmiths, and these farmers chose from a variety of ornamental subjects, and finely detailed roosters, fish, cows, and dragons stylishly pointed the wind direction. These were hammered out of copper or iron. The technological developments of the age appeared in small scale in weathervanes by the late nineteenth century. Some of the developments were steam fire engines and locomotives. Weathervanes are now mass-produced, and their forms still reflect a variety of tastes and trends.

REVISED VERSION

Fragment
corrected.

Appositive

Sentences
coordinated.

Adjective
clause

Long sentence
divided.

Participial
phrase

Phrase shifted
to beginning.

Appositive

Adverb
clause

    In these days of computerized equipment for weather recording and prediction, the oldest weather instrument, the weathervane, is still the most common one. A weathervane is a wind-direction instrument, but it is also an ornament. The pioneer farmers, whittling their weather-vanes out of wood, made them in shapes of simple animals and arrows. Later generations of farmers, who obtained their weathervanes from local blacksmiths, chose from a variety of orna-mental subjects. Finely detailed roosters, fish, cows, and dragons, hammered out of copper or wrought iron, stylishly pointed the wind direc-tion. By the late nineteenth century, the techno-logical developments of the age, such as steam fire engines and locomotives, appeared in small scale in weathervanes. Although weathervanes are now mass-produced, their forms still reflect a variety of tastes and trends.

Exercise 1   Revising: Proofreading   The following paragraph needs to be proofread. On your paper, rewrite it with the needed corrections.

    It is easy to understand why collecting and caring for Tropical Fish are a popular hobby. Many people find a con-stant source of delight in there gorgous coloring. Others are fascinated by the remoteness of their origins. Although some species of Tropical Fish are very expensive. Many species are not. Furthermore because these beautiful little fish adapt easly to home aquariums they are easy to keep and care for. Once acquired they provide many hours of enjoyment.

Exercise 2   Revising: The Paragraph   On your paper, revise the following paragraph. Use the notes at the left as a guide. Proofread it before you hand it in.

Make into appositive.	Block printing is a method of reproducing designs. It is an easy way to make your own
Subordinate in adverb clause.	cards, posters, or prints. The procedure takes a little patience and care. It is a fairly simple one.
Move phrase to beginning.	Draw or trace the design to be printed on a block of wood or linoleum. Cut away a thin
Make into part. phrase.	layer of the surface of the block around the design. You use a knife or special carving tool.
Coordinate sentences.	The block is now prepared. You can make prints. Spread paint or heavy ink on the raised
Correct run-on sentence.	surface, and then press the block against the paper or material to be printed, the design
Divide into two sentences.	transfers neatly, and you can make many copies simply by repeating the process.

Assignment   Revising   On your paper, revise and proof-read the following paragraph.

Elizabeth Blackwell was the first women Doctor in the United States, she overcame a great deal of prejudice to have a career in medicine. She was refused at a number of medical colleges. She was finally accepted at Geneva Medical School in 1847. Faced the prejudice of other students and the instructors. She overcame their prejudice by demonstrating her intelligence and dignity. However others outside the school considered her peculiar. She received her M.D. in 1849, and she was ignored by other Doctors and barred from practice, so with her sister Emily she set up a clinic, and she slowly won the respect of the medical community. Her successful efforts helped reduce prejudice against women in proffesions.

Assignment Checklist

Check your assignment for the following points:

  ✔ 1. Did you combine some sentences?
  ✔ 2. Did you revise the sentence that lacks coherence?
  ✔ 3. Did you vary the sentence beginnings and structures?
  ✔ 4. Did you proofread to correct errors in grammar, usage, spelling, punctuation, and capitalization?

What About Oceanography? Revising an Article

Situation: As a writer for *Science Scene,* you have been asked to revise your first draft of an article about oceanography. Your editor has commented that your article is disorganized and repetitious. Keep the following information in mind as you revise your article.

Writer: you as writer for *Science Scene*
Audience: readers of *Science Scene*
Topic: oceanography
Purpose: to make two unified, coherent paragraphs

Directions: To revise your article, follow these steps.

> *Step 1.* Read over your first draft, on page 395. You have numbered the sentences and want to decide where each sentence fits in your article. Some sentences define oceanography; some tell why it is useful to study the subject. Some sentences are unrelated to the topic and need to be omitted. To help you decide what goes where, set up a worksheet like this:

OCEANOGRAPHY

What is it?	*why study it?*

Sentences that do not deal with either question:

(Continue on page 396.)

WHAT ABOUT OCEANOGRAPHY?

(1) Oceanography is concerned with marine life. (2) Oceanography also studies plant life in the oceans. (3) California has some of the best beaches in the world. (4) The Atlantic Ocean is bounded by Europe and Africa, North and South America, the Arctic Circle, and the Antarctic Circle. (5) To sum up, oceanography is a branch of science dealing with the extent, depth, composition, and temperature of the oceans, and it also deals with the oceans' tides and currents and inhabitants. (6) Numerous government-sponsored and privately funded organizations explore ocean phenomena to learn about the history of life on Earth. (7) For example, the deposits that cover the bed of the ocean are classified according to their origin, and they tell us about early life on the planet. (8) Because three fourths of the earth's surface is water, the oceans are of great importance to us. (9) The American Heritage Dictionary defines oceanography as "the exploration and scientific study of the ocean and its phenomena." (10) In Greek mythology, Oceanus is the god of the oceans.

(11) Oceanographers use the latest equipment, and they go down to the ocean floor, and what they find provides us with a closer look at marine life.

(12) Why study oceanography? (13) One final reason for studying oceanography is that we will learn valuable information about how we can save our natural resources and protect life in the seas. (14) The currents of the Pacific are similar to those of the Atlantic.

Step 2. Each sentence fits in only one of the three categories on your worksheet. Write the number of each sentence in the appropriate space.

Step 3. Identify the function of each sentence listed under *What is it?* and *Why study it?* Use the code below:

   T topic sentence
   S supporting sentence
   C concluding sentence

Discard the remaining sentences.

Step 4. Arrange the supporting sentences in each group in a logical order. Then write a new draft of each paragraph.

Step 5. Review each paragraph, combining sentences as necessary. Then, improve the sentences that are not coherent by dividing them into two sentences or by using phrases and subordinate clauses. Omit extra or repeated words.

Step 6. Write your final draft of the two paragraphs. Proofread them for grammar, usage, spelling, and punctuation.

Unit Assignments

Assignment 1 Select a paragraph that you have already written for a composition assignment. Use the information in this unit to revise your first draft. Then proofread it and make your finished copy.

Assignment 2 Find a paragraph in a magazine, newspaper, bulletin, or other printed matter that you think could be improved. Make the revisions that you think would improve it.

Assignment 3 Write a paragraph using the topic sentence and supporting details that follow these instructions. Eliminate details that are not related to the topic. Then revise and proofread your first draft.

> *Topic sentence:* Anything can go wrong when you care for children.
>
> *Details:*
> Children cry for hours.
> Children lock you out of the house.
> Children get scraped knees.
> Children had measles last week.
> Children won't go to bed.
> Television breaks.
> Children ask for water all night.
> Refrigerator is empty.
> Parents get home late.
> You miss the school dance that night.

Assignment 4 Write a paragraph about a place where you have been. It may be a specific place, such as an arena or a monument, or it may be an area like a city, a seashore, or a mountain. Write about an aspect of it that interested you. Revise and proofread your draft.

(Continue on the next page.)

Assignment 5 Write a paragraph about something that you do well. Describe how you do it. Revise and proofread your draft.

Assignment 6 Write a paragraph about a challenging or difficult task that you have successfully completed. The task could be something like trying out for a team sport, training a pet, making an apology, constructing a school project, or learning how to handle a new responsibility. Tell how you felt before and after the experience. Revise and proofread your first draft.

Revising Your Assignments

For help in revising a first draft, consult the Checklist for Revision on the last page of this book.

Unit Tests

Test 1

A. Number your paper from 1 to 5. Next to each number, write *True* if the sentence is true or *False* if it is false.

1. When you revise a paragraph, first check for unity and coherence, then proofread, and finally, revise the sentences.
2. When you revise a paragraph, you may insert transitional words to create coherence.
3. A sentence that is not coherent can sometimes be improved by rewriting an independent clause as a phrase.
4. One way to combine sentences by subordination is to use a comma and a coordinating conjunction.
5. When revising, remove any supporting sentence that does not contribute to the topic of your paragraph.

B. Number your paper from 6 to 10. Next to each number, write the letter of the term that correctly completes the sentence. You will not use one of the items.

      a. subordination   d. coordination
      b. proofreading   e. variety
      c. revision   f. complex sentence

6. __?__ is the reorganizing and rewriting of a first draft.
7. You form a __?__ when you revise sentences by placing the main idea in an independent clause and the less important idea in a subordinate clause.
8. When you combine short sentences by __?__, you join ideas of equal importance.
9. You can provide __?__ in the sentences in a paragraph by using different beginnings and structures.
10. __?__ is the checking for correct grammar, usage, spelling, capitalization, and punctuation.

(Continue on the next page.)

C. Number your paper from 11 to 15. Next to each number, write the letter of the item that correctly answers the question.

11. Sometimes you can revise two sentences by making one a phrase and combining it with the other sentence. Which one of the following types of phrases is *not* useful for combining sentences?
    a. Appositive phrase
    b. Verb phrase
    c. Participial phrase

12. Which one of the following is *not* an example of revision by coordination?
    a. The rain fell, but we remained dry.
    b. The rain fell; however, we remained dry.
    c. The rain fell. We remained dry.
    d. The rain fell; we remained dry.

13. Which one of the following sentences is *not* an example of revision by subordination?
    a. Amateur photographers take clear pictures when they own good cameras.
    b. Amateur photographers who own good cameras take clear pictures.
    c. Amateur photographers take clear pictures if they own good cameras.
    d. Amateur photographers own good cameras; consequently, they take clear pictures.

14. Which one of the following revised sentences has combined these short sentences with an appositive phrase?
    The old film still entertains audiences. The film is a comedy.
    a. The old film, a comedy, still entertains audiences.
    b. The old film still entertaining audiences is a comedy.
    c. The old film, which still entertains audiences, is a comedy.

15. Which one of the following revised sentences does *not* make this sentence coherent?

Camilla loves to work with numbers, and she wants to be an accountant.

a. Because Camilla loves to work with numbers, she wants to be an accountant.

b. Camilla, who loves to work with numbers, wants to be an accountant.

c. Camilla wants to be an accountant, and she loves to work with numbers.

Test 2

Choose one of the Unit Assignments or a topic suggested by your teacher. Prepare and revise the assignment as directed and hand it in to your teacher.

Unit 10

Expository Writing

Unit Preview

What you write in school is most often **expository**, or explanatory, writing. The purpose of expository writing is usually to explain something to your reader, or audience: How do you get to Shoppers' Plaza from here? How do you make corn muffins? How does a pulley work? What are algae? What is the main idea of *The Red Badge of Courage*? In the unit on developing paragraphs, you learned how to use facts, reasons, and examples to explain a topic sentence. In this unit you will learn the special requirements of various types of explanations.

Directions for getting to a place are one kind of explanation. To provide a framework for a set of directions, begin with a topic sentence and end, usually, with a concluding sentence that brings the paragraph to a definite close. In between, you should include every necessary step. On the other hand, you should *not* include any extra information. Good directions are concise.

Topic sentence
Steps in order

This is the easiest way for you to get a bus to Denver. First, walk from the apartment to the corner of Moreno and Eighth. Then, from there take a number 36 bus going east on Moreno, and get off at Cresta, next to the Thrifty gas station. Next, take a number 11 bus going south on Cresta. The bus will be marked "City Terminal." Stay on the bus till it reaches the end of the line, the terminal. Now walk into the terminal, exit through the main door, and you will find yourself on Tejon Street. Finally, turn left and walk to the Clover Leaf station on the corner. Clover Leaf buses go to Denver almost hourly in the daytime.

Concluding sentence

For Analysis   On your paper, answer the following questions about the directions that you have just read.

1. Into how many main steps are the directions divided?
2. List the first word in each step. How are these words alike?
3. Are all the necessary steps included? Would they be easy to follow?
4. Why do you think the writer included the Thrifty gas station in the directions?
5. Is any unnecessary information given?

In answering the questions about the paragraph, you reviewed some of the main requirements of a good set of directions. This unit will give you practice in writing directions. It will also give you practice in writing other kinds of explanations, including the type of book review in which you explain the ideas of a book. As you write your explanations, you will follow the three steps of the writing process: prewriting, writing, and revising.

10.1   Explaining What Something Is

A basic kind of explanation defines a word. You usually define a word by placing it in a general class and pointing out one or more identifying characteristics, as in the following example.

WORD	*Biology*
CLASS	Science
CHARACTERISTICS	Concerned with life and life processes
DEFINITION	*Biology* is the science that is concerned with life and life processes.

You can express most definitions in a single sentence, but sometimes you may need to explain a word further in additional sentences. The writer of the following paragraph defines a word and expands on that definition.

Model

An anagram is a word or phrase formed by reordering the letters of another word or phrase. For instance, *wolf* is an anagram of *flow, runt* is an anagram of *turn,* and *I do it* is an anagram of *idiot.* An anagram must have exactly the same letters as the original word or phrase. Anagrams have been used to form fictitious names or titles. They also occasionally appear as clues in detective novels. The main value of anagrams, though, is the fun they provide. The cleverest anagrams are those that are closely related in meaning to the words from which they are formed: *enraged* from *angered, cannot stir* from *constraint,* and *voices rant on* from *conversation.*

The writer defines the word *anagram* in the topic sentence. Then the writer expands this definition by giving facts and examples and pointing out important aspects of anagrams that are not mentioned in the one-sentence definition.

Paragraphs that define can be arranged in different ways. In the following paragraph, for instance, the writer begins by explaining the original meaning of a word. The writer continues with a one-sentence definition of the word in its present-day sense and ends by giving three examples.

Model

> The word *slapstick* originally referred to a type of paddle used by actors in comedies. The device was made of two flat pieces of wood bound together at one end but kept loose at the other. An actor could produce a very loud slapping sound by whacking another actor with the stick. Today, *slapstick* refers to any type of comedy that involves loud, boisterous, and zany physical activity. Throwing a pie in someone's face, engaging in a wild chase, riding a horse into a living room—all are typical instances of slapstick humor.

Exercise 1 Writing: The Definition Paragraph

Write a paragraph in which you define one of the words in the following chart. First, write a topic sentence. Then use the other information in sentences that further explain the word. You may include any further details that you think would add to the reader's understanding.

	WORD	CLASS	CHARACTERISTICS	EXAMPLES
1.	*motto*	sentence or phrase	brief catchy expresses a purpose or principle	Be prepared. A stitch in time saves nine. Onward, ever onward.
2.	*conifer*	tree	evergreen bears cones leaves usually needle-shaped	pine spruce hemlock
3.	*ruminant*	animal	four-part stomach chews cud hoofs	sheep cattle giraffes deer

| 4. *sonnet* | poem | has fourteen lines
often follows fixed pattern of rhyme and meter
is sometimes part of a sequence of such poems | Shakespeare's "Shall I compare thee to a summer's day?"
Milton's "When I consider how my light is spent"
Edna St. Vincent Millay's "Euclid Alone Has Looked on Beauty Bare" |

Exercise 2 Writing: The Definition Paragraph
Write a paragraph in which you define another word from the chart in Exercise 1.

Assignment   Prewriting/Writing/Revising   Write a paragraph in which you define one of the following words. In the paragraph provide information about the origin of the word. Consult a dictionary or encyclopedia for necessary information. Revise your paragraph before making a final copy of it.

1. Passport   2. Pandemonium   3. Quixotic

Checklist
Check your assignment for the following points:

✔ 1. Did you write a one-sentence definition that places the word in a general class and then points out one or more identifying characteristics?

✔ 2. Did you expand the definition by giving facts and examples and by pointing out important aspects of the word?

✔ 3. Did you proofread your paragraph for correct grammar, usage, spelling, and punctuation?

10.2 Explaining How to Get to a Place

Writing good directions requires care. Follow these guidelines when you write a set of directions.

Strategies

1. *State what you are going to explain in a topic sentence.* In this way you make the purpose of the paragraph clear.

2. *Divide the explanation into steps and present them in chronological order.* On a sheet of scratch paper, list the steps in the order in which they should be followed. Use the list as you write the supporting sentences that explain the steps.

3. *Use transitional words to introduce some of the steps. First, next,* and *finally* are examples of such words. They help the reader to keep track of the steps. (A list of transitional words appears on page 330.)

4. *Give accurate and complete information.* Include facts that can help the reader understand every direction exactly. Mentioning landmarks is usually helpful. For example, it would be easier for the reader to get off a bus "at the third stop, where you will see the Reliable Pharmacy on the far right corner" than it would be for him or her to depend on counting the stops.

5. *Include only sentences that are essential to the explanation.* Your paragraph will then have unity. Unnecessary information makes directions harder for the reader to follow.

6. *When you can, end the explanation with a concluding sentence.* Such a sentence brings the paragraph to a definite close and indicates to the reader that your explanation is complete.

The writer of the following set of directions observed the six guidelines. The transitional words that signal the beginning of each step are in italic type.

Model

Topic sentence

Steps in chronological order

Concluding sentence

    Driving from Chicago to Detroit is an easy four-and-a-half hour trip because this route is well marked. *First,* drive south from Chicago's Loop on the Dan Ryan Expressway, traveling only twenty minutes to the interchange with the Chicago Skyway. *Then* take the Skyway about five miles until it connects with the Indiana Toll Road. Because these roads merge, there is no need to exit or enter. Just follow the signs for the Toll Road. Continue on the Toll Road about thirty miles until you come to the exit for LaPorte, Indiana. *Now* exit from the Toll Road. Directly beyond the toll booth, you will see the entrance to Interstate 94. *Finally,* enter Interstate 94, going north, which will take you to Stevensville and then will bear east, passing Kalamazoo, Jackson, and Ann Arbor. Interstate 94 will take you directly to downtown Detroit.

The paragraph presents four basic steps in the explanation of how to drive from Chicago to Detroit:

1. Drive south on the Dan Ryan Expressway from the Loop to the Chicago Skyway.
2. Take the Skyway, which becomes the Indiana Toll Road.
3. Exit from the Toll Road at LaPorte, Indiana.
4. Turn onto Interstate 94 going north and then east to Detroit.

Notice that the steps are specific but brief. The writer has given all of the needed information without saying anything extra that could confuse the reader. The writer also has named the roads and given directions in terms of south, north, or east as needed. Approximate mileage or time is included. Finally, the writer has put the steps in chronological order, as they would be followed by the driver.

Exercise 1 Prewriting: Complete Directions The following paragraph gives directions. Some of the steps do not give enough information, however. On your paper, write the numbers of the incomplete steps.

> (1) Anyone interested in the Civil War can easily drive to the Chancellorsville Battlefield from Alexandria, Virginia. (2) First, take Richmond Highway south out of Alexandria for two miles, until you reach the entrance to Route 395. (3) Turn onto Route 395 and continue for a while until you come to the Route 95 exit.   (4) Then turn onto Route 95 going south.   (5) Drive about forty miles to an exit. (6) Next, drive on Route 3 for ten miles to Chancellorsville. (7) As you approach the town, you will see the sign for Chancellorsville National Monument.   (8) Finally, turn right just beyond the sign and drive a half mile to the reception-center parking lot.   (9) You are now ready to begin your walking tour of the battlefield.

Exercise 2 Prewriting: Transitional Words On your paper, list each transitional word in the Exercise 1 paragraph.

Exercise 3 Prewriting: Chronological Order The following sentences are addressed to a person who has never taken a plane before. The steps are out of sequence, however. First, identify the topic sentence and write it on your paper. Then write the rest of the paragraph by giving the steps in the proper chronological order. Add transitional words to some of the sentences.

1. Get off the shuttle bus at the terminal of your airline.
2. At the gate, check in for your seat assignment if you have not yet been given one.
3. At the transportation desk in the lobby of the Center City Hotel, buy a ticket for the airport shuttle bus, which leaves hourly from 7 A.M. to 9 P.M.
4. Enter the terminal and go to the ticket counter.
5. Board the plane when your flight is announced.
6. Board the shuttle bus a block from the hotel, at the corner of Main and Third streets, about an hour and a half before the time of your flight.
7. After leaving the ticket counter, go through the security check, and walk to the gate assigned to your flight.
8. At the ticket counter, confirm your reservation, check your baggage, and get a boarding pass.
9. Here are directions for getting from downtown Center City to your flight.

Exercise 4   Revising: Unnecessary Sentences   The following directions contain facts that do not belong in the paragraph. On your paper, write the numbers of the extra sentences.

(1) If you want to take a pleasant bicycle ride into the country for a picnic, you can bicycle from Littleton to Muir Farm in Buena Vista. (2) First, ride west on the bicycle path along the James River. (3) Pedestrians, joggers, and roller skaters also use the bicycle path. (4) Follow the path around the curves of the river until you reach Waterside Square, where you will see a small park and a gas station at the intersection of three streets. (5) Next, ride down the middle one of the three streets, Route 20, which is also Main Street. (6) The road on the left, Route 16, leads to the Wayside Super Mart. (7) Follow Route 20 through Hillsdale, the next town. (8) As you leave Hillsdale and start up a big hill, the

name of the road will change from Route 20 to Route 117.
(9) Follow Route 117 through the country for approximately
six miles.   (10) Then, just before you reach Muir Farm, you
will see a large wooden sign for it on your right.   (11) Take
the first left turn after the sign, and you will have arrived at
the farm.   (12) Sandy Pond is three miles from the farm.

Assignment 1   Prewriting   *Step 1:* Imagine that you
must write a set of directions for a new friend who has just
moved to your community. The directions will explain how to
get from one place to another—for example, from your friend's
home to a local landmark. Select a trip that is simple enough to
be explained completely in a single paragraph. *Step 2:* Make a
numbered list of steps in chronological order. Save your paper.

Assignment 2   Writing/Revising   Using the chronological list of steps that you prepared in Assignment 1, write a
paragraph of clear directions. Revise your paragraph.

Assignment Checklist

Check your writing assignments for the following points:

1. Did you begin with a topic sentence?
2. Did you present the steps in chronological order, using transitional words to make them clear?
3. Did you present complete and accurate information?
4. Did you include only sentences that are essential to the explanation?
5. Did you end with a sentence that brings the explanation to a definite close?
6. Did you proofread your explanation for correct grammar, usage, spelling, and punctuation?

10.3 Explaining How to Make or Do Something

When you are giving instructions for making or doing something, you should follow most of the guidelines that you use when you write directions for getting to a place. Explaining how to make or do something may be more complex, however. Follow these three additional guidelines.

Strategies

1. *Limit your topic.* You should not try to cover too large a topic. Your topic should be one that you can cover thoroughly in a single paragraph. To find out whether you need to limit your topic further, make some notes on the various steps that you will need to explain. Your paragraph will probably be too long if it needs twelve or more sentences to convey the information. In such a case, change your topic to one aspect of the larger subject.

2. *Define any term that your reader may not understand.* For example, if you are explaining how to pitch a tent, you may need to explain that guy lines are the ropes anchoring the tent to the ground.

3. *Mention any tools and supplies that will be needed.* Mention them early in the explanation so that your reader can begin with all of the needed equipment at hand.

The following paragraph gives an explanation. Notice that the writer has defined the word *crown*. The explanation is complete, and it includes no unnecessary information.

Model

Topic sentence

You don't need to be a botanist to grow a pineapple plant in your home. You need only a pineapple, a narrow-mouthed glass jar, and a good knife. First, cut the cluster of leaves,

Steps in chronological order

called the crown, from the pineapple where the crown and body meet. Leave no fruit attached to the crown. Next, peel the bottom leaves from the crown to expose a half inch to one inch of the core. Then allow the core to dry for one day. After it is dry, put the core in a glass jar in such a way that the core is submerged in water but the leaf-covered part of the crown is held above the water. Keep the core in water until roots sprout, usually within a week or two. Finally, transfer the rooted core to a pot and

Concluding sentence

cover it with soil up to the leaf line. This simple rooting process will produce an exotic house plant for the cost of a piece of fruit.

The explanation tells how to do something. The following paragraph explains how to make something.

Model

Topic sentence

A terrarium—a small garden in a glass case, bottle, or jar—is quite simple to make. For a woodland terrarium, an aquarium tank is ideal. Besides the tank you will need gravel,

Steps in chronological order

charcoal, potting soil, and the plants. To start, cover the bottom of the terrarium with a layer of gravel mixed with lumps of charcoal. Then spread a one- or two-inch layer of potting soil over the gravel. Next, put your plants in. Small ferns are good choices, along with a few seedling evergreens to provide contrast. Use one of

the many kinds of moss as a ground cover.
After you have planted the garden, add water
until the soil is nicely damp and then put on the
lid. Finally, stand the terrarium in a light, fairly
Concluding   cool place. Your terrarium is now finished; it
sentence   should give you pleasure for a long time with a
minimum of care.

Notice that in the topic sentence the writer has defined the
word *terrarium*. The concluding sentence brings the paragraph
to a close on an optimistic note.

Exercise 1   Prewriting: Limited Topics   Some of the
following topics could be successfully developed in a single
paragraph. Other topics are too large. Number your paper
from 1 to 10. Write *Limited* next to the number of each limited
topic and write *Too broad* next to the number of each topic
that is too large. Save your paper.

1. How to iron a shirt correctly
2. How to service and maintain an automobile
3. How to change a bicycle tire
4. How to cut your hair at home
5. How to improve your backhand in tennis
6. How to become an expert carpenter
7. How to draw
8. How to make an omelet
9. How to paint a house inside and out
10. How to pack a carton of breakable objects

Exercise 2   Prewriting: Limiting Topics   In Exercise 1
you decided that some topics were too broad. Limit each of
those topics to one that could be explained in a paragraph.
Write the new topics on your paper.

SAMPLE   How to organize a flea market

ANSWER   How to manage a booth at a flea market

Exercise 3 Writing: Topic Sentences In Exercise 1 you decided that some topics were limited. For each one, write a topic sentence that might introduce a paragraph on the topic.

SAMPLE   How to hang a strip of wallpaper

ANSWER   Hanging wallpaper is not difficult if you know how to do it correctly.

Exercise 4 Prewriting: Chronological Order On your paper, list the transitional words in the paragraph about growing a pineapple plant (*page 413*). Then do the same thing with the paragraph about a terrarium (*pages 413–414*).

Assignment 1 Prewriting Each of the following topic sentences could be developed in a single explanatory paragraph. Select one of the sentences and write it on your paper. Then list in chronological order the steps that would explain the topic. Save your paper.

1. A very attractive and inexpensive bookcase can be built with standard bricks and boards.
2. By following the basic steps, even an inexperienced cook can make ___?___.
3. Although it appears complicated, tying a tie is quite easy.
4. Many people do not know how to organize a record collection properly.
5. Once you know how, it is easy to set a table correctly.

Assignment 2 Writing/Revising Using the planning sheet that you prepared for Assignment 1, write an explanatory paragraph. Add a concluding sentence. Using the Assignment Checklist on pages 416–417, revise your paragraph.

Assignment 3   Prewriting/Writing   Select one topic from each of the following groups. For each topic write a topic sentence and list the steps in order. Save your paper.

THINGS TO DO

1. How to sew on a button
2. How to row a boat
3. How to multiply one fraction by another fraction
4. How to change an automobile tire
5. How to pitch a tent

THINGS TO MAKE

6. How to make tuna salad
7. How to make a wreath
8. How to make a simple piece of pottery
9. How to make a campaign poster
10. How to make a scrapbook

Assignment 4 Writing / Revising   Using one of the paragraph plans that you prepared for Assignment 3, write an explanatory paragraph. End it with a concluding sentence. Then revise the paragraph as needed.

Assignment 5   Prewriting / Writing / Revising   In one paragraph explain how to make or do something that you know well. Revise the paragraph as needed. Include your planning sheet when you submit the finished paragraph to your teacher.

Assignment Checklist

Check your writing assignments for the following points:

✔ 1. Did you limit your topic?
✔ 2. Did you begin with a topic sentence?

  3. Did you mention any needed tools and supplies?
  4. Did you present the steps in chronological order, using transitional words to make them clear?
  5. Did you present complete and accurate information?
  6. Did you include only sentences that are essential to the explanation?
  7. Did you define any terms that your reader might not know?
  8. Did you end with a sentence that brings the explanation to a definite close?
  9. Did you proofread your explanation for correct grammar, usage, spelling, and punctuation?

10.4 Explaining a Process or a Device

Another kind of explanatory paragraph tells how a process or a device works. This kind of paragraph differs in one important way from those that give directions for getting from one place to another or explain how to make or do something. In those paragraphs you give orders to the reader so that he or she can follow the steps:

> First, drive three miles south on Main Street until you reach the bridge.
>
> Turn the dial on the combination lock three revolutions to the right until you reach the number 15.

In a paragraph that explains how something works, however, you do not address the reader directly. Instead, your purpose is to focus on the working of the process itself:

> The first step in solar distillation—using the sun to turn salt water into fresh water—is turning the salt water into water vapor, or mist.

To explain a process, focus on the process itself and follow the other guidelines that you have learned for writing explanations. The following paragraph illustrates those guidelines.

Model

Topic sentence

       Before we can hear a sound, a complicated process must take place. A vibrating object—be it a drum, a vocal cord, or an insect's legs rubbing together—sends out sound waves in every direction, in ever-widening circles. First, air molecules next to the vibrating object are pushed forward with every movement of the object. They move forward until they bump into other air molecules, which force the first molecules back to their original position. The next step in the process occurs when the bumped molecules themselves move forward until they bump into other molecules and return to their starting places. Thus, the "bump and return" movement will continue through the air until a moving air molecule "bumps" into the human eardrum. As it bumps against the eardrum, the drum begins to vibrate. Then the vibrations reach the nerves in the ear that change the vibrations into nerve impulses. The last step in the process takes place when the brain interprets the nerve impulses as sound. We hear! The entire process from vibration to hearing takes only a fraction of a second.

Steps in chronological order

Concluding sentence

    The writer of this paragraph has limited the topic sufficiently. The information is complete and accurate. Each sentence presents a reason in the explanation of the hearing process, and the writer presents the sentences in a logical order. The paragraph begins with a topic sentence and ends with a concluding sentence. Throughout, the writer describes the process without addressing the reader directly.

Exercise 1 Prewriting: Limited Topics Each of the following topic sentences introduces an explanation of how something works. Number your paper from 1 to 5. Write *Limited topic* next to the numbers of the sentences introducing topics that you could cover completely in a single paragraph. Write *Too broad* next to the numbers of the sentences introducing topics that are too broad.

1. The process of tooth decay is simple to explain.
2. The human nervous system is very intricate.
3. There are four principal methods of freezing foods commercially.
4. Over the years many improvements have been made in automobile engines.
5. Salt can be used to make hard water softer.

Exercise 2 Prewriting: Process Paragraphs Paragraphs 1, 2, and 3 are first drafts. All of them explain a process or a device. Evaluate each paragraph. *Step 1:* Seven numbered questions precede the paragraphs. Write them on your paper. You will use them as guidelines. *Step 2:* After each guideline write *Yes* if the writer of Paragraph 1 observed it and *No* if the writer did not. *Step 3:* Then do the same thing for Paragraphs 2 and 3. Put your answers in chart form if you wish.

1. Limited topic?
2. Focus on process?
3. Topic sentence?
4. Chronological order?
5. Information logical and complete?
6. Only essential information included?
7. Concluding sentence?

PARAGRAPH 1

The first way bacteria reproduce is by *fission,* often called cell division. The nucleus splits in two. The rest of the cell grows larger and divides into two parts. The parts separate, each containing half of the nucleus. The parts grow and become full-sized bacteria. Bacteria can also reproduce by *sporulation.* A "baby" cell develops inside the parent cell. As it grows, it breaks through the membrane of the parent cell and becomes a free spore. The spore will then grow into a mature bacterium.

PARAGRAPH 2

An automatic juicer is a great convenience to those who like fresh citrus fruit juice and drink it often. First, the fruit is sliced in half. Then the electrically driven cone of the juicer turns as the fruit is pressed down on it. Finally, as the juice is strained from the pulp, it pours down the spout into the waiting glass. Juice lovers whose time or patience is limited will welcome an electric juicer.

PARAGRAPH 3

Modern as well as ancient peoples have depended on the manufacture of wool for clothes to protect them from the elements. The first step in the manufacturing of wool is the shearing of the sheep in the spring. Shearing is done in the spring so that the sheep's wool will grow back by winter. The second step occurs as the fleece comes off each sheep in a single piece. You can see that the fibers are grouped in tufts or locks. The third step takes place when the fleece is sent to a mill, where the wool is separated into piles of different qualities, depending on the part of the animal it came from. The fourth step is the removal of dirt and oil from the wool in an enormous machine that boils it in detergent. The fifth step is the removal of the oil from the water to make lanolin. The sixth step is the carding of the wool. The seventh step is the spinning of the thread by stretching and twisting it to the desired thickness. Then you wind the wool onto spools. Finally, the spools are put on a loom or a knitting machine.

Assignment 1 **Prewriting/Writing** Plan a paragraph that will explain how one of the following objects works. *Step 1:* Select one of the objects as your topic. *Step 2:* On your paper, write an appropriate topic sentence. *Step 3:* List in order the explanatory steps. Save your paper.

1. A light bulb
2. A can opener
3. Bicycle gears
4. Scissors
5. A pulley
6. A mousetrap
7. A windshield wiper
8. A wheel
9. A faucet
10. A nozzle on a hose
11. A tube of toothpaste
12. A ballpoint pen

Assignment 2 **Writing/Revising** Using the topic sentence and the steps that you developed for Assignment 1, write your paragraph. Then revise it.

Assignment Checklist

Check your writing assignments for the following points:

✔ 1. Did you limit your topic?
✔ 2. Did you explain the working of the process or device without addressing the reader directly?
✔ 3. Did you begin with a topic sentence?
✔ 4. Did you present the steps in chronological order, using transitional words to make them clear?
✔ 5. Did you end with a sentence that brings the explanation to a definite close?
✔ 6. Did you proofread your explanation for correct grammar, usage, spelling, and punctuation?

10.5 Explaining the Ideas in a Book: The Book Review

A book review is a discussion of the ideas and characters in the work. Writing about a book can add to your enjoyment and understanding of it by focusing attention on what is significant about the work.

Book reviews can vary in length from a single paragraph to several paragraphs. Here is a format that you can use.

Procedure

1. *Introductory Sentence.* Begin your review with an introductory sentence that names the author and title of the book and identifies it as fiction or nonfiction.

2. *Brief Description.* Describe the book in a sentence or two. In describing a novel, for example, mention the characters, situation, and setting. The following sentence describes *The Pearl,* by John Steinbeck: "The novel concerns a poor Mexican couple who face serious problems when they become possessors of the largest and most valuable pearl ever discovered." Such a description presents only the essential facts that are necessary to give the reader a general idea of the subject of the book. The following sentence briefly describes a nonfiction work, *The View from a Distant Star,* by Harlow Shapley: "In his thoughtful work, the author investigates the question of whether human beings can survive the contamination of this planet."

   This type of description should not be confused with the longer summary of a book's action or information that you may have written for book reports in the past.

3. *Central Idea.* Continue with a discussion of the central idea of the book. If the book is nonfiction, the central idea will, of course, concern the subject of the book. A biography may explain the reasons for a person's success. A book about science may explain the causes of a natural phenomenon. If the book is

fiction, the central idea probably relates to the conflict within the story: how a character battles against the forces of nature, other people, or certain aspects of herself or himself. In *The Pearl*, for example, the character Kino must struggle with his own greed and with the greed of others when he discovers the valuable pearl.

4. *Evaluation.* Discuss whether the author was successful in presenting his or her central idea to the reader. Was the central idea presented clearly, knowledgeably, and interestingly? As a result, was the book powerful or memorable? Refer to specific passages as you give reasons to support your evaluation. You may indicate whether you liked the book, but this should not be the focus of the evaluation.

5. *Concluding Sentence.* In the last sentence, provide a final evaluation of the book. You may summarize what is significant about the book or describe the impact that it had on you.

The following review uses this format.

Model

Introductory sentence	*Fifth Chinese Daughter,* by Jade Snow Wong, is an autobiography. Not only does it
Brief description	follow the life of a young woman as she matures, but it also gives a view of family life in San Francisco's Chinatown. Jade Snow Wong's family proudly preserved their cultural traditions, trying to rear her with unquestioning respect for her elders and their ideas.
Central idea	Yet the concepts of independence that Jade Snow found in American schools brought her into conflict with her family. Daringly, she

worked outside the family business and earned money for college. Her solution, arrived at slowly and painfully over a period of years, was to find her own place in life as a ceramist. Creating beautiful pottery with her heart and hands, she succeeded as an artist and as a businesswoman in the Chinese community. At first the Wongs opposed her rebellion against their traditional view of the proper role for a woman. Later they came to take pride in her achievements.

Evaluation The author has presented well the conflict of a young person who finds her own ideas to be at odds with those of her family. To some extent, her struggles can be seen as part of the conflict that all young people experience as they grow up. Perhaps the most surprising aspect of the book is the way in which it is told. Following the Chinese tradition of modesty, the author never refers to herself as "I" but always speaks of herself as "Jade Snow" or "she." Her modest life story is more than a pleasant visit to a Chinese American community. It is the story of a courageous young person finding her way.

Concluding
sentence

Exercise Prewriting: The Book Review The kind of book review discussed in this section contains five categories of information: introductory sentence, brief description, central idea, evaluation, and concluding sentence. Each of the following numbered passages represents one of the five categories. On your paper, write the category of each passage next to its number.

1. Anne Frank occasionally tells of short tempers and other human frailties aggravated by stress. But mainly she tells of human courage—the bravery of the Franks' Dutch protectors

and the daily acts of courage on the part of the attic refugees themselves. Anne's remarkable spirit endures. Toward the end of her diary, she is still able to write, "In spite of everything, I still believe that people are really good at heart."

2. *When the Legends Die,* by Hal Borland, is a novel.

3. *The Rock and the Willow* is an exceptionally moving novel.

4. It is the story of an Illinois farm boy who grows to manhood during the Civil War.

5. Ceram's account of the early dwellers in America—their lives and their monuments—is excellently presented. The section that explains what archeology is helps the reader to understand how ruins and artifacts can reveal information about early peoples. Illustrations make Ceram's explanations clear and interesting.

Assignment 1   Prewriting   Select a book, fiction or nonfiction, that you would like to read. Read the book, taking notes on the five types of information needed for a book review.

Assignment 2   Writing/Revising   Using the notes prepared for Assignment 1, write a brief book review. Then revise it. Remember, the purpose of the review is to present an overview and an evaluation of the book.

Assignment Checklist

Check your writing assignment for the following points:

✔ 1. Did you begin by naming the author and title and identifying the book as fiction or nonfiction?

✔ 2. Did you describe the book in a sentence or two?

✔ 3. Did you explain the central idea of the book?

✔ 4. Did you evaluate the author's presentation of the central idea?

✔ 5. Did you end by summarizing what the work achieves?

✔ 6. Did you proofread your book review for correct grammar, usage, spelling, and punctuation?

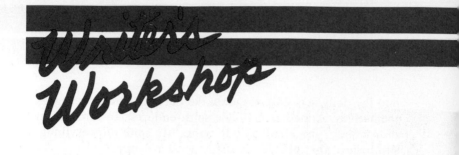

Wilderness Wisdom: Explaining How to Take Care of a Tent

Situation: You write the "Wilderness Wisdom" column in a newsletter called *Backpacking Monthly*. For each issue you collect and prepare information for hikers and campers. This month you have decided to give some tips on taking care of a tent. You will base your advice on some notes that you have in your files. As you plan and write the column, you will keep in mind the following information.

Writer: you as a columnist for *Backpacking Monthly*
Audience: readers of *Backpacking Monthly*
Topic: taking care of a tent
Purpose: to explain the topic in a paragraph of no more than ten sentences

Directions: To write your paragraph, follow these steps.

> *Step 1.* Read "Notes on Tents" on the facing page and decide which details relate to your topic.
>
> *Step 2.* Write a topic sentence for your paragraph.
>
> *Step 3.* In your supporting sentences, explain the various aspects of caring for a tent. Use such words as *first, also,* and *finally* to begin some of your sentences. Use the imperative forms of verbs when you give your instructions, as in "Keep the tent floor clean."
>
> *Step 4.* Write a concluding sentence for your paragraph.

Notes on Tents

Importance of good care
    Correct care insures long use.
    Well—cared—for tent, used 30 days a year, may last
    more than 10 years.
    Large tents are very expensive.

Pitching a tent
    Ideal spot is high, dry, and allows for run—off of
    water if storm comes.
    Do not pitch tent under overhanging branches that
    might fall during storm.
    Guy lines help secure tent.
    Remove twigs, stones (so they will not puncture floor
    of tent).

General use
    Sharp objects can snag and tear tent.
    Long camping trips: remove stakes from tent bottom,
    and lift floor to air the bottom (prevents mildew).
    Tent should not rest in puddles of water for a long
    time.
    Keep tent floor clean: dirt harmful to tent fabrics.
    Ventilate tent through windows or door flap.

Packing a tent
    Dry out tent before packing.
    If drying not possible, spread tent to dry as soon as
    you can.
    Clear away twigs and dirt before packing (reduces
    wear and tear).
    Pack tent stakes separately (protects tent from rips
    or punctures).

Unit Assignments

Assignment 1 Write a paragraph of directions in which you explain to a classmate how to get from your school to your home in one of the following ways. Be exact and mention landmarks whenever you can.

  a. Walking
  b. Taking public transportation
  c. Driving

Assignment 2 Write a paragraph in which you explain one of the following topics to a child of ten. Include only sentences that are essential to the explanation.

  a. How to take part in a home fire drill
  b. How to build a campfire
  c. How to play a home video game

Assignment 3 Choose one of the words listed below. Read about the word in a dictionary or an encyclopedia. Then write a paragraph in which you clearly define the word and give additional information about it.

  a. Alibi   d. Mime
  b. Esophagus   e. Parallel
  c. Hypothesis   f. Sphinx

Assignment 4 Write a paragraph in which you explain how one of the following devices works. Make the paragraph concise.

  a. A pencil sharpener
  b. A flashlight
  c. A lawn sprinkler

Assignment 5 Write a review of one of the books recommended by your school or local librarian. Follow the book-review guidelines that you learned in this unit.

Assignment 6   Write a one-paragraph explanation of one of the following topics. Address the paragraph to an audience of classmates.

    a. How to handle a newspaper route or other job
    b. How to do your favorite dance
    c. How to tune a guitar or another stringed instrument

Assignment 7   Write a one-paragraph explanation of one of the following:

    a. How to make a snowplow stop on skis
    b. How to do a figure eight on skates
    c. How to make a free throw in basketball

Assignment 8   Write a one-paragraph explanation of one of the following processes:

    a. Photosynthesis
    b. The formation of glaciers
    c. A lunar eclipse

Revising Your Assignments

For help in revising a piece of expository writing, consult the Checklist for Revision on the last page of this book.

Unit Tests

Test 1

A. Number your paper from 1 to 5. Next to each number, write *True* if the sentence is true or *False* if it is false.

1. A review of a novel should include facts about an author's life.
2. A definition usually includes the general class in which a word belongs.
3. Expository writing is writing that explains.
4. "How a Spacecraft Is Built" would be a good topic for an explanatory paragraph.
5. A topic sentence makes clear the purpose of a paragraph.

B. Number your paper from 6 to 10. Next to each number, write the letter of the term that correctly completes the sentence. You will not use one of the items.

    a. chronological   d. book review

    b. definition   e. transitional

    c. expository   f. central idea

6. When you give directions, such __?__ words as *first, second,* and *finally* indicate the order of steps.
7. A sentence or paragraph that explains the meaning of a word is called a(n) __?__.
8. Directions for making something must be given in __?__ order.
9. A(n) __?__ presents one reader's reactions and impressions.
10. The __?__ of a book about science might be the formation of volcanoes.

C. Number your paper from 11 to 15. Next to each number, write the letter of the item that correctly answers the question.

11. Which part of a book review describes the characters, situation, and setting of a novel?
    a. Introductory sentence   c. Concluding sentence
    b. Evaluation   d. Brief description

12. Which of the following statements about explaining how to make something is true?

    a. The topic should be limited.

    b. As many details as possible should be included to make the explanation interesting.

    c. Instructions can be written in any order.

    d. A concluding sentence is never necessary.

13. Which of the following statements about an explanation of a process is false?

    a. The steps in the process are presented chronologically.

    b. Only essential information is included.

    c. The explanation should begin with a definition.

    d. The explanation has a topic sentence.

14. Which of the following topics would be suitable for a paragraph about how something works?

    a. Getting from the Severance Hotel to Market Square

    b. Allergy testing

    c. Playing goalkeeper in lacrosse

    d. Making a silver bracelet

15. Which of the following topics would be suitable for a paragraph about how to make something?

    a. Playing a saxophone

    b. Explaining what ecology is

    c. Driving to Houston from Louisville

    d. Building a raft

Test 2

Choose one of the Unit Assignments. Write the assignment as directed and hand it in to your teacher.

Unit 11

Descriptive Writing

Unit Preview

The purpose of writing a description is to bring an object, a place, or a person to life for your reader. The words that you choose can describe sights, sounds, textures, smells, and tastes. A good description is both vivid and precise.

Including specific nouns and verbs makes a description vivid. For example, writing that you rode in a *boat* is not as vivid as writing that you rode in a *rowboat* or sailed on a *cargo ship*. Writing that a person *spoke* is not as vivid as writing that the person *shouted* or *whispered*.

Precise modifiers—adjectives and adverbs as well as participles—add details. For example, you could write that you rode in a *leaky old* rowboat *abandoned at the dock* or that the person shouted *joyfully*.

The following paragraph creates a vivid scene. Notice in particular the words in italic type.

> When spring came, the evening hours were the most exciting of the day. The voices of hundreds of frogs—tree frogs, leopard frogs, and green peepers—*echoed* through the woods until the blackness of night settled in. At the sound of our passing, the frogs became silent, until the whole marsh was filled with an uneasy, unnatural *hush* and only the *rustle* of the cattails could be heard. Then the red-winged blackbirds combatted intrusion not with silence, but, instead, with *raucous*

noise. A series of chortles, bubbles, and loud *chatters* escorted us until we were safely out of sight.

Christopher W. Johnson, Cloquet High School
Cloquet, Minnesota

For Analysis   On your paper, answer the following questions about the description.

1. Words can describe sights, sounds, textures, smells, and tastes. Which of the five types of details does the writer use most in this paragraph? Give at least five examples of that type of detail.
2. On separate lines, copy the words that appear in italic type in the paragraph. Next to each word write a less vivid word or phrase.
3. How would the effect of the paragraph change if the less vivid words were substituted for the words in italic type?

In this unit you will learn how to observe details and how to put those details into vivid words. You also will learn how to organize the details. As you practice describing objects, places, and persons, you will follow the three steps of the writing process: prewriting, writing, and revising.

11.1 Using Sensory Details

Do you notice details in the world around you? To write an effective description, you must first become a careful observer. For example, exactly what color is the shirt that you received for your birthday? Just how loud are the jets that circle your neighborhood in their landing pattern? How sweet are the freshly picked strawberries that you ate for dessert? The heart of descriptive writing is learning to observe details and then putting those details into words for your reader.

11.1a Observing Sensory Details

Consider carefully the person, place, or thing that you are to describe. How does it look, feel, taste, sound, and smell? What you observe—and perhaps write down—will be the **sensory details** associated with your subject. Each of the following descriptions focuses on one of the five senses.

Model: Details of Sight

Mother signed me up for the Junior Cotillion and forced me to go. I used to enter the cotillion room clad in a pink or flowered crêpe de Chine dress made by her, a little sash tying my precocious torso in two like a sack, a frill at my neck and frills at my elbow, pink silk socks and sandals.

Agnes de Mille, *Dance to the Piper*

Model: Details of Taste

Vendors, whose stalls consisted of several shelves screwed to the sides of buildings, guarded a jumble of Hong Kong miscellany . . . sugared coconut, dry fortune cookies, almond cookies, sesame seed cookies, dried litchi nuts, and a thousand other things, pickled, glazed, roasted, or embalmed, all tempting.

Jeffery Paul Chan, "Auntie Tsia Lies Dying"

Model: Details of Smell

. . . the discovery was soon made that Mrs. Todd was an ardent lover of herbs, both wild and tame, and the seabreezes blew into the low end-window of the house laden with not only sweet-brier and sweet-mary, but balm and sage and borage and mint, wormwood and southern-wood. If Mrs. Todd had occasion to step into the far corner of her herb plot, she trod heavily upon thyme, and made its fragrant presence known with all the rest.

Sarah Orne Jewett, *The Country of the Pointed Firs*

Model: Details of Touch

He felt the razor-sharp barnacles bite into his hand, collapse under the pressure, drive their tiny slime-covered shell splinters deep into his flesh.

Arthur Gordon, "The Sea Devil"

Model: Details of Sound

I hear voices from the arbor, low, monotonous, indistinct—and now and again laughter; there are crickets and frogs across the range of the night, everywhere, nowhere. And at long intervals I hear trucks passing along the highway on the south side of the house, in the red cut of the knoll, the high-pitched singing of the tires. There is something unspeakably lonely in that sound. . . .

N. Scott Momaday, *The Names*

Most persons, places, and things that you describe will offer details that appeal to more than one sense. A complete description includes a mixture of the significant sensory details, as in the following passage. In it the writer uses visual details to describe the scene. The writer does not stop there, however; he also gives details from the senses of hearing and touch. The details of sound and touch are identified at the side of the passage.

Model: Mixed Sensory Details

At the bottom of the mountain, a car turned onto the road that leads up to our cabin. It moved slowly along, weaving back and forth, occasionally disappearing behind small ridges and reappearing in a different place. Gradually the two headlights became distinguishable, and

Sound — the low hum of the motor could be heard. The

Sound — car came over the last rise, the gravel popping under the rubber tires. The engine went quiet,

Sound

Sound

Sound, touch

Sound

Sound, touch

and my relatives got out after a long day of driving. The doors slammed as they piled into the cabin, and then all was quiet again except for the stepped-up jolly conversation that came from within. Their still-warm car ticked and cracked as I stood up and clumped across the porch in my heavy untied boots. Before opening the door, I gazed through the dust settling on the driveway at the calm scene around me. The screen door slapped shut, and the warm yellow light engulfed me. My eyes adjusted to the light, and I was quickly swallowed up in the friendliness of the whole family together.

Eric Heywood, Mount Vernon High School
Mount Vernon, Iowa

Exercise 1   Prewriting: Sensory Details   Number your paper from 1 to 10. Write the sense(s)—sight, hearing, touch, taste, and smell—to which each of the following details appeals.

SAMPLE   Yellow bus driving along a highway

ANSWER   Sight, hearing

1. Chuckle
2. Brown suede coat
3. Glass of milk
4. Heavy rain
5. White feather

6. Red balloon
7. Hot corn muffins
8. Smoke
9. Jazz music in the distance
10. Bicycle

Exercise 2   Prewriting: Sensory Details   Divide your paper into three columns headed *Sight, Hearing,* and *Touch.* Under each heading list the details from the following passage that are from that sense. Include sentence numbers.

SAMPLE	(1) Judy, my sister, and I go to bed early, padding across the cold hall floor to our uncle's old room that we share.
ANSWER	Hearing: padding across (1) Touch: cold hall floor (1)

(1) Judy, my sister, and I go to bed early, padding across the cold hall floor to our uncle's old room that we share. (2) Baby pictures of Uncle Dan stare down at us from the room's pink walls. (3) Our feet feel the cold as it seeps up through the hardwood floor into the oval rug covering it, and my eyes fix momentarily upon the huge, ever-present vacuum cleaner resting in the corner so that one can't open the door all the way. (4) We bounce upon the springy, long bed covered with the familiar checkered blankets. (5) Comfortable on the down pillows, we spend half an hour each night whispering and kicking each other before going to sleep. (6) In the dark I stare at the cold glare of the hall light as it shines through the crack in the doorway and reflects off the dresser mirror and picture frames. (7) Its harshness is softened as the voices of those close to me float gently through the glass kitchen door into our room.

Deborah Eisenstein, Mira Costa High School
Manhattan Beach, California

Exercise 3 Prewriting: Sensory Details On your paper, list the five senses, one to a line: sight, hearing, taste, smell, and touch. Next to each category, write the two most pleasant details that you can think of.

SAMPLE	Smell
ANSWER	Smell: Roses, pine trees

11.1b Selecting Sensory Details

A well-written description does not include every detail. Instead, you must choose the sensory details that will help you to carry out your purpose of creating a sharp, deeply felt description.

Model

> There was a sudden hush among the people in the crowd on top of Mount Sinai. Following their gaze, I saw a thin red sliver sitting on top of bands of silver-gray clouds, suspended over the desert wilderness. As I continued to watch, the red crescent became larger, filling out into a semicircle and spilling its pigment onto the clouds and the bleak desert hills. The blood red turned slowly to shades of green and pink and yellow that I have never before or since seen. Then, at the final moment, the sun broke through in a shower of green-gold sparks, bathing the mountains in such beautiful shades of gold that my breath caught in my lungs.

> *(Adapted)*
> *Gillian Kaye, Great Neck North High School*
> *Great Neck, New York*

The writer has created a striking visual description that emphasizes the colors of the rising sun. Of course, she could have included other sensory details, such as the size of the mountains, the sounds of the animal life, or the temperature of the desert. But these details, though interesting, would have marred the impression of sun and sky colors that she was creating. When you write, you sometimes must reject details that are interesting in themselves in order to keep to your purpose of creating a single, sharp impression.

Exercise 4   Prewriting: Sensory Details   Select two of the three objects that follow each of the senses listed. Write them on your paper. Next to each item, write at least one appropriate detail from the sense indicated.

SAMPLE   Sense of taste: A lemon
ANSWER   A lemon: sour, bitter

1. Sense of taste
   a. An apple   b. A chilli pepper   c. Mustard
2. Sense of touch
   a. Sandpaper   b. Linoleum   c. A carpet
3. Sense of smell
   a. A greenhouse   b. A popcorn machine   c. A bakery
4. Sense of hearing
   a. A large clock   b. A fire truck   c. A dog
5. Sense of sight
   a. A T-shirt   b. A wristwatch   c. A fence

Assignment Writing For a week keep a notebook in which you write descriptive details of objects, persons, and places that you see. Record details from all of the senses. You may find that your notebook will furnish topics and details for descriptions that you are later called upon to write.

Assignment Checklist

Check your assignment for the following points:

   ✔ 1. Did you record descriptive details in your notebook?
   ✔ 2. Did you include details from all of the senses?

11.2 Choosing Descriptive Words

Once you know what you will describe and which sensory details you will use, you must choose words that will accurately and vividly convey those details to your reader.

11.2a Using Effective Nouns and Verbs

Use specific nouns and strong verbs in your descriptions. With a specific noun, you can create a precise image. For example, if you use *tree,* your reader will not know whether to picture an evergreen or a leafy tree. *Oak* or *ponderosa pine* is a more specific noun. These words help the reader to form a mental picture.

Verbs, on the other hand, help to create motion in your writing. Strong verbs describe the motion exactly. For example, in the sentence "The flag moved in the wind," *moved* is not a strong verb because it does not indicate whether the flag moved slowly and gently or quickly and vigorously. Either *billowed* or *flapped* would be a stronger verb. In addition, verbs in the active voice are stronger than verbs in the passive voice. A linking verb is the weakest kind of all. "His eyes sparkled brightly" is more vivid than "His eyes were bright."

The following paragraph contains specific nouns and strong verbs.

Model

The white morning light bounces off the waves in glittering ripples. Cold moss-green water darts out and licks my ankles quickly, then retreats. I tread heavily on the solid brown sand, curling my toes in the wet graininess of it. A trail of shallow hollows follows me down the beach, and the sea rushes in again, impatiently erasing them.

Sally Weston, Divine Child High School
Dearborn Heights, Michigan

The specific nouns make the passage vivid. The noun *ripples* describes precisely the pattern of light as it is reflected from the water, and *graininess* captures the texture of sand. In the last sentence, the writer could have written "A line of shallow holes." However, *trail* is better than *line* because it suggests the path along which the writer walked, and *hollows* is better than *holes* because it suggests smaller indentations.

The strong verbs (as well as the participles) create the sense of continuous motion in the description. *Darts out* and *licks* create a stronger picture for the reader than *covers* would have done. Not once does the writer use a weak verb, such as *be* or *have*, or a passive form, such as *is erased* or *am followed*.

Exercise 1   Prewriting: Specific Nouns   Number your paper from 1 to 10. After each number write a noun that is more specific than the one that is listed.

SAMPLE   Store

ANSWER   Bakery

1. Plant
2. Entertainer
3. Sport
4. Fish
5. Shoe

6. Music
7. Metal
8. Fruit
9. Building
10. Dish

Exercise 2   Prewriting: Strong Verbs   Number your paper from 1 to 10. After each number write the more specific verb of the pair.

SAMPLE   Ask, plead

ANSWER   Plead

1. Walk, stroll
2. Bellow, shout
3. Hold, grasp
4. Master, learn
5. Wash, scour

6. Eat, devour
7. Whisper, talk
8. Scare, terrify
9. Gaze, look
10. Gulp, drink

Exercise 3   Revising: Nouns and Verbs   On your paper, rewrite each sentence, using specific nouns and strong verbs.

SAMPLE   The girl played her instrument.

ANSWER   The girl strummed her guitar.

1. There were many colors in the picture.
2. The animal sat in the chair.
3. The children moved around the park.
4. Lightning appeared in the sky.
5. The radio was playing music.
6. The person walked up the stairs.

441

7. The plant was in the garden.
8. The car went down the street.
9. The person entered the building.
10. The person sewed the clothing.

11.2b Using Modifiers

Often you will use modifiers, words that describe, when you re-create sensory details for your reader. One well-chosen adjective or participle can describe a noun; one precise adverb can enhance a verb. A single modifier may be more effective than several. In the following description, notice the modifiers that are in italic type.

Model

On *chilly* mornings I creep into the hallway, smelling coffee boiling on the stove and hearing the *low* voices of my grandparents as they make a fire and prepare breakfast. Then I scamper onto the *bristly* carpet in the dining room and press my *icy* feet against the *warm* air blowing *gently* from the furnace.

Deborah Eisenstein, Mira Costa High School
Manhattan Beach, California

Single modifiers effectively convey the sensory details of this simple description. For example, the writer accurately describes the mornings with the adjective *chilly,* not the word *cold.* She is specific, too, when she uses the adverb *gently* to describe the blowing of the air from the furnace.

Modifiers are not restricted to single words, however. Remember that you can also use prepositional phrases and participial phrases as modifiers.

| NO MODIFIERS | A car passed. |
| ADJECTIVE | A *blue* car passed. |

PARTICIPLE	A *gleaming* car passed.
ADVERB	A car passed *slowly*.
PREPOSITIONAL PHRASE	A car *with a flat tire* passed.
PARTICIPIAL PHRASE	*Moving very slowly,* a car passed.

Exercise 4 Prewriting: Modifiers Number your paper from 1 to 10. After each number write the more specific modifier in the pair of words.

1. Drenched, wet
2. Thirsty, parched
3. Emerald, green
4. Bright, brilliant
5. Glistening, shining
6. Purple, violet
7. Quiet, hushed
8. Deafening, loud
9. Frail, slender
10. Azure, blue

Exercise 5 Revising: Modifiers The following sentences lack modifiers. On your paper, rewrite each sentence, making it more informative and more interesting to the reader by adding at least one modifier. Use phrases as well as single words.

> **SAMPLE**   The storm damaged the trees.
>
> **ANSWER**   The violent storm damaged the elm trees.

1. The aircraft taxied down the runway.
2. The girl sat in a chair in the office.
3. The child watched the movie.
4. The man ran after the bus.
5. The truck pulled up to the door.
6. The woman waited in the station.
7. The hikers climbed the mountain.
8. The candle burned.
9. The hands of the clock moved.
10. The motorcyclist rode along the highway.

11.2c Using Comparisons

Besides using modifiers, you can describe with comparisons. If you want to describe a subject in a striking way, compare it to something that your reader knows but does not ordinarily associate with the subject. Without having to think about it, your reader will instantly identify the characteristic that the two subjects have in common.

The following sentence contains a **simile**, a direct comparison using the word *like* or *as*.

SIMILE   When the curtains opened, the sunlight spread itself like a golden blanket over the old woman's shoulders.

Chiyo Markwell
Woodbridge Senior High School
Woodbridge, Virginia

To describe the sunlight shining through a window, the writer compares it to a "golden blanket," warm and protective.

The second example presents an implied comparison, called a **metaphor**. A metaphor does not use *like* or *as*.

METAPHOR   The taps of his brother's typewriter were small explosions in his ears as he tried to fall asleep.

The writer compares the noise of a typewriter to explosions.

Similes and metaphors are effective when they are fresh and original. Avoid overused comparisons, called **clichés**. Readers have read and heard clichés so often that they are bored by them. Writing that someone is "as pretty as a picture" is not interesting and does not reveal as much about the person as a fresh comparison could. On the other hand, a comparison that is extremely unusual may seem bizarre and distract your reader's attention from your subject.

The following passage contains comparisons that effectively strengthen the description of an arbor. Four of the comparisons, all of them similes, are in italic type.

Model

> The arbor is a square frame building, cool and dark within. Two timbers, *like telegraph poles,* support the high, pitched roof, which is made of rafters and shingles, warped and weather-stained. Inside, on such a day as this, there are innumerable points of light at the roof, *like stars,* too small to admit of beams or reflections. The arbor is a place from which the sun is excluded at midday, a room that is *like dawn or dusk at noon,* and always there is a particular weather inside, an air that is cooler and more fluent than that of the plain, *like wind in a culvert,* and a deeper, more congenial shade. At times you can hear the wind, for it runs upon the walls and moans. . . .
>
> N. Scott Momaday, *The Names*

Because the writer wants the reader to be able to picture the unusual structure of the arbor, he compares its details to familiar things: telegraph poles, stars, dawn or dusk, and wind.

Exercise 6 Prewriting: Comparisons In each of the following sentences, find the comparison and write it on your paper.

SAMPLE   The polished car shines like a new penny.

ANSWER   Polished car is compared to new penny.

1. The earthquake was as sudden as lightning.
2. There was a rumble like thunder.
3. Then the quake shook the house like a cat playing with a mouse.
4. The collapsed garage looked like a broken matchbox.
5. During the quake we were bounced around like basketballs.

Exercise 7   Writing: Similes and Metaphors   On your paper, write a sentence with an appropriate simile or metaphor that describes each of the following subjects.

> SAMPLE   The old baseball glove
>
> ANSWER   The old baseball glove felt like a baby's skin.

1. His walk
2. The muscles of his arms
3. The leafy garden
4. The soprano's voice
5. The trombone music

6. The dog's coat
7. The taste of the orange
8. The windows of the house
9. The sound of the motorcycle
10. The full moon

Assignment   Writing   On your paper, write ten sentences that describe the stores in a shopping center. The sentences need not form a paragraph. Use effective nouns and verbs, and use at least one modifier in each sentence. Use comparisons in some of the sentences.

Assignment Checklist

Check your assignment for the following points:

✔ 1. Did you use specific nouns and strong verbs?
✔ 2. Did you use precise, vivid modifiers?
✔ 3. Did you use comparisons effectively?
✔ 4. Did you proofread your sentences for correct grammar, usage, spelling, and punctuation?

11.3 Describing an Object

Like any paragraph, a descriptive paragraph usually has a topic sentence, in which you introduce the object. Often your topic sentence gives a general impression of the object. A descriptive paragraph may also have a concluding sentence, in which you indicate that the description is complete.

The senses of sight and touch provide you with the details of the object's color, shape, size, texture, and weight. In a careful description you will also include—when applicable —details of taste, smell, and sound.

The following paragraph illustrates how a writer uses details to create a clear impression of a beautiful object.

Model

Topic
sentence

As Fritz continued to walk east, a periwinkle caught his eye. The seashell, so much whiter than the sand that it seemed to radiate its own light, lay before him. He stopped walking again and picked it up to examine it. The shell was not uncommonly large, and its color seemed more faded than it had been in the sand. Yet it was in every way perfect. It was not chipped or broken anywhere; there were no irregularities in its ridges and spirals. The peak was perfectly pointed, the openings at the top formed by smooth curves. Fritz turned it over and over with his fingers. He marveled at the flowing curve that rounded the shell in one continuous line, like a spiral staircase in miniature. He was amazed that something which seemed so fragile had been sturdy enough to survive not merely intact, but perfect.

Comparison

Concluding
sentence

Andrew L. Miller, Westbury High School
Westbury, New York

In the first sentence, the writer introduces the shell. In the second sentence, he describes it with the modifying words "so much whiter than the sand." In the next sentences, the writer uses precise nouns, adjectives, and participles to describe the size, color, and condition of the shell. The comparison with a spiral staircase makes the shape clear to the reader. In his concluding sentence, the writer reinforces the impression of beauty and perfection.

Exercise   Prewriting: Description of an Object   Select three of the following objects. On your paper, make a list of the sensory details associated with each object. If possible, think of an appropriate comparison.

> SAMPLE   An old book
> ANSWER   Rough texture of cloth cover
>   Light blue water stains on dark blue cover
>   Crackling sound when book is opened
>   Brittle, yellow pages
>   Musty smell like that of a basement

1. A kitten
2. A small calculator
3. A piece of jewelry

4. A clock
5. A tree
6. A surfboard

Assignment 1   Writing   On your paper, describe each of the following objects in a sentence. Each sentence should include details from only one sense. Identify that sense. Be sure to save your paper.

> SAMPLE   A carpet
> ANSWER   The carpet felt soft and thick. (*Touch*)

1. A pair of scissors
2. A football
3. A section from an orange

4. An onion
5. A church bell

Assignment 2   Prewriting   Review the work that you completed for Assignment 1. Select one of the sentences containing details from a single sense. Now make a list of details from the other senses associated with that object. Save your paper.

448

SAMPLE	The carpet felt soft and thick. (*Touch*)
ANSWER	*Sight:* large oriental designs with cobalt blue as the dominant color; faintly shiny surface; knotted beige fringe at both ends
	Smell: slightly musty

Assignment 3 Writing/Revising Using the list that you completed for Assignment 2, write a brief paragraph that describes the object that you chose. Then revise your paragraph.

Assignment 4 Prewriting/Writing/Revising *Step 1:* Select one of the following topics for description. *Step 2:* On your paper, make a list of the sensory details associated with it. *Step 3:* Using this information, write a descriptive paragraph for your classmates to read. *Step 4:* Revise your paragraph.

1. A favorite article of clothing
2. A portable radio
3. A video game
4. A comfortable chair
5. Roller skates

Assignment 5 Prewriting/Writing/Revising *Step 1:* Find an unusual object to describe. *Step 2:* On your paper, make a list of all the sensory details associated with the object. *Step 3:* Write a paragraph describing the object without revealing its name. *Step 4:* Revise the paragraph. You might read your paragraph to your classmates and teacher to see if they can guess what the object is.

Assignment Checklist

Check your writing assignments for the following points:

  ✔ 1. Did you include a topic sentence that states what your paragraph will describe?
  ✔ 2. Did you include carefully selected sensory details?

✔3. Did you use precise, vivid words and effective comparisons?

✔4. Did you proofread your paragraph for correct grammar, usage, spelling, and punctuation?

11.4 Describing a Place

Every location is unique. Even two scenes within a few yards of each other are different. Your purpose as a writer is to capture in words the one-of-a-kind quality that every place has.

11.4a Using Sensory Details

Although a place is sometimes thought of only in terms of sight, it may also offer details of smell, taste, sound, and touch. For example, in an industrial city you can often smell the smog created by factories and cars, taste the chemical pollution in the air, hear the roar of the traffic, and in the summer feel the heat of the sun's rays. By choosing precise modifiers and an occasional comparison to convey the sensory details, you can create a powerful description. The following description includes details from all four senses.

Model

	As I walk down the street, I am assaulted by the sights and sounds of the bazaar. The
Sight, touch	milling people crowd around me, pressing me into walls and other pedestrians. The very scents of life are in the air: the tangy aroma of
Smell	lamb curry simmering over an open flame, of a
Smell	young goat on a spit, of espresso in a small
Touch	café. Dust hangs heavy in the hot, still air as I stop to look at something and am harangued by

Sound	the owner in a high-pitched foreign language. I
Sound	hear the harsh sound of a coppersmith beating
Sight	copper over what looks like an overly large
	bolt, its top round and scarred from previous
Smell	workings. The people around me stink of un-
	washed bodies and the animals they work with.
	Every now and then, someone nestles up
Touch	against me and gives me a quick pat down,
	trying for my wallet before darting into the
Sound	crowds. On all sides the cacophony rises as
	dealers argue over whose goods are better.

Kevin Ruddell, Rancho High School
North Las Vegas, Nevada

Notice that in his concluding sentence the writer returns to the sense of noise and confusion described in the topic sentence.

Exercise 1   Prewriting: Sensory Details   The following list contains three sensory details from an imagined scene of a bridge at night. On your paper, add five more sensory details that might complete a description of the scene. Do not write sentences; simply list descriptive details.

1. The sound of traffic driving across the bridge
2. The sight of a coal barge
3. The feel of fog

11.4b Using Spatial Order

A special consideration in describing a place is the organizing of the details. Since you want to re-create the scene for your readers, you must present the details in an order that readers can follow. The most effective way is to use spatial order—that is, to arrange the details in the order in which they exist in space. Present them as they would be seen—from left to right, from top to bottom, from foreground to background, and so on. The most natural way of viewing the scene is best. For example, in describing a room, the best way to organize the details often is to start at the entrance and proceed in whatever direction you would actually follow in viewing the room.

Notice how the writer of the following description makes the spatial order clear by using phrases that suggest direction. The phrases appear in italic type.

Model

Garden viewed from yard	Following the calls of the black starlings, Diana walked toward her garden. *From the yard* she appraised the neat rows that she had made
Garden seen from nearer vantage point	in the rich soil. *Coming closer,* she could see the small healthy plants, a few inches high now, spread new leaves to the sun. She *walked along*
Garden seen from path	*the path,* admiring the feathered green of her carrots and the broad purple cabbage leaves.
A close-up view	She *squatted down* on her heels to watch the quiet progress of a spider as it built its fine web between the stalks of two milkweed plants.

Amanda Yskamp, Brookline High School
Brookline, Massachusetts

Exercise 2   Prewriting: Spatial Order   The sentences in the following description need to be arranged in spatial order. Determine a logical sequence for the sentences. On your paper, write the sentences (and their numbers) in the correct order. Save your paper.

(1) Fragile white cobweb strings wave at me from the ceiling before I reach the last step. (2) In the right-hand corner, there are more stacks of cardboard boxes heaped with faded striped blankets. (3) Coming down uneven and narrow basement steps, I find it difficult to see at first. (4) Once

I am in the basement, the first dim shape I see is a dress-maker's dummy in the left-hand corner. (5) Finally, I spot a jar of my favorite kind of pickles. (6) Along the right wall, colorful jars of fruit preserves and vegetables weigh down a dusty shelf. (7) A few cardboard boxes are bunched along the center wall. (8) Above the last step hangs a man's checked wool overcoat. (9) They are overloaded with fat red and gold books, some old 78 records without covers, and yellowed magazines.

Exercise 3   Prewriting: Spatial Order   Take out your paper from Exercise 2. On it underline each word or phrase that makes clear the spatial order of the details in the basement room.

Assignment 1   Prewriting   *Step 1:* Sit or stand in a room in your home. On your paper, list all the specific details that would be necessary to re-create this room in a reader's imagination. *Step 2:* Decide on a location from which to view the room—perhaps a doorway or a chair in the corner. *Step 3:* Arrange the details as you see them from the location that you have chosen. You are still at the list-making stage. Do not actually write the description. Save your list with the details in order.

Assignment 2   Writing/Revising   Using the list that you made in Assignment 1, write a paragraph describing the room. Then revise your paragraph.

Assignment 3   Prewriting   *Step 1:* Think of an outdoor scene that made an impression on you. *Step 2:* List details of the scene to use in a description. *Step 3:* Now arrange the details in spatial order. Save your list.

Assignment 4   Writing/Revising   Using the list that you made in Assignment 3, write a paragraph describing the outdoor scene. Then revise your paragraph.

Assignment Checklist

Check your writing assignments for the following points:

✔ 1. Did you include carefully selected sensory details that capture the uniqueness of the place?
✔ 2. Did you use specific, vivid words and effective comparisons?
✔ 3. Did you arrange the details in spatial order?
✔ 4. Did you use words and phrases, as needed, to tie the details together?
✔ 5. Did you proofread your paragraph for correct grammar, usage, spelling, and punctuation?

11.5   Describing a Person

When you describe someone, your purpose is to convey to your reader the person's individual qualities.

11.5a   Describing Physical Characteristics

The following description of Babe Ruth gives a memorable picture of the physical characteristics of this famous baseball player. Notice that the writer has used precise modifiers (in italic type) in the carefully selected details.

Model

Height	He is *six* feet in height, or close to it, with an *unshapely* body that features a *tremendous,*
Build	*barrel-shaped* torso that tapers down into *too-small* legs and an *amazingly fragile* and *delicate*

Head
Eyes
Nose

Mouth
Teeth
Hair

pair of ankles. But his head is even more re-markable. It is *enormous, too large* even for his *big, bulky* frame. His eyes are *brown, small,* and *deep-sunk,* but *clear* and *bright.* His nose is *flat* and *pushed in.* Nobody did it for him; it grew that way. It gives him a *quaintly appealing porcine* look, emphasized by the *little, glittering* eyes. His mouth is *large* and *thick-lipped* and featured by *fine white* teeth. His hair is a *dark brown, almost black,* and *crisp* and *curling.*

Paul Gallico, "His Majesty the King"

When you describe a person, your topic sentence should usually convey a general impression of age, height, and body structure. Your reader will want to know whether the person is small or large, fat or thin, muscular or delicate.

Then describe the head and face, including the hair and eyes. Try to find just the right modifiers. For example, you can describe hair color as reddish brown, but you can describe it even more precisely as chestnut, auburn, or mahogany. As you describe the facial features, go beyond eye color to describe the shape of the eyes and the eyebrows. The nose is a prominent feature that is often forgotten. It may be large, small, long, thin, flat, pointed, broad, turned up, straight, crooked. The mouth, too, is unique and can be described in many ways to convey its individuality.

Finally, include sensory details other than visual details if they add to the unique portrait of the subject. The quality of the person's voice is significant. Sometimes, too, you can include the fragrance of perfume, after-shave lotion, or a fresh-smelling soap as part of your description. In describing the textures of hair and skin, you can include details from the sense of touch.

Exercise 1 Prewriting: Description of a Person
Certain details in the following passage describe the physical characteristics of one man. On your paper, copy each numbered category. After it write the words from the passage that describe the category.

SAMPLE   Height

ANSWER   Height: "tall"

> The general . . . was a tall man past middle age, for his hair was a vivid white; but his thick eyebrows and pointed military moustache were as black as the night. . . . His eyes, too, were black and very bright. He had high cheekbones, a sharp-cut nose, a spare, dark face.

> Richard Connell, "The Most Dangerous Game"

1. Age
2. Hair
3. Eyebrows
4. Moustache

5. Eyes
6. Nose
7. Other facial characteristics

11.5b Using Details That Suggest Personality

People, of course, are more than the sum of their physical characteristics. They have personalities. Often a person's physical characteristics give some hint of the personality within. For example, facial expressions can reveal much about an individual. A smile, a frown, the curl of a lip can each suggest personality. Movements, as well, can be enlightening. The twitching of fingers, bitten fingernails, confident gestures while speaking—all tell something about individual temperament. Posture, carriage, and gait, too, can reveal such characteristics as pride or shyness. Finally, people's choice of clothing often reveals something of their nature.

To add interest to your description of a person, you can use physical details that suggest personality, as the writer of the following paragraph has done.

Model

> On the right wall hangs a portrait of my great-grandfather and his wife. In the portrait my grandfather stands dressed in his ship captain's uniform. His thick black hair is tightly plastered to his scalp, and his ebony eyes look right through me and scrutinize everything. Next to my great-grandfather sits my great-grandmother, posed stiffly, dressed in rich red velvet. She has a translucent complexion, her features are delicate and chiseled, and her expression is melancholy but confident.

> *Teri Kaplowitz, George W. Hewlett High School*
> *Hewlett, New York*

From this brief description, the reader knows that the captain is an imposing figure whose uniform, "tightly plastered" hair, and observant eyes suggest a man of authority and control. The writer also hints at her great-grandmother's personality. Although the captain's wife appears "delicate" and "melancholy," she gives the impression of confidence.

Exercise 2 Prewriting: Description of a Person
The following description of a woman suggests some of her personality traits. On your paper, list two traits, along with the words from the paragraph that suggest them.

> Doña Henriqueta was not even as tall as Doña Esther, but plumper. She had a light olive complexion and a mass of dark brown hair so wavy it burst when she undid her braids. She never did household chores without singing, accompanying herself by imitating a guitar that plinked and plonked between the verses of her song. Her features were good-looking, almost soft, not like her temper.

> Ernesto Galarza, *Barrio Boy*

Assignment 1 Prewriting *Step 1:* Divide your paper into four columns headed *Sight, Hearing, Smell,* and *Touch.*

Step 2: Observe a person carefully and record sensory details in the proper columns. *Step 3:* When you feel that you have completed the lists, cross out details that seem weak or unnecessary. Save your paper.

Assignment 2   Writing/Revising   Using the details selected in Assignment 1, write a paragraph describing the individual whom you observed. Revise your paragraph.

Assignment 3   Prewriting   *Step 1:* Write two column headings on your paper: *Physical Characteristics* and *Physical Details That Suggest Personality*. *Step 2:* Observe someone and collect details for both columns. *Step 3:* When you have finished your lists, cross out unnecessary or uninteresting details. Save your paper.

Assignment 4   Writing/Revising   Using the details selected in Assignment 3, write a paragraph describing the person whom you observed. Try to bring the person to life in your description. Then revise your paragraph.

Assignment 5   Prewriting/Writing/Revising   Write a one-paragraph description of a real person. Write it for a friend in another community who is going to meet this person at a bus terminal or an airport. Because your friend has never seen the person, your description must be exact. Revise your paragraph before making a final copy of it.

Assignment 6   Prewriting/Writing/Revising   Imagine a person who lives in an interesting house or apartment building that you pass regularly or a person who works in an unusual office that you have seen. Imagine the person's physical characteristics and personality. Then write a one-paragraph description of that individual. Include physical characteristics that reveal personality. Revise your paragraph before making a final copy of it.

Assignment Checklist

Check your writing assignments for the following points:

✔ 1. Did you write a topic sentence that gives an overall impression of the person?
✔ 2. Did you include carefully selected sensory details that capture the uniqueness of the person?
✔ 3. Did you include some details that suggest the personality of the individual?
✔ 4. Did you use precise, vivid words and effective comparisons?
✔ 5. Did you proofread your paragraph for correct grammar, usage, spelling, and punctuation?

Inside a Haunted House: A Description

Situation: You are the set designer for *Gothic,* a new play that takes place in the living room of a haunted mansion. The producers have asked you for a description of the proposed set. As you plan and write the description, you will keep in mind the following information.

Writer: you as a set designer
Audience: producers of the play
Topic: living room of a haunted mansion
Purpose: to describe the set in a single paragraph

Directions: To write your paragraph, follow these steps.

> *Step 1.* To get ideas for the set, you made notes about how the room might look. You wrote the notes as quickly as possible, and you let your imagination have free rein. The notes appear on the facing page. Read the notes carefully to refresh your memory.
>
> *Step 2.* Make a sketch of the room, indicating where you would place each item that you want in your set.
>
> *Step 3.* Using your notes and your plan of the room, write a paragraph in which you describe the room. Use spatial order in your description. Do not use every detail from the notes, and add additional details if you wish. Be sure to include a topic sentence.

<u>Notes</u>

What does the living room of a haunted
mansion look like?

Dim lights. Dusty. Dark. Furniture like
crouching monsters. Cobwebs in every
corner. An old suit of armor. Musty
smell. Large portraits of ancestors on
wall. Walk into the room — it feels
very cold. The rug gives off clouds
of dust. Large overstuffed sofa covered
with a sheet. Pair of dark leather arm-
chairs. Some furniture so worn that
stuffing is visible. On a rickety
table, ornate three pronged candle-
holder. Big antique desk covered with
cobwebs. Books are leatherbound,
obviously old. Stretch of wall—perfect
place for a secret panel. Old spotty
mirror. Small windows. Leaded panes.
Imposing mantelpiece over cavernous
fireplace. Cobwebs over logs in the
wood bin. Not enough lamps.
A stuffed owl.

Unit Assignments

Assignment 1 On a visit to a relative's house, you have been given a household object as a birthday present. When you write home, you describe the object in one paragraph of your letter. First, choose the object to write about—for example, a poster or a cassette player. Then write the paragraph so that your reader(s) can visualize the object in detail.

Assignment 2 Observe a public place, such as a post office, a park, or a shopping center, and write a paragraph describing it. Limit your topic to one part of the place, concentrating on details that will re-create it for your reader.

Assignment 3 Observe the people in a public place, and write a paragraph that describes one of them. Begin with a general impression of the person's size and age, and then go on to precise details.

Assignment 4 In a paragraph describe someone you know well. Include details, such as facial expressions and a way of walking, that give this person individuality. Select at least one or two details that suggest personality.

Assignment 5 In a paragraph describe a room in the home of a friend or a relative. Write your description as if you were standing in one part of the room, and arrange your details as you might see them from that vantage point. Try to convey the atmosphere of the room.

Assignment 6 Imagine that you have left a handbag, a wallet, a musical instrument, or an item of sports equipment on a bus. In one paragraph describe that object so clearly that the person who is in charge of lost property at the bus company will be able to recognize it when it is turned in by the driver.

Assignment 7 Find a color photograph of an attractive or interesting place. In a paragraph, describe that place. Include specific details to show what makes the place attractive or interesting.

Assignment 8 In a paragraph describe one of your favorite possessions. Begin with your general impression of the object. Write your paragraph for a friend who has never seen the object that you are describing.

Revising Your Assignments

For help in revising a description, consult the Checklist for Revision on the last page of this book.

Unit Tests

Test 1

A. Number your paper from 1 to 5. Read the following passage. Next to each number, write the letter of the item that correctly answers the question.

> (1) The wind was blowing through my hair. (2) From somewhere far below, music and cotton candy smells drifted up to me. (3) They would fade, grow stronger, fade, grow stronger. (4) I heard the gears grind and clack as they worked to spin the gigantic Ferris wheel in which I was a passenger. (5) Sights and sounds of the country fair rushed upward, backward, forward, toward me, and I experienced the topsy-turvy feeling in my stomach as excited butterflies did cartwheels. (6) I was alone in the seat, alone to look at the world spread out before me—the booths with their bright lights and sounds; the rides that spun, whirred, and twirled; and the people, different, all shapes and sizes.
>
> *Patricia Ann Crowe, Oconee County High School*
> *Watkinsville, Georgia*

1. Which of the following does the passage describe?
   a. A windy day   c. A sports event
   b. A circus   d. A ride on a Ferris wheel
2. Which verb in Sentence 4 describes the noise of the gears?
   a. Heard   b. Worked   c. Clack   d. Spin
3. In Sentence 6 what is described as having "bright lights"?
   a. Booths   b. Rides   c. Seat   d. World
4. In Sentence 6 which verb does *not* describe the rides' motion?
   a. Spun   b. Was   c. Twirled   d. Whirred
5. Which of the following sentences contains details that appeal to the senses of hearing and smell?
   a. Sentence 1   b. Sentence 2   c. Sentence 3   d. Sentence 4

B. Number your paper from 6 to 10. Read the following passage. Next to each number, write the letter of the item that correctly completes the sentence.

I remember standing atop a little hill midway between the town and the sea. It was one of my favorite spots, and on some days I would spend hours on end there, disturbed only by the occasional goat wandering by on the deeply rutted trail.

Looking east from the hill, one saw the broad, sparkling, empty expanse of the beach, blindingly white in the glare of the sun. The emerald waters of the Mediterranean lapped at the sands, and, farther out, the water turned a deeper and deeper shade of blue, until it melted into the perfect blue of the sky on the distant horizon. On most days a shrimp boat could be seen chugging down the coast, and on other, more rare occasions, dolphins would leap about, far offshore.

Dan Staley, Woodrow Wilson High School
Long Beach, California

6. The description moves directly from details of the hill to details of the __?__.
   a. sky   b. beach   c. water   d. horizon
7. The descriptive details are arranged in __?__.
   a. chronological order   c. spatial order
   b. topical order   d. order of importance
8. The modifier that does *not* describe the expanse of the beach is __?__.
   a. white   b. sparkling   c. emerald   d. broad
9. The verb that describes the movement of the water is __?__.
   a. lapped   b. turned   c. melted   d. would leap
10. The modifier that describes the waters of the Mediterranean is __?__.
    a. perfect   b. blindingly   c. sparkling   d. emerald

Test 2

Choose one of the Unit Assignments. Write the description as directed and hand it in to your teacher.

Unit 12

Narrative Writing

Unit Preview

The purpose of **narration** is storytelling. The simplest kind of story is a single paragraph that narrates one incident—a series of related actions that take place within a short space of time. Stories about longer or more complex events may contain many paragraphs. Nonfictional narratives, such as autobiographical and biographical writing, are based on fact. Fictional stories, on the other hand, come directly from the author's imagination.

The following paragraph tells an incident.

Beginning: first action	While waiting alone for my parents to return from their shopping trip one evening, I detected a strange rustling coming from the kitch-
Second action	en. Curious, I set down my mystery novel and left my comfortable seat in the living room. The
Third action	scratching noise got louder. As I entered our darkened kitchen, the intruder flashed past me. A
Fourth action	metal can clanged to the floor next to me. I still have no clue as to how that baby raccoon got
End	into our kitchen.

Like all narratives, this incident answers the question "What happened?" It contains other important features of all narrative writing. For example, when you write a narrative, you tell the actions in chronological order—the order in which they occur. You give the narrative a definite beginning and a definite end, as well as a high point that creates suspense or excitement. Early in a narrative, you must introduce the characters—the people who participate in the actions. You also must establish the setting—the time and the location of the actions.

For Analysis On your paper, answer the questions about the preceding narrative paragraph.

1. What settings does the writer present in the narrative?
2. The writer's parents are mentioned in the first sentence of the paragraph. Are they characters in the narrative? Why or why not?
3. Would a sentence about what the parents bought while they were shopping belong in the paragraph? Why or why not?
4. In which sentence does the writer present the action that is the high point of the narrative?

The paragraph about the noise made by a raccoon shows that even a brief incident can be the topic of a complete narrative. In this unit you will learn how to narrate incidents, how to maintain one point of view in a narrative, and how to write dialogue. You will also learn how to write longer narratives. As you create your narratives, you will follow the three steps of the writing process: prewriting, writing, and revising.

12.1 Narrating an Incident

Choosing a Topic

Choosing a suitable topic is the first step in writing a narrative about an **incident**—a series of connected actions that occur within a few hours or on a single day. Choose an incident that is simple enough to be told in one paragraph. You may decide to narrate a true incident. In that case, you will write about actions that really happened and about the real people who performed the actions.

On the other hand, you may choose to narrate a fictional incident, for which you will invent the actions, the people, or both. Fictional actions and people do not have to come solely from your imagination, however. They may come from one of your own experiences, which you can narrate as fiction by changing details as you wish. The actions of other people may also help you to think of a fictional incident. For example, if you see an athlete winning the discus throw, you may imagine what would have happened if the athlete had lost the contest. Or you may imagine what happened the first time the athlete tried to throw the discus.

Planning the Narrative

After you have chosen your topic, plan the narrative carefully. An incident must have (1) a beginning, (2) a high point, and (3) an end.

1. The beginning introduces the situation. In it you present both the **characters**—the people who perform the actions—and the **setting**—the time and location of the actions.
2. The high point is the action that creates the most excitement or suspense.
3. The end contains the final actions of the story.

As prewriting, list the actions that you wish to narrate. Your list should include the actions of all three parts of the narrative. Make sure that you have listed the actions in chronological order.

Writing the Narrative

As you write your narrative about an incident, keep in mind the following guidelines.

Strategies

1. *Present the subject in a topic sentence,* usually the first sentence.

2. *Include information about the people and the setting* early in the narrative. With such information readers can clearly understand the incident. However, do not include more information than the reader needs.

3. *Tell the actions in chronological order,* according to your list.

4. *Use transitional words.* Such words as *first, soon, next,* and *later* are like signposts for your reader.

5. *Write a concluding sentence* to bring the incident to a definite end.

In the following narrative (from a longer account), the writer recalls a true incident.

Model

Topic sentence	I started up the ladder of the water tower again. I didn't look up; I didn't look anywhere.
Actions in chronological order	I began to climb with a rhythm—left, right, left, right. All the time I was thinking, "I've got to do it. I can't be afraid." I made progress. Eventually I made it past the spot where I had stopped before. Still I climbed—left, right, left,
High point	right. After what seemed an eternity, I reached the top. I carefully climbed over the rail and stood on the platform that surrounded the
Concluding sentence	tower. I had made it.

Warren Weckesser, Northport High School
Northport, New York

The writer of this narrative used definite beginning and ending sentences. The only character is the writer himself: the "I" who is climbing a water tower. The tower is the setting of the actions. The writer's transitional words, *Eventually, Still,* and *After*, emphasize the chronological order of the climb.

Exercise 1   Prewriting: Chronological Order   The sentences in the following autobiographical incident are not in chronological order. On your paper, write the sentences (with their original numbers) in the correct order.

(1) Finally succumbing to irresistible temptation, two of us slipped out of camp after dark, armed with a tape recorder.   (2) Waves of rhythmic chanting, in time with the drums, drew us closer and closer.   (3) One Saturday evening during our stay on the island, the drums started beating as usual but gradually got louder, and it was soon obvious that a celebration was being held very near our camp.   (4) Even before our hearts reached our throats, we were scurrying back to camp.   (5) More torches ignited, and voices and drums rose to stunning climaxes.   (6) Gradually, trembling figures dressed in ornate costumes became visible, their wiry arms clutching the wildly flickering torches.   (7) At first, only torches were visible, moving as if independently, in widening concentric circles.

Eric Fleischauer, Hardaway High School
Columbus, Georgia

Exercise 2   Prewriting: Transitional Words   On your paper, list the transitional words or phrases in the following passage. Next to each word, write its sentence number.

(1) At the radio audition, I was scared to death.
(2) As the song started on its last chorus, I started on my last fingernails.   (3) Then I heard the news introduction.
(4) Finally, Dave, the disc jockey, looked up, smiled, and pointed at me.

(5) "This is Deborah Deggs with the twelve o'clock report . . ." (6) Later, "This has been the twelve o'clock news."

(7) I sat back, took a deep breath, and heard the news close and another song start. (8) Soon Dave came into the studio, where I was still shaking. (9) "Fine job," he said.

(10) Now it is ten months later, and I sit in the D.J.'s chair, cuing novice newspersons.

(Adapted)

Deborah Deggs, Alvin High School
Alvin, Texas

Exercise 3 Writing: Narration The following chronological list contains the actions in an incident. Write a narrative paragraph based on these details. Use transitional words as needed.

1. Packed the car full of camping gear
2. Locked the front door
3. Started off on the trip
4. Traveled through an isolated part of the mountains
5. Passed sign: "Next gas station 25 miles"
6. Car started to sputter
7. Pulled over to the side of the road
8. Driver jumped out of car
9. Driver raised hood and checked engine
10. Small child said, "Did you know the gas gauge was on empty before we stopped?"

Assignment 1 Prewriting/Writing *Step 1:* Think of a true experience—your own or someone else's—that you can narrate in a single paragraph. For example, the experience might be a humorous incident, or it might be one that illustrates something about human nature. *Step 2:* Plan your paragraph. Begin by selecting the actions, including a high point. Then list the actions in chronological order. *Step 3:* Create a topic sentence and a concluding sentence for the paragraph. Save your paper.

Assignment 2   Writing/Revising   Using the list and the sentences that you prepared in Assignment 1, write a paragraph in which you narrate the incident. Be sure that your narrative makes clear who the characters are and what the setting is. Then, using the Assignment Checklist, revise the paragraph.

Assignment 3   Prewriting/Writing/Revising   Think of an imaginary incident or a real incident that you can use as the basis of a fictional narrative. For example, the incident might concern making a discovery or meeting an unusual person. Plan and write a paragraph that narrates the incident. Make sure that the narrative has a definite beginning and a definite end and that it clearly presents the characters and the setting. Then revise the paragraph.

Assignment Checklist

Check your writing assignments for the following points:

1. Did you present the subject in a topic sentence?
2. Did you make clear who the characters are and what the setting is?
3. Did you present the actions of the incident in chronological order, using transitional words as needed?
4. Did you include a high point?
5. Did you conclude with a sentence that brings the narrative to a definite end?
6. Did you proofread your paragraph for correct grammar, usage, spelling, and punctuation?

12.2 Point of View

You can write a narrative from one of two points of view: from the viewpoint of a participant or from the viewpoint of an outsider.

When you narrate an incident in which you have participated, you use **first-person narration.** You are the "I" who tells the actions. (For more information about the first-person and third-person forms of pronouns, see page 7.) Autobiographical narratives—narratives about events in your own life—are written in the first person. You can also write fiction in the first person.

The other type of storytelling is **third-person narration.** As you tell a true incident or a fictional story in the third person, you use the pronouns *he, she,* and *they* to refer to all of the people in the narrative when you do not use their names. Biographical narratives—narratives about other people's lives —are written in the third person. The following examples illustrate the difference between first-person and third-person narration.

FIRST-PERSON NARRATION
> Rising at seven to find the dark clouds gathering outside *my* window, *I* thought nature was warning *me* that this might be a stormy day.

THIRD-PERSON NARRATION
> Rising at seven to find dark clouds gathering outside *her* window, *she* thought nature was warning *her* that this might be a stormy day.

You must keep your point of view consistent throughout any paragraph or composition. If you begin a narrative in the first person, use that form throughout. Similarly, if you begin a narrative in the third person, you may use the pronoun *I* only in direct quotations.

The following paragraph (from a longer narrative) is autobiographical and, therefore, is told in the first person.

Model: First-Person Narration

We soon reached Poland. I was more excited than I had ever been as the day approached when I would finally meet my grandmother. For thirteen years I had tried to imagine what our meeting would be like. At last I saw her. She was hanging out clothes to dry on the line that stretched before the small thatched house. As I ran toward her, I felt an unbelievable rush of emotion, like a tremendous white light glowing within me. Suddenly I felt as if I had spent my entire life prior to that moment in a darkened room. The radiance that was our love and joy burst forth, revealing everything. I knew that I had a place in a family and in a people that I had never known before. I had a place in a nation that I had never appreciated before. And most important, I had within myself all the strength and fortitude that my family and people and nation seemed to personify.

Michael Dzialo, New Rochelle High School
New Rochelle, New York

Notice that the writer of the paragraph is consistent in his point of view. He uses the pronoun *I* throughout. He describes the setting as it appeared to him. Most important, he tells how he felt at the prospect of meeting his grandmother, and then he tells how the actual meeting made him feel.

Notice, too, that the paragraph has the characteristics of any well-told narrative. In the first sentence, for example, the writer establishes the setting. In the second sentence, the topic sentence, he introduces the main characters. He also establishes what the paragraph will be about. Then the writer narrates chronologically the details leading up to the meeting, which is the high point of the paragraph. In the concluding sentence, he summarizes what the meeting meant to him.

The following paragraph (from a longer work) is about Zelda Fitzgerald, an American writer and the wife of the author F. Scott Fitzgerald. Because the paragraph is biographical, it is written in the third person.

Model: Third-Person Narration

Even as a child, Zelda was not unaware of the effect she created. She possessed early a certain command over others, making them do what she wanted them to do. She also had a knack of drawing attention to herself. Stories about her escapades abound in Montgomery. There is one about when Zelda, having nothing better to do on a fine summery day, called up the fire department and told them that a child was caught on a roof and couldn't get down. Then Zelda got a ladder, climbed up to the roof of her own house, pushed the ladder away and waited. The fire engine came, clanging its bell, and the neighbors rushed out to see where the fire was. There Zelda sat marooned, and delighted by the commotion.

Nancy Milford, *Zelda: A Biography*

Notice that the writer consistently refers to the main character as "Zelda" or "she." In the topic sentence, the writer presents an observation about Zelda Fitzgerald. In the next three sentences, she elaborates on the same idea. The writer expresses these ideas in the third person, never using the word *I* in presenting them. In the rest of the paragraph, she narrates in chronological order the actions in an incident that illustrates the observation. In the concluding sentence, she brings the incident to an end.

Exercise 1 Prewriting: First-Person Narration The

following passage is written in the third person. On your paper, rewrite the passage. Change the point of view to the first person, writing as if you were Tim. Remember that your rewriting will include changing the third-person forms *they* and *their* to the first-person forms *we* and *our*.

Tim spent many summer days searching for Indian arrowheads and hatchet heads near his home in Missouri. His friend Girard always searched with him. One day they decided to explore a hilly area near a creek. They arrived at the creek early in the morning, and by lunchtime they had found nothing. They stopped to eat sandwiches, then continued their search. As the afternoon wore on, they became hot and exhausted from walking up and down hills with their heads bent toward the ground so that they would not miss anything. Tim was just about to suggest giving up for the day when something partially buried in the ground caught his attention. He yelled for Girard to join him and then slowly uncovered the object. It was a rose quartz hatchet head, one of the most beautiful objects that he had ever found. As they walked home, Tim was glad that he had not given up one minute earlier.

Exercise   2   Prewriting: Third-Person   Narration
The following passage is written in the first person. Rewrite the passage, changing the point of view to the third person. To refer to the main character, use a name and the pronoun *he* or *she*.

Last fall, I agreed to be the properties manager for my school play. I thought it would be fun to gather chairs, dishes, and pictures for the play. I had no idea that I would also have to find a sofa, a radiator, and a stove. The sofa was no problem. I found it in a storeroom in the school basement. Getting the radiator and the stove was more difficult. By calling every plumbing and heating supply store for miles around, I finally found one fifteen miles away that had an old radiator. However, I had to pick up the radiator at the store and take it to the town dump after the play was over. To get the stove, I called every appliance store in town. Finally, in exchange for a listing in the program, the owners of one store agreed to lend me a stove for the two performances of the play. By the opening night, I had the sofa, the radiator, the stove, and all of the small items in place, but I was almost too tired to enjoy the performance.

Exercise 3 Writing: First-Person Narration Write a first-person narrative paragraph based on the following notes about getting a job. Add details as you wish.

1. Waited outside the manager's office
2. Secretary said manager would see me
3. Walked into office
4. Shook hands
5. Explained that I wanted to apply for job as waitress
6. Mentioned lack of experience
7. Manager smiled and asked about my clothing size
8. Did not know why he asked
9. Manager gave me light blue dress and small white apron
10. Got the job

Assignment 1 Prewriting / Writing / Revising Write a paragraph in which you narrate a brief incident in the life of a family member or a friend. Interview the person to get the details of the incident. Write your narrative in the third person. Then, using the Assignment Checklist, revise your work.

Assignment 2 Prewriting / Writing / Revising Select a significant but brief incident that occurred in your life before you were ten years old. It should be an incident that you would enjoy sharing with a reader. For example, you might choose to write about your first day in school, a time when you received an important letter or package in the mail, a time when you did a difficult thing, a time when something frightened you, or a time when something made you happy. In an autobiographical paragraph, narrate the incident for a friend. Then revise your narrative.

Assignment Checklist

Check your assignments for the following points:

✔ 1. Did you use a consistent first-person point of view in narrating an autobiographical incident?

✔ 2. Did you use a consistent third-person point of view in narrating a biographical incident?

✔ 3. Did you present the actions in chronological order?

✔ 4. Did you write a topic sentence and a concluding sentence that give the narrative a definite beginning and end?

✔ 5. Did you proofread your narrative for correct grammar, usage, spelling, and punctuation?

12.3 Using Dialogue in Narration

You have considered the structure of a narrative and the two points of view from which you can tell a true or fictional story. Now you need to learn more about presenting your characters and their conversations.

To the extent that you can, include the conversation as well as the actions of your characters. You can do so in either of two ways: (1) You can present a conversation directly, by giving the exact words that the characters say. (2) You can present the conversation indirectly, by simply summarizing what the characters say.

> DIRECT Joan's voice trembled as she whispered to Carole, "I have some wonderful news."
>
> INDIRECT Joan's voice trembled. She whispered as she told Carole that she had good news.

Direct reporting of speech is more lively than indirect reporting. Unless the speech of a character is very long, use the exact words. When you write the exact words of a conversation between your characters, you are using **dialogue**.

The Purposes of Dialogue

In writing dialogue, you have two purposes.

First, you want to make the characters come alive as your reader hears them speak. What people say reveals much about the sort of people they are. Rather than telling your reader that "Nat was selfish" or "Lenore was intelligent," you can present Nat's and Lenore's own words to show your characters' personal qualities. Make your characters' way of expressing themselves suit their ages, education, and general background as well as their personalities.

To the quoted words, add explanatory details that make clear which character is speaking and *how* he or she is speaking. The following phrases in italic type are examples of explanatory details.

> *Meredith demanded angrily,* "Just how long did you expect me to wait?"
>
> "The bus is always late just when I have to be on time," *Michael answered slowly.*

Your second purpose in writing dialogue is to use it as a way of telling some actions of the narrative. Through dialogue you can actually tell some of a story in a form that is interesting and easy to read.

The following excerpt is from a short story that takes place in a large northern city. In it the writer presents the exact words of four characters. He also uses such explanatory details as "Charley said."

Model

> "Hi," Blackie said. "Where are you from?"
> "Marion County," T.J. said.
> We laughed. "Marion County?" I said. "Where's that?"
> He looked at me as if I was a stranger too. "It's in Alabama," he said, as if I ought to know where it was.
> "What's your name?" Charley said.

"T.J.," he said, looking back at him. He had pale blue eyes that looked washed out, but he looked directly at Charley, waiting for his reaction. He'll be all right, I thought. No sissy in him, except that voice. Who ever talked like that?

"T.J.," Blackie said. "What's your real name? Nobody in the world has just initials."

"I do," he said. "And they're T.J. That's all the name I have."

His voice was resolute with the knowledge of his rightness, and for a moment no one had anything to say.

Borden Deal, "Antaeus"

The dialogue reveals what the characters are like. It shows that Charley, Blackie, and the narrator (teller of a story) are suspicious of the new boy, T.J. It also shows that T.J. is confident. In addition, by showing how T.J. wins the approval of the other boys, the dialogue presents an action of the narrative. Notice that the speech of the boys sounds natural. It suits their ages and backgrounds.

The Format of Dialogue

The pattern of punctuation and paragraphing in a dialogue follows certain conventions. There are three basic rules.

Rule   Put the spoken words in quotation marks.

Rule   Start each spoken sentence with a capital letter.

Rule   Begin a new paragraph each time the speaker changes.

See pages 243–245 if you need more information on punctuating direct quotations.

Exercise 1   Prewriting: Dialogue   Number your paper from 1 to 12. Write *Indirect* beside the number of each sentence or sentence group that presents a speaker's words indirectly. Then rewrite the sentence or sentence group so that it presents the character's words directly, in quotation marks.

12.3

Format of Dialogue

Write *Direct* beside the number of each sentence or sentence group that already presents the speaker's words directly.

1. As Brian and Michelle were walking to the summer theater, Michelle told him that she was planning to try out for the leading part in the play.
2. "Are you really?" Brian replied with some surprise.
3. "Yes," answered Michelle. "Are you surprised that a person who is sometimes shy would try out for the lead?"
4. Brian said that he was surprised.
5. "There's a story behind my interest in the theater," Michelle announced.
6. Brian asked her to tell the story.
7. "Last summer, when I was at camp, I forced myself to try out for a part in the camp play. As I listened to others read their lines, it seemed to me that something was missing in the readings."
8. Brian asked if she had been nervous.
9. Michelle said that she had been nervous at first. However, the nervousness disappeared as she stepped onto the stage and read the lines as she thought they should be read. When she finished, there was applause.
10. "That must have given you a wonderful feeling," Brian said. "Are you still shy?"
11. Michelle said that although she was still somewhat shy with people, she was always confident onstage. In fact, she wanted to be an actress.
12. "I'd certainly like to have your confidence," Brian said.

Exercise 2 Writing/Revising: Dialogue The following paragraph contains information for a dialogue, but it has no direct quotations. On your paper, rewrite the passage as dialogue. Convey the information in quoted words and in explanatory details. At the beginning you will need to include a sentence or two that present the setting and the characters. After writing your dialogue, revise it.

Sue Ellen arrived home at dinnertime to find her brother David reading a magazine. He told her that their parents both had to work late and would not be home for dinner. Sue Ellen asked David whether dinner was ready. He replied that he was hoping she would get the dinner. They had a discussion, deciding in the end that they would prepare the meal together. They had to decide what they wanted to eat and who would prepare each part of the meal.

Assignment 1   Writing / Revising   Consider the following situation.

Who: A fifteen-year-old boy or girl, one or both parents, and a brother or a sister

What: A conversation between the boy or girl and the parent(s), with the brother or sister making occasional remarks

Where: A room in the family's home

When: Monday evening

Why: The boy or girl wants permission to stay out two hours later than usual on Friday night.

Imagine the dialogue that might develop in this situation. Write the dialogue, including explanatory details. Introduce the setting and the characters in a sentence or two at the beginning. Try to make each person's speech distinctive. After writing your dialogue, use the Assignment Checklist as a guide to revising it.

Assignment 2   Writing / Revising   Listen carefully to a short radio or television discussion, noticing the different ways in which the speakers talk. Observe their choice of words, whether they finish what they start to say, and whether they express themselves clearly. Take notes on the conversation. Then record their words in writing as well as you can remember them. Use direct quotations when you can. Finally, revise your work.

Assignment 3 Prewriting/Writing/Revising Write a fictional dialogue between two characters that presents a situation and brings it to a conclusion. Try to make the situation and the dialogue seem real. Revise your dialogue before making a final copy of it.

Assignment Checklist

Check your assignments for the following points:

✔ 1. Did you reveal the personalities of the characters through the dialogue?
✔ 2. Did you tell some of the actions of the narrative in the dialogue?
✔ 3. Did you use correct punctuation and paragraphing?
✔ 4. Did you proofread your work for correct grammar, usage, spelling, and capitalization?

12.4 Writing a Longer Narrative

When you narrate a simple incident that has only a few actions, you include all of the actions in one paragraph. Sometimes, however, you need to write a fictional or true story with many actions. In a longer narrative of two or three pages, you must place each group of closely related actions in a paragraph of its own. In addition, you must give the longer narrative an appropriate structure.

Planning the Narrative

Conflict. You usually build the actions of a longer narrative around a **conflict,** a situation or problem that must be settled at the end. The conflict may be between two people: two teammates competing for the same starting position on a basketball team. The conflict may be between a person and a force of nature: a rancher struggling to save an orange grove during a sudden freeze. The conflict may also take place within the mind and feelings of one person: the main character deciding whether to spend a vacation visiting a new friend or staying home to be with old friends.

Climax. In a longer narrative, as in a narrative of a brief incident, you should plan to tell the actions in chronological order, leading up to a high point, or **climax,** in which the conflict is greatest. For example, in the basketball story that is mentioned in the previous paragraph, there may be a contest to see which of the two teammates will play in an important game. After the climax, the actions lead to a conclusion, in which the conflict is usually resolved. In the basketball story, one of the players may be chosen to start in the important game.

After you have decided on the conflict or situation that you will write about, plan the other important elements of your narrative. First, determine the characters and the setting that you will present. Then, so that you will be able to write your narrative effectively, make a chronological list of the actions, including the climax and the ending. Finally, before you begin writing, decide whether to use the first-person or third-person point of view.

Writing the Narrative

As you write your longer narrative, keep in mind the following guidelines.

Strategies

1. *In the beginning establish the setting and introduce the important characters.* Also, establish the point of view of the narrative. When possible, suggest the conflict. Present all of the information in a way that will capture your reader's attention.

2. *Tell the actions in chronological order,* according to your prewritten plan. Place each group of related actions in its own paragraph. After you introduce the conflict, work up to the climax and resolve the situation in the end. Very often the end of a story follows soon after the climax.

3. *Use dialogue* to show what your characters are like and to tell some of the actions of the story.

4. *Maintain the point of view that you established at the beginning.* For example, if you use the first-person point of view, you must tell all the actions as they appear to the narrator, the "I" in the story. You can tell what the narrator is thinking and feeling, but you will not be able to reveal the thoughts and feelings of any other characters.

The following first-person narrative is fictional. Notice how the writer presents the characters and how she creates and resolves the conflict in the story. Notice, too, that she tells the actions in chronological order.

Model

The Gift

Beginning	I met Gertrude as part of our Girl Scout project. We were to go to elderly people's homes in our town and do little odd jobs. To decide who went where, we drew names, and,
Main character introduced	well, I came up with Gertrude Hinkle. Gertrude is the oldest person in our town: she is ninety-four years old. She still lives in her own
Setting introduced	home and takes care of herself. At first, I was nervous. My mom's and dad's parents died

when I was little. I never knew my grand-parents, and I didn't know any other elderly people. But after my first visit with Gertrude, my nervousness vanished.

The first day I helped her do her dishes. She told me about her family. She had come from a large family with five boys and three girls. She was the youngest of the family and the only remaining member.

The next Saturday I went back and helped her clean her house. She told me more about her family and herself. When I was ready to leave, she asked me to come back on Monday. I did not ask why and cheerfully said I would.

On Monday I arrived at her house just after school was out. Scattered around the living room were square pieces of cloth. She told me that she was making a patchwork quilt for the granddaughter of one of her nieces. The pieces of cloth were all separated into colors and ar-ranged in a pattern. I went to Gertrude's house every day after school for nearly a month. She taught me how to sew the pieces of cloth to-gether evenly. Each piece had some sentimental meaning to her—each told a story—and she told me the stories.

When the quilt was finished, we both sat back and stared at it. So much had been put into it, not just work but the lives of many people—people I had never known but felt I knew from her stories. Tears were in Gertrude's eyes as we took the quilt and packed it in a box. Both of us felt sad to send away the work that had given us many good times together. I would

Climax · have loved to keep the quilt myself. However, I said nothing as we wrapped the box in brown paper so that it was ready to mail.

Two days later a package arrived at my house. I knew what it was. Attached to the outside was a note that read:

> Dear Sally,
>   You worked hard on this. It's only fair that you should have it. I hope the quilt brings you as many memories as I have.
>   Love,
>   Gertrude

End · I went to thank Gertrude immediately, but she wasn't there. A neighbor said that she had gone to see relatives for a few days.

(*Adapted*)

Brenda Harms, Mt. Vernon High School
Mt. Vernon, Iowa

In the beginning of her narrative, the writer presents the setting, Gertrude's home, and the main characters, Gertrude and Sally. Although no dialogue appears in the story, the writer tells what Gertrude and Sally talked about and did. In addition, the letter presents Gertrude's words in a way that reveals her personality. When Sally receives the quilt, the conflict—between Sally's wish to keep the quilt and Gertrude's original plan to send it to a relative—is resolved.

Notice that the writer has provided a title. After you have written and revised the first draft of a narrative, you will probably want to select a title for it. Your title should refer to an important part of the narrative but should not be so unusual that it sounds odd. Also, the title should not reveal too much about what happens in the narrative.

Exercise 1   Prewriting: Conflict   On your paper, write a sentence describing a conflict that could develop from each of the following situations. The conflict that you describe should be of the type listed after the situation.

> SAMPLE   *Situation:* Both the track team and the drama club have practice immediately after school.
> *Type of conflict:* Within the mind and feelings of one person
>
> ANSWER   A student wants to belong to both groups but cannot attend both practices.

1. *Situation:* A hurricane is approaching the town.
   Type of conflict: Between a person and a force of nature
2. *Situation:* A child is going to camp for the first time.
   Type of conflict: Within the mind and feelings of one person
3. *Situation:* You do not realize that your birthday present for your best friend has gotten lost in the mail.
   Type of conflict: Between two people
4. *Situation:* Reyna is sailing a boat on a windy day.
   Type of conflict: Between a person and a force of nature
5. *Situation:* Two teams are participating in a championship softball game.
   Type of conflict: Between two people

Exercise 2   Writing: Dialogue   The writer of "The Gift" chose to concentrate on telling the actions of the story without using dialogue, which would have made the narrative longer. Choose the second, third, or fifth paragraph of the story and rewrite it, using dialogue. Make the words of Sally and Gertrude consistent with the way in which the writer presents them in the story.

Assignment 1   Prewriting   Select a significant event that you or a member of your family experienced. It should be an event that you would like to share with a reader. On your paper, list the setting, the characters involved in the actions, the conflict, the actions that led up to the climax, the climax itself, and the end. Finally, list the point of view from which you plan to narrate the event. Save your paper.

Assignment 2   Writing / Revising   Using the notes that you developed for Assignment 1, write a nonfictional narrative of two or more pages. Be sure to introduce the characters, the setting, and (if possible) the conflict at the beginning of the narrative. Place all related actions in the same paragraph. Then, using the Assignment Checklist, revise your narrative.

Assignment 3   Prewriting / Writing / Revising   Write a fictional narrative of two or more pages that includes at least two main characters. Include dialogue. Then revise your narrative.

Assignment Checklist

Check your writing assignments for the following points:

  ✔ 1. Did you build the actions of the narrative around some kind of conflict that is resolved at the end?
  ✔ 2. Did you present a climax in your narrative?
  ✔ 3. Did you present the actions in chronological order?
  ✔ 4. Did you place each group of related actions in a paragraph of its own?
  ✔ 5. Did you present the setting and introduce the main characters in the beginning of your narrative?
  ✔ 6. Did you use dialogue to reveal the personalities of your characters?
  ✔ 7. Did you keep your point of view consistent?
  ✔ 8. Did you proofread your narrative for correct grammar, usage, spelling, and capitalization?

The Rescue: A Personal Account

Situation: You are a high school student named Johanna Bates. Last week you rescued a woman from a burning building. After an account of the rescue appeared in the local newspaper, the editor of your school magazine asked you to write an account of the incident. As you write, you will keep in mind the following information.

Writer: you as Johanna Bates
Audience: readers of the school magazine
Topic: your rescue of Mrs. Salazar
Purpose: to narrate an experience in the first person

Directions: To write your narrative, follow these steps.

Step 1. To see which details interested the magazine editor, read the newspaper account of the rescue that appears on the facing page.

Step 2. Narrate the incident in the first person. Organize your sentences in chronological order, using transitional words as needed. Be sure that your narrative builds to a high point, or climax. Add information and descriptive details about the rescue that will make it vivid to your readers.

Step 3. In your concluding sentence, sum up what the experience meant to you.

Student Saves Woman from Burning Building

A student at James High is credited with saving the life of 84-year-old Esther Salazar, who was overcome by smoke in her apartment at 39 Locust Street yesterday. Passing the building on her way home from school, Johanna Bates saw smoke coming from a second-story window. Thinking quickly, she ran to the nearest alarm box and summoned the fire department.

While waiting for the firefighters to arrive, she heard Mrs. Salazar calling out from her first-floor window. Miss Bates ran into the building, entered the Salazar apartment, and helped the woman to safety. Mrs. Salazar was suffering from smoke inhalation.

Firefighters arriving on the scene saw the two women emerge from the building just before clouds of gray smoke poured out of the front door. A paramedic treated Mrs. Salazar while firefighters worked for two hours to put out the blaze. Damage to the building was extensive, but no injuries were reported.

When interviewed, Miss Bates commented that she did not feel particularly brave. "I couldn't just stand there and watch her. Anyone would have done what I did."

Firefighters stated that Miss Bates's quick action probably saved the woman's life.

Buyin... ...a bargain
How ...

Think ...
the bui...
Anyon...
proba...
just ...
but ...
arr...
w...

...mmoned

Any...
way ...
on h...
pour...
apar...
the ...
Pass...
calli...
scho...
Stre...

Unit Assignments

Assignment 1 Recall a brief incident in your life during the past few years, an incident that you would like to share with a reader. Tell the actions of the incident so clearly that the reader will be able to understand exactly what happened.

Assignment 2 Find a news story and retell it in one paragraph as an interesting incident. The narrative should consist of a short sequence of actions. It should have a topic sentence and a concluding sentence. Be sure that the story is simple enough to be told in a single paragraph.

Assignment 3 Recall a significant event that happened in your life several years ago. Instead of writing about that event in the first person, write about it in the third person, as though it happened to someone else. Be sure to be consistent in using the third-person point of view.

Assignment 4 Recall a time when one person's words caused an event to happen in a certain way. Retell that event in a narrative about two pages long, using dialogue where it is appropriate. If you cannot recall an actual event, narrate an imaginary one. In this case write *Fiction* at the top of your paper.

Assignment 5 Write a longer fictional narrative from the first-person point of view. In the beginning establish who the characters are and what the setting is.

Assignment 6 Write a brief narrative about an incident that occurred in connection with one of your main interests, such as a sport, a hobby, or music.

Assignment 7 Recall an interesting incident that you witnessed in a public place, such as a store, a school, or a playing field. Narrate that incident as though you had been a participant in it.

Assignment 8   Narrate a true or fictional event that occurs in an unusual place. Pay special attention to describing the setting at the beginning of the narrative.

Revising Your Assignments

For help in revising a narrative, consult the Checklist for Revision on the last page of this book.

Unit Tests

Test 1

A. Number your paper from 1 to 5. Next to each number, write *True* if the sentence is true or *False* if it is false.

1. An autobiographical narrative is a story about a person's life that is written by someone else.
2. In a narrative the characters' dialogue should suit their ages, education, general background, and personalities.
3. All biographical writing uses first-person narration.
4. A narrative is always told from the viewpoint of a participant.
5. A narrative may be either nonfictional or fictional.

B. Number your paper from 6 to 10. Next to each number, write the letter of the term that correctly completes the sentence. You will not use one of the items.

    a. third person   d. climax

    b. dialogue   e. first person

    c. conflict   f. setting

6. The high point of a longer narrative is known as the __?__.
7. The __?__ is the time and location of the action in a narrative.
8. A story in which the writer uses the pronouns *he, she,* and *they* to refer to all of the characters is told in the __?__.
9. __?__ is the conversation between characters in a narrative.
10. A longer narrative establishes a __?__ that must be resolved.

C. Number your paper from 11 to 15. Next to each number, write the letter of the item that correctly answers the question.

11. In which order are narratives written?
    a. Increasing order of importance
    b. Spatial order
    c. Chronological order
    d. Decreasing order of importance

12. Which of the following is *not* a transitional word?

    a. Next   b. Soon   c. Anywhere   d. Later

13. Which of the following pronouns does a writer use in telling a first-person narrative?

    a. I   b. She   c. He   d. You

14. Which of the following statements is *not* true of dialogue?

    a. It helps a writer to make the characters come alive.

    b. It presents conversations indirectly.

    c. It may include some actions of the narrative.

    d. It needs quotation marks for correct punctuation.

15. Which of the following statements is *not* true of the beginning of a longer narrative?

    a. It should capture the reader's attention.

    b. It introduces the important people in the narrative.

    c. It indicates the setting of the narrative.

    d. It summarizes the actions in the entire narrative.

Test 2

Choose one of the Unit Assignments. Write the assignment as directed and hand it in to your teacher.

Writing a Persuasive Essay

Unit Preview

Essays present thoughts, observations, opinions, and happenings that you want to share with others. Your own experience provides the basis of an essay. An important type of essay is the persuasive essay. A **persuasive essay** presents and supports an opinion.

Like other types of essays, a persuasive essay is organized in a specific way. The introductory paragraph presents the opinion, the body paragraphs support it, and the last paragraph states a conclusion. When you are writing a persuasive essay, always keep these two points in mind:

1. The purpose of a persuasive essay is to convince readers that your opinion is correct. All the ideas in the essay should work to accomplish this purpose.
2. A persuasive essay is written to an audience of readers—the people you would like to accept your opinion. Your audience can be one person—a friend, for instance—or many people—all residents of your community, for example.

The following paragraph introduces a persuasive essay. In this introduction the writer presents an opinion and addresses it to a specific audience.

When I pushed aside something I didn't like at dinner, my parents used to tell me to think about "the poor starving children in other countries." That didn't make any sense to me.

What did I have to do with hungry children in other parts of the world? For the last year, however, I've been exchanging letters with a boy my age in the Sudan in Africa. He has opened my eyes to hunger, poverty, and malnutrition. I now realize how fortunate I am. I also believe that people like me should sacrifice occasionally—giving up a new tape or record or an extra pair of shoes—and share our good fortune with those whose lives are far more difficult than ours.

For Analysis   Read the following numbered items. Write the answers on your paper.

1. Copy the sentence that best states the writer's opinion.
2. In a sentence, identify the audience.
3. Make a list of a few ideas that the writer could use in the rest of the essay to support the opinion.

By analyzing the opinion, the audience, and possible supporting ideas of one essay, you have prepared yourself to write a persuasive essay. As you work on your essay in this unit, you will follow the three steps of the writing process: prewriting, writing, and revising.

13.1 Recognizing Opinions

The purpose of persuasive writing is to convince a reader that your opinion is correct. An **opinion** states a personal view or belief that cannot be *proved* to be true. This simply means that there can be different opinions on the same subject. We evaluate opinions according to how reasonable each is.

Here is an example. Some residents of a community have become upset because the city's streets and parks are littered with bottles. They submit a proposal to the city council asking the city to set up a recycling center. Having such a center, they say, will encourage people to turn in their empties, not discard them. The city council, on the other hand, says that the recycling center will not pay for itself and that the city cannot make up the difference. The council proposes an antilitter campaign instead. The local newspaper then publishes an editorial calling for a bottle deposit ordinance. Stores would be asked to charge a deposit of five cents a bottle, to be refunded when the bottle is returned.

Each of the three opinions answers the problem of litter in a different way. Since none of the opinions can be proved to be correct, each group must attempt to persuade the others to accept its opinion.

Another way of understanding opinions is to contrast them with facts. **Facts** are statements that can be proved true.

Mount Everest is 29,028 feet tall.

Born in 1856, Woodrow Wilson was the twenty-eighth president of the United States.

Her eyes are blue.

A statement of fact is not suitable as a topic of a persuasive essay. The reason is simple: no one needs to be persuaded to accept an established fact. However, you can use facts in a persuasive essay to support your opinion.

Exercise   Prewriting: Facts and Opinions   Number your paper from 1 to 10. Write *Opinion* beside the number of each item that expresses an opinion. Write *Fact* next to each item that states a fact.

1. The Land Rover swerved off the road and flipped over.
2. He was too old to be admitted to the park for half price.
3. The government should force reclamation of strip-mining lands.
4. Life on a farm is superior to life in a big city.
5. Trout fishing is a spiritual experience.
6. Airline travel is nicer than it used to be.
7. The cafeteria offers high prices and bad food.

8. This year there were more hurricanes than last year.

9. Sky diving is thrilling.

10. He was the sport's greatest champion—and biggest crybaby.

Assignment Prewriting Read the editorials, opinion columns, and letters to the editor in several issues of your school and community newspapers. Copy one example of each of the sentences described below.

1. A sentence that expresses an opinion about a school issue or problem

2. A sentence that expresses an opinion about a community issue or problem

3. A sentence that expresses an opinion about a national issue or problem

4. A sentence that proposes a solution to a school, community, or national problem

Continuing Assignment Prewriting *Step 1:* List five opinions that you would like to write about. *Step 2:* Underline two that you can write about from personal experience. Save your paper.

Assignment Checklist

Check your Continuing Assignment for the following points:

✔ 1. Did you write five sentences that are opinions, not facts?

✔ 2. Did you underline opinions that you can write about from personal experience?

13.2 Selecting and Limiting a Topic

Prewriting for a persuasive essay begins with selecting and limiting a topic. It may be tempting to begin writing your essay immediately, but time spent on prewriting will help you clarify your ideas and provide a clear direction for your essay.

13.2a Selecting a Topic

Selecting a topic for a persuasive essay can be quite easy. If you are like most people, you have an abundance of opinions. When asked to write a persuasive essay, your biggest problem may be deciding which opinion to focus on. There will be times, however, when no opinion that you want to write about comes immediately to mind. The following questions may then be helpful to you. After each question, a possible response is given.

1. What activities, issues, or ideas do I feel strongly about?
   Example: safeguarding the environment
2. Have I experienced anything recently that made me think that a person or a group should change their minds about something? That some specific action should be taken?
   Example: building a better swimming pool for the town
3. What problems do I know about that need solving, and what are the solutions to these problems?
   Example: teen-age unemployment
4. What issue has produced disagreement and debate lately among my friends, my classmates, or members of the community?
   Example: the school sports program
5. What have I read recently that I agreed or disagreed with?
   Example: aid to underdeveloped countries

These questions should suggest topics that are of interest to you and that come from your own experience and ideas. In choosing a topic for a persuasive essay, it is very helpful to talk over your topic ideas with others or to do research. Nevertheless, the topic you choose should generally be one that you have a genuine interest in and already know something about.

Exercise 1 Prewriting: Persuasive Essay Topics
Number your paper from 1 to 10. Write *Suitable* beside the number if the topic is appropriate for a persuasive essay. Write *Unsuitable* if the topic is not appropriate.

1. Summers: a time for work as well as play
2. The value of competition
3. Swimming: the perfect form of exercise
4. The manufacturing of modern aircraft
5. Our town's most urgent problem
6. The year's best film
7. An account of the first voyage of Columbus
8. The life of Jane Addams
9. Signers of the United States Constitution
10. Democracy: the best political system

13.2b Limiting a Topic

When you have a topic in mind, you will want to make sure that it is specific. A broad topic such as "Sports" or "The environment" will not help you to write an effective persuasive essay. If you have selected a broad topic, you can make it specific, or limit it, by asking yourself another set of questions.

1. Can I limit my topic to a person, group, or example?
   BROAD Sports
   LIMITED School sports

2. Can I limit my topic to a part of the subject?
   BROAD The environment
   LIMITED Water pollution

3. Can I limit my topic to a specific event or place?
   BROAD   Politics
   LIMITED   School elections

4. Can I limit my topic to a specific audience?
   BROAD   Computers
   LIMITED   Students of computer science

The following list shows how a broad topic can lead to a limited topic.

BROAD TOPIC	LIMITED TOPIC
Travel	Traveling in the Northwest
Careers	Making a career decision
Science	Biology
Dress	Current fashions
Music	Rock music
Sports	Professional athletes
Politics	The upcoming election in our community

Exercise 2   Prewriting: Limiting Topics   The three numbered sentences are ways of limiting an essay topic. Use each statement to limit the topics that follow it. Write each limited topic on your paper.

SAMPLE   Limit the topic to a single group.
            Helping people

ANSWER   *Limited topic:* Our responsibility to refugees

1. Limit the topic to a part of the subject.
   a. The impact of high technology
   b. Skills needed for career success
2. Limit the topic to a specific event or place.
   a. Travel
   b. Sports
3. Limit the topic to a specific audience.
   a. Mathematics
   b. Music

13.2c Expressing an Opinion

You should now express your topic as an opinion. State the opinion in a complete, declarative sentence. This **opinion statement** is important because it will guide the rest of your work on the essay. Rewrite the statement if it does not accurately express the opinion that you want your readers to accept. Here is an example of an opinion statement that would be appropriate.

TOPIC	Sports
LIMITED TOPIC	School sports
OPINION STATEMENT	Every student ought to have the opportunity to participate in a sports program.

Not all opinions are suitable for a persuasive essay, however. There are three points that you should keep in mind when you write your opinion statement.

1. *An opinion statement should express more than a personal preference.*

    NOT SUITABLE
    > Green is a wonderful color.
    > I will not watch baseball on television.

    These sentences simply express personal likes and dislikes. They may be strongly held opinions, but a writer cannot support them with reasons that other people will accept.

2. *An opinion statement should not be based strictly on a feeling or a hunch.*

    NOT SUITABLE
    > We are the happiest family on the block.
    > Next year, I'm sure we'll have a 10-0 record.

An opinion statement that expresses only a feeling or a guess is difficult to support and thus unsuitable for an essay.

3. *An opinion statement should be as specific and clear as possible.*

NOT SUITABLE
>   Violence is bad.
>
>   Toxic wastes are a problem.

These opinion statements are not suitable for an essay because they are too general or too vague. The first statement expresses an idea that most people agree with. In fact, the statement says little. The second statement is also general, and it does not say why or how the problem should be solved.

The opinion statements that follow are suitable for a persuasive essay.

SUITABLE
>   Our community needs a recycling center to aid energy conservation and to discourage littering.
>
>   Because computers are widely used, students should take a computer literacy course.

These opinion statements are suitable for an essay for three reasons. (1) They express more than a personal preference. (2) They are based on logic, not a feeling or a hunch. (3) They are stated specifically and clearly.

Exercise 3   Prewriting: Opinion Statements

Number your paper from 1 to 10. Write *Suitable* beside the number of each opinion statement that is suitable for a persuasive essay. Write *Unsuitable* beside the number of each opinion statement that is not suitable.

1. I bet the talent show will be great.
2. Administrators have the right to censor a school newspaper.

3. Schools should award credit for work experience.

4. I like the Truck Stops.

5. There is more emphasis on teamwork in basketball than in any other sport.

6. Our Constitution calls for separation of church and state.

7. The Olympic Games have become too commercialized.

8. The most outstanding characteristic of Americans is their friendliness.

9. Peace is important to everyone.

10. All students ought to be required to take a foreign language.

Exercise 4   Prewriting: Opinion Statements

Rewrite three of the following opinions so that they are specific enough to be used as opinion statements in an essay. Add whatever details are needed to make each opinion clear and definite.

> **SAMPLE**   Our school should do something about career planning.
>
> **ANSWER**   Once a month, our school should sponsor career panels made up of local employers and professionals.

1. The driver training program needs improvement.

2. Television commercials make you want to buy things you don't need.

3. Personal stereos are changing the world.

4. It should be harder (easier) to become an American citizen.

5. Volunteer work is vital to society.

Assignment   Prewriting   Write an opinion statement suitable for a persuasive essay about each of the following topics. Limit a topic sufficiently before writing the statement.

1. Grades
2. Driving age
3. Community issues
4. Highway safety
5. Work

Continuing Assignment Prewriting *Step 1:* Using the questions on page 500, list three topics for a persuasive essay. *Step 2:* Underline the three topics that interest you the most. Add these to the two topics you underlined for the Continuing Assignment on page 499. *Step 3:* Limit the five topics by using the questions on pages 501–502. *Step 4:* Write opinion statements for three of the limited topics. Save your paper.

Assignment Checklist

Check your Continuing Assignment for the following points:

✔ 1. Did you list five topics that you have an opinion about?
✔ 2. Did you limit each of the topics?
✔ 3. Are your opinion statements specific and clear?

13.3 Planning Your Persuasive Essay

The next step is to plan your persuasive essay. This step involves considering your audience, listing and selecting ideas, and organizing your ideas in an outline.

13.3a Considering Your Audience

Thinking about your audience is important in any kind of writing. It is particularly important in persuasive writing because you want readers to accept your opinion. Often, you want your audience to take some sort of action based on your opinion. By knowing who your audience is and anticipating their reactions, you have a better chance of convincing them.

To help you think about your audience, here are four questions to consider.

1. Who is my audience?

2. What is likely to be my audience's attitude toward my opinion?
3. How much does my audience know about the subject of my opinion?
4. What terms should I define for my audience?

Here is an example of an opinion statement, followed by answers to each of the questions.

OPINION STATEMENT
> Every student ought to have the opportunity to participate in a sports program.

ANSWER TO QUESTION 1
> School administrators

ANSWER TO QUESTION 2
> My audience favors a sports program but is concerned about its cost. They probably feel academic programs are more important than sports.

ANSWER TO QUESTION 3
> My audience knows a lot about the subject, especially finances. But they may not know what sports mean to students.

ANSWER TO QUESTION 4
> I must be sure to define the term *sports*. By *sports* I mean any kind of exercise such as ballet, gym classes, and intramurals—not just the major team sports like football.

Exercise 1   Prewriting: Identifying an Audience

Number your paper from 1 to 5. For each opinion, list one possible audience for a persuasive essay.

SAMPLE   To improve driving skills, a driver "apprenticeship" program should be started.

ANSWER   Local police

1. The cultural contributions of (choose an ethnic group) deserve a wider recognition by all.

2. Bicycle lanes should be designated on major streets in our community.
3. An annual award to a student for service to our city should be instituted.
4. Although it is entertainment, the television series (choose one you watch and enjoy) also has a message for viewers.
5. People make a great mistake when they judge someone on appearance alone.

Exercise 2   Prewriting: Considering the Audience

Select two of the opinions and the audience you named for them in Exercise 1. Answer the following questions for each audience.

1. What is the audience's attitude toward the opinion?
2. How much does the audience know about the subject?
3. What terms might have to be defined for the audience?

13.3b Listing and Selecting Ideas

The questions you asked about the audience should suggest how to begin supporting your opinion. Supporting ideas can include facts, examples, statements by authorities, and personal experiences that back up your opinion. Such supporting ideas form what is known as an argument. An **argument** is reasoning presented to persuade an audience to accept an opinion.

To begin listing supporting ideas, read your opinion statement and ask yourself, "Why should someone agree?" Another approach is to write down your opinion statement and follow it with the word *because*.

Every student ought to have the opportunity to participate in a sports program because

Facts   Statements by authorities
Examples   Personal experience

Suppose you were writing an essay on the importance of a full school sports program, an essay for an audience of school administrators. You might list the following ideas.

1. My grandfather suffers from disease partly caused by lack of exercise when he was young.
2. Exercise from early age important for health
3. School no fun without sports
4. Some athletes will be denied pro careers.
5. Sports are enjoyable.
6. Sports relieve stress.
7. Without sports program, what will students do after school?
8. Exercise gives you a feeling of well being.
9. Sports teach teamwork and self-discipline.
10. Sports help you mature.
11. Band and drill team won't be able to perform at sports events.
12. Saw newspaper report of study that showed children and teenagers in U.S. don't get enough exercise
13. Exercise from early age on important for good health

You should go through your list of supporting ideas and decide which ideas will help your argument in the essay. To make the decision, use these questions as a guide.

1. Is the idea closely related to my opinion?
2. Is the idea important?
3. Will the idea help to persuade my readers?

In the list of ideas above, these questions would eliminate Idea 3 (won't persuade most readers), Ideas 4 and 7 (not closely related to the opinion), and Idea 11 (not important). Because the other ideas are important and support your opinion, you would probably want to use them in the essay.

Ideas 12 and 13 contain facts that could be found from research. Although many persuasive essays are written entirely from personal experience, a few facts gained from research can show your audience that your opinion is reasonable and well supported.

Exercise 3 Prewriting: Related Ideas On your paper, copy the three opinions that follow. Under each opinion, list the ideas (identified by letters) that are closely related to the opinion and will help persuade a reader.

> SAMPLE   *Opinion:* A major league baseball game is a social event.
>
> a. Crowd is interesting
> b. Plenty of time to talk, relax
> c. Win or lose, you meet people.
> d. Can be seen on TV
>
> ANSWER   a, b, c

1. *Opinion:* Cooking requires the skills of a laboratory scientist.
   a. Recipes often are long and complex.
   b. My father likes to cook.
   c. Timing must be precise.
   d. Can't miss a step or omit an ingredient
   e. Recipe books are often attractive.
2. *Opinion:* The evolution of health care has created new problems for patients.
   a. High cost of treatment
   b. Care usually not personal
   c. Doctors are highly trained.
   d. Hospitals have become large, sometimes frightening.
   e. Hospital food is often poor.
3. *Opinion:* For their own good, human beings should treat the natural world with great care.
   a. Tropical rain forests produce oxygen.
   b. Hawaii is one of the most beautiful states.
   c. Atmosphere shields us from harmful radiation.

d. Polar ice caps help determine weather.

e. Many animal species sustain our food chain.

13.3c Organizing and Outlining Your Essay

After you have listed and selected your ideas, you need to organize them in an order that the reader can easily follow. To do so, divide the ideas into groups. Put all related ideas in the same group. Then arrange the ideas within each group as a main idea with two or more ideas that support it. If there is a main idea that has no supporting ideas, devise two or more supporting ideas and add them to the group. If there are supporting ideas without a main idea, devise a main idea to go with them.

For a persuasive essay, the only effective way of organizing your main ideas is in order of importance. You usually present the least important main idea first and build up to the most important. Sometimes, however, you may choose to give the most important main idea first for special emphasis.

Now you are ready to write an outline. In an outline the main ideas on your list become **main headings,** and the supporting ideas become **subheadings**. The introductory and concluding paragraphs of an essay are usually listed as main headings in the outline. For a short essay, there is no need to outline them further.

Always start a main heading with a Roman numeral followed by a period. Start a subheading with a capital letter followed by a period. Subheadings are indented. Except for the introduction and conclusion, a main heading must always have at least two subheadings.

The ideas on sports from page 509 can be outlined as follows. The main ideas have been placed in their order of importance, beginning with the least important. Notice that some ideas have been reworded. Notice, too, that the opinion statement is placed at the beginning of the outline.

> *Opinion statement*: Every student ought to have the opportunity to participate in a sports program.

I. Introduction
II. Sports as source of enjoyment
   A. Relieve stress
   B. Give a sense of well-being
III. Sports as helping you mature
   A. Teach teamwork
   B. Teach self-discipline
IV. Sports as important to lifelong health
   A. Findings of national study of exercise
   B. Should begin at early age
   C. Example: Grandfather's illness
V. Conclusion

The preceding outline is a **topic outline**—one in which the headings are stated in words, phrases, or clauses. Topic outlines are used most often. There are two other kinds of outlines. A **sentence outline** is arranged in the same way, but its headings and subheadings are expressed in complete sentences. A **rough outline,** on the other hand, is simpler. It consists of main ideas only and is helpful in planning the more detailed topic outline.

Exercise 4   Prewriting: Outlining   On your paper, arrange the following main headings and subheadings in topic outline form. List main headings II, III, and IV in order of importance, from most important to least important. You may list subheadings in any order that seems logical. Do not use subheadings for the introduction or conclusion.

> *Opinion statement:* Violence shown in television programs for children should be reduced or eliminated.

MAIN HEADINGS	SUBHEADINGS
TV already too violent	Teach positive values
Conclusion	Just as enjoyable as
Nonviolent children's shows	violent shows
Introduction	Can cause violent behavior
Shows influence behavior	Adult shows filled with violence
	Can teach acceptance of
	violent behavior in others
	Even TV sports violence-filled

Assignment Prewriting Using the opinion statement you wrote for the Assignment on page 505, consider the audience, list supporting ideas, and select the ideas that you will actually use in your essay. Arrange these ideas in a topic outline.

Continuing Assignment Prewriting *Step 1:* Select one of the opinion statements you wrote for the Continuing Assignment on page 506, and consider the audience. *Step 2:* List supporting ideas and select ones you want to use in your persuasive essay. *Step 3:* On your paper, write the opinion statement and arrange your ideas in a topic outline, listing the main ideas in order of importance. Save the outline for the next step of your essay.

Assignment Checklist

Check your assignments for the following points:

    ✔ 1. Did you use the questions on pages 506–507 as you considered your audience?

    ✔ 2. Did you list and select your ideas?

    ✔ 3. Did you prepare a topic outline with the main headings arranged in order of importance?

13.4 Writing the Introductory Paragraph

The introductory paragraph of a short persuasive essay should interest the reader in the topic and present the opinion statement. In addition, any special terms that you will use in the essay should be defined in the introductory paragraph. Keep the following suggestions in mind when you write an introductory paragraph.

Strategies

1. *Write to your audience.* You can do so by being your own audience. Consider what might interest you about your subject. Then try to convey in words the most interesting aspect of it.

2. *Include your opinion statement as one sentence.* This sentence need not be the first one in the paragraph. In fact, an opinion statement is likely to come at the end or near the end. You may need to revise your opinion statement as you write the paragraph.

3. *Be direct.* Do not search for fancy words and impressive-sounding generalizations. In other words, be yourself.

4. *Be brief.* If your opening paragraph is more than six or seven sentences, you may be using material that belongs elsewhere in your essay.

In this unit you have studied the planning of a persuasive essay on the importance of school sports. The following model is a possible introductory paragraph for such an essay. To begin the paragraph, the writer uses a reference to the ancient Greeks. The reference puts the subject in perspective and also links the writer's opinion with the "wisdom of the Greeks." The last sentence of the paragraph is the opinion statement.

Model

The ancient Greeks believed that the purpose of education was a sound mind in a sound body. Today, however, we are in danger of setting aside the wisdom of the Greeks by neglecting one aspect of education. Because of budget problems, our school sports program may not exist next year. This action would eliminate not only major team sports like football and basketball but also gymnastics, tennis, swimming, gym classes, and intramural programs. I believe that sports, defined as school-sponsored exercise of any kind, have an important place in education. In fact, every student ought to have the opportunity to participate in a sports program.

This paragraph effectively introduces the essay because it interests the reader in the topic, defines an essential term to be used later, and presents the opinion statement.

Exercise 1 Writing Number your paper from 1 to 3. Evaluate each of the following introductory paragraphs. If the paragraph is interesting, defines important terms, and presents an opinion statement, write *Effective* next to the paragraph number on your paper. If the paragraph does not do one or more of these, write *Ineffective* on your paper. Also give one or more reasons for labeling a paragraph *Ineffective*.

PARAGRAPH 1

In this essay I want to say that people should not let their popularity determine how they feel about themselves. In this essay I will present several reasons to support this opinion. First, I will introduce the essay. It's hard to define popularity. Popularity can make you feel good or bad about yourself. So if you wear certain clothes, say certain things in a certain way, listen to certain music, and act like everyone else, people will like you. Then you can be happy. But what does this happiness really mean?

PARAGRAPH 2

lo·bot·o·my. The dictionary defines this word as surgery on or removal of a lobe of the brain. Anyone who has seen the movie *One Flew over the Cuckoo's Nest* knows what a lobotomy can do to your personality. The hero was funny and rebellious before surgery. He was as lively as a turnip afterwards. I have been watching rock videos every day for the last year and have discovered something as a result. Rock videos are the electronic equivalent of a lobotomy.

PARAGRAPH 3

For fifteen years our swim team has boarded a bus after school for a twenty-minute ride across town. The team leaves the bus, enters a building in a run-down neighborhood, and goes to a locker room that looks like a room in an abandoned factory. The locker room, however, is pleasant compared to the pool area, which is dark, chilly, and dirty. You would not jump into the pool itself unless you were forced to. The swim team does because our school does not have a pool.

Exercise 2   Revising: Introductory Paragraphs

Select a paragraph that you labeled *Ineffective* in Exercise 1 and revise it.

Assignment   Writing   Write an introductory paragraph for a persuasive essay on one of the following topics.

1. Parents should attend one full day of classes at school.
2. Nutrition should be a required course in high school.
3. Students should be given discounts by local merchants.
4. News media give accurate (distorted) views of the world.
5. Being an only child (one of several children) is an advantage.

Continuing Assignment   Writing   Write an introductory paragraph for the essay you outlined for the Continuing Assignment on page 513. Save your paper.

516

Assignment Checklist

Check your assignment for the following points:

✔ 1. Did you include your opinion statement somewhere in the introductory paragraph?
✔ 2. Did you define important terms?
✔ 3. Did you introduce your opinion in a way that will interest your readers?

13.5 Writing the Body of Your Essay

The paragraphs in the body of a persuasive essay support and develop your argument. Writing the body of a persuasive essay is similar to writing an effective paragraph. In a well-written paragraph, each sentence supports the main idea stated in the topic sentence. In a persuasive essay each paragraph supports the opinion statement of the introductory paragraph.

When you make your initial attempt at writing the body of the essay, consider it a first draft. Do not rush your writing, but do not get bogged down worrying about a single word or sentence. You can make needed changes in your work later.

13.5a Following the Outline

Rely on your outline as you write the body of the essay. Your task is to put together sentences and paragraphs that express the ideas and relationships in the outline. To do so, you may need to add some more supporting ideas.

Usually, a main heading and its subheadings are the basis for one paragraph. Base the topic sentence of each of your paragraphs on the main heading.

The following model shows how a writer turns an outline into the body paragraphs of an essay. These paragraphs are based on the outline that appears on page 512.

Model

I. Introduction	The ancient Greeks believed that the purpose of education was a sound mind in a sound body. Today, however, we are in danger of setting aside the wisdom of the Greeks by neglecting one aspect of education. Because of budget problems, our school sports program may not exist next year. This action would eliminate not only major team sports like football and basketball but also gymnastics, tennis, swimming, gym classes, and intramural programs. I believe that sports, defined as school-sponsored exercise of any kind, have an important place in education. In fact, every student ought to have the opportunity to participate in a sports program.
II. Sports as source of enjoyment	First of all, sports are a source of enjoyment. This may not seem important in a school, where learning is the main goal. Nevertheless, the enjoyment of sports can affect the academic
A. Relieve stress	environment. Vigorous exercise helps to relieve stress. High levels of stress are known to block concentration and to lower achievement. Regu-
B. Give a sense of well being	lar exercise also brings a sense of physical well-being. Students who feel energetic are certain to be better students than those who are listless.
III. Sports as helping you mature	In addition, sports help students mature. Anyone who regularly plays a team sport learns the value of teamwork. Students learn that each
A. Teach teamwork	individual must do his or her part if a team is to perform well and that the combined efforts of individuals can lead to extraordinary results.
B. Teach self-discipline	Any sport, team or individual, teaches students self-discipline. To excel in a sport, from aerobic dancing to volleyball, an individual must have self-discipline to practice, compete, and improve.

IV. Sports as important to lifelong health	Most important, school sports provide a basis for lifelong health. Recently, a government survey showed that children and teen-
A. Findings of national study of exercise	agers were not exercising enough. The government has recommended more exercise activities in schools because they establish good exercise
B. Should begin at early age	habits that help prevent heart problems and other diseases in later life. I can give a personal
C. Example: Grandfather's illness	example. My grandfather suffers from osteoporosis, a weakening of the bones. His doctor says the condition is partly due to the fact that Grandfather did not exercise regularly when he was a young man.

Exercise 1 Writing   In this exercise you will work with an outline of the body paragraphs of a persuasive essay. In the paragraphs that follow the outline, each sentence has a number. On separate lines of your paper, copy each Roman numeral and each capital letter of the outline. Next to each numeral or letter, list the number or numbers of the sentences in the essay that match the corresponding heading or subheading in the outline.

Opinion statement: Americans have forgotten that there is still an energy crisis.

    II. Consumption of energy
        A. Gasoline and driving
        B. Other forms of energy
    III. Conservation of energy
        A. Recycling
        B. Use of renewable sources
    IV. Politics of energy
        A. U.S. still dependent on foreign countries
        B. Political situation still uncertain

    (1) In the mid-1970s after the Arab oil embargo, consumption of energy was a national concern.   (2) The federal

government considered an emergency rationing plan that would allow drivers to buy gasoline once or twice a week.   (3) Americans curtailed their driving and consumption of gasoline voluntarily, however, and auto companies produced more fuel-efficient vehicles.   (4) Now, despite high prices, consumption of gasoline and the miles driven per year by Americans have begun to increase again.   (5) Moreover, the consumption of other forms of energy, such as home-heating oil and natural gas, has also increased.   (6) No one seems to remember when the temperature of office buildings was regulated by the government, and homeowners were asked to keep their thermostats at 65 degrees during cold months.

(7) In the 1970s there was an emphasis on many types of energy conservation.   (8) Recycling and the use of renewable energy got a lot of attention.   (9) Recycling centers for paper, bottles, and metal were set up in communities throughout the nation.   (10) In the 1980s, although some states have passed bottle-deposit laws, some recycling centers have closed and many people again view cans and bottles as trash.   (11) During the 1970s money was also invested in renewable forms of energy—for example, solar power and wind power.   (12) As time went on, however, money has also been withdrawn from research in renewable energy.

(14) Nevertheless, the politics of energy have not changed. (15) The United States is still dependent on foreign countries for a significant share of its energy.   (16) The goal of energy independence has not been achieved.   (17) At the same time, the political situation that used to frighten people has not changed.   (18) There is no peace in the Middle East.   (19) If anything, that region of the world is less stable than it was, and a cutoff of oil supplies remains a threat.   (20) Still, Americans do not seem to care.

13.5b Using Transitional Words

Transitional words guide your reader through your essay. They show relationships between the ideas in your sentences and between the ideas in your paragraphs. Some of the most common transitional words and phrases are listed below according to the ways in which you can use them.

TO INDICATE TIME
> after, at the same time, finally, later, meanwhile, next, simultaneously, soon, then, until

TO INTRODUCE EXAMPLES
> one, another, for example, for instance

TO INDICATE RESULTS
> as a result, consequently, hence, therefore, thus

TO SHOW OTHER LOGICAL RELATIONSHIPS
> accordingly, also, however, if so, in addition, in fact, in view of this, nevertheless, on the other hand, similarly, since, then, yet

Exercise 2   Prewriting: Transitional Words   On your paper, write the transitional word or phrase that is most appropriate for each blank in the following paragraph from a persuasive essay. Be careful to express the correct logical relationship between ideas. Use each transitional word or phrase only once.

also	finally	however
as a result	for example	

Doing volunteer work is an excellent way of preparing yourself for a career. If you choose your work carefully, you will be able to gain experience that will help you to get a job later. __1__, if you want to work with children someday, you can do volunteer work in a day camp. Doing volunteer work __2__ can give you a chance to work at a job that you know little about. You will be exposed to actual working conditions, and __3__ you will learn whether you like the job. You may not, __4__, be able to work at a job that requires special training. __5__, doing volunteer work will give you a good feeling because you will be helping other people.

Assignment 1   Prewriting   The following passage is the introductory paragraph of a persuasive essay. On your paper, make a list of ideas that you could use to develop the topic. Then write a topic outline for two body paragraphs that would follow the introduction.

Education is usually associated with things like schools, books, lectures, and computers. I would like to suggest an important resource that is neglected in discussions of education: people. We do not study people, and we certainly do not take notes on what they say—unless they are classroom teachers. Nevertheless, we learn from the people we are close to. From several of my close friends and relatives, I've received an education almost equal to the one I've received in school.

Assignment 2   Writing   Write the two body paragraphs that you outlined in Assignment 1. Save your paper.

Continuing Assignment   Writing   Write a first draft of the body paragraphs for which you wrote an introductory paragraph in the Continuing Assignment on page 516. Save your paper.

Assignment Checklist

Check your writing assignments for the following points:

- ✔ 1. Did you follow your outline?
- ✔ 2. Did you give information that fully develops the points in the outline?
- ✔ 3. Did you use appropriate transitional words?

13.6   Writing the Concluding Paragraph

The final paragraph helps the reader to grasp the full meaning of a persuasive essay. As a reminder to your readers, the concluding paragraph should restate the opinion statement in different words.

OPINION STATEMENT
> Every student ought to have the opportunity to partici-
> pate in a sports program.

RESTATED IN CONCLUDING PARAGRAPH
> Sports are not a luxury; sports should be for everyone.

There are three main ways of bringing an essay to a definite close.

Strategies

1. *Call for a specific action based on your argument.* Many persuasive essays end with a call to action of some sort. The essay on school sports could be concluded using this strategy.

   Model

   > I realize that our school faces serious budget prob-
   > lems and that maintaining excellent academic programs is
   > a priority. However, I believe that the school administra-
   > tion should meet and reconsider the decision to eliminate
   > the sports program. Sports are not a luxury; sports should
   > be for everyone.

2. *Introduce a personal judgment or reaction.* The essay on school sports could end with the writer's personal view.

   Model

   > I am not an expert on school finances. I do think,
   > though, that school sports are not a luxury. Sports should
   > be for everyone. I believe that dropping the sports
   > program could be a terrible mistake in the long run. The
   > money saved would ease the budget problem over the
   > next few years, but the cost in the well-being of students
   > now and in later life could be great. I think that is too
   > high a price to pay.

3. *Summarize the main points of the essays.*

Model

>Sports have many benefits. They are a source of pleasure for students because they relieve stress and give them a sense of physical well-being. Sports teach values that are essential to maturity, such as teamwork and self-discipline. Finally, school sports lay a foundation for good health throughout one's life. Thus, I believe sports are not a luxury; sports should be for everyone.

The three methods presented here are not the only ways of concluding an essay. For instance, you can use a quotation or a question to end an essay. Regardless of the method used, a good concluding paragraph should leave the reader with a clear understanding of the main idea of your essay.

Exercise   Prewriting: Concluding Paragraphs   The following are concluding paragraphs. On your paper, write *Summary, Call for action,* or *Personal reaction* to show which of the three methods the writer of each paragraph uses to conclude the essay.

PARAGRAPH 1

As I have shown, high school students should have the courage to be individualists. Peer-group pressure usually emphasizes outward things, like dress and ways of spending leisure time. Also, the pressure to conform can sometimes be dangerous, as when a group dares someone to do something. Finally, when a teen-ager grows up, there will not be anyone around to tell him or her what to do. High school students should start thinking for themselves now.

PARAGRAPH 2

The most convincing thing I can say, however, has to do with the feeling I have when I play a piece of music well. My hands and the piano keys seem to be one, and the sound seems to come from me, not the instrument. I lose all sense of where I am. Only the notes of the piece are important. Music, then, is the one thing I can't live without.

PARAGRAPH 3

   As my examples show, my summer job at the day-care center was the most important experience of my life. I had to be outgoing to make shy children like LaShawn join in our games, and I had to be patient while children struggled to learn tasks like tying their shoes. Finally, I had to be organized to make sure that we got back from the park by lunch time and that all of the toys were put away before it was time to leave.

Assignment   Writing   Write a concluding paragraph for the essay that you developed in Assignments 1 and 2 on pages 521-522. Use a method of concluding the essay that will leave your reader with a clear understanding of your opinion. Save your paper.

Continuing Assignment   Writing   Write the concluding paragraph of the essay for which you have written the introductory and body paragraphs in the Continuing Assignments on pages 516 and 522. Before you write the paragraph, look over the different ways of concluding an essay that are discussed in this section. Save your paper.

Assignment Checklist

Check your assignments for the following points:

   ✔ 1. Did you call for a specific action, introduce a personal reaction, summarize the essay, or use another effective method of bringing the essay to a close?
   ✔ 2. Does your concluding paragraph leave the reader with a clear understanding of your opinion as you have presented it in the essay?
   ✔ 3. Did you restate your opinion statement in the concluding paragraph?

13.7 Revising and Finishing Your Essay

The literal meaning of the verb *revise* is "to see or look again." Revising is looking at your work again from the point of view of your audience. In other words, you are reading to discover where your audience might become confused or bored. A good way of seeing the paper from your reader's point of view is to read it aloud. Another way is to have someone else read or listen to the first draft.

To revise your essay, you have to be willing to change it. You have several options for correcting a problem: removing material, inserting new material, rewriting, reorganizing, or a combination of these. The option that you choose depends on the problem. Sometimes you will know exactly what to do. At other times you will need to experiment with the options.

Reviewing the Content

See whether each part of your essay says what you want it to say. Answer these questions:

1. Does the introductory paragraph include a clear and specific opinion statement?
2. Will the introductory paragraph interest the reader in the subject of your opinion?
3. Does the body of the essay present reasons, facts, and other types of support that will persuade the reader to accept your opinion?
4. Does the concluding paragraph include a restatement of your opinion statement, and does it bring the essay to a definite close?
5. Are any of the sentences unrelated to the presentation of your opinion? Remove any that are.
6. Does any part of the essay need more supporting ideas? If so, add new material to your sentences or write new sentences.

Checking Sentences and Word Choices

After reviewing your first draft for what it says, examine it again for the way in which you expressed your ideas.

Strategies

1. *Check the length of your sentences.* Be alert for too many short sentences in a single paragraph. When this occurs, you can often combine some of the sentences. Also be alert for long, complicated sentences. You may have tried to combine too many ideas. A long sentence can often be divided into simpler sentences that are more easily understood.

2. *Check the coordination and subordination of the ideas in your sentences.* Such coordinating conjunctions as *and* and *but* and such subordinating conjunctions as *although, when,* and *because* show relationships between ideas. For further help on revising sentences, see pages 363–388.

3. *Check the transitional words in your sentences.* Transitional words make the ideas of your essay flow logically and smoothly.

4. *Check your word choices.* Be sure that your word choices express your ideas as precisely as possible. Try out new words in your essay, but be sure to use them correctly. Do not use a word simply to impress the reader.

Proofreading

The last step in revising the draft is proofreading it—reading it for errors. Check your work for correct punctuation, capitalization, and spelling. Proofreading also includes checking your essay for correct grammar and usage. For example, be sure that your composition contains no sentence fragments or run-on sentences.

Choosing a Title

After revising the first draft of your essay, you will probably want to select a title for it if you have not already done so. An essay title should reflect the idea of the essay in a way that will interest the reader. A few key words taken from your opinion statement or from your restatement of it in the concluding paragraph will usually make a good title. Possible titles for the sports essay in this unit are "Sports Are for Everyone" or "School Sports Are Not a Luxury."

Preparing the Finished Paper

You can prepare the finished paper when you are satisfied with your revisions and have proofread the revised essay. As you copy the essay, remember that neatness and accuracy will make a good impression on your reader. Always proofread your essay for errors made in copying.

You will find guidelines for preparing the finished paper on pages 258–259. Use them with any alterations that your teacher suggests.

Exercise 1 Revising: The Paragraph The parts of the following paragraphs from a letter that are in italic type need revision. Each part has a number. Three possible ways of revising each part are listed after the paragraph. Copy the numbers on your paper. After each number write the letter of the revision that will most improve the paragraph.

You, Mrs. Rashad, have been upset with me. (1) *Because I've been ignoring your son.* You believe I'm being rude for no reason. I would like to convince you that there are good reasons for my behavior. I believe Ralph has a lot to learn about friendship.

Last summer our scout troop went on a wilderness camping trip. (2) *Everything had to be carried in backpacks.* Each group of four scouts carried two tents, two tarps, a cookstove, and groceries, as well as sleeping bags and personal belongings. (3) *In my group one scout could carry few of the group supplies.* His pack was almost full with his own supplies. Therefore, the remaining three of us (4) *sustained the weight of* his share of the load. We were willing to help him until we reached camp and discovered that he had a radio and a pillow in his pack. (5) *Those were bulky and unnecessary supplies for a camping trip, and on the way back, he had to carry his share of the group supplies.*

1. a. Remove sentence.
   b. Remove the word *Because*.
   c. Combine with previous sentence: *You, Mrs. Rashad, have been upset with me because I've been ignoring your son.*

2. a. Remove sentence.
   b. Rewrite sentence: *Before we could set up camp, we had to carry all of our supplies into the woods in backpacks.*
   c. Combine with previous sentences: *Last summer our scout troop went on a wilderness camping trip, and everything had to be carried in backpacks.*

3. a. Combine with next sentence: *In my group one scout could carry few of the group supplies because his pack was almost full of his own supplies.*
   b. Remove sentence.
   c. Rewrite sentence: *Therefore, in my group one scout was able to carry only a few of the group supplies.*

4. a. Change word: *held up*
   b. Change word: *shouldered*
   c. Change word: *accepted*

5. a. Separate into two sentences: *Those were bulky and unnecessary supplies for a camping trip. On the way back, he had to carry his share of the group supplies.*
   b. Rewrite sentence: *On the way back, he had to carry his share of the group supplies.*
   c. Remove sentence.

Exercise 2   Revising: The Essay as a Whole   Rewrite the paragraphs of the following essay. Convert the last two sentences of the first paragraph into an opinion statement. Omit any unnecessary information. Also, separate sentences that are too long and combine sentences that are too short. Finally, replace the three incorrect words in the passage.

Technological change is hailed in this country as evidence of our ingenuity and dedication to greater efficiency. That praise is probably justified most of the time. However, not all technological changes are improvements. Electronic banking is one those doubting changes. I despise electronic banking. I believe it should be abolished.

My checkbook is under my control. An electronic banking machine is not. When I use a banking machine, I am made to believe that I am controlling the transaction, however. I am asked questions on the screen—the machine presents itself as my servant!—and I punch keys to answer. I seem to be controlling the transaction. The money is dispensed by the machine in a neat pile. As a "report card" in my mastery of the process, I am rewarded with a printed receipt that lists the date and time, the amount of the transaction, and my account balances. Throughout this sequence I am at the mercy of the machine. If the machine decides I have insufficient funds, I cannot show it my checkbook balance, if the machine dispenses too much money, I cannot give it back, and if the machine keeps my bank card, I cannot get it back.

Worse yet. The banking machine completely depersonalizes banking. Human tellers may not be as fast or as accurate as a machine. They are generally friendly and attentive. (At the rate things are going, you will soon have to make an appointment to see a human teller.) Moreover, tellers are usually helpful with problems and can straighten out a snarled transaction on the spot. A banking machine, on the other hand, is either friendly nor helpful.

When I do business at a banking machine, I come away with a feeling of my own powerlessness, not of astonishment at the technology. I am insured that the machine can do everything a human teller can do, but as a customer, I have found a smile from a bank employee can be as important as efficiency, and although I have little hope that it will happen, I would like to see banking machines permanently retired from service. I'm serious about this.

Assignment   Revising   You have written the body paragraphs and the concluding paragraph of an essay for Assignment 2 on page 522 and for the Assignment on page 525. Revise these paragraphs according to the guidelines in this section. Then prepare a final copy of your work.

Continuing Assignment   Revising   Revise the essay that you have been developing in the Continuing Assignments in this unit. Read your first draft several times as you revise and proofread it. Then prepare the finished paper. Proofread it carefully.

Assignment Checklist

Check your assignments for the following points:

✔ 1. Did you revise your persuasive essay so that it says what you wanted it to say?
✔ 2. Did you revise your essay so that your opinion is clearly presented and well supported?
✔ 3. Did you improve the wording of your essay as you read it over?
✔ 4. Did you proofread your final draft for correct grammar, usage, spelling, and punctuation?
✔ 5. Did you choose a suitable title?
✔ 6. Did you prepare the finished paper according to your teacher's guidelines and proofread it carefully?

The Contest: Writing a Persuasive Essay

Situation: You are a high school student who has decided to enter the Civic Association's annual essay contest. This year the topic is "The Best Thing About Our Community." You have a copy of the contest rules. As you plan and write the essay, you will keep in mind the following information.

Writer: you as a contest entrant

Audience: a community panel, including teen-agers and adults

Topic: your opinion on the best thing in the community

Purpose: to plan and write a 350-word persuasive essay that presents your opinion

Directions: To write your essay, follow these steps.

Step 1. Read the contest rules on the facing page.

Step 2. As a start on prewriting, make notes on the questions that follow. Write your notes quickly, jotting down whatever comes to your mind in response to each question.

> What do I enjoy most in the community?
> What is the community known for?
> What makes the community special?

Step 3. Read your notes and put a check beside the things about the community that interest you. Choose the aspect that you like best, and cross out items that are not related to it.

Step 4. Write down any other ideas that occur to you about your topic.

Step 5. Write an opinion statement. It should clearly express your opinion. *Example:* "The Crafts Museum is the best thing about our town."

Step 6. Prepare an outline of main headings and subheadings. Remember that your word limit probably will allow for only four or five paragraphs in all. Make sure that the flow of ideas supports your opinion statement.

Step 7. Write the first draft of your essay. Start with an introductory paragraph that includes your opinion statement and will interest readers in what you are about to say. Then write the body paragraphs, giving each one a topic sentence. Finally, write the concluding paragraph.

Step 8. Reread your essay and revise it.

Essay Contest Rules

1. This year the essay topic is "The Best Thing About Our Community."
2. The contest is open to all high school students.
3. Essays must not exceed 350 words.
4. Essays will be judged on the basis of persuasiveness, style, and originality.
5. The decision of the judges will be final.
6. Students may submit only one essay each.
7. Essays must be submitted to the Civic Association by April 10.
8. The three winning essays will be printed in the *Herald-Times*.

Unit Assignments

Assignment 1   Write an essay to convince others that they should try your favorite hobby, sport, or after-school activity. Use transitional words to emphasize logical relationships. Write a concluding paragraph that summarizes the main ideas of your essay.

Assignment 2   Write an essay that makes a convincing case for an unusual personal goal. Write for a specific audience: a good friend or a relative. Place your opinion statement at the beginning of your introductory paragraph.

Assignment 3   Write a persuasive essay that presents an opinion about a state or national issue. Before you write the essay, research a few facts to support your opinion. Place your opinion statement at the end of the introductory paragraph, and write a concluding paragraph that calls for a specific action.

Assignment 4   Write an essay that expresses your opinion about the value of watching television. Write for an audience of your classmates, and write a concluding paragraph that expresses a personal reaction.

Assignment 5   Write a persuasive essay in which you present and support an opinion about a significant school issue. To gather facts for the essay, interview a few students and, perhaps, a teacher or an administrator. Write for an audience of students and teachers.

Assignment 6   Write an editorial that could appear in the local newspaper. Read a few issues of the newspaper to select a subject to write about and to study how the editorials are written.

Assignment 7   Imagine that you are governor of your state. Write a persuasive essay that you as governor will deliver in a radio broadcast. The essay should offer an opinion on a matter that is important to all residents of your state.

Assignment 8   Write an essay that expresses your opinion about a certain kind of dance or music. Write for an audience who may disagree with your opinion. Write a concluding paragraph that expresses a personal judgment or reaction.

Revising Your Assignments

For help in revising an essay, consult the Checklist for Revision on the last page of this book.

Unit Tests

Test 1

A. Number your paper from 1 to 5. Next to each number, write *True* if the sentence is true or *False* if it is false.

1. The concluding paragraph of a persuasive essay may summarize the main points made in the body paragraphs.
2. When you revise a persuasive essay, you should check to see that you have effectively supported your opinion.
3. An opinion statement must appear in the body of a persuasive essay.
4. In an outline for a persuasive essay, you may use chronological order or order of importance.
5. You limit an essay topic by making it more general.

B. Number your paper from 6 to 10. Next to each number, write the letter of the item that correctly completes the sentence. You will use all but one of the items.

    a. transitional words   d. argument
    b. order of importance   e. outline
    c. proofreading   f. revising

6. An important part of planning an essay is preparing an __?__.
7. An __?__ is reasoning presented to persuade an audience to accept your opinion.
8. Removing, rewriting, and reorganizing material are ways of __?__ an essay.
9. Checking your work for correct punctuation, capitalization, and spelling is called __?__.
10. *Finally, furthermore,* and *therefore* are examples of __?__.

C. Number your paper from 11 to 15. Next to each number, write the letter of the item that correctly answers the question.

11. Which of the following is a suitable opinion for a persuasive essay?
    a. A personal preference
    b. A hunch
    c. A logical, specific statement
    d. A statement of fact

12. Which of the following is the next step after selecting a limited topic for a persuasive essay?
    a. Writing an opinion statement
    b. Writing an outline
    c. Organizing the information
    d. Writing an introduction

13. Which of the following is a guideline for writing an introductory paragraph?
    a. Include the subheadings from your outline.
    b. Compile the major details.
    c. Include your opinion statement.
    d. Develop your main points.

14. Which of the following is a guideline for writing the body of a persuasive essay?
    a. Add supporting ideas as they are needed to make your ideas clear.
    b. Review your first draft.
    c. Summarize your main points.
    d. Check your spelling and punctuation.

15. Which of the following is *not* a guideline for revising a persuasive essay?
    a. Remove sentences that have little to do with your topic.
    b. Write an opinion statement.
    c. Check the length of your sentences.
    d. Check your sentences for correct grammar and usage.

Test 2

Choose one of the Unit Assignments. Write the essay as directed and hand it in to your teacher.

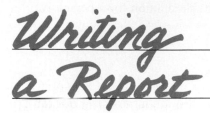

Unit 14

Writing a Report

Unit Preview

A report communicates information on a specific topic. The following two paragraphs begin a report on ocean beaches.

	The Life of a Beach
Footnote number Statement of topic	The wind blows steadily, ocean currents sweep past, the tide rises and falls, waves break and recede. The product of these and other forces is a beach. However, change a single force, such as wind direction, "and the beach changes or even disappears."[1] The fate of a beach is largely determined by the interaction of four natural forces: the level of the sea, the waves, the wind, and the currents.
Footnote number	Of the four forces, the level of the sea is the most powerful. The position of a beach changes as the level of the sea rises and falls. Since the sea level along the coastline of the United States is rising, most of our beaches are being pushed inland, some at the astonishing rate of ten meters per year.[2]
Footnotes	[1] Allan E. DeWall, "Getting Acquainted with Beaches and Coasts," *Science and Children,* Oct. 1980, p. 13. [2] U.S. Army Corps of Engineers, *Report on the National Shoreline Study* (Washington, D.C.: U.S. Government Printing Office, 1971), p. 36.

The opening of the report clearly states the topic about which the reader will receive information. Each sentence, as in the sample, communicates information about the topic.

A report is based on information that you collect from books, magazines, newspapers, and other sources. You use footnotes in a report for two reasons. First, they acknowledge where you have found the facts, the ideas, and the quotations used in a report. Second, they are a service to the reader who wishes to explore the topic further.

For Analysis   On your paper, answer the following questions about the report on ocean beaches.

1. Which of the following items of information would you expect to find in the report? You may choose more than one answer.
   a. Facts about wave and wind action
   b. Recreational uses of beaches
   c. The effects that storms have on ocean beaches
   d. Facts about currents that run close to shore
2. Which of the following sources could the author use to collect information for this report?
   a. Facts about wave and wind action
   b. A book on coastal marine life
   c. An almanac
   d. A newspaper
3. Two sentences in the sample are followed by footnote numbers. Briefly explain why each is footnoted.

In this unit you will write a report. After selecting and limiting a topic, you will gather and organize information and present it as clearly and efficiently as possible in your report.

14.1 Selecting and Limiting a Topic

The purpose of doing research for a report is to inform yourself. The purpose of writing a report is to inform your audience. The report topic that you select should offer an interesting question for you to answer through research. You should not select a topic that you can write about from your experience alone. A topic based only on your experience is appropriate for an essay, but not for a report.

Your report topic should be limited, or specific, for two reasons. First, a limited topic will guide your research and writing. You will know the precise area to research, and when you begin writing, you will know exactly what you are trying to accomplish. Second, a limited topic can be thoroughly discussed in a report. A broad topic, such as "The oceans," cannot possibly be covered adequately, even in a report of ten or twenty pages.

To limit your report topic, ask the following questions:

1. Can I limit my topic to one part of the subject?
2. Can I limit my topic to one person, one group, or one example?
3. Can I limit my topic to a brief time period?
4. Can I limit my topic to one event or place?

The following example shows how you can limit a topic:

QUESTION	ANSWER
What report topic am I interested in?	I'm interested in the raising of corn.
Can I limit my topic to one part of the subject?	Yes, I'm interested mostly in the detasseling of corn.
What do I want to find out about it?	I want to find out why and how corn is detasseled.
Is there any further way to limit the topic?	Yes, the time element—I want to find out why the detasseling is done at a certain time every year.
What will be the purpose of my report?	My report will explain why farmers detassel corn, how they do it, and when they do it.

Now you need to make sure that you can discuss your limited topic thoroughly in a short report of 300 to 750 words. You may have to select, limit, and test several topics before finding one that can be treated in a short report.

Test a topic by checking the amount of information on it that is available to you. A good place to start is a general encyclopedia. Specialized encyclopedias and reference books may also be helpful. Next, check the library card catalog (*Unit 21*) for books on your topic. A glance at the index and the table of contents in these books will quickly tell you whether they will be useful. For locating magazine articles, the standard reference work is the *Readers' Guide to Periodical Literature (Unit 21),* which indexes articles according to subject and author.

There may be so much material on your topic that you cannot possibly discuss it fully in 300 to 750 words. In that case, you will need to limit your topic further. On the other hand, if you cannot find at least two sources on your topic, it is too limited. The decision that your topic is too general or too limited does not mean that you have to reject it completely. The material that you found as you tested your topic may suggest related topics that are better suited to a short report.

When you are assigned a report topic, limit it and test it for available information just as you would a topic of your own choosing.

Exercise 1 Prewriting: Report Topics On your paper, rate each of the following report topics by writing *Good, Too general,* or *Not appropriate.*

SAMPLE	Visiting the town of my ancestors in Ireland
ANSWER	Not appropriate

1. Soccer
2. Geography
3. What I learned about people by working in a restaurant

4. The settling of the Southwest
5. The growth of women's rights
6. The Confederate surrender at Appomattox
7. The life cycle of an insect
8. The launching of a hot-air balloon
9. Why I love the outdoors
10. How a solar cell works

Exercise 2   Prewriting: Report Topics   Under each of the following topics, three possibilities for a limited topic are given. On your paper, write the letter of the one possibility that is both limited enough and appropriate for a report topic.

1. Nutrition
   a. Three rules for good nutrition
   b. You are what you eat
   c. Nutritious foods

2. Inventions
   a. The age of electronics
   b. The Industrial Revolution
   c. The first flying machine

3. Gardening
   a. Why mulching the soil in a garden helps the plants
   b. I love gardening because I love to see things grow
   c. Gardening is easy

4. The consumer
   a. Let the buyer beware
   b. The unjustified expense of some skin-care products
   c. I never take advertising seriously

5. Famous people
   a. American geniuses
   b. The other Thomas Jefferson: inventor and architect
   c. War heroes

Assignment   Prewriting   List five topics that would be suitable for reports. For each topic, write two appropriately limited topics.

Continuing Assignment   Prewriting   *Step 1:* List five topics that you would like to know more about. *Step 2:* Select three that especially interest you. Limit each topic. *Step 3:* Test the limited topics by checking sources, and select one topic that is suitable for a report. Write down your limited topic.

Assignment Checklist

Check your assignments for the following points:

   ✔ 1. Did you select topics that require research?
   ✔ 2. Did you limit the topics?

Check your Continuing Assignment for this additional point:

   ✔ 3. Did you find sources that have information on your chosen topic?

14.2 Gathering Information

Once you have limited your topic, you are ready to begin a list of sources that you intend to use. You can make this list, called a **working bibliography,** on a sheet of paper. However, for a report it is more convenient to list each source on a separate three-by-five-inch index card, called a **bibliography card.**

14.2a Preparing Bibliography Cards

The information that you list on a bibliography card and the form in which you list it depend upon the kind of publication that you are using.

Books.   List the author's name (last name first), the book title (underlined), the city where the publisher is located, the publisher's name, and the year of publication. (The titles that you would underline appear in italic type in print.) Note the punctuation of the following example:

> Smith, Whitney. The Flag Book of the United
>   States. New York: William Morrow, 1970.

Magazines and Newspapers.   List the author's name (last name first), the title of the article (in quotation marks), the name of the magazine or newspaper (underlined), the date of publication, the section in which the article appears (for newspaper articles only), and the page numbers of the article. For a magazine or newspaper article that runs on consecutive pages, list the first and last page numbers of the article (for example, *pp. 1–3*). For an article that does not run on consecutive pages, list the number of each page on which the article appears (for example, *pp. 1, 60*). If the author of the article is not given, begin the listing with the title of the article. Note the punctuation of the following examples:

> MAGAZINE   Horst, John. "Making a Sundial." Country
>   Journal, March 1980, pp. 97–99.
>
> NEWSPAPER   "Train Snarls Downtown Traffic." Champaign-
>   Urbana News Gazette, 6 Jan. 1982,
>   Sec. A, p. 5.

Encyclopedias.   Because the author of an encyclopedia article is often not given, begin your listing with the title of the article (in quotation marks). Then list the title of the encyclopedia (underlined) and the year of publication of the edition that you are using, as in this example:

> "Computers." Encyclopedia Americana. 1977 ed.

The following are sample bibliography cards.

Bibliography Card: Book

Author ———
Title ———
Place of publication ———
Publisher ———
Date of publication ———

Smith, Whitney. *The Flag Book of the United States*. New York: William Morrow, 1970.

Bibliography Card: Magazine Article

Author ———
Title of article ———
Name of magazine ———
Date of publication ———
Page numbers of article ———

Horst, John. "Making a Sundial." *Country Journal*, March 1980, pp. 97–99.

Exercise 1   Prewriting: Bibliography Listings   Use the following information to write bibliography card listings. For this exercise write the listings on a sheet of paper. Be sure to use correct punctuation.

AUTHOR	TITLE	PUBLICATION FACTS
Books		
1. Norma Miller	*Freshwater Fish*	Ten Speed Press Berkeley, California 1973

2. Rodney Rodriguez *Notable American*   Green Mountain
                     Musicians   Publishers
                                          Grafton, Vermont
                                          1959

3. Larry Kettlekamp *Tricks of Eyes and* William Morrow
                     Mind: The Story of and Company
                     Optical Illusion   New York, N.Y.
                                           1974

Magazines

4. Maxine Woo   "Drifting   *Geography*
                    Continents"   July 1976
                                         pp. 15–18

5. Harlow Womack   "The Roots of   *Performer*
                    Country Music"   December, 1982
                                         pp. 51–60

6. Not given   "Is Antarctica   *Newsweek*
                    Shrinking?"   5 October 1981
                                         pp. 72–74

Newspapers

7. Not given   "Local Driver   *Fithian Daily Record*
                    Wins Indy 500"   31 May 1981
                                         Sec. C, p. 1

8. Candy Gotschal   "This Record   *Elkville Enquirer*
                    Was Made   5 February 1978
                    to Be Broken"   Sec. D, pp. 1, 12

Encyclopedias

9. Gerhard Maerker "Tallow"   *World Book Ency-
                                         clopedia,* 1979 ed.

10. Not given   "Japanese Art"   *Collier's Encyclo-
                                         pedia,* 1980 ed.

14.2b Taking Notes

You are now ready to begin taking notes from the sources
that you have listed on your bibliography cards. The following
note-taking strategies can save you time and effort.

Strategies

1. *Write your notes on index cards.* Use either three-by-five-inch or four-by-six-inch cards. When you have finished your research and are ready to make an outline, you will find it easier to arrange your notes if they are on index cards.

2. *Make a guide card.* On one card write your topic and a few questions about it that you would like answered. These questions will help guide your reading and note taking.

3. *Skim an article or a chapter quickly to determine its content.* If it applies to your limited topic, reread it carefully. (See Unit 18 for instructions on skimming.)

4. *Write the author's last name and an abbreviated title in the upper right corner of each note card.* For an article in which the author is not given, write the abbreviated title only.

5. *On each card make notes on only one idea.* You can then rearrange your note cards easily. For instance, suppose that you are researching a report on the problems of deep-water drilling for oil. A paragraph in a magazine article discusses two different problems. Even though this information is in a single paragraph of the article, make a separate card for each problem.

6. *Write a summary of important information.* In a summary you briefly state the author's point in your own words. (See Unit 18 for further information on writing a summary.) To save time and space, you may write a summary in phrases rather than in complete sentences. Copy directly from the source only when you find a comment that is difficult to express in your

own words. Copy a direct quotation exactly and enclose it in quotation marks. Your notes may contain ideas, facts, and statistics.

7. *At the bottom of the card, write the number of the page from which the idea or quotation is taken.* If the idea comes from more than one page, list all of the page numbers (for example, *pp. 12–14*). If the idea comes from an encyclopedia article, also write the volume number of the encyclopedia.

8. *Write a subject heading in the upper left corner of each card.* This heading will identify the main idea of the card. Subject headings will help you to rearrange your cards for your outline. They will form some of the main headings and subheadings of your outline.

Two examples of note cards follow. The first note is a direct quotation.

Note Card: Direct Quotation

Subject heading
Author
Abbreviated title

Note (direct quotation)

Page reference

Dyeing of clothing material Gruenbaum, Before 1776

"Although the only dye that could be ordered was indigo (a blue dye), the colonists were clever and found ways to make warm and exciting colors."

p. 22

The second note is taken from a magazine article. The note contains a summary of the author's information.

Note Card: Summary

Subject heading ⌐ *Robots on assembly line   Friedrich,*
Author ───────── *"Robot Revolution"*
Abbreviated title ⌐

Note
(summary) ─── *Robot on assembly line can replace
ten human workers. Works
twenty-four hours a day. Each
of two arms can perform
a different task.*

Page reference ─── *p. 72*

Exercise 2   Prewriting: Note Cards   Read the following passage from a reference book and the three note cards taken from it. On your paper, state which card would be most useful for writing a report. Give two reasons for your answer. Explain why the other two cards would be less useful.

    Before the development of writing, objects were often used to record and communicate information. For centuries shepherds carried small bags of pebbles containing one pebble for each member of the herd. If an animal was sold, a pebble was discarded. If additions were made to the flock, pebbles were added. Some shepherds used sticks to record the number of sheep in their flocks. Each animal was represented by a notch in a stick. Ancient peoples used notched sticks to record numbers of other things, as well as the passage of time. On a calendar stick, for instance, days were indicated by notches, while weeks were indicated by grooves. In Australia the Boinji people used sticks as "picture postcards." Pictures conveying a message, such as a summons to a tribal meeting or a warning of danger, were carved on batons or small wooden tablets. The batons or tablets were delivered by messengers and thus were called "messenger sticks" by the Boinji.

Note Card 1

> Communicating without written words   Porter,
>   Signs and Writing
>
> Among ancient peoples "objects were often used to record and
> communicate information." Shepherds carried bags of pebbles.
> Each pebble represented a member of the flock. Adding or
> removing a pebble meant that an animal had been added to or
> removed from the herd. Notched sticks were used for counting
> things and as calendars. The Boinji of Australia used "messenger
> sticks"—pictures carved on batons or wooden tablets delivered by
> messengers.
>
> p. 102

Note Card 2

> Communicating without written words   Porter,
>   Signs and Writing
>
> Objects
>   1. Bags of pebbles, shepherds
>   2. Notched sticks as calendars
>   3. "Messenger sticks" as postcards, Boinji in Australia
>
> p. 102

Note Card 3

> Communicating without written words   Porter,
>   Signs and Writing
>
> Ancient peoples able to communicate effectively without words:
> "Before the development of writing, objects were often used to
> record and communicate information."
>   Examples:
>   1. Shepherds used pebbles to count animals in herds
>   2. Notched sticks used to count and to record time
>   3. Carved batons or wooden tablets used as "picture postcards"
>   by an Australian tribe
>
> p. 102

Exercise 3 Prewriting: Note Cards You are writing a report explaining how stage lighting is used in the production of a play. Make a note card with the subject heading "Kinds of stage lighting." On the card write a note on the following passage from Volume 19 of *The World Book Encyclopedia*. The passage is from the article "THEATER/Lighting and Sound" on p. 188d. Do not quote more than a sentence or two of the passage.

> Lighting for the stage is divided into (1) specific illumination, (2) general illumination, and (3) special effects. *Specific illumination* concentrates on a limited area. It is used principally for lighting the acting areas, which require strong emphasis. *General illumination* is used to light the sets and background elements, and to blend the lighting of acting areas. It is also used to provide a gradual change between brilliantly lighted acting areas and less intense lighting on the background. *Special effects* refer to a variety of lighting techniques and instruments. Typical examples include projections of clouds and stars, fires, and rainbows.

Assignment 1 Prewriting Prepare three bibliography cards for a report on one of the following topics:

1. Exploration for oil
2. Animal communication
3. Television program ratings

Assignment 2 Prewriting Find a short article in a magazine. Read the article and prepare two note cards based on it. In addition to the note on each card, include a subject heading, the author's last name, an abbreviated title, and the page reference.

Continuing Assignment Prewriting In the Continuing Assignment on page 543, you selected and limited a topic for your report. Now prepare bibliography cards for at least three sources for your topic. Then prepare at least fifteen note cards on your topic. Save your note cards and your bibliography cards.

Assignment Checklist

Check your assignments for the following points:

    ✔ 1. Did you make a bibliography card for each source?

    ✔ 2. Did you write a subject heading, the author's last name, an abbreviated title, and a page reference on each note card?

    ✔ 3. Did you summarize information from sources on your note cards?

    ✔ 4. If you wrote down direct quotations, did you copy them exactly and enclose them in quotation marks?

14.3 Organizing Your Information

A thesis statement and an outline help you to organize your information. Your **thesis statement** is a single sentence that states the main idea of the report. Making a report outline is essentially a matter of sorting your note cards according to their subject headings. The following steps describe the process of sorting your note cards and arriving at a thesis statement.

Procedure

1. *Reread all your note cards.* Make sure that each card has a subject heading, source identification, and page reference.

2. *Separate your note cards into stacks that contain similar ideas.* Use the subject headings as a guide.

3. *Read through each stack of note cards and select the most important subject heading.* This subject heading will become the main heading of the stack. The other subject headings will become the subheadings.

4. *Make a rough outline based on the subject headings of each stack of note cards.* A **rough outline** consists of main headings only.

5. *Read over the subject headings and use them to create a thesis statement.* Your thesis statement tells what the report will describe, prove, or explain. Make sure that the main headings of your rough outline support the thesis statement. Eliminate any headings and cards that do not.

For example, suppose that you are writing a report on the life of the gray whale. Arranging your note cards by main headings, you construct the following rough outline:

Physical characteristics of the gray whale
Fall migration from Arctic feeding grounds
Spring migration from Mexican lagoons
Whale as an endangered species

Migration is the aspect of the gray whale's life that interests you most. As a result you will base your thesis statement on the second and third headings of the rough outline.

Thesis Statement: The gray whale migrates between Arctic feeding grounds and Mexican lagoons, where its young are born.

Looking at your notes, your rough outline, and your thesis statement, you see that the main headings on the physical characteristics of the gray whale and on the whale as an endangered species are not relevant to your thesis statement. These headings should be eliminated from the rough outline, and the notes on them should be set aside.

The following steps will turn your rough outline into a topic outline.

Procedure

1. *Put the main headings in an order that seems logical for your topic*—for example, chronological order, spatial order, or order of importance. Be sure that each point relates directly to the topic of the whole report.

2. *Assign a Roman numeral to each main heading.* Begin with Roman numeral *I* for the introductory paragraph, and number the main headings consecutively. The concluding paragraph will be your last heading. (The introductory and concluding paragraphs will be discussed later. For a short report, there is no need to outline these paragraphs further.)

3. *Review each stack of note cards again to look for subheadings to list under each main heading.* As you did with the main headings, arrange the subheadings of each stack in an order that is logical for your topic.

4. *Assign a capital letter to each subheading.* Be sure that your note cards are arranged in the order in which you will use them.

When you have finished this process, you should have a thesis statement and an outline similar to the following:

Thesis Statement: The gray whale migrates between Arctic feeding grounds and Mexican lagoons, where its young are born.

   I. Introduction
  II. Fall migration of the gray whale
     A. Migrates south to Mexican coastal lagoons
     B. Young born and nursed in warm-water lagoons
     C. Fat in blubber coat only source of food for adult

III. Spring migration of the gray whale
    A. Migrates north with young to feeding grounds
    B. Spends warm-weather months off Alaskan coast
    C. Feeds in plankton-rich Arctic waters until fall
IV. Conclusion

The preceding outline is a **topic outline.** In a topic outline, the headings are single words, phrases, or clauses. However, your teacher may ask you to make a sentence outline. In a sentence outline, all of the headings are complete sentences.

Exercise Prewriting: The Topic Outline On your paper, make a topic outline that develops the given thesis statement. The outline structure that follows the thesis statement shows the number of main headings and subheadings that you will need. Use only the note cards that are directly related to the thesis statement. Use subject headings from the note cards as the main headings for the body of the report. The information in the notes will provide the subheadings. Save your outline.

Thesis Statement: Taking pleasing photographs is not difficult if you know the basics of picture taking and lighting.

  I. Introduction
 II. __?__
    A. __?__
    B. __?__
    C. __?__
    D. __?__
III. __?__
    A. __?__
    B. __?__
    C. __?__
IV. Conclusion

(Continue on the next page.)

Note Card 1

Features of a simple camera   Lamson,
                                                          "Your Camera"

Lens and shutter positioned in front of film. Shutter button moves
shutter up and down to allow light to pass through lens and focus
on film. When turned, winding knob brings new film behind lens
for next shot.

p. 12

Note Card 2

Basics of good picture taking   Fertig,
                                                       Better Photographs

Always keep lens clean. Stand close enough to subject; otherwise,
you lose detail. Avoid rapidly moving subjects because picture will
probably be blurred. Hold camera steady and squeeze shutter
button.

p. 87

Note Card 3

Basics of effective lighting   Cardenas,
                                                              Outdoors

Bright sunlight best for picture taking. Direction of sunlight: from
behind you or from the side. (Shooting directly into the sun usually
results in an overexposed picture.) Flash (a small bulb or light that
can be attached to camera) can be used outdoors to eliminate
shadows.

p. 101

Note Card 4

Kinds of film	Fertig, Better Photographs

Many brands of black-and-white and color film on the market.
Black and white less expensive to buy and have developed.

p. 9

Assignment   Prewriting   On your paper, make a rough outline for a report based on one of the following thesis statements. Include at least two main headings in addition to the introduction and the conclusion. You may consult reference books for information.

1. Although many citizens of the United States opposed the purchase of Alaska in 1867, the value of the territory soon became apparent to everyone.
2. Before clocks were invented, people used other methods to tell time.

Continuing   Assignment   Prewriting   Working from the notes that you took for the Continuing Assignment on page 551, make a rough outline of main headings. Then write a thesis statement and make a topic outline.

Assignment Checklist

Check your assignment for the following points:

  ✓ 1. Did you write at least two main headings that will support the thesis statement that you chose?
  ✓ 2. Did you consult reference books if you needed more information?

Check your Continuing Assignment for these points:

✔ 3. Did you sort your note cards by subject heading?
✔ 4. Did you write a thesis statement that clearly expresses the main idea of the report?
✔ 5. Did you make a rough outline?
✔ 6. Did you make a topic outline that is based on your thesis statement and includes all of the important points?

14.4 Writing Your Report

14.4a Writing the First Draft

Your notes, your thesis statement, and your outline will guide you through the writing of the first draft. Write your draft in the third person—that is, avoid using the pronoun *I*. The use of the first person is not appropriate in a report.

The Introductory Paragraph

Begin your report with an introduction. For a short report, the introduction is usually one paragraph. In the introductory paragraph, you present the thesis statement of the report and capture the interest of the reader. After reading the introductory paragraph, your reader should know what the report is about and want to continue reading it.

Notice that the following introductory paragraph first presents the topic of the report, whales, and then presents the thesis statement. The thesis statement is in italics.

Model

Whales are unique because of their combination of size, grace, and intelligence. Yet whales are no different from other animals in certain ways. One example of their similarity to other animals is the migration of some whales. *The gray whale migrates between Arctic feeding grounds and Mexican lagoons, where its young are born.*

The Body

The body of a report supports and develops the thesis statement. When you write the body of the report, follow your outline carefully. In a short report of 300 to 750 words, you will usually need one paragraph to cover each main heading and its subheadings. Before you begin a paragraph, review your notes in the appropriate stack of cards. You will also refer to them as you write the paragraph. The topic sentence of each paragraph will be based on a main heading of the outline. Use the subheadings to form the important points of each paragraph.

Write the first draft carefully, but avoid worrying over a single sentence. After the draft is written, you will have an opportunity to revise both the wording and the organization.

The Concluding Paragraph

The concluding paragraph helps the reader to grasp the full meaning of your report. In it you restate the main points of the report and summarize what the report has shown. The following paragraph concludes the report on the migration of the gray whale.

Model

> Thus, gray whales, like many other animals, migrate twice a year to be in an advantageous environment. They are in the best feeding grounds when they need to eat and in the safest waters when their young are born.

Exercise 1 Writing: The First Draft On your paper, write a first draft of an introductory paragraph for a report on taking photographs. Use the thesis statement and notes from the exercise on pages 555–556.

Exercise 2 Writing: The First Draft On your paper, write a first draft of one of the body paragraphs for a report on taking photographs. Use the outline that you prepared and the notes given in the exercise on pages 555–556.

14.4b Acknowledging Sources

Footnotes

You must give credit to your sources of information. **Footnotes** identify the sources of information that you have used on each page. The following rules will help you know where to use a footnote in the text of your report.

Rule Footnote your source when you quote an author's exact words.

You should quote only when the author's exact wording is crucial. Do not quote commonly known information that appears in more than one source, even though it is new to you.

Rule Footnote your source if the idea that you present is the author's, even though you have not used the author's exact words.

Rule Footnote your source when you give figures or statistics taken from the source.

Footnote Forms.   Footnotes identify the author and the publication from which you took an idea, quotation, or statistic. Footnote forms vary. Your teacher may ask you to use the following forms or may give you a different form to use.

FOOTNOTE FOR A BOOK

[1] Whitney Smith, The Flag Book of the United States (New York: William Morrow, 1970), p. 39.

FOOTNOTE FOR A MAGAZINE ARTICLE

[2] John Horst, "Making a Sundial," Country Journal, March 1980, p. 97.

FOOTNOTE FOR A NEWSPAPER ARTICLE

[3] "Train Snarls Downtown Traffic," Champaign-Urbana News Gazette, 6 Jan. 1982, Sec. A, p. 5.

FOOTNOTE FOR AN UNSIGNED ENCYCLOPEDIA ARTICLE

[4] "Computers," Encyclopedia Americana, 1977 ed., Vol. 3, p. 428.

You may find that you need to footnote the same source more than once in a report. It is not necessary to write out the full footnote for a source already credited. The shorter forms for subsequent footnotes for one source are as follows:

[5] Smith, p. 11.

[6] "Computers," p. 429.

Footnote Numbering. The first footnote in a report is numbered *1*. The number appears in the text of the report immediately following the information that you have taken from the source. The same number is placed at the beginning of the footnote, slightly above the line. Footnotes are generally numbered consecutively throughout a report.

Footnote Placement. The footnotes that go with a page of a report are sometimes grouped at the bottom of that page. When placed at the bottom of a page, footnotes are single-spaced. Three lines are left blank between the text and the footnotes. Alternatively, all of the footnotes may be listed on a separate page at the end of the report. The page is headed "Notes" and is placed just before the bibliography. Footnotes on a separate page are double-spaced. The first line of each footnote is always indented.

The Bibliography

The **bibliography** is the list of all of the works that you have acknowledged in your footnotes. It is the last page of the report. The bibliography is compiled from the information on your bibliography cards. Bibliography entries follow the forms used for bibliography card listings.

In a bibliography the entries are arranged in alphabetical order. An entry with no author named is alphabetized by the first word of the title, not counting *A, An,* and *The.* The first line of a bibliography entry starts at the left margin, and succeeding lines are indented.

Exercise 3   Writing: Footnotes   On your paper, convert the following listings to footnotes. Use the item number as the footnote number.

> SAMPLE   1. Goldman, Andrew. *The Way of the Dolphin.* Boston: Houghton Mifflin Company, 1975. Pages 7–10.
>
> ANSWER   [1]Andrew Goldman, *The Way of the Dolphin* (Boston: Houghton Mifflin Company, 1975), pp. 7–10.

1. Loomis, Robert D. *All About Aviation.* New York: Random House, 1964. Page 6.
2. Jack Meltzer. "Urban Renewal." *World Book Encyclopedia.* 1979 ed. Volume 20. Page 174b.
3. Kanabayashi, Masayoshi. "In Japan, Most Guys Pestering You to Buy Insurance Are Gals." *Wall Street Journal,* 25 March 1981, Sec. 1. Page 1.
4. Phillips, Phoebe, and Dunnan, Nancy. *Album of Roses.* New York: Viking Press, 1978. Pages 12–15.
5. Ajemian, Robert. "Zealous Lord of a Vast Domain." *Time,* 30 March 1981. Page 27.

Assignment 1   Writing   Write a first draft of an introductory paragraph for a report on methods of food preservation. Use the following thesis statement and outline.

> *Thesis statement:* Modern methods of food preservation were developed during the nineteenth century.

I. Introduction
II. Canning in jars and bottles
    A. Process involves sealing food in airtight containers and heating to destroy organisms that cause spoiling
    B. Invented in 1796 by French chef Nicolas Appert, who won government award for invention
    C. First done in United States in Boston plant opened in 1820 by William Underwood

Assignment 2 Writing Using the thesis statement and the outline in Assignment 1, write a first draft of a body paragraph for a report on food preservation.

Continuing Assignment Writing Using the thesis statement and outline that you prepared in the Continuing Assignment on page 551, write the first draft of your report. Include footnotes and a bibliography.

Assignment Checklist

Check your assignments for the following points:

✔ 1. Does your introduction capture the reader's attention?
✔ 2. Did you include the thesis statement in the introductory paragraph?
✔ 3. Is the topic sentence of each body paragraph based on a main heading of the outline?
✔ 4. Did you develop each body paragraph with details from your outline and notes that support both the topic sentence of the paragraph and the thesis statement of the report?

Check your Continuing Assignment for these additional points:

✔ 5. Did you write a concluding paragraph for your report?
✔ 6. Did you acknowledge with footnotes any ideas or quotations taken from your sources?
✔ 7. Did you prepare the bibliography correctly?

563

14.5 Revising and Finishing Your Report

Revising the First Draft

Finishing your first draft is an accomplishment. Now you need to read your draft slowly several times, with an eye to improving it. The following strategies for revising will help you to improve your paper.

Strategies

1. *Check your draft against the outline* to make sure that you have covered the points in the right order. If the outline has not worked well in some places, consider departing from it slightly to solve the problem. During this first reading, also make sure that the draft says what you want it to say. You do not want to force your reader to guess at the information that you are trying to convey.

2. *Read the draft for clarity.* Combine short sentences (*pages 363–380*) or divide long ones (*pages 381–384*) if doing so will express your thoughts more clearly.

3. *Read the draft for correct grammar, sentence structure, and word choice, as well as for effective transitions.* Correct any errors in sentences. Revise any sentences that are wordy or unclear.

4. *Proofread the draft to correct errors* in spelling, capitalization, and punctuation.

After you have revised your draft, select a title, if you have not already done so. Your title should reflect your topic in an interesting way.

When no further additions or changes are necessary, you may write or type your final draft.

Preparing the Finished Report

The finished report should make a good impression on your reader. You will find guidelines for preparing the finished paper in Unit 5, on page 258. However, your teacher may ask you to use different guidelines.

So that you can see a report that has been correctly prepared, the first page of a report is given here. Footnote and bibliography pages for the entire report are shown after the model report page.

Fred Simms
English 2190A
April 5, 19__

Report title   Frankenstein's Misunderstood Movie Monster

Introductory paragraph   Motion pictures are often based on books. Because the two forms are so different, the story told in a book is frequently changed in order to make the motion picture. In fact, sometimes the story or characters in a book are

Thesis statement   altered so much that the motion picture bears almost no resemblance to the book on which it is supposedly based.

Body paragraph   The novel <u>Frankenstein</u> was written by Mary Wollstonecraft Shelley and published in 1818. Victor Frankenstein and his monster quickly became the subjects of plays and, in this

Footnote number   century, of many motion pictures.[1]

Body paragraph   Movies present Victor Frankenstein as a mad scientist and the monster as an unstoppable

Footnote
number

killer, who lurches from one crime to another.[2]

In time, "Frankenstein" has become the name

Footnote
number

popularly attached to the monster himself.[3]

The motion picture versions of Frankenstein and

his monster, however, are far different from the

characters in the novel.

Notes page

Notes

[1] Ivan Butler, The Horror Film (New York: A. S.

Barnes, 1967), p. 40.

[2] Carlos Clarens, An Illustrated History of the

Horror Films (New York: Putnam, 1967), p. 63.

[3] "Frankenstein," Encyclopaedia Britannica, 1975 ed.,

Vol. IV, p. 280.

[4] Clarens, pp. 67—69.

[5] "Frankenstein."

Bibliography page

Bibliography

Butler, Ivan.   The Horror Film.   New York: A. S. Barnes,
     1967.

Clarens, Carlos.   An Illustrated History of the Horror
     Films.   New York: Putnam, 1967.

"Frankenstein."   Encyclopaedia Britannica.   1975 ed.

Exercise 1   Revising: Introductory Paragraphs

Read the following drafts of an introductory paragraph. On your paper, tell which is the better introductory paragraph for a report called "The Basics of Picture Taking." Briefly explain the reasons for your choice.

1.   Taking pictures is fun—a little expensive perhaps, but fun. Taking pleasing photographs is not difficult. Pay attention to what you are doing. You will get better pictures that way.

2.   Taking pictures is fun. Looking at your pictures is even more fun—unless the subjects are fuzzy or too dark to distinguish. You don't have to be disappointed in your photographs. Taking pleasing photographs is not difficult if you know the basics of picture taking and lighting.

Exercise 2   Revising: Sentences   Some of the numbered sentences in the following report draft need revision. For each sentence, write on your paper the letter of the revision that will improve the report.

(1) Taking a good picture requires a little planning. (2) According to Emily Fertig, "At first your preparations will seem awkward and you may lose some good shots, but with practice you'll prepare for a picture quickly and smoothly." (3) I will now discuss the basics. (4) Before you use your camera, make sure that the lens is clean.

(5) Fertig tells you how to clean it. (6) When you are ready to take a picture, Fertig recommends that you stand close enough to the subject to fill the frame of the camera viewfinder.[1] (7) Otherwise, you will lose the details that make a picture interesting. (8) Avoid rapidly moving subjects. (9) Pictures of rapidly moving subjects will probably be blurred. (10) When you are ready to take a picture. (11) Hold the camera still and squeeze the shutter button. (12) Fertig says that it will reduce camera movement.[2] (13) I will now discuss the basics of lighting.

(14) Your careful preparations will be defeated if you do not pay attention to lighting. (15) Bright sunlight is ideal for

picture taking, and so you should try to compose your pictures so that the sun is behind you or to the side.   (16) If you shoot directly into the sun, "you might get lucky, but you'll more likely get an overexposed picture."[3]

(17) A flash—a small bulb or battery-powered light that can be attached to the body of the camera—is normally used indoors.   (18) However, it can also be used outdoors. (19) According to Enrique Cardenas, a professional photographer, if your subject is in the shadows but is within ten feet or so, a flash will help illuminate the subject.   (20) The resulting photograph will have greater clarity and detail.

1. Sentence 2
   a. Eliminate the quotation marks.
   b. Remove the sentence.
   c. Add a footnote number.

2. Sentence 3
   a. Remove the sentence.
   b. Rewrite the sentence: *I will now discuss the basics of photography*.

3. Sentence 4
   a. Make the sentence the beginning of the next paragraph.
   b. Rewrite the sentence: *Make sure the lens is clean*.
   c. Remove the sentence.

4. Sentence 5
   a. Rewrite the sentence for clarity: *Fertig mentions three ways that you can safely clean the lens glass*.
   b. Add a footnote number.
   c. Give the full name of the author.

5. Sentences 8 and 9
   a. Combine as follows: *Pictures of rapidly moving subjects will probably be blurred*.
   b. Combine as follows: *Avoid rapidly moving subjects because pictures of them will probably be blurred*.

6. Sentence 10
   a. Remove the fragment.
   b. Combine the fragment with the following sentence: *When you are ready to take a picture, hold the camera still and squeeze the shutter button.*
7. Sentence 12
   a. Remove the sentence.
   b. Rewrite the sentence for clarity: *Fertig says that squeezing the shutter button will reduce camera movement.*[2]
   c. Remove the footnote number.
8. Sentence 13
   a. Make the sentence the beginning of the next paragraph.
   b. Remove the sentence.
9. Sentence 15
   a. Rewrite the sentence: *Take pictures only in bright sunlight.*
   b. Divide the sentence into two sentences: *Bright sunlight is ideal for picture taking. You should try to compose your pictures so that the sun is behind you or to the side.*
10. Sentence 19
    a. Add a footnote number.
    b. Divide the sentence into two sentences.

Assignment   Revising   Revise the paragraphs that you wrote for Assignments 1 and 2 on pages 562–563.

Continuing Assignment   Revising   *Step 1:* Revise the first draft of the report that you wrote for the Continuing Assignment on page 563. *Step 2:* Prepare the finished paper. Submit your outline with the finished paper.

Assignment Checklist

Check your assignments for the following points:

   ✔ 1. Did you revise and proofread your report?
   ✔ 2. Is your finished paper neat and free of errors?

Project Helios: Organizing Data

Situation: You are a member of the Mission Control team working on the Helios Project, a deep-space probe that is currently sending back information about the outer reaches of the solar system. The data on page 571 represent some of the probe's findings for the planet C3x. Every bit of information, logged as it is received and not in any particular order, is coded with a number. This number (for example, *3105*) refers to one of four general categories of information. You are to organize these data as preparation for writing a Project Report. As you do, keep the following facts in mind.

Writer: you as member of Mission Control
Audience: director of Mission Control
Topic: information about Planet C3x
Purpose: to organize data into categories and to prepare an outline

Directions: To organize the data, follow these steps.

Step 1. Set up a three-by-five-inch index card for each item of incoming information listed. Write the code number in the upper left corner and the planet name in the upper right corner. Write the data as your notes.

Step 2. Group together all cards with the same code numbers. Use the "Key to Codes" on page 571 to provide the category of information, and write the category next to the code number.

Step 3. Arrange the categories of information (groups of cards on the same subject) in a logical order, and make a topic outline.

INCOMING DATA--PROJECT HELIOS

Planet: C3x   Survey site: #3

5103   average surface temperature: minus 62.3 degrees
        Celsius

5103   gaseous atmosphere composed of oxygen, nitrogen,
        argon, and several other trace gases

4809   surface covered by a sheet of ice

4809   average depth of surface ice: 2400 meters

5506   evidence of former volcanic activity

4809   average altitude of land mass: 1830 meters

3105   area of land mass: 13,200,000 square kilometers

3105   land mass has an area equivalent to one tenth
        of the earth's surface

5506   western portion of land mass consists of a chain
        of islands covered by ice; eastern portion is
        solid bedrock under ice

5103   average precipitation in the form of snow
        amounts to 50 centimeters per planetary year

5506   rock underlying surface covering of ice is
        composed mainly of granite with small amounts
        of copper, nickel, iron

Key to Codes	
CODE NUMBER	CATEGORY OF INFORMATION
3105	Aerial Survey Data
4809	Surface Survey Data
5103	Climate
5506	Geological Data

571

Unit Assignments

Assignment 1 Write a report that answers a question that you have wondered about but never had answered (for example, Why do leaves change color in the fall?).

Assignment 2 Write a report on a job that you are interested in. The report should answer some or all of the following questions: What are the duties of the job? What training is needed for the job? Does the job involve the operation of equipment, machines, or vehicles? If so, does the operator need special training?

Assignment 3 Write a report about a historic site (a structure or a place) in your area. Ask your school or public librarian for help in locating sources of information. If possible, visit the site to gather first-hand information. Report on the history of the site and give a physical description of it.

Assignment 4 Write a report on women's or men's fashions in the 1890s or in some other period that ended at least twenty years before you were born. Include a description of the clothes that a person wore to school or work and the clothes that a person wore for a special occasion such as a party or a wedding.

Assignment 5 Write a report on a recent scientific or medical discovery. Include a clear explanation of the new information and the reasons why it is important. You may mention its direct or indirect effect on people's lives and its significance for the future. You may also include information on the people involved in the discovery or the history of the research that led to it.

Assignment 6 Write a consumer report on a product, such as an automobile, a camera, a bicycle, or any household appliance. The report should answer the following questions: What are the strong points of the product? What are the weaknesses? How does the product compare with others on the market?

Assignment 7   Prepare a report on one of the topics in Assignments 1 to 6. Give your report orally, using your outline and notes. After you have given your report, submit your outline, your note cards, and a written bibliography. (See Unit 20 for information on oral presentations.)

Revising Your Assignments

For help in revising a report, consult the Checklist for Revision on the last page of this book.

Unit Tests

Test 1

A. Number your paper from 1 to 5. Next to each number, write *True* if the sentence is true or *False* if it is false.

1. Your report topic should be specific, so that you can thoroughly explain it.
2. For a written report, you should choose a topic that requires you to gather information.
3. On each note card, you should make notes on only one idea.
4. You must always include page numbers on your bibliography cards.
5. After you write your report, you should outline it.

B. Number your paper from 6 to 10. Next to each number, write the letter of the term that correctly completes the sentence. You will not use one of the items.

    a. summary   d. introductory paragraph
    b. footnote   e. concluding paragraph
    c. subject heading   f. outline

6. The thesis statement of a report is presented in the __?__.
7. In the upper left corner of a note card, you should write a(n) __?__.
8. A good __?__ makes writing your first draft easy.
9. When you quote an author's exact words in a report, you must give credit in a(n) __?__.
10. One way to take notes is to state the author's point in your own words in a(n) __?__.

C. Number your paper from 11 to 15. Next to each number, write the letter of the item that correctly answers the question.

11. What is the term for a single sentence that tells the main idea of a report?
    a. Topic outline   c. Thesis statement
    b. Introduction   d. Final draft

12. What is the term for a list of all the works you have acknowledged in footnotes?
    a. Bibliography
    b. Introductory paragraph
    c. Outline
    d. Body

13. Which one of the following should *not* be included on a note card?
    a. Subject heading
    b. Source identification
    c. Page reference
    d. Publication date

14. Which one of the following is *not* true of footnotes?
    a. They can vary in form, depending on the source.
    b. They are used when you quote an author's exact words.
    c. They are used only in very long reports.
    d. They are used when you are presenting an author's idea.

15. Which one of the following is *not* included in the finished paper?
    a. Introductory paragraph
    b. Concluding paragraph
    c. Bibliography
    d. Note cards

Test 2

Choose one of the Unit Assignments or a topic that your teacher suggests. Write the report as directed and hand it in to your teacher.

Writing
Business
Letters

Unit Preview

On many occasions, you will find it necessary to write a business letter. Regardless of your reason for writing, your letter should always be neat, courteous, and concise.

The business letter on the next page contains all the information necessary to the person who will receive it.

For Analysis   On your paper, answer the following questions about the business letter.

1. What is the purpose of the letter?
2. What is the item being ordered?
3. What are the features of the item?
4. How much will the total order cost?
5. How will payment be made?
6. Where will the item be sent?

In this unit you will learn how to write business letters for three purposes: to request information, to place an order, and to suggest an adjustment for unsatisfactory merchandise. As you write your business letter, you will follow the three steps of the writing process: prewriting, writing, and revising.

```
            65 Longfellow Lane
            Greensboro, NC   27405
            March 19, 19__

            Folk Crafts Incorporated
            P.O. Box 34
            Rye, NY   10580

            Dear Sir or Madam:

            In the February issue of Crafts America
            magazine, I noticed your advertisement for
            hand-crafted jewelry boxes.

            Please send me one solid cedarwood jewelry
            box with polished brass hinges and natural
            finish.   I would like the magenta velvet
            lining.   The total price is $15.95.

            I have enclosed a money order for $20.90.
            This includes the cost of the jewelry box
            and $4.95 for postage and handling.

            Because this jewelry box will be a gift,
            please fill my order by April 17.

            Sincerely,

            John V. Corliss

            John V. Corliss

            Enclosure
```

15.1 Features of Business Letters

Parts of the Business Letter

Heading.   The heading consists of three lines in the upper right corner of your stationery or on the left, depending on which form you use. The first line gives your street address or route number. It also has your apartment number, if you have one. The second line gives your city, state, and Zip Code. You may spell out the name of your state, use the standard abbreviation, or use the Postal Service abbreviation (*page 231*). The third line gives the month, day, and year.

Inside Address. The inside address usually consists of four lines. The first line gives the name and possibly the business title of the person who will receive the letter. The second line consists of the name of the company or agency, if any. The third line contains the person's or the company's street address or postal box number. The fourth line gives the city, state, and Zip Code. To be consistent, refer to the state here by the same method you used in your return address.

Salutation. The salutation is the greeting. In it, capitalize the first word and all nouns. If you do not know the name of the person to whom you are writing, use *Dear Sir or Madam.* Place a colon after the salutation.

Body. The body of the letter contains the paragraphs that state your business. Leave an extra line of space between the salutation and the first paragraph. Also leave an extra line of space between paragraphs.

Complimentary Close. The complimentary close appears below the last paragraph. It goes on either the right or left side of your paper, depending on which letter form you use. Make sure it aligns with the first word of the heading or of the inside address. Always capitalize the first word. Place a comma after the complimentary close.

Signature. The signature is, of course, your name. Always write it in longhand, even if you type your letter. Place your signature under the complimentary close, and be sure to write your full name. If your letter is handwritten, print your name under your signature. If your letter is typed, type your name under your signature. Be sure to leave enough space in which to write your name.

Forms of Business Letters

The two most frequently used styles of business letters are the block style and the modified block style. In the **block style,** start all parts of the letter at the left margin. Leave adequate margins on all sides of your letter. Use the block style only when you are typing your letter.

Block Style

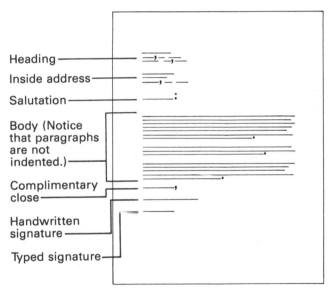

In the **modified block style,** the heading, the complimentary close, and the signature appear on the right. You may indent paragraphs, as shown in the following example, or you may start paragraphs at the left, as shown in the block style. Leave adequate margins on all sides of your letter. You can use the modified block style when either handwriting or typing your letters.

Modified Block Style

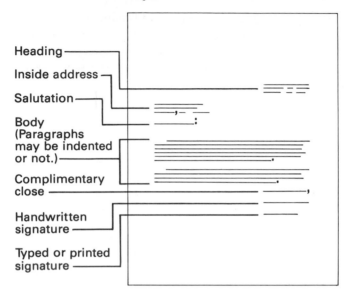

Heading

Inside address

Salutation

Body
(Paragraphs
may be indented
or not.)

Complimentary
close

Handwritten
signature

Typed or printed
signature

Addressing the Envelope

Whether you are using a long or a short business envelope, write the address slightly below the center on the front of the envelope. The address should contain the same information found in the inside address on your letter. However, you should use the Postal Service abbreviations on envelopes.

In the upper left corner of the envelope, place your return address. The first line should contain your full name; the second line, your street address; and the third line, your city, state, and Zip Code. Again, use the Postal Service abbreviation for your state.

Folding and Inserting the Letter

Follow the steps shown in the diagrams for folding letters for both long and short envelopes.

Procedure

Long Business Envelopes

1. Place the letter on your desk face up.

2. Fold the bottom of the letter up, slightly less than one third of the way.

3. Fold the top of the letter down to within about ½ inch of the first crease.

4. Put the letter into the envelope, inserting the last crease first.

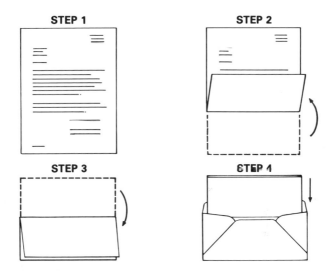

STEP 1 STEP 2 STEP 3 STEP 4

Short Business Envelopes

1. Place the letter on your desk face up.

2. Fold the bottom of the letter up to within ½ inch of the top edge.

3. Fold from right to left about one third of the way.

4. Fold from left to right to within ½ inch of the right side.

5. Put the letter into the envelope, inserting the last crease first.

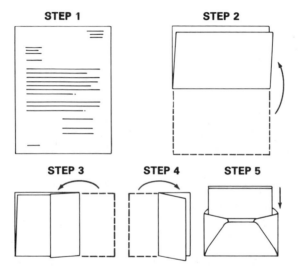

STEP 1 **STEP 2** **STEP 3** **STEP 4** **STEP 5**

Use the following strategies when writing business letters.

Strategies

1. *Use unlined paper measuring 8 ½" x 11".*

2. *If possible, type your letter. If not, use black or blue ink.* Do not use pencil.

3. *Make certain that both the heading and the inside address are complete.*

4. *Make certain that your letter is neat.* Reread it carefully to see that there are no errors in typing, spelling, grammar, or punctuation. Remember that the person to whom you are writing does not know you. You will want your letter to create a favorable impression.

5. *Choose an appropriate complimentary close.* Appropriate ones include *Yours truly, Very truly yours, Sincerely yours,* and *Yours sincerely.* Remember to place a comma after the complimentary close.

6. *Do not use informal language.* Avoid slang and contractions.

7. *Be sure that the envelope is correctly and clearly addressed and that it shows your complete return address.*

Exercise 1 Prewriting: Parts of Business Letters
Number your paper from 1 to 4. Rewrite the following letter parts, correcting all errors in form.

1. Very sincerely yours
2. August 6, 19—
   Fargo, North Dakota 58102
   11 Ashburton Place

3. Dear Professor Henderson
4. 135 West Ninth Avenue
   Sioux City, Iowa 51102
   Costa Bros. Groceries

Exercise 2 Writing: The Business Letter Using the information in the following list, write a business letter on a sheet of unlined paper. Use the modified block style. Add appropriate punctuation where needed. Then fold your letter to fit a long envelope.

1. Heading: 126 Leverett Street North Stonington
                Connecticut 06359 April 5 19—
2. Inside address: Optics Incorporated 45 West
                Washington Street Chicago Illinois
                60602
3. Salutation: Dear Sir or Madam
4. Body: I am an amateur astronomer. I would like to purchase a reflecting telescope. Please send me your free catalogue that describes the binoculars, microscopes, and telescopes that you have available. In addition, please send

me your free brochure, "Tips for Telescopes." Thank you very much.

5. Complimentary close: Yours truly
6. Signature: Reyna Gomez

Exercise 3   Revising: Parts of a Business Letter   On a sheet of unlined paper, revise the following letter, using the block style. Correct all errors in form and placement. Then fold your letter to fit a short envelope.

June 7, 19—
Carthage, Miss. 39051

1050 S. 19th St. NW   12 Briarhill Lane
Mr. Daniel Ikeda
Washington, D. C. 20036
Consumer Product Safety Commission

Dear Mr. Ikeda,

I read an article in *Consumer News* in which safety features of the new car models were discussed. I am curious about the findings of the Consumer Product Safety Commission.

Please send me the free brochure offered by your commission.

I have enclosed a self-addressed, stamped envelope. Thank you very much.

sincerely
Terry Roberts

Assignment   Writing   *Step 1:* In your newspaper, find a short letter to the editor. Rewrite the letter on an unlined sheet of paper, using the modified block style. Use the address of your newspaper. If you do not know the editor's name, make up a name. Use your own return address. *Step 2:* On your paper, draw a long envelope. Address it to the newspaper. Fold your letter to fit a long envelope.

Assignment Checklist

Check your assignment for the following points:

✔ 1. Did you include appropriate punctuation?

✔ 2. Did you arrange the parts of your letter correctly for the modified block style?

✔ 3. Did you fold your business letter properly to fit a long business envelope?

✔ 4. Did you address your envelope correctly?

✔ 5. Did you proofread your letter for correct grammar, usage, spelling, and punctuation?

✔ 6. Did you proofread your envelope for correct spelling and punctuation?

15.2 The Request Letter

One kind of business letter that you may have to write is the request letter. When you do, be certain that you state your purpose for writing, provide necessary background information, make your request clearly, and conclude with a courteous statement. The letter on page 586 contains all the information needed.

Use the following strategies when writing request letters.

Strategies

1. *State your request briefly, clearly, and courteously.*

2. *Make certain that your letter contains all the information necessary.*

Exercise 1   Prewriting: The Request Letter   On your paper, write the numbers of the statements that you would include in a request letter for a catalogue. There are some statements that you will not use.

1. Please send the catalogue that includes photographs of carved ivory figures.

```
                              2612 Alamagorda Drive
                              Albuquerque, NM  87107
                              April 29, 19__

            Director
            Albuquerque Parks and
              Recreation Department
            1117 Main Street
            Albuquerque, NM  87003


            Dear Sir or Madam:
```

Purpose

```
                  I am interested in finding work for
            the summer.
```

Background

```
                  I have been told that the Parks and
            Recreation Department will hire school-age
            boys and girls this summer.
```

Request

```
                  Please send me information about the
            kinds of jobs that are open, the age
            limits, and the wages.
```

Courteous statement

```
                  I have enclosed a self-addressed,
            stamped envelope.  Thank you very much.

                           Yours truly,

                           Brad Ratchford
                           Brad Ratchford
```

2. My aunt would like to visit Juneau.
3. Sometimes these figures are carved in wood.
4. I collect Alaskan ivory figures.
5. The *Folk Arts* listing mentioned several available catalogues.
6. Thank you very much.
7. I understand that there is no charge for the catalogue.
8. One of your catalogues does not include photographs.

9. A few months ago, *Folk Arts* magazine listed The Adler Collection as an important source for Alaskan art.

10. The Adler Collection also includes rare scrimshaw.

Exercise 2   Writing: The Request Letter   On an unlined sheet of paper, write a request letter in the modified block style. Use the statements that you selected in Exercise 1, in correct sequence. For the inside address, use The Adler Collection, Box 2-1737, Anchorage, Alaska 99509. Use your own return address.

Assignment   Writing   *Step 1:* On an unlined sheet of paper, write a letter to the director of a summer camp requesting the following information: the dates the camp is open, the cost of attending, and a list of the camp's activities. Use the modified block style. Make up a name and address for the camp and its director, but use your own return address. *Step 2:* Draw an envelope on your paper, and address it to the camp.

Assignment Checklist

Check your assignments for the following points:

✔ 1. Did you include all the necessary parts of the business letter?

✔ 2. Did you state your request briefly, clearly, and courteously?

✔ 3. Did you include all the necessary information?

✔ 4. Did you use the modified block style?

✔ 5. Did you address your envelope correctly?

✔ 6. Did you proofread your letter for correct grammar, usage, spelling, and punctuation?

✔ 7. Did you proofread your envelope for correct spelling and punctuation?

15.3 The Order Letter

Another kind of business letter that you need to know how to write is the order letter. Many companies furnish order blanks with their catalogues or in magazines, but frequently you will have to order without such forms. The following letter shows the necessary contents of an order letter: purpose, details of the purchase, arrangement for payment, and reference to the payment enclosed, if applicable.

129 Old South Street
Natchitoches, LA 71457
May 4, 19__

Stone Novelty Company
Box 2018
East Middlebury, VT 05740

Dear Sir or Madam:

Purpose

In the movie <u>My Side of the Mountain</u>, one of the characters has a wooden dancing doll that taps its feet when the player keeps time on a board. Our country—western school band would like to purchase some of these.

Details of purchase

My music teacher says that your company calls them Limberjacks and that they sell for $7.95 each. Will you please send me two (2).

Arrangement for payment

I have enclosed a money order for $17.90 to cover the cost of the dancing dolls and $2.00 for handling.

Yours truly,

Michael A. Rowe

Michael A. Rowe

Enclosure

Use the following strategies when writing order letters.

Strategies

1. *Include all necessary information about the item you wish to purchase:* the quantity of each item in words and in numbers in parentheses, the name of the article, the model number if there is one, the size, the color, and the price. The more information you provide, the more certain you can be that you will receive the exact merchandise that you want. If required, give the weight of the item. Handling and shipping costs are often determined by weight.

2. *Be sure to give the date and number of the catalogue,* if you are ordering from a catalogue.

3. *Specify how you intend to pay for the merchandise.* Do not send cash through the mail. Checks or money orders are preferred.

4. *Explain briefly if there is any reason that you must have the merchandise delivered by a certain date.* Be sure to include that date in your letter.

5. *Type or write the word* Enclosure *in the bottom left corner of your letter* if you have enclosed a money order or a check. Make sure it aligns with the left margin. *Enclosure* alerts the reader to the fact that a separate item accompanies your letter.

Exercise 1   Prewriting: The Order Letter   On your paper, write the numbers of the statements that you would include in an order letter for yarn. There are some statements that you will not use.

1. The Icelandic wool that your shop sells is also appealing.
2. Please mail me 5 skeins of natural wool yarn.
3. I have enclosed a money order for $28.95.

4. I would like yarn that is heather-colored.

5. The natural wool yarn is produced locally.

6. My next project will probably be a child's sweater.

7. In order to complete my knitting project, I must order additional yarn from your shop.

8. Each skein sells for $5.00.

9. My total purchase is $25.00, plus $3.95 for handling.

10. This natural wool yarn is item number 2-145 in your catalogue.

Exercise 2   Writing: The Order Letter   On an unlined sheet of paper, write an order letter in block style. Use the statements that you selected in Exercise 1, in correct sequence. The inside address is The Yarn Emporium, 5 Foxhill Road, Winchester, Virginia 22601. Use your own return address.

Assignment   Writing   *Step 1:* On an unlined sheet of paper, write a letter to a sporting goods store in which you order a pair of running shoes. Be sure to include all necessary information. Use the modified block style. Make up a name and address for the store, but use your own return address. *Step 2:* Draw an envelope and address it to the store.

Assignment Checklist

Check your assignments for the following points:

✔ 1. Did you include all the necessary parts of the letter?

✔ 2. Did you include all the necessary information—item, quantity, model number, size, color, price, weight?

✔ 3. Did you give the catalogue date or number?

✔ 4. Did you specify the terms of payment?

✔ 5. Did you use the modified block style?

✔ 6. Did you address your envelope properly?

✔ 7. Did you proofread your letter for correct grammar, usage, spelling, and punctuation?

✔ 8. Did you proofread your envelope for correct spelling and punctuation?

15.4 The Adjustment Letter

You will need to know how to write an adjustment letter when merchandise you have bought is defective or otherwise unsatisfactory. Notice that the following letter of adjustment does two things: it states the problem and it suggests a solution. Notice also the courteous tone of the letter.

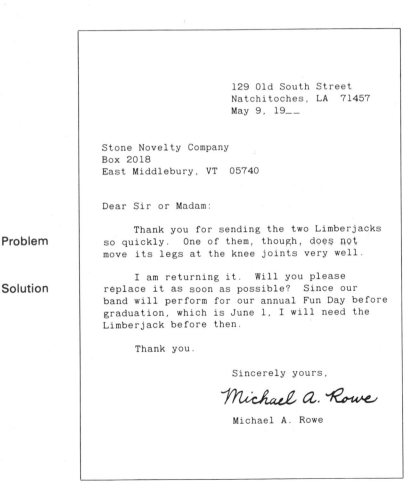

129 Old South Street
Natchitoches, LA 71457
May 9, 19__

Stone Novelty Company
Box 2018
East Middlebury, VT 05740

Dear Sir or Madam:

Problem

Thank you for sending the two Limberjacks so quickly. One of them, though, does not move its legs at the knee joints very well.

Solution

I am returning it. Will you please replace it as soon as possible? Since our band will perform for our annual Fun Day before graduation, which is June 1, I will need the Limberjack before then.

Thank you.

Sincerely yours,

Michael A. Rowe

Michael A. Rowe

Use the following strategies when writing adjustment letters.

Strategies

1. *State the problem clearly.* If the merchandise is defective or otherwise unsatisfactory, explain.

2. *Suggest a solution.* You may ask for your money back, or you may suggest that the merchandise be replaced.

3. *Be courteous.* It is all right to express your disappointment if you do so politely, but do not express anger.

Exercise 1 Prewriting: The Adjustment Letter On your paper, write the numbers of the statements that you would include in an adjustment letter. There are some statements that you will not use.

1. Thank you very much.
2. Now I will never complete my project in time!
3. My natural wool yarn order arrived promptly.
4. The Yarn Emporium employs careless people.
5. Would you please send me 5 skeins of heather-colored yarn.
6. I am returning the yarn and would like a replacement.
7. I received lavender-colored yarn instead.
8. In the future, I will not conduct business with your shop.
9. However, I ordered the heather-colored yarn.
10. My friends have all been warned about The Yarn Emporium!

Exercise 2 Writing: The Adjustment Letter On an unlined sheet of paper, write an adjustment letter using the modified block style. Use the statements that you selected in Exercise 1, in correct sequence. The inside address will be The Yarn Emporium, 5 Foxhill Road, Winchester, Virginia 22601. Use your own return address.

Exercise 3 Writing: The Envelope On your paper, draw an envelope. On it, write the address from Exercise 2 and your own return address.

Assignment Writing *Step 1:* On an unlined sheet of paper, write an adjustment letter to a record club asking for a replacement for a defective cassette tape. Be sure to include all necessary details. Use the block style. Make up a name and address for the record club, but use your own return address. *Step 2:* Draw an envelope on your paper, and address it to the record club.

Assignment Checklist

Check your assignment for the following points:

- ✔ 1. Did you include all the necessary parts of the business letter?
- ✔ 2. Did you state the problem clearly and courteously?
- ✔ 3. Did you include all necessary details?
- ✔ 4. Did you suggest a solution?
- ✔ 5. Did you use the modified block style?
- ✔ 6. Did you proofread your letter for correct grammar, usage, spelling, and punctuation?
- ✔ 7. Did you proofread your envelope for correct spelling and punctuation?

Career Day: Posters

Situation: Your school is planning Career Day so that students can meet and talk with guest experts in various career fields. As secretary of the Planning Committee, you have been asked to order the posters that will be distributed throughout the school and community to advertise the event. As you write, keep in mind the following information.

Writer: you as secretary of the Planning Committee
Audience: local printing company
Topic: posters for Career Day
Purpose: to provide information for printers

Directions: To write your letter, follow these steps.

Step 1. Read the minutes of the Planning Committee's last meeting.

Step 2. Write an order letter to Robinson and Sons, Printers. Their address is 271 South Street. Tell Robinson and Sons what information you want on the posters, how many posters you need, and when you will need them. Inform them that you are enclosing a money order for $35.00 as a deposit.

Minutes of Planning Committee Meeting, March 18

The meeting was called to order at 3:00 P.M. by
Elaine Hauser.

The members of the committee made the following
recommendations for Career Day:

1. Career Day will be held in the school cafeteria on
   Saturday, April 23, from 10:00 A.M. till 4:00 P.M.

2. Booths will be set up around the room. Each booth
   will have a sign indicating the particular field
   or profession it represents.

3. Students will have an opportunity to talk with
   representatives from these areas: computer
   science, publishing, auto mechanics, veterinary
   medicine, dairy farming, teaching, social
   services, accounting, restaurant management, and
   many others.

4. At 11:30 there will be a slide show presented by
   the combined branches of the United States
   military.

5. There will be special appearances by:

   Lawrence DiGiovanni, a graduate of our school
   who is now with the United States Forest
   Service

   Thelma Tamura, a former student at our school
   who is now a set designer with Angelo Studios
   in Hollywood

   The mayor of our city, the Honorable Dennis
   J. Deegan

6. Refreshments will be served from 12:30 till 1:30.

CAREER DAY

Robinson and Sons, Printers

271 South Street
555-1233

Unit Assignments

Assignment 1 You and a friend plan to raise rabbits to sell to the pet stores in your area. Write a letter to the United States Department of Agriculture to request a list of publications that will give you information about the care and raising of rabbits. The address is

> United States Department of Agriculture
> Office of Communications
> Room 507A
> Washington, DC 20250

Assignment 2 In the November issue of *Teen Years* magazine, you saw an advertisement for return-address labels. For $2.00 plus 40 cents postage, you can order any name, address, and Zip Code up to four lines printed in black on white. The gummed labels are 1 ¾" long and are boxed in quantities of 1000. Order a box for yourself from

> Walter Kline, Inc.
> 3008 State Street
> Colorado Springs, Colorado 80904

Assignment 3 From the A.Z. Deane spring and summer catalogue, order the following item for your vacation: #5771 Deane's Camp Bag, $35.00 postpaid. It comes in three colors: green, red, and blue. You also want one #6382 Correcto Compass, $6.00 postpaid. The address is A. Z. Deane Company, Springfield, Maine 04487.

Assignment 4 The address labels that you ordered in Assignment 2 contain a spelling error. Write to the company about the mistake and ask for a corrected set of labels.

Assignment 5 The compass that you ordered in Assignment 3 has points that cannot be read at night. You have found one at a local store that you like better. Write a letter to the A. Z. Deane Company, returning the compass and asking for a refund.

Revising Your Assignments

For help in revising a letter, consult the Checklist for Revision on the last page of this book.

Unit Tests

Test 1

A. Number your paper from 1 to 5. Next to each number, write *True* if the sentence is true or *False* if it is false.

1. In the modified block style, all parts of the business letter start at the left margin.
2. The complimentary close of a business letter is always followed by a comma.
3. The business envelope includes the same information found in the inside address and the return address in your letter.
4. Your signature is never handwritten in a business letter.
5. Cash is the easiest and safest way to pay for merchandise in an order letter.

B. Number your paper from 6 to 10. Next to each number, write the letter of the term that correctly completes the sentence. You will not use one of the items.

a. heading
b. salutation
c. modified block style
d. adjustment letter
e. block style
f. order letter

6. *Dear Sir or Madam* is a proper __?__ to use if you do not know the name of the person to whom you are writing a business letter.
7. When you write a(n) __?__, you should include the purpose, details of purchase, arrangement for payment, and reference to payment enclosed.
8. All parts of the letter start at the left margin in the __?__ business letter.
9. The __?__ consists of three lines in the upper right corner of your stationery and gives your full address and the date.
10. A letter that states a problem and that suggests a solution is called a(n) __?__.

C. Number your paper from 11 to 15. Next to each number, write the letter of the item that correctly answers the question.

11. Which of the following would you write to obtain a free booklet on energy conservation from your local government?

    a. Adjustment letter
    b. Order letter
    c. Request letter

12. Which of the following would you write to obtain a porcelain figurine that you saw in a catalogue?

    a. Order letter
    b. Request letter
    c. Adjustment letter

13. Which of the following would you write to receive the correct model of a sleeping bag that you wanted instead of the model that you received?

    a. Adjustment letter
    b. Request letter
    c. Order letter

14. Which of the following does *not* belong in a business letter?

    a. Inside address   c. Salutation
    b. Informal language   d. Heading

15. Which of the following is *not* a strategy for writing a business letter?

    a. Choose an appropriate complimentary close.
    b. Reread your letter carefully to correct errors.
    c. Write the letter in pencil.
    d. Make certain that the heading and the inside address are complete.

Test 2

Choose one of the Unit Assignments. Write the assignment as directed and hand it in to your teacher.

Part Three

Related Skills

Where can you apply your writing skills? How can you speak and listen more effectively? Where can you find information on subjects that you want to know about? In Part Three you will find ways to improve important skills that you use often for work in your English class, in other school subjects, and in your outside activities. Whether you need to use the library, to give a speech, or to take a test, you can use these units as resources in carrying out your assignment.

By becoming familiar with the information and strategies provided in these units and by referring to them often, you will develop skills that you can apply to all your projects and assignments.

Unit 16

Spelling Skills

16.1 How to Study Spelling Words

Use the following steps to study words that you wish to learn to spell.

Procedure

1. *Look at the word and study its letters.*

2. *Pronounce the word* and associate the letters in it with their sounds.

3. *Write the word,* concentrating on any difficult letter combinations.

4. *Check your spelling* to see whether it is correct.

5. *Study the word* until you have memorized its spelling.

16.2 Spelling Rules

16.2a Making Nouns Plural

A **singular noun** names only one person, place, thing, or idea. A **plural noun** names more than one. You can improve your spelling if you learn the rules for changing the spellings of nouns in order to make them plural.

Regular Plurals

Most nouns in English form their plurals according to certain rules. Study the rules that are listed on the following pages.

Rule Form the plural of most nouns by adding -s to the singular.

hat	record	bicycle
hats	records	bicycles

Rule If a noun ends in s, x, z, ch, or sh, add -es to form the plural.

gas	ax	adz
gases	axes	adzes

Rule To form the plural of a common noun that ends in y preceded by a consonant, change the y to i and add -es.

lady	penny	fly
ladies	pennies	flies

Rule If a *proper noun* ends in y preceded by a consonant, add only -s to form the plural.

Fred and Nina Grady	Germany
the Gradys	the two Germanys

Rule If a noun ends in y preceded by a vowel, add -s to form the plural.

key	delay	boy
keys	delays	boys

Rule To form the plural of a letter, symbol, number, or word that has been italicized (or underlined) for special attention (*page 253*), add an apostrophe and -s ('s). Do not underline the plural ending.

Jeff didn't make his *j*'s right when he wrote *adjust* and *joy*.

Shelly used *3*'s and ***'s to make a border on her paper.

Rule If a noun ends in *f* or *fe,* you usually change the *f* to *v* and add *-es* to form the plural.

	wife	half	loaf
	wives	halves	loaves
BUT	spoof	belief	
	spoofs	beliefs	

Rule To form the plural of a noun that ends in *ff,* add only *-s.*

cliff	sheriff
cliffs	sheriffs

Rule If a noun ends in *o* preceded by a vowel, add *-s* to form the plural.

stereo	duo	tattoo
stereos	duos	tattoos

Irregular Plurals

For some nouns, there are no rules that you can follow to form the plurals. In such cases, you should memorize the correct plural forms or check them in your dictionary. The following are examples of some kinds of irregular plurals.

1. Nouns that end in *o* preceded by a consonant. You form the plural of some of these nouns by adding *-s.* To others, you add *-es.* For certain words either *-s* or *-es* is correct.

ADD *-s*	avocado	piano	silo
	avocados	pianos	silos
ADD *-es*	echo	hero	potato
	echoes	heroes	potatoes
ADD *-s* OR *-es*	cargo	motto	mosquito
	cargos	mottos	mosquitos
	cargoes	mottoes	mosquitoes

To form the plural of a *proper noun* that ends in *o* preceded by a consonant, add only *-s*.

Jean and Sal Ferraro	Filipino
the Ferraros	Filipinos

2. Nouns that change their spelling:

woman	ox	child
women	oxen	children

3. Nouns that have the same form for plural as for singular:

Iroquois	bellows	sheep

Compound Nouns

Rule To form the plural of a compound noun (*pages 4–5*) that is written as one word, change the last word in the compound to its proper plural form. To form the plural of a compound noun that is hyphenated or written as two or more words, make the most important word plural.

crosswalk	stepchild	father-in-law
crosswalks	stepchildren	fathers-in-law

Assignment 1 Noun Plurals On your paper, write the plural forms of the following singular nouns. Then write a paragraph or brief story using all of the plural nouns.

1. elf	5. moose	9. baby
2. church	6. rodeo	10. house
3. valley	7. camera	11. roof
4. appendix	8. squash	12. goose

16.2b Adding Endings

The following rules for adding endings other than the plural (*-s* and *-es*) will enable you to spell many words.

Doubling the Final Consonant

Sometimes when you add an ending to a word, you must double the final consonant of the base word. However, you may have trouble deciding when to double the consonant and when not to. Here are some rules that may help. Because the rules about doubling the consonant are rather complicated, the following discussion begins with the cases in which you should *not* double the consonant.

1. If you are adding an ending that begins with a consonant, do *not* double the final consonant of the base word.

slap	develop	hat
slaps	development	hatful

2. If the base word ends with one consonant preceded by more than one vowel, do *not* double that final consonant.

read	appear	clean
reading	appearance	cleaner

3. If the base word ends with two consonants, do *not* double the final consonant.

remark	ask	spell
remarkable	asked	spelling

You double the final consonant only if you are adding an ending that begins with a vowel. If the ending begins with a vowel, there are only two times when you *do* double the final consonant. Here are the rules for those two instances.

Rule   Double the final consonant *if* the word has only one syllable and ends with one consonant preceded by a vowel.

plan	hot	sun	stop
planning	hotter	sunny	stopped

Rule Double the final consonant *if* the word has more than one syllable, ends with a single consonant preceded by a single vowel, and has the stress on the last syllable.

allot	occur	propel	control
allotted	occurrence	propeller	controller

Use the following questions to help you decide whether to double the final consonant when you add an ending to a word.

	Yes	No
1. Does the ending begin with a vowel?	?	?
2. Does the base word end with one consonant preceded by one vowel?	?	?
3. Does the base word have only one syllable?	?	?
4. Does the base word have more than one syllable, and is the most stress on the last syllable?	?	?

If you answer Yes to any three of these questions, then you should double the final consonant of the base word before you add the ending.

Dropping the Final e

Rule If a word ends with silent *e*, drop the final *e* when you add an ending that begins with a vowel.

use	like	code	sense
using	likable	codify	sensible

Rule If a word ends in *c* or *g* followed by silent *e*, you usually keep the *e* before an ending that begins with *a* or *o* in order to preserve the soft sound of the *c* or *g*.

peace	courage	trace
peaceable	courageous	traceable

Rule If a word ends with silent *e,* you usually keep the final *e* when adding an ending that begins with a consonant.

	definite	like	hope	nine
	definitely	likeness	hopeful	ninety
BUT	due	argue		
	duly	argument		

Changing Final *y* to *i*

Rule If a word ends in *y* preceded by a consonant, change the *y* to *i* before adding any ending except *-ing.*

	merry	busy	spy	study
	merriment	busily	spied	studying
BUT	shy	dry		
	shyly	dryness		

Rule If a word ends in *y* preceded by a vowel, do not change the *y* to *i* before adding an ending.

pay	employ	convey
pays	employer	conveyed

Assignment 2   Adding Endings   There are seven rules (given on pages 606–608) for adding endings to words. *Step 1:* Choose a chapter in one of your textbooks, and find in it examples of all the rules. Try to find at least five examples for each rule. Make seven columns on your paper, and write the words in groups. *Step 2:* Take one word from each of the seven groups and use its plural form in a sentence.

16.3 Spelling Patterns

If you learn the rules for spelling letter combinations that are particularly troublesome in English, you will be a better speller. Two of these problem combinations are *ie/ei* and the *-sede, -ceed,* and *-cede* word endings.

The *ie*/*ei* Pattern

The following rules will help you decide what to do when you know that a word has an *i* and an *e* but you do not know which one comes first.

Rule Use *ie* whenever the vowel combination has a long *e* sound (as in *belief*) unless the letter *c* comes right before the pair of vowels.

	field	achieve	chief
	yield	grief	receive
BUT	seize	leisure	protein

Rule Use *ei* after *c* or when the sound is not long *e*.

	their	seismic	heifer
	conceit	forfeit	foreign
BUT	friend	sieve	glacier

Rule If the vowel combination has a long *a* sound (as in *eight*), always spell it with *ei*.

reign   neigh   weigh   vein

Remember that if the two vowels are pronounced separately in the word, they are spelled in the order of their pronunciation.

science   society   being

The "Seed" Sound Pattern

The "seed" ending sound has three spellings: *-sede, -ceed,* and *-cede.*

1. Only one word ends in *-sede: supersede.*
2. Three words end in *-ceed: proceed, succeed,* and *exceed.*
3. All other words end in *-cede: accede, concede, recede,* and so on.

The spelling *s-e-e-d* does not occur as an ending in any word. It is used only in words that have to do with seeds: *seeded, reseed, seedling,* and so on.

16.4 Pronunciation and Spelling

Certain types of pronunciation errors often lead to errors in spelling. If you learn to avoid those errors, your spelling will improve. You should always check your dictionary for the pronunciations of words that you are unsure of, and note the letters that spell the sounds.

Extra Syllables.   Sometimes people misspell a word because they include an extra syllable when they say the word. For instance, *arthritis* and *remembrance* may be misspelled because people pronounce them with four syllables instead of three. Such errors also occur in the words in the following list. Be careful not to add extra syllables when you pronounce or spell them. The number after each word tells how many syllables it has.

athlete (2)	disastrous (3)	laundry (2)
athletics (3)	grievous (2)	mischievous (3)

Omitted Sounds.   Sometimes people misspell a word because they omit a sound when they pronounce the word. The following list provides examples of such words. Be careful to include the sound or sounds indicated by the underlined letters when you pronounce or spell these words.

accidentally	February	library
environment	government	particular

Transposed Letters.   Sometimes people write the letters in the wrong order because they pronounce them in the wrong order. Such errors often occur in the words in the following list. Be sure you pronounce and spell the underlined letters in the proper order.

bre<u>th</u>ren	ene<u>m</u>y	<u>per</u>form	<u>pre</u>scribe
cava<u>lr</u>y	mode<u>rn</u>	<u>per</u>spire	rel<u>ev</u>ant

Homophones.   Words that have the same pronunciation but different spellings and meanings are called **homophones**. They, too, can cause trouble in spelling. Be sure that you know the spelling and meaning of each word in the following list of homophones.

bridal, bridle	shone, shown
buy, by, bye	sole, soul
capital, capitol	some, sum
pedal, peddle	who's, whose

Commonly Confused Words.   Some other sets of words are not homophones, but they are similar enough in sound and spelling to create confusion. It is helpful to distinguish the meanings of such commonly confused words. Here are a few examples. (See also Usage Notes, pages 194–213.)

accent, ascent, assent	hold, hole, whole
access, excess	loose, lose
formally, formerly	statue, statute, stature

Assignment   Pronunciation and Spelling   Choose three sets of words from the list of Homophones and three sets from the list of Commonly Confused Words. On your paper, write a sentence (or two, if necessary) using each set of words correctly, and underline the words from the lists.

SAMPLE	bridal, bridle
ANSWER	My aunt and uncle were married on horseback. She wore a white <u>bridal</u> gown as they rode away down the <u>bridle</u> path.

16.5   Other Spelling Helps

After you have learned all the preceding spelling rules and patterns, there are still more things you can do to improve your spelling. This section suggests some strategies that will help you to improve your spelling.

Strategies

1. *Develop your own methods of word study.* Knowing the rules and patterns of spelling will help.

2. *Keep lists of troublesome words.*

3. *Create memory aids,* called mnemonic (nĭ-MŎN'ĭk) devices, for difficult words. For example:

> *Emma* is in a **dilemma**.
> The **principal** is my *pal*.
> There is an *arc* in **arctic**.
> There is an *end* in **friend**.

4. *Think carefully about what words sound like and look like.*

5. *Whenever you are unsure of the spelling of a word, check it in your dictionary.*

Other Spellings of Some Sounds

Sometimes it is difficult to locate a word in your dictionary when you do not know how to spell it. You may have to guess the spelling of the word and then check other possible spellings until you find the correct one. You already know which letters usually stand for the various sounds in English. The following list suggests where to look for a word when it does not begin the way you expect.

CONSONANT SOUNDS	OTHER SPELLINGS
f, as in *frog*	*ph,* as in *photography*
j, as in *juice*	*g,* as in *gentle*
k, as in *kite*	*c* or *ch,* as in *coat* and *chorus*
n, as in *nice*	*gn, kn,* or *pn,* as in *gnome, knock,* and *pneumonia*
r, as in *ring*	*wr,* as in *write*
s, as in *sing*	*ps* or *c,* as in *psalm* and *cider*

VOWEL SOUNDS	OTHER SPELLINGS
a, as in *ate*	*ei,* as in *eight*
i, as in *island*	*ei,* as in *Einstein*
u, as in *urn*	*e* or *ea,* as in *ermine* and *earn*

16.6 Frequently Misspelled Words

Certain words are misspelled so often that many writers consider them problem words. Some troublesome words were given earlier in this unit. The following list gives twenty-five more for you to master.

all right	exaggerate	parallel
business	excellent	really
captain	interesting	recommend
committee	misspell	separate
deceive	mortgage	straight
development	nickel	success
disappear	occasion	usually
disapprove	occurred	valuable
embarrass		

Assignment   Learning New Words   Choose ten words from the list of Frequently Misspelled Words. On your paper, write a sentence using each word. Study your words, using the method suggested on page 612. Then exchange lists with a classmate and, using the sentences each of you wrote, take turns giving one another a test on the listed words.

Unit 17

Vocabulary Skills

Your **vocabulary**—the words you use when you speak or write and the words you understand when you listen or read—is one of the things that help you to communicate with others. If you can use and understand a wide variety of words, you will be able to communicate effectively in any situation. In this unit you will learn how to improve your vocabulary.

17.1 How to Learn New Words

Strategies

1. *Keep a list of words that you want to learn.* Use a special place in your notebook for this list.

2. *Look up the meanings of the words and write them in your notebook.*

3. *Study these words from time to time.*

4. *Look for these new words in your reading, and try to use them in your writing.*

5. *Add prefixes and suffixes to words that you already know* in order to create other words.

6. *Memorize new words and their meanings.*

17.2 Using Context to Get Meaning

When you are reading and you come to a word you do not know, you can often figure out the meaning of the word by using the context in which it appears. **Context** means "the general setting in which something appears." For an unknown word, the context is the overall sense of the words and ideas that surround it. By thinking about the meanings of those words and ideas that you *do* know in a passage, you may be able to figure out the meaning of a word you do *not* know.

There are four things to look for in the context that can help you to derive the meaning of a word: the sense of the passage, synonyms, examples, and comparison or contrast.

Sense of the Passage.　To use context effectively, look in the passage for clues to the meaning of the word. Then use your own knowledge and experience to help you figure out what the word must mean in that particular context.

> Like the previous studies, the latest report confirmed that smoking has a **deleterious** effect on health and should, therefore, be discouraged.

You could figure out that the word *deleterious* means "harmful" from the following clues: (1) your own prior knowledge that smoking is harmful, and (2) the statement that smoking should be discouraged.

Synonyms.　Sometimes a writer will restate or define an unfamiliar word. If you know the meaning of the synonym given in the restatement or definition, you can figure out the meaning of the unknown word.

> In spite of the lawyer's appeal, the presiding judge remained **obdurate**; that is, unyielding.

The writer of this sentence assumes that you know the meaning of *unyielding* and uses that word to define *obdurate*.

The following words often signal restatement:

| or | which means |
| that is | in other words |

Examples.   An example can explain an unfamiliar word or concept. By showing you what kinds of things the word refers to, the writer helps you to figure out the meaning of the word.

> The coach suspended the player for his many **infractions** of the rules; for example, coming late to games, breaking training, and missing practice.

The examples that are given in the preceding sentence are instances of breaking or failing to follow rules; therefore, you can guess that *infractions* must mean "violations."

The following words often signal examples:

| as | such as | for example |
| like | especially | for instance |

Comparison or Contrast.   A comparison or contrast of a familiar word or idea with an unfamiliar word can make the unfamiliar word more understandable. To use this kind of clue, you must be able to recognize whether the two words or ideas are being compared or contrasted, and you must know the meaning of one of the words. If they are being *compared,* the unfamiliar word should have about the *same* meaning as the word or idea with which it is being compared.

> The new Ritz Hotel is as **opulent** as a palace.

The comparison between the Ritz Hotel and a palace tells you that *opulent* must mean "rich."

The following words often signal comparisons:

| as | like | similar to |
| the way that | as if | as though |

If the words are being *contrasted,* the unfamiliar word should mean the *opposite* of the familiar word or idea to which it is being contrasted.

> The medication was intended to **alleviate** the pain; instead, the treatment only worsened the injury.

The contrast between *worsened* and *alleviate* indicates that *alleviate* means "to reduce or relieve."

The following words often signal contrast:

but	however	on the other hand
instead	although	on the contrary
unlike	as opposed to	

Assignment Context *Step 1:* Find in a newspaper or magazine a paragraph that contains from four to eight words whose meanings you are unsure of. Underline those words; then cut out the paragraph and fasten it to a piece of notebook paper. Try to use the context to figure out the meanings of the words. *Step 2:* On a second piece of paper, write the words in alphabetical order. Beside each word write the meaning that you think the word has in the article. Next, find each word in your dictionary, and compare the dictionary definition to the one that you wrote. If your definition is inaccurate, write the correct meaning under the word on your paper. Be sure to select the dictionary meaning that fits the context in which the word is used. *Step 3:* Now exchange articles (but not definitions) with a classmate. After each of you has read the other's article, take turns telling what you think is the meaning of each underlined word.

17.3 Getting Meanings from Word Parts

If you learn the meanings of roots, prefixes, and suffixes, they can help you to figure out the meanings of words that you do not know.

617

Roots.   Because many words in English have Latin or Greek origins, learning the meanings of some Latin and Greek roots can be very useful to you. One **root**, the central or basic element of a word, can give you the meanings of several English words. For example, *audition, audible,* and *auditorium* all come from the Latin root *-audi-,* meaning "hear." In some cases the spelling of the root changes when it becomes part of an English word. The hyphens before and after the roots in the tables that follow indicate that they may appear at the beginning, in the middle, or at the end of words.

COMMON LATIN ROOTS

Root	Meaning(s)	Examples
1. -aud(i)- (-audit-)	hear	audition, audible
2. -ce(e)d- (-cess-)	go, move, yield	proceed, concession
3. -duc- (-duct-)	take, lead, draw	induce, abduct
4. -fac(t)- (-fect-, -fic-)	make or do	factory, effect
5. -fund- (-fus-)	pour	refund, transfusion
6. -pon- (-pos-)	place or put	component, position
7. -port-	carry, bear	transport, portable
8. -scrib- (-script-)	write	subscribe, manuscript
9. -tract-	draw, pull, drag	attract, traction

COMMON GREEK ROOTS

Root	Meaning(s)	Examples
1. -aut- (-auto-)	self	autobiography, autograph
2. -biblio-	book	bibliography, bibliophile
3. -bio-	life	biography, amphibious
4. -graph-	write	graphology, monograph
5. -log- (-logo-)	word, speech	biology, dialogue
6. -mon- (-mono-)	alone	monologue, monopoly
7. -phil-	love, be fond of	philology, philosopy
8. -phon-	sound, voice	phonograph, telephone

Prefixes. A **prefix** is a letter or a group of letters placed before a word or a root to make a new word. When you add a prefix to a base word, the spelling of the base word does not change. The meaning of a prefix can be a clue when you are figuring out the meaning of an unfamiliar word. For example, because *mis-* means "wrong or wrongly," you can figure out that *misinterpret* must mean "to interpret wrongly."

Prefix	Meaning(s)	Examples
1. ad- (a-, ac-, af-, al-, ap-)	to, toward, in the direction of	adverb, affix
2. de-	reversal, removal	decode, defrost
3. dis-	not, opposite of	disagree, disable
4. in- (il-, im-, ir-)	not or without	illegal, inactive
in- (il-, im-, ir-)	in or into	immigrate, irradiate
5. inter-	among or between, together	international, interlock
6. mis-	wrong or wrongly, lack of	misgovern, mistrust
7. pre-	earlier or before	prearrange, precaution
8. re-	back, again, against	rearrange, react

Suffixes. A **suffix** is a letter or a group of letters placed at the end of a root or a word. Suffixes change the function and sometimes the meaning of a word. The spelling of the root or base word may change when a suffix is added. You should observe and learn these spelling changes.

Suffix	Meaning(s)	Examples

These suffixes make verbs out of nouns or adjectives:

1. -fy	make, cause to be	purify, humidify
2. -ize	cause to be or become, make into, become	dramatize, materialize

These suffixes make nouns out of verbs or adjectives:

Suffix	Meaning(s)	Examples
1. -cy (-ity, -ty, -y)	state, quality, or condition	hesitancy, capability, modesty
2. -er (-or)	one who, that which	writer, helper
3. -ion (-ation, -ition, -tion)	act or process, result of, state of being	migration, civilization
4. -ness	state, quality, or condition of being	literateness, quietness

These suffixes make adjectives out of nouns or verbs:

1. -able (-ible)	capable or worthy of, inclined to	adaptable, fashionable
2. -ous	having, full of, like	joyous, harmonious
3. -some	characterized by	awesome, quarrelsome
4. -y	full of, like	creamy, peachy

This suffix makes adverbs out of adjectives:

1. -ly	in a way that is	gradually, modestly

Assignment 1   Roots   For each of the Latin and Greek roots listed on page 618, write on your paper two examples that are not given on those pages. Then write sentences using those words. You may use several words in one sentence if you wish. Underline your words. Be prepared to explain what each word means, based on what you know about the meanings of the roots. Use your dictionary if necessary.

Assignment 2   Prefixes and Suffixes   Using the affixes listed on pages 619–620, make as many new words as you can from each of the following base words. You may combine one or several prefixes or suffixes or both with the base words. Write the new words on your paper, and be prepared to explain how the meanings of the affixes combine with the meanings of the base words to give new meanings. You may change the form or spelling of the base word if necessary.

SAMPLE   claim

ANSWER   acclaim, disclaim, reclaim, acclaimer, claimable, acclamation, disclaimer, reclamation, reclaimable, reclaimer

1. credit   4. mobil   7. mature
2. act   5. compose   8. arrange
3. advantage   6. locate   9. mystery

17.4 How to Choose the Best Word

Once you have enriched your vocabulary with new words, you will want to be sure that you are using the *best* word in any situation. To do so, you need to learn about synonyms and about the difference between denotation and connotation.

Synonyms

Over the centuries, the English language has incorporated words from many other languages. As a result, English has a large vocabulary, rich in **synonyms,** words that have nearly the same meanings.

Of course, no two words mean exactly the same thing. Because there are always slight differences in meanings, many dictionaries include paragraphs about groups of synonyms. Such paragraphs explain the various shades of meaning.

A closer look at *dark* and four of its synonyms will illustrate the shades of meaning that synonyms have. You can see the special meaning of each adjective when it is paired with an appropriate noun, as follows:

Dark	"without light; having no lights on": *dark* room
Dim	"not clear, lacking in clarity": *dim* memories
Murky	"foggy; cloudy; smoky": *murky* afternoon
Obscure	"unclear to the mind": *obscure* ideas
Shadowy	"seen in poor light": *shadowy* figure

When you choose a synonym, pick the one that fits best in the context.

Denotation and Connotation

All words have both denotations and connotations. The **denotation** of a word is its dictionary meaning. **Connotation** refers to the attitudes and feelings that the word suggests or implies.

For example, two words that mean "bright and quick-witted" are *clever* and *shrewd*. However, while *clever* may be used to describe any intelligent, quick-thinking person, *shrewd* includes in its connotation "having an awareness of other factors." This connotation can, in turn, be either positive or negative.

> Ann is a **clever** student; she always does well on tests.
>
> Ann **shrewdly** reviewed the last chapter of the book before the final exam.
>
> Ann **shrewdly** sat behind the best student in the class.

You need to be aware of the connotations of words in order to read, write, and speak effectively. All forms of literature, particularly poetry, depend heavily on connotations. When you recognize the connotative values of words, you will enjoy your reading even more. If you are trying to write persuasively, you should use words whose connotations contribute most strongly to your point of view. If you are aware of the negative and positive connotations of words, you can choose the most appropriate words when you speak or write.

Assignment **Understanding Connotations** Choose five pairs from the following sets of synonyms. For each pair, write one or two sentences to show the contrast between the connotations of the two words. You may use different forms of the words, if necessary. Underline the two words in your sentence(s).

> SAMPLE   promise, pledge
>
> ANSWER   John <u>promised</u> that he would never be late again, but his promises aren't worth much.
>
>   Mervin <u>pledged</u> his entire fortune to help rescue the stricken city.

1. young, childish
2. car, limousine
3. inexpensive, cheap
4. proud, haughty
5. pretend, fake
6. calamity, misfortune
7. mistake, blunder
8. merry, hilarious

17.5 Using the Dictionary

If you wish to find the meaning or the pronunciation of a word, or other information about it, you need to know how to use your dictionary.

Locating a Word

Guide Words. Printed at the top of each page of a dictionary are **guide words** that help you to locate words easily. The guide words name the words that appear first and last on the page. For instance, if the guide words are *shoe* and *short,* you would find on that page any word that comes in alphabetical order between *s-h-o-e* and *s-h-o-r-t.*

Entry Words. An **entry word** in a dictionary is the word that is being defined. The **entry** is all the information that is given about the word: its pronunciation, part of speech, definitions, and so on. The entry word shows the correct spelling of the word. It is usually printed in boldface type and divided into syllables by dots or hyphens. This syllabication tells you where to divide the word at the end of a line of writing.

Using a Pronunciation Key

Pronunciations.   A dictionary also shows how to pronounce a word. The pronunciation is printed inside parentheses, brackets, or bars and follows the entry word. Most dictionaries contain a complete **pronunciation key** near the front of the dictionary and a shorter pronunciation key at the bottom of each page or each pair of facing pages. The key shows how to interpret pronunciation symbols. Because pronunciation keys vary from one dictionary to another, you should become familiar with the particular system that your dictionary uses.

Parts of a Dictionary Entry

Definitions.   Dictionaries provide definitions, or meanings, of words. Although some words have only one meaning, many have more than one. When an entry word has more than one meaning, each meaning is numbered. Sometimes, to make the meaning of the word clear, the definition may include a sample sentence. The dictionary may also include a map, a chart, or a picture to clarify a meaning. Because a word may have many meanings, you should read all the definitions to find the one that makes sense in the context in which you found the word.

Parts of Speech.   Dictionaries identify the part of speech of a word. The following abbreviations are used in most dictionaries. They usually appear after the pronunciation.

n.	noun	*adj.*	adjective
pron.	pronoun	*adv.*	adverb
v. or *vb.*	verb	*prep.*	preposition
vt. or *v. tr.*	transitive verb	*conj.*	conjunction
vi. or *v. intr.*	intransitive verb	*interj.*	interjection

Synonyms. Because the English language contains so many synonyms, dictionaries often list synonyms for an entry word and explain their connotations. Some dictionaries also list **antonyms,** words that have opposite meanings.

Homographs. Words that are spelled alike but have different origins and different meanings are called **homographs.** They may also have different pronunciations and syllabications. Homographs are usually listed as separate entry words in a dictionary and are identified by **superscripts,** small raised numerals placed before or after the words. When homographs are listed, you may need to read all the definitions of each entry to find the meaning that is appropriate to the context in which you found the word.

Labels. When appropriate, dictionary entries include usage labels, such as Nonstandard, Colloquial or Informal, or Slang. Such labels are a guide to the correct use of words.

Etymologies. The **etymology** of a word is its origin and history. The etymology is given in brackets or parentheses after the pronunciation or at the end of the entry. Often an etymology gives additional insight into the meaning of a word.

Assignment Improving Your Vocabulary Find an interesting article in a newspaper or magazine. Make note of any words that are new or confusing to you. When you have found five to ten new words, list them in your notebook. Look up the meanings, and copy them beside the words. Write a new sentence for each word. Then try to use each new word in your conversation or writing during the next week.

Unit 18

Study
Skills

To perform well in your classes and to write well, you need to be able to read efficiently. You also need to know how to take notes. Taking notes will help you to remember what you read. This unit will help you to develop both your reading and your note-taking skills.

18.1 Reading Skills

There are several ways in which you may improve your reading skills. The SQRRR, skimming, and scanning are all reading methods that you will find useful when you study.

18.1a SQRRR Reading Method

The SQRRR reading method is a way of analyzing, organizing, and retaining information that you read. **SQRRR** stands for *Survey, Question, Read, Recite,* and *Review.* The following reading selection is used to show you how the SQRRR reading method works.

WORLD WAR I

In the early 1900s, Europe was faced with serious problems. Countries were arguing among themselves. At the same time, they were building up their armies. By 1914 Europe seemed about to explode.

War in Europe

The war started with a quarrel between Austria-Hungary and Serbia. There was bitterness between these two countries because some Serbs were ruled by Austria-Hungary. On June 28, 1914, a Serb shot and killed an Austrian archduke. One month later, Austria-Hungary declared war on Serbia. World War I had begun. On one side were the **Allied Powers**, which included France, Great Britain, Russia, Belgium, and later Italy. On the other side were the **Central Powers** (Germany, Austria-Hungary, and Turkey).

Battles took place involving millions of troops. It soon became clear that neither side would win a quick victory. Armies dug trenches separated by an area called **no man's land**. Anyone moving in no man's land was in grave danger.

America Attempts Neutrality. American leaders tried to make sure that the United States stayed neutral. Even so, most Americans hoped for an Allied victory. The United States had strong cultural ties with Great Britain. Also, Americans were reminded of the help from France during this country's fight for independence.

The steps of the SQRRR method are explained in the following paragraphs.

Survey. The first step is to survey the reading selection. To survey means to read all section titles, subheadings, and terms in boldface or italic type. Then, examine all illustrations. Finally, read any summary paragraphs or lists in the selection. A survey of the selection you just read tells you the following:

The topic is World War I. (selection title)

The war was fought in Europe. (subheading)

The war was fought between the Allied Powers and the Central Powers. (boldface terms)

The fighting involved a no man's land. (boldface term)

America was neutral when the war began. (subheading)

Question. The next step is to ask yourself questions that will be answered by reading the selection. The questions are based on the material that you find in your survey. You could ask yourself the following questions after a survey of the reading selection:

> When did World War I begin?
> Why did the war begin?
> What nations were the Allied Powers?
> What nations were the Central Powers?
> What was no man's land?
> Was America completely neutral?

Read.   Read the selection for information that will answer your questions. Write down the questions and take notes if that will help you to remember. Be alert for information that is not covered by your questions.

Recite.   When you have finished reading, ask yourself each question and then answer it. You can do this silently, aloud, or in writing. If there is information in the selection that you did not anticipate, think of additional questions for that information. Then answer those questions.

Review.   Review by asking and answering your questions again. Ideally, you should do this within twenty-four hours. Do not look at your notes or the reading selection. When you have finished, check your answers against your notes or the selection. Continue reviewing until you can answer each question correctly.

Assignment 1   SQRRR Reading Method   Read the following selection, using the SQRRR reading method. On your paper, write the letters of the correct answers to the three questions that follow the passage. There is more than one answer for each question.

THE ROARING TWENTIES

The 1920s have been called the "Roaring Twenties." There were so many new ways of doing things, and so much was happening at once, that it seemed an exciting time to be alive.

A Transportation Revolution

After World War I, Americans began to build large numbers of cars. By 1920 there were about eight million cars in the United States. As more Americans became car owners, the United States became a "nation on wheels." Farm families no longer lived in isolation. Now they could drive into town to shop and see friends. Since people could drive to work, more suburbs grew up around cities. Many people spent their vacations taking long road trips. **Cottage camps** (the first motels) were found along the nation's highways. So were gas stations and garages.

By 1930 over twenty-three million cars were registered in the United States. The car business meant employment for many Americans. New jobs opened up everywhere, from the factory to the gas station. More than anything else, cars provided the prosperity of the 1920s.

Airplanes had been used in World War I, at first for scouting, then for fighting. During the 1920s, improvements were made in airplanes. Airports were built, and mail and passenger service got under way.

The nonstop flight of Charles A. Lindbergh from New York to Paris in 1927 made people more interested in air travel. Overnight, "Lucky Lindy" became a national hero. In 1928 Amelia Earhart was the first woman to fly across the Atlantic. She, too, was treated as a hero.

The Radio and Motion-Picture Boom

On November 2, 1920, station KDKA of Pittsburgh went on the air to broadcast the results of the presidential election. Soon everyone was talking about the radio. A San Francisco newspaper reported, "There is radio music in the air, every night, everywhere." By 1929 the United States had ten million radio sets and about seven hundred and fifty radio stations. A nationwide hookup of one hundred and twenty stations made it possible for millions of Americans to hear Herbert Hoover take his presidential oath of office on March 4, 1929.

629

The motion-picture industry also boomed during the 1920s. First came the silent films. Then in 1927 came the "talkies"—pictures with sound. Many actors and actresses became well known to people throughout the United States. As many as one hundred million people went to the movies every week to see such stars as Mary Pickford and Rudolph Valentino.

1. Which of the following statements can you make after a survey of "The Roaring Twenties"?
   a. The Roaring Twenties were a time of change.
   b. Fewer changes took place in the 1930s than in the 1920s.
   c. Cars and airplanes were part of a transportation revolution.
   d. By 1929 there were more than twenty-nine million radios in the United States.
   e. Radio and motion pictures became popular in the 1920s.

2. Which of the following questions would you use to guide your reading of the selection?
   a. What changes took place during the Roaring Twenties?
   b. Why was the United States "a nation on wheels"?
   c. Who was President during the Roaring Twenties?
   d. What were the 1920s like in other countries?
   e. How did the motion-picture industry develop during the 1920s?

3. Which of the following answers will help you to remember important information in "The Roaring Twenties"?
   a. The number of cars increased, airline service began, and radio and motion pictures became popular.
   b. Herbert Hoover took the presidential oath of office on March 4, 1929.
   c. Many new businesses were created when the United States became "a nation on wheels."
   d. Radio dramatically changed communications in the United States.
   e. Airplanes were used for scouting in World War I.

Assignment 2   SQRRR   Find a magazine article and read it, using the five steps of the SQRRR reading method.

18.1b Skimming and Scanning

Skimming and scanning are additional ways of helping you read more efficiently. They save time. When you use these methods, you do not read every word of a selection.

Skimming

Skim a reading selection when you want to get a general idea of the content.

Use the following strategies when you skim a selection.

Strategies

1. *Read the title of the selection.*

2. *Read the first two or three paragraphs.* Introductory paragraphs usually tell you a lot about a selection.

3. *Read the first and last sentences of all other paragraphs.*

4. *Read subheadings, and notice words in boldface or italic type.*

5. *Read the last paragraph.* The final paragraph often summarizes the content.

Because reading material is organized in different ways, you will have to adjust your skimming techniques. For instance, the introductory paragraphs may not tell you much about the content. On the other hand, a selection may begin with a complete summary of the content.

Scanning

Scan a reading selection when you are looking for specific information, such as a date or a formula.

Use the following strategies when you scan a selection.

Strategies

1. *Know exactly what you are looking for before you start scanning.* Keep in mind key words related to the information you want.

2. *Glance down the pages or columns to find key words.* Use these clues: section titles, subheadings, words in boldface or italic type, first and last sentences of paragraphs, and illustrations.

Assignment 3 Skimming   Read the following questions. Then skim the reading selection. On your paper, answer the questions about the passage, using the strategies for skimming.

1. What is the reading selection about?
2. What four things in the first paragraph show how the sun is active?
3. What did the astronomers discover?
4. What words in boldface type give you an idea about the content of the reading selection?
5. What group of words in the final paragraph helps summarize what the reading selection is about?

The Sun Gives a Continuous Performance

Sunspots are regions of gases that are cooler than the rest of the sun's surface, so they look dark. Vast solar flares shower outer space with intense radiation that can be dangerous for space travelers. Hundreds of areas of seething gases, up to 800 km in diameter, make the sun's surface look like a pot of boiling breakfast cereal. Streamers of exploded gases rise hundreds of thousands of kilometers above the surface.

The sun has a bright halo, called the **corona**, always present but only visible during total eclipses. The **solar wind** is shot out like spray from a turning garden sprinkler or sparks from a fireworks pinwheel.

Recently astronomers have discovered that the sun pulses in and out. These pulsations occur every two hours and forty minutes. Astronomers hope that these impulses will help them learn more about the inside of the sun.

The sun puts on one dramatic act after another. It is the only star close enough to Earth to study in detail. No wonder many scientists devote their lives to understanding what happens on the sun.

Assignment 4 Scanning Read the following questions. Then scan the reading selection. On your paper, answer the questions about the passage, using the strategies for scanning.

1. What are two labor laws passed in the 1930s?
2. Why were the labor laws of the 1930s passed?
3. What is another name for the National Labor Relations Act?
4. When was the Wages and Hours Act passed?
5. What does the passage say about a minimum wage?

The New Deal Adopts Labor Laws

Many laws of the 1930s were passed just to lift the American people out of the Great Depression. However, several of these laws are still important today. Two of these laws had to do with workers. President Roosevelt believed that workers should be protected in the right to join labor unions and to bargain collectively (in groups) with employers. In 1935 Congress passed the *National Labor Relations Act* (often called the Wagner Act), which stated that the government would protect these rights.

Roosevelt also believed that the country would be more prosperous if wages were increased and working hours reduced so that persons with no jobs could be given employment. *The Wages and Hours Act* of 1938 said that the regular work week of all persons making goods to be sold in interstate commerce (outside the states where they were made) should be limited to forty hours. It also said that the least a worker could be paid was forty cents an hour. This minimum wage has been increased several times since then.

18.2   Note-Taking Skills

18.2a   How to Take Notes

To study efficiently, you also need to know how to take notes efficiently. The simple act of writing something down will help you to remember it.

Remember that note taking is a selective process. You must first decide what is important enough to include in your notes.

Use the following strategies when taking notes.

Strategies

1. *Write your notes in your own words.*

2. *Use words and phrases, not complete sentences.* Use mostly nouns and verbs. Omit articles (*a, an, the*). Use adjectives and adverbs sparingly.

3. *Use abbreviations and symbols when possible.*

4. *Pay close attention to words in boldface and italic type, in quotation marks, or in another color in order to determine what is important.*

5. *Watch for words and phrases that signal main points.* Examples include *first, then, finally, in summary, in conclusion, most important, more important, the reason for, the causes of, the result was, for instance, for example,* and so forth.

6. *Separate your notes from different classes.*

7. *Review your notes shortly after you write them.*

8. *Write your notes in ink.* Pencil will fade or blur.

Before writing any notes, read a sentence through. Make sure that you understand it. Then decide which words are the important ones. In the following example, all important words have been underlined.

In early <u>1913</u> <u>Fennel Jackson</u>, <u>discouraged</u> by his consistent <u>bad luck</u>, <u>left</u> <u>Chicago</u> and journeyed <u>to</u> <u>Rapid City</u>, South Dakota.

Just from looking at the underlined words, you learn when Fennel Jackson left, why he left, where he left from, and where he went. Your understanding is enhanced by all of the words in the sentence, of course. Otherwise, they would not have been used. To grasp the basic information contained in the sentence, however, you need only those words that are underlined.

Once you have determined what is important, you are ready to write your notes. Because you cannot underline words in textbooks and encyclopedias, you must write your notes on a piece of paper. The following examples show how you might take notes from the statement that you just read about Fennel Jackson.

NOTE   1913, F. Jackson discouraged by bad luck. Went Rapid City from Chicago

You may want instead to use your own form of shorthand for taking notes. If you do, be sure that you understand your symbols and abbreviations and that you use them consistently. Otherwise, you may not be able to read your own notes.

NOTE   1913; J., discouraged, Chicago ⟶ Rapid C.

Both notes contain a shortened form of Fennel Jackson's name. If you think you might forget his name, then you should use his full name. Notice also that South Dakota has not been referred to. If you think you might forget where Rapid City is, then you would refer to South Dakota as SD.

Assignment 1   Note Taking   On your paper, write only the underlined words that you would include in notes on the following passages.

1. In a rain forest on <u>an</u> island in the <u>Philippines,</u> <u>there</u> are <u>twenty-four</u> people living in the Stone Age. <u>Members</u> of the <u>Tasaday</u> tribe live in <u>caves</u>, do not farm, do not use weapons or <u>pottery</u>, and make fires with <u>wooden</u> sticks and <u>dry</u> fibers.

2. **Bait-and-Switch Advertising**. <u>This</u> is the <u>single</u> most <u>common</u> kind of <u>fraud</u>. A store advertises a product that has already <u>been</u> sold or is so <u>bad</u> that no one <u>would</u> want it. This product, the "<u>bait</u>," is designed only to bring you into the store. <u>When</u> you say you don't want it, a salesperson tries to "<u>switch</u>" you to a so-called quality product—<u>one</u> that <u>costs</u> you more money and brings the store more profit. Bait-and-switch advertising is forbidden by law, but the consumer should be alert nevertheless.

Assignment 2   Note Taking   On your paper, list all of the key words in the passages in Assignment 1. Then write notes on the passages.

18.2b How to Write a Summary

A **summary** is a brief statement of the important ideas in a reading selection. You will find that a summary is an economical way of taking notes on a reading assignment. It is also a form of note taking that you use when you are doing research for a written or oral report.

Use the following strategies when writing a summary.

Strategies

1. *Look for key words and use them in your summary.*

2. *Do not use complete sentences.*

3. *Use as few words as possible without being too brief and therefore inaccurate.*

4. *Write the summary in paragraph form.*

The key words in the following passage are underlined. Notice how they are used in the summary that follows the passage.

ORIGINAL   A typical <u>atoll</u> is shaped like a rough <u>circle</u>, made up of several sandy <u>islets</u> <u>separated</u> by <u>surge</u> <u>channels</u>. Through these channels, the irregular tides of the central Pacific flush the shallow <u>central</u> <u>lagoon</u> <u>enclosed</u> by the atoll. . . . An atoll gets its ringlike shape because it was a <u>collar</u> of <u>coral</u> <u>around</u> the perimeter of a <u>sinking</u> <u>volcanic</u> cone.

William H. Amos, *Wildlife of the Islands*

SUMMARY   Atoll: circle of islets separated by surge channels and enclosing a central lagoon; formerly coral collar around sinking volcanic cone

Assignment 3 Summary Turn to "The Roaring Twenties" on page 628. On your paper, write down the key words for each paragraph of the selection. Then write a summary of each paragraph. Use the strategies on this page.

Unit 19

Listening
Skills

19.1 The Importance of Listening

Although many of us take listening for granted, it is an important part of communication, and it requires attention and practice to be effective. Good listening, like good speaking, is necessary for the successful oral exchange of information.

Listening is different from hearing. When you really listen, you think about what you are hearing. Listening is a skill, which you can practice and learn. Although the emphasis in this unit is on listening to speeches and formal presentations, you use many of the same skills in other situations as well.

Occasions for Using Listening Skills

As a student you probably spend about half of your school day listening. You listen to your locker mate in the hallway, to your teachers in the classroom or gym, to your principal on the intercom, and to your friends in the cafeteria. At home you listen to your family conversing at mealtime, to a news commentator on television, to a friend or a relative on the telephone, or to a song on the radio. In other settings you listen to a clerk in a store, to actors in a movie or a play, or to an airline pilot during a flight.

Kinds of Listening

On different occasions you need to listen in different ways. A situation may require listening for information, critical listening, conversational listening, recreational listening, or a combination of these. For each kind of listening, you have a different purpose and you need a different kind of effort and understanding. For example, you might listen to a song purely for enjoyment, or you might try to understand the words so that you can write an interpretation for a class assignment. In both cases you would be listening to the same material, but your purpose and your level of attention would be quite different. In the first case, you would be doing recreational listening. In the second case, you would be combining listening for information and critical listening.

In informational listening, critical listening, and conversational listening, it is important for you to be an active listener. **Active listeners** weigh information and evaluate what they are hearing. In contrast, **passive listeners** are uninvolved in what they are hearing. They allow their minds to wander, being alerted only when the speaker pauses, changes pace, or gives special emphasis to key words or phrases. Passive listeners often have trouble telling the difference between fact and fiction, between dependable information and a slick sales talk, and between digressions and supporting examples.

Assignment 1 Active Listening On your paper, write a sentence or two for each situation listed, telling why it is important for each participant to be an active listener.

1. Two friends planning a party
2. An interview for a summer job
3. A physician's consultation with a patient
4. A teacher's conference with a student
5. A coach discussing strategy with team members

Assignment 2 Kinds of Listening In your notebook or on separate paper, keep an accurate account of the time you spend listening during one entire school day. For each entry, note the kind of listening you did: informational, critical, conversational, recreational, or a combination. Then write down whether you were an active or a passive listener. Bring your record to class and compare it with those of your classmates.

19.2 Getting Ready to Listen

Good listening starts with a positive attitude. You want to listen to get as much as possible out of what is being said. In addition, there are several other ways that you can prepare yourself to be an active and effective listener.

The Setting

When you are about to listen to someone speak, whether it is a formal speech or a casual conversation with a friend, you should be comfortable and free of distractions so that you will be able to concentrate. You will also be showing your attention and interest, which are necessary for successful communication. The following strategies will help you to improve your setting for listening.

Strategies

1. *Arrive early or on time,* and be ready to begin listening at the scheduled starting time for the class, presentation, or conference.

2. *Get your note-taking materials ready ahead of time.* Do not shuffle paper or dig for a pencil after the speaker has begun. Put unrelated books and other materials away.

3. *Sit in a comfortable but alert position,* keeping the speaker in your line of sight. Do not gaze around the room or out the window.

4. *Listen quietly and avoid distracting yourself and others.* Make yourself aware of unconscious habits that might distract the speaker, other listeners, or yourself, such as tapping your pencil or cracking your knuckles. Do not whisper or motion to other members of the audience.

5. *Clear your mind of other concerns* so that you can concentrate. Keep a positive attitude, plan to be interested, and expect to benefit from what you hear.

Things to Know Before Listening

Some prior knowledge about the topic and the speaker will usually help you to listen effectively. You will be prepared to evaluate the information and the speaker's knowledge of the subject if you give them some thought ahead of time. Ask yourself questions like the following to prepare for active listening:

1. What is the speaker's topic? What do I already know about it? How can I find some information on the topic?
2. Who is the speaker? What qualifies the speaker to talk about this subject?
3. What is the speaker's purpose—to inform, to persuade, or to entertain?
4. What is my purpose in listening?
5. Do I expect to be interested? Do I have a positive attitude and an open mind? Am I prepared to change my mind?

Assignment 1   Distractions to Listening   Make a list of all the physical and mental distractions that affect your listening during one entire day. Then note next to each entry whether the distraction was one that you could have prevented or one that was beyond your control.

Assignment 2   Preparing to Listen   *Step 1:* Before an upcoming class report, school assembly, club meeting, or televised speech or documentary, find out as much as you can about the topic and the speaker. Ask yourself the questions listed on page 641, and prepare yourself as fully as possible to be an active listener. *Step 2:* Following the event, write a paragraph explaining how your preparation affected your listening. Point out specific ways in which your preparation did or did not help you to listen.

19.3 Listening for Information

Often you listen actively to gain knowledge from another person. The speaker may give an announcement, some instruction, a report, an explanation, or a demonstration. The information may be presented formally or informally.

ANNOUNCEMENT	Your principal announces that school will be dismissed early, due to bad weather.
	Your parents announce that an exchange student will be living with your family.
INSTRUCTION	Your science teacher gives instructions for taking the final test.
	Your neighbor instructs you on caring for her yard while she is on vacation.
REPORT	Your club's treasurer reports on finances.
	On the way to school, your friend reports on the band's concert tour.

EXPLANATION	Your English teacher explains the difference between a simile and a metaphor.
	Your sister explains why she needs you to take over her paper route.
DEMONSTRATION	The Drama Club members demonstrate stage lighting, set design, and make-up procedures in an assembly.
	Your father demonstrates how to make a perfect omelet.

As an active listener, you should be alert for certain kinds of help that the speaker may provide. These are the speaker's way of letting you know what is most important, how the information is organized, or that you should be prepared for another important point. Here are some strategies to use when you listen for information.

Strategies

1. *Listen for signals.* During the first few moments, an effective speaker may state a purpose, outline central ideas, or give important background information. These are signals for what you can expect in the rest of the presentation. A good speaker also uses signals throughout the speech to alert you to key points or to shifts in focus.

   SIGNAL OF PURPOSE
   "My purpose is to show . . ."
   "I would like you to learn about . . ."

   SIGNAL OF BACKGROUND INFORMATION
   "Let me explain how this situation came about."

   SIGNAL OF KEY POINTS
   "This topic has two main parts."
   "I have three ideas on how to . . ."

643

SIGNAL OF SUPPORTING MATERIAL
"Let's take an example . . ."
"That reminds me of the time . . ."
"In a recent survey, . . ."

2. *Listen for transitions.* Transitional words and phrases connect different ideas, information, or sections of a speech. Like signals, transitions tell you what the speaker considers important. They help you to follow the organization of a speech.

TRANSITIONAL WORDS   "Instead . . ."
"Next . . ."
"Consequently . . ."

TRANSITIONAL PHRASES   "Another problem is . . ."
"Now let's turn to . . ."
"As a result . . ."

3. *Listen for summaries.* A good speaker gives a cue before making a summary. A summary statement may come within a speech or at the end. It restates the purpose, a main idea, or some key information. It emphasizes important points and gives you a chance to catch anything you might have missed. You should listen for summary cues, and then pay special attention to the summary itself.

SUMMARY CUES   "What I have been saying adds up to . . ."
"Let me summarize in this way."
"Before I go on, let's review . . ."

4. *Listen for main ideas.* Your purpose in listening for information is to grasp the speaker's main ideas. A good speaker will direct you to these key points by using signals, transitions, and summaries.

5. *Listen for supporting details.* A good speaker provides support for every key point or main idea. Some

19.3

Information

of this support may be important information that you need to remember. For example, if you are listening to instruction or to a demonstration, you need to learn every step. In other cases, such as a report, you may need the supporting information only to understand and remember the main idea.

6. *Listen to take notes.* Taking notes (*pages 634–635*) makes you listen attentively and helps you remember what you have heard. You should listen for a few moments to get a sense of the speaker's direction, and then begin taking notes. Jot down the specific purpose, the thesis statement (*page 506*), the main ideas, and at least one supporting point for each main idea. If you have trouble identifying any of these points, make a note of the problem. Jot down any questions or points of disagreement that occur to you. Your notes are to serve you as simple reminders. They should be brief and specific instead of lengthy and detailed. Do not try to write down everything you hear.

Assignment 1   Forms of Information   In your notebook or on separate paper, list the five forms of information given on page 642. During one school day, keep track of the information that you listen to. Write down at least one example for each of the five forms of information.

Assignment 2   Listening for Signals   Listen to a report, a demonstration, or a speech on radio or television. While you are listening, write in your notebook or on separate paper all the signals that you hear the speaker give. Then review your list and identify each signal, using the names of the signals given on pages 643–644.

19.4 Critical Listening

Critical listening does not necessarily mean listening to find fault. It means listening intelligently, judging the value of what you are hearing before you accept it or reject it.

When you listen critically, you listen to evaluate, to judge, or to analyze a message, a presentation, a speech, or a discussion. You must listen critically to any persuasive speech —that is, when the speaker wants you to agree, to take action, or to give support. You should also listen critically to television, radio, and films—especially to advertisements, news commentaries, and political messages.

Critical listening requires that you first understand what the speaker is saying. Only then can you evaluate, judge, or analyze what you hear. Your own background and your knowledge of a subject help you to listen critically. You may react to a speaker's message in any of these ways:

I understand and agree because . . .

I understand and agree in part, but I have the following reservations.

I understand what you are saying, but I need time to think it over before I judge.

I understand what you are saying, but I do not accept your position (your reasoning, or your evidence) because . . .

In listening critically, you can ask yourself questions that will help you to evaluate a presentation. You need to consider the subject matter, the organization, the supporting material, and the language. Then you will be prepared to decide whether you accept or reject what the speaker is saying.

1. Is the speaker well prepared on the subject?
2. Is the speaker objective?
3. Do the main ideas make sense individually? Taken together, do they cover the subject completely?
4. Does the speaker support the main ideas?

5. Does the speaker explain any contradictions in the evidence?
6. Does the speaker make statements that you think may be wrong?
7. Is the language clear, vivid, concise, and appropriate for the audience? Are special terms defined? Does the speaker avoid using clichés, slang, and poor grammar?

You should also consider the speaker's attitude toward the audience. Often the success or failure of a presentation depends on how well the speaker understands the needs of the listeners.

8. Has the speaker considered the listeners' interests, background, and level of understanding?
9. Is the speaker enthusiastic and involved in the subject? Does the speaker want the audience to be enthusiastic and involved as well?
10. Is the speaker helpful in answering questions?

You may also find that the way in which a speaker delivers the presentation affects your understanding.

11. Does the speaker talk clearly, loudly enough, and at an appropriate pace?
12. Does the speaker maintain eye contact with the audience?
13. Does the speaker move about and use gestures and facial expressions effectively?
14. Does the speaker use visual aids effectively?

It is important to be objective when you evaluate any presentation. Do not assume that a humorous, skillfully delivered speech always has accurate and reliable content. On the other hand, a nervous or awkward speaker may have a valuable message to convey in spite of difficulties in delivering the speech.

Assignment   Critical Listening   Your teacher will give each student three sheets of colored paper (red, green, and yellow) to use for a signal system. Red means "I do not understand what you are saying." Green means "I understand and I agree with your point." Yellow means "I understand but I disagree with what you are saying." Use these papers in English class for two days. Hold them up whenever appropriate, when either your teacher or another student is speaking. At the end of the second session, discuss how the signal system affected those who were speaking.

19.5 Responsive and Courteous Listening

Many listening situations provide you with the opportunity to respond to the speaker. One way of responding is through simple courtesy. You can express your appreciation by listening quietly and attentively, by thanking the speaker, and, in some settings, by applauding.

Often you can respond by asking questions or by offering comments. Be sure to save your questions or comments until the speaker has finished the presentation. The following list suggests some ways to respond.

Strategies

1. *Ask directly to have something explained or restated.*

   "Would you please explain what you mean by . . . ?"

2. *Paraphrase briefly* what you think the speaker meant. Then ask whether you have understood clearly.

   "I believe that you said. . . . Did I understand you correctly?"

3. *Bring up a related point or an alternate view* that has occurred to you while listening. Be sure that your comment will be interesting to other listeners as well.

"I think that another reason might be . . ."

4. *Ask for more information* or for suggestions about further study or action.

"Would you please give us some suggestions for . . ."
"What can we do about . . . ?"
"Where can I find more information about . . . ?"

Be sure to make your question or your comment brief and direct and to state it in a strong, clear voice. Remember to be polite and respectful and to thank the speaker for responding.

You should never feel timid about asking questions. The speaker's goal is to convey a message to you so that you understand. That goal will be accomplished only with your active participation as a listener.

Assignment   Responsive Listening   Listen to a televised editorial or a political speech. Take notes on two or three points to which you have one of the following reactions:

a. You agree strongly.   c. You want more information.
b. You do not understand.   d. You disagree strongly.

Then work each of your reactions into a well-phrased question or comment that you would say to the speaker if you had the opportunity. Write down your comments and questions, and bring them to class.

Unit 20

Speaking Skills

20.1 Occasions for Speaking

Many times each day you need to speak to other people. The situations vary, the purposes are different, and the occasions range from very casual to quite formal and serious. Sometimes you can plan what you will say and how you will say it. At other times you need to speak without preparation. In this unit you will learn basic steps that will help you to prepare and deliver both informal talks and formal speeches.

20.1a Kinds of Speeches

Depending on the occasion, the purpose, and the audience, a speech may be either **formal** or **informal.**

FORMAL SPEAKING
SITUATIONS
As a candidate for student office, you speak at a school assembly.

A senator gives a prepared statement at a press conference.

INFORMAL SPEAKING
SITUATIONS
You introduce a new student to your homeroom class.

A senator answers reporters' questions at a press conference.

In addition to being either formal or informal, a speech is either prepared or impromptu. For example, a class report is a **prepared speech.** You have time to gather information and organize your material before you speak. An **impromptu speech** is one that you make on the spur of the moment. For example, you may be asked to make an unscheduled announcement or to accept an award.

20.1b Purposes of Speaking

When you are a speaker, your purpose is to inform your listeners, to persuade them, or to entertain them. Sometimes you have more than one purpose. For example, you may want to *inform* your listeners about an issue and also to *persuade* them to take some action on it.

While you are considering your purpose in speaking, you must also think about your listeners. In fact, what you know about your audience should affect all the decisions you make in planning your speech.

Speaking to Inform. When your purpose is to inform, you want to increase your listeners' knowledge about your subject.

> You explain and demonstrate to your scout troop how to tie basic knots.

Speaking to Persuade. When your purpose is to persuade, you want to make your listeners change their minds or take some action.

> You explain in a student assembly why each class should sponsor a foster grandparent.

Speaking to Entertain. When your purpose is to entertain, you want your listeners simply to enjoy hearing you speak. Sometimes you want to entertain your audience while you are informing or persuading them. In such cases you may include an amusing anecdote or some unusual facts in an informative or a persuasive speech.

> You tell the Photography Club about your adventures mountain climbing in Alberta.

Assignment   Purpose and Audience   For each topic listed, write on your paper (a) whether the speech would be formal or informal; (b) what the purpose would be; and (c) who would be a suitable audience.

1. The need for new bleachers in the football stadium
2. Computers in the classroom
3. How *not* to run a car wash
4. Support for public television
5. Economic forecasting: a look at the next decade
6. How to build a kite

20.2 Planning Your Speech

Making a speech is easier if you take one step at a time. The following steps make up the process of preparing and giving a speech:

1. Selecting and limiting a topic
2. Gathering information
3. Organizing your speech
4. Preparing and rehearsing your speech
5. Delivering your speech

20.2a Selecting and Limiting Your Topic

A **subject** is a broad category, such as music, nutrition, or scuba diving. A **speech topic** is a particular portion of a subject. It must be narrow enough for you to cover effectively in your speech.

SUBJECT	SPEECH TOPIC
Computers	How we can use computers in English class
Politics	The role of women in government today
Sports	What to look for when buying skis

Often in school your subject or your speech topic is assigned. At other times you need to think up a topic by yourself. Think about your interests, your experiences, and the things you know about. Then select a topic for a speech in the same way that you would for a paragraph, an essay, or a report (*pages 299–301, 497–500, 539–541*).

You will need to limit your topic to make it narrow enough for you to cover well and to make it suitable for the occasion. To do so, you will have to consider your general and specific purposes, your thesis statement, your audience, and your time limit.

General and Specific Purpose

Your **general purpose** is either to inform, to persuade, or to entertain, or perhaps a combination. Your **specific purpose** is a statement of exactly what you want your audience to do or to think as a result of your speech. You need to consider your general and specific purposes when you limit your topic and plan your speech, but you will not state these purposes directly to your audience.

GENERAL PURPOSE	SPECIFIC PURPOSE
To inform	I want my audience to learn the difference between racquetball and handball.
To persuade	I want my audience to agree that the school board should include a student member.
To entertain	I want my audience to be amused by my experiences in my summer job at the daycare center.

Your Thesis Statement

Your thesis statement (*page 506*) tells your audience what you are going to talk about. It should be specific and clearly stated. The preceding specific purposes are changed into thesis statements in these examples.

GENERAL PURPOSE	THESIS STATEMENT
To inform	Today I will explain three differences between racquetball and handball: the court, the hitting techniques, and scoring.
To persuade	I would like to tell you how the students, the school board, and the entire community would benefit from having a student on the board.
To entertain	Let me tell you what fun and good feelings I had when I worked at the daycare center last summer.

Your Audience

As you select and limit your topic, think about your listeners' interests and background. Ask yourself these questions: Who are my listeners? Will they be interested in my topic? What do they already know about this topic? How do I want to affect my audience? Keep these questions in mind as you study the rest of this unit and whenever you plan a speech.

Time Limits

You should have some idea of how much time is allotted for your speech. If you do not know, discuss the time limit with your teacher or the person in charge. The time allowed will affect how much you need to limit your topic. It will also guide you as you organize and rehearse your speech.

Assignment   Selecting and Limiting a Topic

Step 1: On your paper, list a speech topic for each of the following subjects:

1. An interesting experience you have had
2. An organization or a project that you already know about or that you want to know about
3. An issue that you feel strongly about

Step 2: For each of your topics, write a general purpose and a specific purpose. *Step 3:* For each topic write three thesis statements, one for each of these situations:

   a. A ten-minute speech to your English class
   b. A five-minute talk to a sixth-grade class
   c. A twenty-minute speech to a group of adults

Make your thesis statements consistent with your specific purposes. Save your paper.

20.2b Gathering Information

You should gather information for a speech in much the same way as you would for an essay or a report (*pages 502–503 and 543–545*). Depending on your purpose and your topic, you may be able to draw on your own knowledge and experience, or you may need to consult books and articles. You may also wish to interview an expert on the subject or to get information from television and radio broadcasts. If time allows, you can also write or telephone organizations and agencies to ask for specific information.

It is particularly important in a speech to give information that is clear and complete. A listener cannot stop to review or to look up a word the way a reader can. Be sure to define any difficult or specialized terms, and include examples or illustrations to clarify your point. For some topics, you may need to give background information. Statistics such as census data, percentages, and survey results can sometimes be helpful. Be careful, however, to give only enough statistics to help your listeners, and not so many that you confuse them. Quotations and the opinions of experts often provide interesting support for your points. Be careful to quote only material that is concise, clear, and related to your topic.

Assignment   Gathering Information   From the Assignment on page 655, select one of the speech topics and the thesis statement that you wrote for a ten-minute speech to your English class. *Step 1:* Make a list of the information or supporting material that you already have about your topic. *Step 2:* List the kinds of information that you need to gather on the topic. Also list specific questions that you need to have answered. *Step 3:* List all the sources that you can think of that might provide the material and the answers that you need. *Step 4:* Find the needed information, and take accurate notes. Keep a record of your sources. Save your notes.

20.3 Organizing Your Speech

Like an essay or a report, your speech should have an introduction, a body, and a conclusion. As you organize your material, make an outline (*pages 508–509*) that includes main headings, subheadings, and specific supporting information. This procedure will help you to present your material clearly, to remember what you want to say, and to estimate how much time your speech will take. It will also help your audience to follow your thoughts and to remember your important points.

The Body of Your Speech

When you develop the main points of your message, you should organize your material into main headings and subheadings. The main headings are your major points. The subheadings are your reasons, facts, and evidence. How many main headings you include depends on your specific purpose, your audience, and the length of your speech.

You should arrange the main headings of your speech in an appropriate order for the subject that you are discussing.

Topical Order. Arrange your headings by topics when your subject matter has distinct parts.

> The federal government has three branches: the executive, the legislative, and the judicial.

Chronological Order. Use chronological order for a speech topic that involves a set of steps or a historical progression.

> I will explain the steps for building a bookshelf.

Spatial Order. Use spatial order when your subject involves physical or geographical relationships.

> Here is a good way to lay out a campsite.

Problem-Solution Order. Many persuasive speeches involve explaining a problem and then looking at possible solutions to find the best one.

> Declining school enrollment is an expensive problem.

The Introduction to Your Speech

Once you have decided on the content and organization of your speech, you can plan an effective introduction. You need to accomplish several things in the opening sentences. Use the following strategies to create a forceful introduction.

Strategies

1. *Capture your listeners' attention.* A question or a startling fact can be an effective beginning. In some cases, a quotation or a bit of humor is appropriate.

2. *Create interest in your topic.* You might open your talk by referring to a personal experience or by relating your topic directly to your listeners' experience.

3. *Give your thesis statement.* Let your listeners know exactly what you are going to talk about.

4. *Reveal your plan for the speech.* Give signals (*page 643*) to tell your listeners how you have organized your message.

5. *Develop a positive relationship with your audience.* Show that you know about your subject and that you are relaxed and confident in speaking. As a result, your audience will be receptive, comfortable, and attentive as they listen to your speech.

The Conclusion of Your Speech

The purpose of your conclusion is to sum up your speech and to end on a strong and interesting note.

Different kinds of speeches need different kinds of conclusions. An informative speech might end with a summary or a review of major points. Your persuasive speech could finish with a challenge or a call for action. Your entertaining speech might close with a quotation, an anecdote, or even a question.

Your conclusion, like your introduction, should be clearly linked to your topic and suitable to your audience.

The Content and Wording of Your Speech

When you decide what to include in your speech, think about how much material your listeners can handle at one time. Also consider your audience when you decide on the wording of your presentation. Be sure that your language is neither too easy nor too difficult. Take time to define specialized terms. Use words that are vivid and specific to hold your listeners' attention. For example, the words *shuffled* and *marched* are more vivid and specific than *went*. Be careful also to make your wording appropriate to the formality or informality of the occasion.

Signals and transitions (*pages 643–644*) help your listeners to follow what you are saying. Let your audience know that you are moving on to the next step in your discussion. If your speech will take longer than a few minutes, insert an occasional summary to help your audience keep track of your important points. The more you help your listeners, the better they will understand your message.

Because listening is different from reading, you should use simpler sentences in speaking than you would in writing. It is usually a good idea to use sentences in which the subject of your sentence is near the beginning. Otherwise, your listeners may get lost in subordinate clauses or modifying phrases and miss your point. Of course, your sentences should not be all alike. Vary your sentence structure and sentence length to avoid monotony.

Assignment Organizing Your Speech   Use the thesis statement and the information that you gathered for the Assignment on page 656. Select a suitable order for organizing your speech. Then write an outline, an introduction, and a conclusion for your speech. Save your papers.

20.4 Delivering Your Speech

After you have outlined your speech, you need to plan for delivering it to your audience. Careful preparation will ensure a successful presentation.

20.4a Preparing to Deliver Your Speech

All speakers experience some nervousness before they face an audience. If you are well prepared, however, you can be confident of giving a good speech.

Note cards.   Instead of writing out your speech word for word, you can use note cards to guide you in speaking. You are more likely to speak naturally and to put your audience at ease if you speak from notes rather than recite a memorized speech or read a prepared text. You will also be able to maintain eye contact with your listeners and to avoid fumbling with papers if you speak from note cards.

Each card should contain no more than one of your major points, with its subheadings and supporting material. Instead of complete sentences, write down only key words and phrases. Include names, dates, and statistics as memory aids. Write clearly and do not crowd your notes, for you will need to refer to them quickly and easily. You may wish to use two different colored inks to distinguish your major points from your subheadings and supporting material. Number each card so that you can keep your notes in order.

Rehearsing.   You should be very familiar with what you are going to say. Rehearsing will help you to speak naturally, maintain eye contact, and reduce nervousness. It will also give you a chance to time your speech.

Using your note cards, rehearse your speech aloud several times. Use a tape recorder if one is available. If you get mixed up or if you forget what you want to say, make changes on your cards. If possible, have a friend or a relative listen.

20.4b Presenting Your Speech

When you finally stand before your audience, your main concern will be what you have to say. However, you should also think about your voice, facial expression, eye contact, gestures, and posture. All of these affect your listeners' ability to concentrate on your message.

Voice. Your voice should express your enthusiasm about your subject and should emphasize key points in your speech. Avoid speaking in a monotone, and do not speak too quickly. Pause occasionally for emphasis or to signal a new idea. Speak loudly enough to reach those in the back of the room, and pronounce your words distinctly.

Facial Expression and Eye Contact. Your facial expression can show determination, puzzlement, surprise, or delight. When you describe a serious problem, let your face reflect your concern. If you think about what you are saying, rather than about how nervous you are, your face will naturally show your feelings about the subject.

Just as in conversation, you should look directly at people when you speak to a group. Look around the room, and make contact with all parts of your audience rather than with only one or two people. Avoid staring at your notes, at the floor, or at the back wall of the room.

Gestures and Posture. Your posture should be natural. Stand straight but not stiffly. Relax, but do not slouch or lean on a desk or lectern. Feel free to walk around while you talk if it helps you to relax.

Use gestures as you would in conversation. Let your movements be a natural expression of what you are saying. Try not to let them seem artificial and rehearsed. If you use props or visual aids, be sure to hold them so that everyone can see.

Assignment Delivering Your Speech Use your notes, outline, introduction, and conclusion from the Assignment on page 659. Prepare note cards and rehearse your speech several times. Then deliver your ten-minute speech to your class.

Unit 21

Library Skills

Whether you are looking for a good novel or for information for a class report, your school or public library is an excellent source. This unit will help you to find and use the many resources found in most libraries.

21.1 How to Locate Books

Fiction

Books in the fiction section of a library are alphabetized by the authors' last names. If two authors have the same last name, the books are arranged alphabetically by the first name. For example, a novel by Charlotte Brontë would come before one by Emily Brontë. All novels written by the same author are arranged alphabetically by title. For example, Ernest Hemingway's *A Farewell to Arms* would come before *For Whom the Bell Tolls*. The words *A, An,* and *The* at the beginning of a title are ignored in alphabetizing.

Nonfiction

Many public libraries and most school libraries use the Dewey decimal system to classify nonfiction and also plays and poetry. The system was named for Melvil Dewey, who invented it. Dewey arranged subjects in ten groups numbered from 000 to 999.

The Dewey Decimal System

000–099	General Works	500–599	Science
100–199	Philosophy	600–699	Technology
200–299	Religion	700–799	Fine Arts
300–399	Social Sciences	800–899	Literature
400–499	Language	900–999	History

Dewey subdivided the ten groups so that every subject would have a number. For example, 652.3 is the number for typing. The number is in the 650s, the business section of the 600s. The digits that come after the decimal point help to define the exact subject. You do not have to memorize Dewey numbers, because they are posted in libraries. You simply need to know that the numbers will help you to find books.

Biography

The biography section of a library is arranged alphabetically by the last names of the persons whom the books are about. For example, a biography of John F. Kennedy would come before one of Martin Luther King, Jr.

Collective biographies, books that contain short biographies of a number of people, are treated differently. Such books are given a Dewey classification in the 920s. For example, Eve Merriam's *Growing Up Female in America: Ten Lives* is classified as a collective biography.

Assignment 1 Arrangement of Fiction On your paper, list the following books in the order in which you would find them on the fiction shelves of a library.

1. *A Crack in the Sidewalk,* by Ruth Wolff
2. *Shadows on the Rock,* by Willa Cather
3. *Twenty Thousand Leagues Under the Sea,* by Jules Verne
4. *Animal Farm,* by George Orwell
5. *Jane Eyre,* by Charlotte Brontë
6. *The Snow Goose,* by Paul Gallico

Assignment 2   Arrangement of Biography   On your paper, list the following books in the order in which you would find them on the biography shelves of a library.

1. *The Story of My Life,* by Helen Keller
2. *Barbara Jordan: A Self-Portrait,* by Barbara Jordan and Shelby Hcaron
3. *Nisei Daughter,* by (and about) Monica Sone
4. *Geronimo's Story of His Life,* edited by S. M. Barrett
5. *Barrio Boy,* by (and about) Ernesto Galarza
6. *Houdini: A Pictorial Life,* by Wilbourne Christopher

21.2 The Card Catalog

The **card catalog** is a cabinet that contains drawers with cards arranged in alphabetical order. The purpose of the card catalog is to let you know what books are in the library and where to find them.

To know where to find a book, you must look at the number in the upper left corner of the card. That number is the **call number,** or the Dewey classification and subdivision number (*pages 662–663*). The call number directs you to the appropriate shelf in the library. Books of fiction are also listed in the card catalog, but they do not have call numbers. Instead they may have the letters FIC or the author's initials.

Each nonfiction book has three kinds of catalog cards. From all three kinds of cards, you can learn the following facts about a book: the name of the author, the complete title, the subject, the publisher, the publication date, the number of pages, and the call number. If a book contains illustrations, maps, or bibliographies, these may be indicated on the cards.

Author Cards.   On an **author card,** you will find the name of the author listed to the right of the call number. Below the

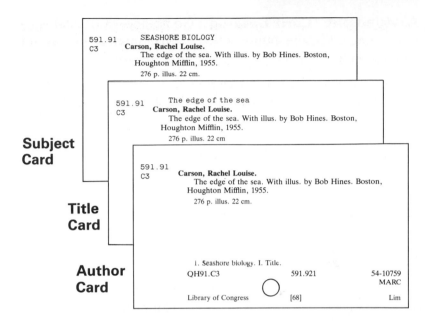

Subject Card

Title Card

Author Card

call number, you will find the initial or the first few letters of the author's last name. Author cards are especially useful when you want to know what books a particular author has written.

Title Cards. On a **title card,** you will find the title of the book to the right of the call number and above the author's name. Title cards are very useful when you do not know the name of the author of a particular book.

Subject Cards. On a **subject card,** you will find the subject of the book to the right of the call number, on the line above it. At the bottom of the card, you will find numbered references to all of the subject cards under which a book is listed. The same book may be listed under several different subjects. Subject cards are useful when you want to know what books have been written about a particular subject.

Assignment   Card Catalog   Go to the card catalog in your library. List the author, title, and call number for each of the following.

1. A book about swimming
2. A book about photography
3. A biography of an American artist
4. A book about a type of music
5. A book of poetry by Nikki Giovanni
6. A play or a book about the theater
7. A book about nutrition
8. A Spanish-English dictionary

21.3   General Reference Books

Dictionaries

Most libraries have both unabridged dictionaries and desk dictionaries in the reference section. Words that do not appear in a desk dictionary may often be found in a larger, unabridged dictionary. (See pages 623-625 for more information about using a dictionary.) There are also specialized dictionaries on such subjects as jazz, psychology, and mathematics. There are dictionaries of rhyming words, abbreviations, and slang, as well as dictionaries for many foreign languages.

When you are writing, you may also have need of a dictionary of synonyms, such as *Roget's II: The New Thesaurus* and *Webster's New Dictionary of Synonyms*. Use these two as you would an ordinary dictionary. However, when using *Roget's International Thesaurus,* you should first consult the index. It will refer you to the correct word in the section that contains lists of synonyms.

Assignment 1   Dictionaries   Using appropriate dictionaries in your library, carry out the following instructions. Write the answers on your paper.

1. Find a definition of the slang expression *with it*.
2. Define the French word *chercher*.
3. Define the Spanish word *alianza*.
4. Find at least two rhymes for *curb*.
5. Find out what the abbreviation *COD* stands for.

Encyclopedias

Another basic reference is the **encyclopedia,** which is generally a set of volumes that contains alphabetically arranged articles covering a wide range of subjects. Some articles have accompanying maps, charts, and illustrations.

You can locate articles in an encyclopedia either through a direct alphabetical search of the volumes by subject or through using the index. The index is a vital part of the encyclopedia. Use it as a guide to every place in the encyclopedia where your topic is discussed.

There are many encyclopedias available today. The ones listed here are found in most libraries.

The World Book Encyclopedia
Compton's Encyclopedia
The Encyclopedia Americana
The New Encyclopaedia Britannica

Assignment 2   Encyclopedias   Using encyclopedias in your library, write the answers to the following questions. Remember that using an index often saves time.

1. In what field is Shirley Verrett well known?
2. Give the name of a painting by Georgia O'Keeffe.
3. What was the Trail of Tears?
4. Who invented the saxophone? How many reeds does it have?
5. In what field is Minoru Yamasaki well known?
6. List two ballets by the choreographer George Balanchine.
7. Who was the first governor to be elected in Puerto Rico? How many terms did he serve?
8. How many events are there in a women's gymnastic meet?

Almanacs and Yearbooks

These annual publications specialize in current information. In them you can find such information as the top ten news stories of the year, the number of field goals made by a specific team in the NBA, the names of government officials, and lists of major disasters throughout history. If you cannot find a particular fact listed as a heading in the index, look under a related topic. If, for instance, you cannot find information about award-winning plays under *Plays,* look under *Theater* or *Drama*. The following are frequently used almanacs.

> *The Hammond Almanac of a Million Facts, Records, Forecasts*
>
> *The Information Please Almanac: Atlas and Yearbook*
>
> *The World Almanac and Book of Facts*
>
> *The Guinness Book of World Records*

Assignment 3   Almanacs   Using an up-to-date almanac in your library, write the answers to the following questions.

1. Who wrote the song "When Irish Eyes Are Smiling"?
2. Where is the United States Naval Academy?
3. Who won the Nobel Prize for Literature in 1980?
4. How many secondary schools does New Mexico have?
5. In what year was "The Star-Spangled Banner" designated the anthem of the United States?

Atlases and Gazetteers

Atlases are books of maps. They vary in the regions that they cover and in the types of maps that they contain. Some cover small areas, while others represent the whole world. Some have maps of the moon; some have oceanographic maps. The following are frequently used atlases.

> Hammond's *Ambassador World Atlas*
>
> *National Geographic Atlas of the World*

Rand McNally Cosmopolitan World Atlas
The World Book Atlas

Gazetteers are dictionaries of place names, including the names of such geographical features as mountains and rivers. The entries give the pronunciation as well as the location of the place, along with such information as size or population. Some gazetteers are part of atlases, such as Hammond's *Ambassador World Atlas*. Other gazetteers, such as *Webster's New Geographical Dictionary,* are entire books.

Assignment 4 Atlases and Gazetteers Using an atlas or a gazetteer in your library, find and copy on your paper the population of the following places. Tell also whether each place is a city, a town, a province, or a state.

1. San Juan, Puerto Rico
2. North Adams, Massachusetts
3. St. Mary's, Ontario
4. Driggs, Idaho
5. Manitoba, Canada
6. Montana, USA

21.4 Biographical Reference Books

Sometimes you may need more information about a person than can be found in an encyclopedia, especially when that person is still living. There are several biographical reference books you can turn to.

Current Biography is a monthly publication about living people. Each year the publications are collected in a bound volume called *Current Biography Yearbook.* The lengthy biographies in this work are accompanied by photographs and lists of sources. There is also an index of the people covered during the previous ten years and obituaries of prominent people who died during the year covered by the volume.

Who's Who in America and other volumes of this type are additional sources of information about living people. Many libraries have these volumes: *Who's Who in the World, Who's Who Among Black Americans, Who's Who of American Women,* and *Who's Who in Canada.*

Assignment   Biographical References   Using appropriate biographical works in your library, identify the following persons by writing a phrase on your paper. Include the person's dates, if possible.

SAMPLE   René Dubos

ANSWER   microbiologist, pioneer in development of antibiotics (1901–1982)

1. Anne Tyler
2. Margaret Bourke-White
3. Edwin H. Land
4. Julian Bond
5. Diana Nyad

6. Toshiro Mifune
7. Toni Morrison
8. James Galway
9. John B. Anderson
10. Tracy Austin

21.5   Literary Reference Books

Quotation Dictionaries

Dictionaries that contain famous sayings and their sources are called **quotation dictionaries.** They generally provide the complete quotation, its source, and the name of the person who said or wrote it. To find the quotation, you can look under the subject or one of the key words in the quotation. If, for instance, you wanted to know who said "Love is blind," you could look under "love" or "blind." Two of the more well-known quotation dictionaries are Bartlett's *Familiar Quotations* and Stevenson's *Home Book of Quotations.*

Literature Indexes

Short works such as poems, short stories, and some plays are often found in collections. If you want to find a particular work, you can use a literature index to find out which collections include it. The index will tell you the full title of the work, its author, and a list of collections in which it appears. If you need a particular short story, consult *Short Story Index*. Look for poems in *Granger's Index to Poetry*. To find the source of many plays, look in *Play Index*. School libraries may not have these volumes, but most public libraries do.

Assignment   Literature References Using an appropriate reference book in your library, supply on your paper the information asked for in the following items.

1. A collection that contains *Our Town,* a play by Thornton Wilder
2. The author and source of the quotation "Water, water, everywhere, / Nor any drop to drink"
3. A collection containing the poem "Nothing Gold Can Stay" by Robert Frost
4. The author and source of the quotation "Beauty is truth, truth beauty"
5. A poem about each of the following subjects: music, the sea, friendship, baseball, liberty

21.6 The *Readers' Guide*

If you want up-to-date information about such subject areas as world events, science, or the arts, magazines are one of the best sources. To find which magazines have articles useful to you, consult the *Readers' Guide to Periodical Literature*. It lists articles in more than 180 periodicals.

The accompanying illustration shows part of a column in the *Readers' Guide*. Articles are indexed alphabetically by subject and author. Notice that the subject and author entries are in boldface type. Under them are entries for articles. Each article entry includes the following information: title, author,

A Portion of a *Readers' Guide* Page

Author entry	**SITTLER, Joseph** Driven to deeper reflection. Chr Cent 97:311 Mr 19 '80 **SIZEMORE, Judy**
Title of article	Make recycled-glass wind chimes. il Mother Earth News 62:100-1 Mr/Ap '80 **SKATERS** Soul on ice: the skaters to watch in the Olym-
Author of article	pics. L. Ramsey. il Glamour 78:202-3+ Mr '80 **SKATING** *See also* Roller skating

Study and teaching

Discipline on the rocks [Canadian ice skaters: interview by S. Clark] E. Burka. pors Macleans 93:6-7 Mr 10 '80

Subject entry	**SKI racing** Little matter of Russian roulette [Canadian
Name of magazine	team at World Cup] H. Quinn. il Macleans 93:32-3 Mr 17 '80 **SKIERS** Little matter of Russian roulette [Canadian team at World Cup] H. Quinn. il Macleans
Volume number	93:32-3 Mr 17 '80 **SKIN**
Page numbers	Hey freckle face, you're cute! J. Biondi. il Teen 24:47-8 Mr '80

Care and hygiene

Date of magazine	Proper soap and water: how to find your skin's best friends. P. R. Jackson. il House & Gard 152:32+ Ap '80 Rites of spring for skin. K. Brady. N Y Times Mag p84 Mr 23 '80

Sports: how they affect your skin. Glamour 78:290 Ap '80
This spring unmask a fresh new face. il Glamour 78:258-9 Ap '80

Diseases

"See also" reference	*See also* Psoriasis

Fish

Shark skin and locomotion. C. W. McCutchen: S. A. Wainwright. Science 207:1004-5 F 29 '80

Subhead	**Reptiles** Lipid barrier to water exchange in reptile epi-

dermis. J. B. Roberts and H. B. Lillywhite. bibl f il Science 207:1077-9 Mr 7 '80
SKIPTON Castle. England. See Castles—England
SKIS and skiing

Illustrated	Cross-country skiing. S. C. Nilve. il Harp Baz 113:10-12+ Mr '80

Study and teaching

Anybody can ski, says Ed Lucks, and that in- cludes the handicapped and the blind. F. W.

Portraits	Martin. il pors People 13:44+ Mr 31 '80 **SKIS Rossignol (firm)** See Sporting goods

industry—France
SLAUGHTER, Dinny
Don't miss out on the morels! il Mother Earth News 62:99 Mr/Ap '80

"See" reference	**SLAVE labor camps.** See Concentration camps

name of magazine, volume number, pages on which the article appears, and date of the magazine. An entry also indicates whether the article contains portraits, illustrations, maps, or a bibliography.

Assignment 1 *Readers' Guide* Use the *Readers' Guide* to find an article on two of the following subjects. On your paper, copy the complete entry for both articles. Include author, date, title, magazine, page, and volume number.

1. a musical performer   4. careers
2. the environment   5. a film star
3. motorcycles   6. a well-known author

Assignment 2 Reference Books List on your paper the reference books mentioned in this unit that you would consult to find each of the following.

1. Information about a prominent American female poet

2. The location of Pikes Peak

3. Background information about ecology

4. The meaning of *morose*

5. A synonym for *naive*

6. The author who wrote "Parting is such sweet sorrow"

7. A magazine article about the space shuttle

8. A map of Greenland

Test-Taking Skills

22.1 Preparing for a Test

The first thing that you should do in preparing for a test is to establish a study routine. You will learn and retain more by studying regularly than by cramming before a test.

Place and Time.   Study in a place where you are comfortable and will not be interrupted. The fewer distractions there are, the more you will be able to concentrate. Do not have the television, radio, or stereo playing while you study.

You can do some studying for a test with classmates, friends, or members of your family. For instance, one person can ask questions and the other can answer them. However, be honest with yourself about how much you are really accomplishing. Remember that individuals, not groups, take tests. If you find that your attention strays from the subject, perhaps you should study alone.

Try to study at the same time each day. That way, studying will become a habit. Pick a time when you feel fresh and energetic. Do not try to study for hours at a time without a break. Study for 25 to 45 minutes, and then take a short break.

Emphasis of Studying.   Your teacher may indicate what material will be covered in the test. If your teacher tells you to reread certain pages or chapters in the textbook, be sure that you do. Pay close attention to any unit or chapter summaries in your textbook. Also review definitions and all words or phrases in boldface or italic type.

Your class notes should also tell you what material your teacher considers important. Review them carefully. Also review the written assignments that you have done since the last test. The emphasis of the assignments may well be the emphasis of the test.

Active Studying. Effective studying is active studying. Merely rereading your notes, assignments, and textbook will not completely prepare you for a test. Study actively by doing the following: (1) Review what you already know about the subject before you begin studying. (2) As you study, write questions that you think might be asked on the test. (3) Ask yourself the questions and answer them from memory after you have finished reviewing your notes and other study materials. Find the answers that you did not know. Then, study them until you can also recite them from memory.

All of the points that you just read will help you to prepare for a test. The following strategies will help you to perform well on a test.

Strategies

1. *Assemble all of the materials you will need for the test:* paper, pens, pencils, rulers, and so forth.

2. *Skim through the entire test before you answer any of the questions*, if there is adequate time. Doing so should make you feel more confident.

3. *Read the directions very carefully.* For example, do the directions instruct you to answer Questions A *and* B or Question A *or* B?

4. *Do exactly what the directions call for.* If you are asked to give three reasons, give only three, not two and not five. If you are asked to give facts, give facts and not opinions.

5. *Watch the time.* Usually you will not be asked to do more than you can do in the alloted time. Be certain that you allow time for each question.

6. *Get a good night's sleep and have a good breakfast.* You can perform better if you feel well.

7. *Stay calm.* It is natural to be a little nervous, but if you have prepared well, you can approach the test with confidence.

Assignment   Preparing for a Test   On your paper, write *Good study habit* or *Poor study habit* next to the number of each of the following statements.

1. Study your class notes.
2. Have a friend quiz you.
3. Study with music playing in the background.
4. Review your written assignments.
5. Study only what you do not know.
6. Take a break every three hours.
7. Study in a quiet place.
8. Write a list of practice questions.
9. Cram all night before a test.
10. Study at a different time each day.

22.2 Taking a Test

There are three basic types of test questions: objective, short answer, and essay. **Objective** and **short-answer** test your recall of important facts and ideas. They usually have only one correct answer. An **essay question** may evaluate both recall of specific information and more general knowledge of a subject. An essay question is also a test of your writing ability.

Objective Questions

There are three types of objective questions: true-false, multiple-choice, and matching. Each requires slightly different test-taking strategies.

True-False Statements. In a true-false test, you must indicate whether a statement is true or false. Most true-false statements are simple and direct, much like this example:

> All living things need oxygen to stay alive.
> T_?_   F_?_

Use the following strategies when responding to true-false statements.

Strategies

1. *Read each question carefully before answering it. If any* part is not true, the statement is *False.*

2. *Be alert for words that mean that there are no exceptions* to the statement. Those words include *all, none, always, no, never,* and *only.*

3. *Be alert also for words that mean that there are exceptions* to the statement. Those words include *most, generally, some, few, sometimes,* and *may.*

4. *Consider any other key words* before deciding that a statement is true or false.

Suppose you were asked to respond to this true-false statement: "All living things need oxygen to stay alive." The first word that you should notice is "all." It is important because it indicates that there are no exceptions. In addition, there are other key words that deserve your consideration. The words *living, need, oxygen,* and *alive* are also important in determining that the answer is *False,* because some living things (certain forms of bacteria) do not need oxygen.

Multiple-Choice Questions. In multiple-choice questions you are asked to choose the correct answer from a list of possible answers. They usually follow this format:

> The smallest state in the United States is (a) Hawaii (b) Delaware (c) the District of Columbia (d) Rhode Island (e) none of the above.

Use the following strategies when answering a multiple-choice question.

Strategies

1. *Read the question carefully and try to answer it before you look at the choices.*

2. *Read all of the choices before you answer.*

3. *Eliminate the choices that you know are wrong,* if you are not certain of the answer. Then pick the best answer from those that are left.

4. *Do not make wild guesses.* On some tests you may be penalized for guessing.

Look again at the example multiple-choice question. If you follow the strategies before answering this question, you might find that you can answer it before looking at the choices. If not, you might first eliminate answer (c) because you know that the District of Columbia is not a state. You might next eliminate answer (a) because you know that both Delaware and Rhode Island are smaller than Hawaii. Possibly you could next eliminate answer (e) because you know that either Delaware or Rhode Island is in fact the smallest state in the United States. You have now narrowed your choices down to two. Because you have analyzed the question and its possible answers, you now have a better chance of answering the question correctly: (d) Rhode Island.

Matching Questions. In matching questions you are asked to match items that have something in common. Usually you must match the items in one column with those in the other. Often there will be more items in the second column than in the first, so that there will be possible answers that you do not need, as in this example:

> Match the names in the right column with the correct descriptions in the left column. You will not use one of the names.

_?_	1. U.S. President	a. Ralph Waldo Emerson
_?_	2. Famous poet	b. Franklin Pierce
_?_	3. Social worker and author	c. Harriet Tubman
		d. Wilbur Wright
_?_	4. Leader of the Underground Railroad	e. Jane Addams
		f. Dolley Madison
_?_	5. Pioneer in aviation	

Use the following strategies when answering matching questions.

Strategies

1. *Read the directions carefully to see if you may use an answer more than once or if there are possible answers that you will not need.*

2. *Match first those items that you know with certainty.*

3. *Look for clues in the remaining items.* For instance, if the question contains a variety of items to be matched, do the particular items call for a matching person, thing, place, date, or idea?

4. *Cross off answers as you use them,* if your teacher permits it, so that you will not mistakenly use them twice.

Look again at the example matching question. If you read the directions carefully, you learned that you would not use one of the names. If you looked at the items in the second column, you may have seen many names that you recognized. For instance, you may have recognized the names of Ralph Waldo Emerson, Wilbur Wright, Harriet Tubman, and Dolley Madison. If so, you would be left with only two items that you would have to consider more carefully. Since you know that there has never been a woman President, you would know that Franklin Pierce is the "U.S. President," leaving only the name of Jane Addams for "Social worker and author."

Assignment 1   Objective Questions   On your paper, write *True* for those statements that are true and *False* for those that are false.

1. You should carefully read every word in a test item before answering it.
2. If any part of a true-false item is true, mark the item *True*.
3. Even though you may be penalized for wrong answers, you should always guess at items that you do not know.
4. In a matching test, it is best to answer first the items for which you are sure of the answers.
5. If you are not certain of the answer in a multiple-choice item, the best strategy is first to eliminate the choices that you know are wrong, and then to mark one of those that are left.

Assignment 2   Objective Questions   On your paper, write the answers to the questions that follow this true-false statement.

One difference between humans and animals is that humans can use tools, but no animals can.

1. What word in the statement might lead you to believe that there are no exceptions?

2. Is it necessary to know the meaning of *tools* in order to know the answer? Why or why not?

3. If you knew that some animals use sticks and stones to help them find food, could you answer the question? Explain.

Short-Answer Questions

In some short-answer questions, called fill-in-the-blank, you must supply a missing word or phrase in a sentence. Look at the following example.

> Because of the canals and waterways of the __?__, ships can sail between the Atlantic Ocean and the Great Lakes.

In answering other short-answer questions, you will write a brief answer of a few words or one or two sentences after the question. The following question requires an answer of two sentences.

> When was the American Red Cross founded and what is one service that it provides?

Use the following strategies when answering short-answer questions.

Strategies

1. *Read the question carefully.* Look for clues to the answer in the wording of the question.

2. *If you are not certain of the answer, write what you do know.* You may receive some credit.

3. *Use complete sentences in your answers unless you are instructed not to.* If, for instance, the question asks "Who is the inventor of the phonograph?" begin your answer "The inventor of the phonograph is. . . ."

Suppose you were to answer the example question: "Because of canals and waterways of the __?__, ships can sail between the Atlantic Ocean and the Great Lakes." If you follow the strategies, you will find an important clue in the phrase "between the Atlantic Ocean and the Great Lakes." It is important because it refers to a definite geographic location. That phrase will help you to recall the correct answer: the Saint Lawrence Seaway.

Look again at the question: "When was the American Red Cross founded and what is one service that it provides?" Because you have been asked two questions, you know that your answer will consist of two sentences. "The American Red Cross was founded in 1881" answers the question *When?* and "One service that it provides is distributing clothing to victims of peacetime disasters" answers *What?*

Assignment 3 Short-Answer Questions On your paper, write the answers to the questions that follow this fill-in-the-blank question.

> *Kidnapped, Treasure Island,* and *A Child's Garden of Verses* were all written in the nineteenth century by a man named __?__.

1. What words should you pay special attention to before attempting to answer the question?
2. If you knew who wrote any of the three books mentioned, could you answer the question? Why or why not?
3. Would you have to have read any or all of these books in order to answer the question? Why or why not?
4. Suppose that you knew that these books were for young people. Suppose also that you knew the name of only one male writer for children in the nineteenth century. Should you write his name to complete the statement? Explain.

Assignment 4 Short-Answer Questions On your paper, write the answers to the questions that follow this fill-in-the-blank question.

> Arithmetic, geometry, algebra, and calculus are all branches of the science known as __?__.

1. What are the key words that you should notice?
2. Is it possible to know the answer before reading the entire question?
3. If you thought that you knew the answer, should you read the entire question anyway?
4. Would you have to know what calculus is in order to answer the question? Explain why or why not.

Essay Questions

An **essay question** requires a short essay written in a limited time. You may be asked to discuss, describe, explain, compare, contrast, summarize, or illustrate. To follow those directions correctly, you must know what the directions mean.

DIRECTIONS	MEANING
compare	point out likenesses
contrast	point out differences
describe	give details
summarize	give main points briefly
list	mention but do not explain
explain	give reasons for
name	list by actual name
discuss	consider all aspects of subject
illustrate	provide examples

Essay questions can be more complex than other types of test questions. Read them with care so that you will know exactly what is asked of you. Study the following examples:

Compare and contrast the reactions of Maurice and Maralyn to the ordeal described in *Staying Alive!* (10 points)

Name three Latin American leaders that we have studied this semester and explain why they were important. (15 points)

Use the following strategies when you are answering essay questions.

Strategies

1. *Read the directions carefully.* You may be given a choice of questions to answer. If so, read all of the questions before you choose.

2. *Allot the time that you will spend on each question according to the number of points that it is worth.* You should spend more time on a question worth twenty-five points than on one worth fifteen. Sometimes all questions have equal value. Then, apportion your time according to how detailed your answer must be.

3. *Start with the question that you are most familiar with.*

4. *On scratch paper jot down names, dates, facts, or formulas required in your answer, and arrange them in appropriate order or in outline form.* Suppose you were to answer the second of the example essay questions: "Name three Latin American leaders that we have studied this semester and explain why they were important." After you think of three leaders —Toussaint L'Ouverture, Simón Bolívar, and Benito Juárez, for example—plan your answer by making notes or by making an outline.

5. *Be specific in your answer, but do not pad it with unrelated details.* A concise answer that is detailed and well organized will receive more points than a long answer that is padded and disorganized.

6. *Reread the question after you have finished your answer to be certain that you have done all that you were asked to do.* Sometimes you may be asked to do two things, such as *list* and *discuss*. Be certain that you have done both.

7. *Reread your answer to be certain that you have made no errors in grammar, usage, spelling, or punctuation.*

Assignment 5 Essay Questions Number your paper from 1 to 5. Match the test direction words in the second column with the correct definitions in the first column. You will use all but one of the items.

__?__ 1. give main points briefly

__?__ 2. consider all aspects of subject

__?__ 3. provide examples and give details

__?__ 4. point out likenesses and differences

__?__ 5. list by actual name and give reasons for

a. list

b. compare and contrast

c. discuss

d. illustrate and describe

e. name and explain

f. summarize

Assignment 6 Essay Questions Find an essay question in your literature or social studies textbook. Answer it, using the strategies on pages 684–685.

Index

Abbreviations: capitalization of, 224, 228-229; punctuation with, 231-232
Action verbs: defined, 14; transitive and intransitive, 19-20
Active voice, defined, 156
Adjectives: adverbs modifying, 30; articles as, 22; comparison forms, 186-188; defined, 21; diagramed, 79; distinguished from -*ly* adverb, 32-33; nouns used as, 24-25; participial phrases used as, 101; placement, 22; possessive nouns used as, 25; possessive pronouns used as (pronominal adjective), 25-26, 117-178; predicate, 74-75; prepositional phrases used as, 94; proper, 24; proper, capitalization of, 228; with -*ly*, 32-33
Adjective clauses: defined, 111-112; diagramed, 132, 133; essential clause, 113; nonessential clause, 113; subordinate clause as, 111-112; subordinating conjunctions in, 112; subordinating with, 370-371
Adjustment letter, 591-592
Adverbs: comparative and superlative degrees, 189; comparison, 186-188; conjunctive, 44; defined, 28; diagramed, 79; distinguished from -*ly* adjective, 32-33; modifying adjectives, 30; modifying adverbs, 31; modifying a verb, 29-30; prepositional phrases used as, 95
Adverb clauses: defined, 114-115; introducing, comma after, 235; diagramed, 133-134; subordinate clause as, 114-115; subordinating conjunctions in, 115; subordinating with, 373
Almanacs, 668
Antecedent: agreement of pronoun with, 170-171, 172-173; defined,

6; pronoun reference, 183-184
Antonyms, 625
Apostrophe: in contractions, 247; to form plural letters, numbers, 247-248; to show possession, 246-247
Appositives: defined, 96; phrases, 96-97, 378; *we, us* used with, 181-182
Appositive phrases: defined, 96; diagramed, 129; essential, 96-97; nonessential, 96-97; revising sentences with, 378; as sentence fragments, 123-124
Argument, 508
Articles: *a, an, the,* 22, 184
Author: in bibliography, 545-546; in card catalog, 664-665; finding, for given title, 665; on note cards, 548
Auxiliary (helping) verbs: defined, 16; list of, 17

Bibliography, final, 566
Bibliography cards, 543-545; for books, 545; for magazine articles, 545
Body: of essay, 517-519; of letter, 578-580; of report, 559; of speech, 656-657
Book reviews, 421-424
Business letters, 577-592. *See* Adjustment letter; Envelopes; Order letter; Request letter.

Call numbers, 664-665
Capitalization, 221-229
Card catalog, 541, 664-665
Characterization, 468, 485
Chronological order: organizing events, 329-331
Clarity. *See* Coherence.
Clauses: adjective, 111-113; adverb, 114-115; defined, 108; diagraming, 132-135; essential,

686

113; independent (main), 108; misplaced, 191-193; nonessential, 113; noun, 115-116; sentence fragments as, 124-125; subordinate (dependent), 109-110, 111-113, 114-115, 115-116; subordinating conjunctions, 115, 116

Clichés, 444

Climax, 484

Coherence: in paragraphs, 328-329, 359-360

Collective nouns: agreement with verb, 163-164; as antecedents, 172; defined, 5, 163-164

Colloquial language, 144

Colon, 241-242

Comma, 233-235, 236-238: with adverb clause, 235; with dates and addresses, 238; with direct address, 236; with independent clauses, 234, 236; with interjections, *no, yes,* 235; after introductory expressions, 234-235; with modifiers, 234; with nonessential appositives, 237; with nonessential phrases and clauses, 237-238; with parenthetical expressions, 237; with participial phrases, 235; with prepositional phrases, 234; with quotation marks, 244; to separate sentence parts, 236-238; in series, 233-234; with subordinate clauses, 234

Common noun, defined, 4

Comparison: comparative degree, defined, 186; correct usage, 189-190; irregular modifiers, 188; one-syllable modifiers, 186-187; positive degree, defined, 186; superlative degree, defined, 186; three-or-more-syllable modifiers, 187; two-syllable modifiers, 187; using *less, least,* 187; using *than, as,* 182

Comparison and contrast, 342-345, 508

Complements: compound object, 71; defined, 69; diagramed, 80-82, 83-85; direct object, 70;

indirect object, 70-71; after linking verb, 73-74; objects, defined, 69; subject, 73-74

Complete predicate, 65-66

Complete sentence: defined, 123; subordinate clause in, 109-110

Complete subject, 64

Complex sentence: defined, 120; diagramed, 137

Complimentary close, 578-580

Compound-complex sentence, 121

Compound nouns: defined, 4-5; hyphen with, 4-5; plurals, 605

Compound predicate, 62

Compound prepositions, list of, 35

Compound sentence: comma between clauses, 236; defined, 118-119; diagramed, 136

Compound subject: defined, 61-62; verb agreement, rules for, 160-161

Concluding paragraph, 522-523 559

Concluding sentences: defined, 296; of speech, 658; writing, 317-318, 403, 408, 413, 559

Conflict, 483-484

Conjugation of a verb, defined, 150-151

Conjunctions: coordinating, 38-39, 119, 126; correlative, 40; defined, 38; distinguished from prepositions, 43-44; kinds of, 38; subordinating, 41-42, 126

Conjunctive adverbs: connecting independent clauses, 44; defined, 44; list of, 44; semicolon with, 240

Connotation, 622

Context, for word meanings, 615-616

Contrast. *See* Comparison and Contrast.

Coordinating conjunctions: comma before, 236; connecting independent clauses, 39, 119, 126, 239-240; list of, 38; semicolon in place of, 239-240

Coordinating sentences, 364, 367-368

Correlative conjunctions, list of, 40

Dangling modifier, 192-193
Dash, 250-251
Declarative sentence: defined, 57; punctuation, 231; subject and predicate in, 66-67
Definition paragraph, 403-405
Definitions, in dictionary entries, 624
Demonstrative pronoun: defined, 9; used as an adjective, 26
Denotation, 622
Dependent clause. *See* Subordinate clause.
Descriptions: comparisons in, 444-445; effective use of modifiers in, 442-443; effective use of nouns and verbs in, 439-440; models of, 434-435, 438, 440, 442, 444, 445, 447, 450-451, 452, 454-455, 457; purpose of, 402; sensory details in, 433-438
Descriptive writing, 402-432. *See also* Descriptions.
Dewey decimal system, 662-663
Diagraming, 77-85, 128-137
Dialogue: format of, 480; in narration, 478; punctuation of, 243
Dictionaries: parts of, 624-625; uses of, 623-625; types of, 666
Dictionary entry, parts of: antonyms, 624; definitions, 624; entry word, 623; etymologies, 625; parts of speech, 624-625; pronunciation, 624; superscripts, 625; synonyms, 625; usage labels, 625. *See also* Guide words; Homographs; Pronunciation key.
Directions, writing, 407-409
Direct object: defined, 70; diagramed, 80-81
Direct quotation: defined, 221; in narratives, 578; quotation marks in, 243
Double negative, 199
Double subject, 199

Encyclopedia listings, in bibliography, 546
Encyclopedias, 544, 667

Envelopes, of business letters: addressing, 580; folding and inserting, 560-583; types of, 581-582. *See also* Business letters.
Essay. *See* Persuasive essay.
Essay questions, 683-684
Etymologies, 625
Exclamation point, 232
Exclamatory sentence: defined, 58; subject and predicate in, 68
Expository writing, 402-431

Facts, 498
Fiction: arrangement in library, 662; Dewey classification of, 663; finding source of, 671
Fill-in-the-blank questions, 681-682
First-person narration, 473, 485-486
Footnotes: forms, 560-561; numbering of, 561; placement of, 561; rules for, 560
Formal speeches, 650
Fragment. *See* Sentence fragment.
Free-flow writing, 281-282

Gender: agreement of pronoun with antecedent, 172-173; defined, 172; personal pronoun, 7
Gerund: distinguished from participle, 102-103; defined, 102; used as noun, 102, 178
Gerund phrase: defined, 103; diagramed, 130; used as a noun, 104
Greek roots, common, 618
Guide cards, 547
Guide words, 623

Heading, of business letter, 577, 579, 580
Helping verb. *See* Auxiliary verb.
Homographs, in dictionary entries, 625
Homophones, 611
Hyphen: at the end of a line, 249-250; in compound modifier, 249; in compound noun, 4; in compound words, 249; in

fractions, 250; in numbers, 250; with *all-, ex-, self-,* 249; with prefixes, suffixes, 249

Idioms, 144
Imperative sentence: defined, 58; subject and predicate in, 67
Impromptu speeches, 651
Indefinite pronouns: agreement with antecedents, 171-172; defined, 10-11; list of, 11; plural, 162-163; singular, 162; used as adjectives, 26
Independent clauses: commas in a series, 234; conjunctive adverb with, 44, 119, 240; coordinating conjunction in, 39, 119, 126; coordinating strategies, 364; coordinating words, 367-368; defined, 39, 108; semicolon with, 119, 239-240; subordinating conjunction with, 41, 109-110, 115
Index, in general reference works, 666-667
Index cards, 547
Indirect object: action verb with, 71; defined, 70-71; diagramed, 81
Indirect quotation: defined, 243; in narratives, 478; quotation marks in, 243
Infinitive: defined, 105; distinguished from prepositional phrases, 105; functions, 105; *to* understood, 146
Infinitive phrase: defined, 106; functions, 106-107; as sentence fragment, 123-124
Informal speeches, 650
Inside address, 578, 579, 580
Instructions, writing, 412-414
Intensive pronoun, defined, 10
Interjections, defined, 46
Interrogative pronoun: defined, 10; in noun clause, 116; used as adjective, 26; *who, whom,* 179-180
Interrogative sentence: defined, 58; punctuation, 232; subject and

predicate in, 67
Intransitive verb: defined, 19; linking, 15-16
Introduction strategies, for a speech, 657-658
Introductory paragraph, 514-515, 558
Inverted word order, 167-168
Irregular verbs: defined, 147; list of, 148-149; past participle of, 99-100
Italics, 253

Jargon, 144

Latin roots, common, 618
Letters. *See* Adjustment letter; Business letters; Order letter; Request letter.
Library skills, 662-673
Linking verbs: defined, 15; list of, 15-16, 20, 74; predicate adjective with, 75; predicate nominative with, 74; subject complement with, 73-74
Listening: active, 639, 641; for information, 642-643; for notes, 645; passive, 639; for signals to key points or shifts in focus, 643-644; critical, strategies for, 646-647; for supporting details, 644-645. *See also* Critical listening.

Main verb: defined, 16; in verb phrase, 16-17
Manuscript form, 258-259
Matching questions, 679
Mechanics, defined, 220
Metaphors, 444
Misplaced modifier, 191-192
Misspelled words, common, 616
Modifiers: commas in series, 234; comparison of, 186-188, 189-191; compound comparison, 190; compound, hyphen with, 250; dangling, 192-193; diagramed, 79; *-er, -est,* 186-187, 189-190; illogical comparisons, 190-191;

irregular, list of, 188; *less, least,* 187, 188; misplaced, 191-193; *more, most,* 187, 189; one-syllable, 186-187; positive, comparative, superlative, defined, 186; three or more syllables, 187; two-syllable, 187; usage, list of, 194-213
Multiple-choice questions, 679

Narration, types of: first-person 473-475; incident, 467-470; third-person, 473, 475.
Narrative: dialogue in, 478; longer, 483-487; models of, 469, 474, 475, 479-480, 484-485; planning a, 483-484; strategies for writing and revising a, 469, 484
Narrative writing, 466-495
Nonessential phrases and clauses, commas with, 237-238
Nonfiction: arrangement in library, 663; classification of, 663, finding source of; 671-673. *See also* Call numbers.˜
Nonstandard language, 145
Note cards: bibliographical form of, 545-546; for direct quotation, 548; examples, 548, 549, 550; for speeches, 660; strategies for, 547; for summary, 549
Notes: strategies for taking, 547-548, 634-635; use of summary in, 636-637; use of underlining in, 635
Noun clause: defined, 115-116; interrogative pronoun in, 116; subordinate clause as, 115-116; subordinating conjunctions in, 116
Nouns: as antecedent, 6-7; collective, 5, 163-164; common, 4; compound, 4-5; defined, 3; ending in *s,* agreement with verb, 164-165; kinds of, 3; possessive, defined, 25-26; possessive form, 246-247; proper, 4; titles and names, agreement with verbs,

165-166; used as adjectives, 24-25
Number, defined, 158
Numbers, 254-256; in dates, street numbers, page numbers, 255-256; in writing time, 255

Object, describing an, 446-448
Object (of sentence): compound, defined, 71; diagramed, 80-81; direct, defined, 69; indirect, defined, 70-71; of verb, 19
Object of preposition, 35
Opinions, 497-498
Opinion statement, 503-504
Order: chronological, 409-410, 413-414, 467, 470, 508, 657; of importance, 337-339, 507; problem-solution, 657; spatial, 451-452, 507, 657; topical, 657
Order letter, 588-589
Outlining, 511-512, 553-555

Page references, on note cards, 548
Paragraphs: coherence, 328-329, 359-360; chronological order of events, 329-331; concluding sentences, 296, 317-318; coordinating (combining) strategies, 364; coordinating words, 367-368; coordination, defined, 363-364; defined, 295-297; developing by comparison and contrast, 343-345; incoherent sentences, revising, 381-382; order of importance, 337-339, 511; organizing details, 334-335, 337-339; proofreading, 390-392; revising sentences (coordination) 363-364; revising sentences (subordination), 370-371, 373; revising sentences with phrases, 376-377, 378; selecting a topic, strategies, 299-301; sentence beginnings, 386-387; sentence structure, 388; spatial order

(location), 334-335; subordinating (revising) sentences, 370-371, 373; subordination, defined, 370; supporting sentences, 296, 308-309, 310-311, 312-313; topic sentence, 296, 304-305; transitional words and phrases, 330, 334-335, 339, 344-345; unity, 297, 357-358; using examples, 310-311; using facts, 308-309; using reasons, 312-313; variety in sentences, 385-387, 388

Parentheses, 251

Parenthetical expressions, commas to set off, 237

Participial phrase: as sentence fragment, 123-124; comma after, 235; defined, 101; diagramed, 129-130; introductory, comma after, 235; revising sentences with, 376-377; used as adjective, 101

Participle: defined, 98; distinguished from gerund, 102-103; in verb phrase, 100; past, 99-100; present, 99; used as adjective, 98-99; used as verb, 99-100

Passive voice, defined, 156

Period, 231-232

Person, describing a, 454-457

Person (of pronoun): agreement of pronoun with antecedent, 173

Personal pronouns: defined, 7; possessive, 7, 25-26, 177-178, 247

Persuasive essay, 496-537; audience of, 506-507; models of, 515, 518-519, 523-524; opinion statement in, 503-504; organizing ideas for, 511-512; outlining, 511-512; purpose of, 496; selecting and limiting topics for, 499-502; strategies for writing, 514, 523, 527

Phrases: appositive, 96-97; commas in a series, 234; defined, 93; gerund, 103-104; infinitive, 106-107; introductory, comma after, 234-235; misplaced, 191-193; participial, 101;

prepositional, as adjectives and adverbs, 93-95; as sentence fragments, 123-124; verbal, 98-104, 106-107

Place, describing a, 450

Point of view, 473, 485. *See also* First-person narration; Third-person narration.

Possessive, form singular, plural, 25, 247

Possessive pronouns (pronominal adjective): as adjectives, 25-26, 177-178

Predicate: complement as part, 69; complete, 65-66; compound, 62; simple, 60

Predicate adjective: compound, 75; defined, 74; diagramed, 81-82

Predicate nominative: compound, 74; defined, 74; diagramed, 81-82; linking verb with, 74; verb agreement, 168

Prefixes and suffixes: defined, listed, 619-620; hyphen with, 249

Prepared speeches, 651

Prepositional phrase: as adjective, 35-36, 94; as adverb, 35-36, 95; defined, 35, 93-94; diagramed, 128-129; distinguished from infinitive, 105; introductory, comma after, 234; as sentence fragment, 123-124

Prepositions: compound, 35; defined, 34; distinguished from conjunctions, 43-44; distinguished from infinitives, 105; list of, 34; object of, 35

Prewriting, defined, 270-271

Process and device paragraphs, 417-419

Pronominal adjective (possessive pronoun), 25-26, 177-178

Pronoun antecedents: agreement in gender, 172-173; agreement in number, 170-171; agreement in person, 173; indefinite, agreement, 171-172

Pronoun case: defined, 174; nominative, 175; objective, 175-176; possessive, 177-178

Pronouns: agreement with

Similes, 444, 445
Simple predicate, 60
Simple sentence, defined, 118
Simple subject, 59
Skimming, strategies for, 631
Slang, 144
Spatial order, organizing details, 334-335
Speeches: audience and purpose of, 651-652; and compositions, contrasted, 657-658; delivery, 660-661; gathering information for, 655-656; organizing, 656-659; selecting and limiting topic of, 652-653
Speeches, kinds of: formal, 650; impromptu, 651; informal, 650; prepared, 651
Spelling problems, 610-611
Spelling rules, 603-610
Spelling strategies, 612
Study skills, 626-637. See Notes; Scanning; Skimming; SQRRR Reading Method.
Subject (of sentence): complete, 64; compound, 61-62; simple, 59
Subject complement, defined, 73-74
Subject heading, in note cards, 548
Subjects: agreement with *every, many a,* 168-169; agreement with verb, 160-163, 163-165, 165-166; amount and time, agreement with verbs, 166; collective nouns as, 163-164; compound, 160-161; indefinite pronoun as, 162-163; indefinite pronouns, agreement with verbs, 162-163; indefinite pronouns, list of, 162; inverted word order 67, 167-168; nouns ending in *s,* 164-165; titles and names, 165-166
Subject-verb agreement: with auxiliary verb, 158; collective nouns, 163-164; compound subjects, 160-161; *every* and *many a,* 168-169; indefinite pronouns, 162-163; intervening words and phrases, 159; inverted word order, 167-168; nouns ending in *s,* 164-165; predicate nominatives, 168; titles and

names, 165-166; words of amount and time, 166
Subordinate clause: as sentence fragment, 123-124; defined, 41, 109-110; commas in a series, 234; in complete sentence, 109-110; in compound complex-sentences, 121; relationships to independent clauses, 109-110; relative pronoun in, 112, 180-181; subordinating conjunction with, 41-42, 112, 115, 116; used as adjective, 111-112, 113; used as adverb, 114-115; used as noun, 115-116
Subordinating conjunctions: defined, 41-42, 115; list of, 115
Summary: defined, 636; strategies for writing, 637
Supporting sentences: defined, 296; example, defined, 310-311; fact, defined, 308-309; reason, defined, 312-313; writing, 308-309
Synonyms: as clue to unfamiliar words, 615; choosing among, 621-622; defined, 615, 621; in dictionaries, 625. See also Connotation.
Synonyms, dictionaries of, 666

Tests, kinds of: essay, 683-685; objective, 677-680; short-answer, 676, 681-682
Tests: preparing for, 674-675; strategies for taking, 677, 678, 679, 681, 684-685
Thesis statement, 552-553, 645, 654. See also Opinion statement.
Third-person narration, 473
Title, choosing a, 528
Titles: alphabetizing of, 662; in bibliography, 545-546; capitalization of, 224; on library cards, 664, 665; quotation marks in, 244
Topic: selecting for writing, 283-284, 299-301, 467-469, 499-501, 539-541; for speech, 652-653

Acknowledgments (continued)

The Publisher also wishes to thank all the students whose names appear in this textbook for granting permission to use their writing as models. The editors and the Publisher have been solely responsible for selecting the student writing used as models.

From *Wildlife of the Islands* by William H. Amos. Published in 1980 by Harry N. Abrams, Inc., New York. Reprinted by permission.   Adapted from pp. 476–477 and 492–496 in *Freedom's Trail* by Richard A. Bartlett, Clair W. Keller, and Helen H. Carey. Copyright © 1979 by Houghton Mifflin Company. Used by permission.   Excerpt by Ben Black Elk, from *I Have Spoken: American History Through the Voices of the Indians* by Virginia Irving Armstrong, Swallow Press, 1971. Reprinted with the permission of The Ohio University Press, Athens, Ohio.   From "Auntie Tsia Lies Dying" by Jeffery Paul Chan. Used by permission of the author.   From *The First Book of Surprising Facts* by Frances N. Chrystie, copyright © 1956, used by permission of Franklin Watts, Inc.   From "The Most Dangerous Game" by Richard Connell. Copyright, 1924 by Richard Connell. Copyright renewed, 1952 by Louise Fox Connell. Reprinted by permission of Brandt & Brandt Literary Agents, Inc.   From *Dance to the Piper* by Agnes de Mille (Little, Brown and Company, 1952). Used by permission of Harold Ober Associates, Inc.   From the short story "Antaeus" by Borden Deal. Copyright © 1961 by Southern Methodist University Press. Used by permission of The Borden

Credits

Checklist for Revision

As a guide in revising your writing, consider the following questions:

✔ 1. Did you cover your topic thoroughly?

✔ 2. Did you remove any information not directly related to your topic?

✔ 3. Did you include a topic sentence or a thesis statement?

✔ 4. Did you present your information in a logical order?

✔ 5. Did you use transitional words and phrases to emphasize the order of your ideas?

✔ 6. Did you write an appropriate conclusion?

✔ 7. Did you use words and details that are suitable for your audience?

✔ 8. Did you achieve your purpose for writing?

✔ 9. Did you vary the length and structure of your sentences?

✔ 10. Did you use accurate and precise words?

✔ 11. Did you use the correct forms for reports and letters?

✔ 12. Did you avoid using sentence fragments, run-on sentences, and other incorrect sentence structures?

✔ 13. Did you use correct usage, spelling, punctuation, and capitalization?

✔ 14. Did you carefully proofread your finished copy?